To my parents, Will and Bessie Nabors,
my wife and children, and to
the Nabors family

Table of Contents

Foreword

For the legislative historian, now conditioned to the existence of convenient means of tracing U.S. legislative history from current Congressional calendars, many official catalogs or the almost countless checklists and services that have been published over the past 25 years, it seems scarcely credible that 32 volumes of the U.S. Statutes at Large, published from 1789 to 1903, contained no references to statutory bill numbers- an essential element in identifying the progress of legislation. Now that Congress can routinely introduce as many as 30,000 pieces of legislation in a two-year session, the bill number has assumed great significance as the usual means of tracking current status into law.

But for the historian seeking a description of legislative intent for laws enacted during the first century of the Republic, the search heretofore has been initially impeded because there was no reference in the statute books to bill numbers even if the searcher had access to early bill prints. Not only is there a dearth of documentation to describe intent before 1900, but there has been nothing to assist with this basic process of numerical identification even if the public law or chapter number of the legislation was known. As this checklist will reveal, bill numbers for this early period could be obtained only by tedious and generally inconvenient reference to the official Journals of the proceedings of the Senate and House of Representatives. Having now checked all of these reference for us from these journals and other little-noticed sources, Mr. Nabors makes a fundamental contribution to the job of researching legislation enacted from 1789 to 1903.

This work was very much inspired by necessity and by its author's fortunate proximity to an incomparable collection of legislation and Congressional records of proceedings in the American-British Law Division of the Library of Congress. Mr. Nabors has been one of the principal managers of this collection for many years and for those who approach it, a mentor with singular knowledge of its organization and function. For those of us who have been privileged to know him in Washington, this knowledge has on countless occasions expedited "trips to the Hill" that could have otherwise consumed days. His patience and conscientious concern to assist a truly enormous public through a maze of documents that describe nothing less than the evolution of American government, are personal qualities that made this checklist finally possible. It has been at least ten years in preparation. The time that it will now save historians, librarians and archivists probably cannot be measured.

Ellen P. Mahar
Librarian, Covington
 & Burling
Washington, D.C.

J. S. Ellenberger
Librarian, Shearman
 & Sterling
New York City

Acknowledgments

I wish to express my sincere appreciation to many persons
from the private, public, academic, and government community.
To the General Counsel, John J. Kominski, my peers and
co-workers at the Library of Congress. The Senate librarian,
Roger K. Haley and his staff who provided invaluable exchange of
insights and friendship. The Diplomatic branch at the National
Archives, Messrs. Jerry Haines, who several years ago let me
examine the original laws in the vault, and Ronald Swerczek and
Sally Marks who tolerated my many hours of encroachment. To
Nancy Taft Wynn, Dr. and Mrs. Donald Sham, who offered their
unyielding talents which was invaluable. Dawud B. Ziyad,
Assistant Professor, University of the District of Columbia, who
first inspired me to proceed in the completion of this work. To
Jack Ellenberger and Ellen Mahar, who took an immediate interest
in this gigantic project, and encouraged its completion. To
Minnie N. Height, Virginia Garrett, and Reba Burrus, who offered
timely suggestions and my demanding deadline - - - - overnight.
Lastly, my friends and colleagues who have sensed and shared the
emergence of an age in which the exploration of human conscious-
ness in all its aspects is restored.

The author claims all responsibility for this project and
its creation. The time devoted for the completion of this work
was done during his leisure hours. The author has made every
effort to produce results of absolute accuracy, but apologizes
for any errors and omissions that may have occurred.

Introduction

This key is intended to provide a systematic reference to the numbers of the U.S. Congressional bills and joint resolutions which became law from the 1st Congress (1789) through the 57th Congress (1903). The number assigned to a bill when introduced in the Congress provides the most direct historical reference for tracing legislative history. It should be noted that by its very nature this study is tabular in form with annotations and explanation whenever necessary.

No legislative bill numbers were used in the Statutes at Large prior to March 3, 1903. With the exception of the date, which always has been used, the only identifiers given the laws in the Statutes at Large were the chapter numbers. These were assigned in one sequence to all laws upon receipt and the numbering was started anew each session. Therefore, when the two categories -- public and private -- were classified and separated for publication in the Statutes at Large, discontinuity occurred in the number sequence of each. Since this checklist includes only public laws you will find breaks in the numbering sequence of the Chapters caused by the omission of the private laws.

The line of demarcation to determine the private and public laws is not easily defined until the publication of the Statutes at Large was transferred to the General Services Administration by Reorganization Plan No. 20. (Federal Register, Volume 15, Number 101, May 25, 1950, p. 3178).

Prior to 1950 no rules determined the division of laws into private or public acts. There are, however, certain considerations which have been followed in order to determine the class into which a law should be placed. In arriving at the conclusion, an act was always examined and considered as a unit,

rather than paragraph by paragraph, in order to identify the
intent of Congress when the act was passed. That determination
was based upon the debate of the legislation as it appeared in
the Congressional Record; the nature of the legislation; its
effect and scope; whether it amended previous classed
legislation; and upon personal opinion.

Legislation classed generally as public may be listed as
that in which the interest of the government are paramount,
particular, or outweighs the other considerations of the act
and/or the interest of the public as a whole is affected.
Legislation classed generally as private may be stated to
include that which is passed for the particular benefit of an
individual or group of individuals, in the enactment of which
the government of public has no direct or immediate interest.
In borderline cases the general practice is to classify the law
as public; that is the present practice of the General Services
Administration.

Even though the assignment of numbers of bills is extremely
important in tracing their legislative histories, "The numbering
of bills apparently started during the 15th Congress. It seems
that beginning with the congress House bills were numbered
continuously through a congress, and remained alive beyond the
first session. Until the 30th Congress, Senate bills were
numbered beginning with 1 for each session and appear to have
died at the end of the session". [1]

---

(1) Schmeckebier, Lawrence F. Government publications and
     their use. 2d rev ed. Wash., D.C.
     Brookings Institution 1960, p. 169

While the House, in 1817, adopted the policy of numbering the bills consecutively, it was not until 1847 that the Senate began using the same numbering system as in the House and some uniformity achieved. However, the key identifier, the bill number was not included in the U.S. Statutes at Large along with the chapter number, brief title/synopses, and approval date of law. Bill numbers were (and are) important to the committees and the Members of Congress because they consider, report, and debate the bills primarily on basis of the assigned number. In the absence of bill numbers assigned at the time of introduction, searchers must rely upon other sources and identifiers. However, the House and Senate Journals, which are the only official record of Congressional activity required by the Constitution, are excellent sources for tracing legislative histories, especially for the period from 1789 to 1903. These were the sources used in compiling this checklist.

The House and Senate Journals are also excellent supplementary tools to be used with the Indexes to the debates as explained in the "Users Guide" to this checklist.

The difficulties, caused by the omission of bill numbers prior to 1903, have been recognized by those interested in developing histories for academic, legislative or judicial reason. Each legislative history had to be developed on a case by case basis, there being no overall finding list which could be used. Hence, this publication should create a significant and expedient source for beginning legislative research for the period covered, making it possible for librarians and researchers in the legal community to save a significant amount of time.

Legislative histories can be essential to any individual who needs to understand the statutory intent and meaning of the law.

Eugene Nabors

1.		2.	3.	4.	5.
Public Law/Resolution		Statutes at Large	Page	Date	Bill No.
Chapter	Number				

1. Chapter -   This is the primary identifier from 1789-1903 for
                the beginning of each law, public or private.
                1st-84th Congress.

    Number -   This identifies the public law number or public
                resolution number.

2. Statutes at Large - Laws of a given Congress are published
                         in the final and permanent form.

3. Page - Inclusive pagination of the law's beginning and end
            page citation.

4. Date - The date the law was approved by the President.

5. Bill Number - The most important item when introduced but
                   was omitted in the Statutes at Large from
                   1789-1903.

    Indexes to the earlier volumes of the debates are poor,
necessitating almost page by page examination. To avoid this
process, the index to the Senate and House Journals may be used,
checking the table of bills in the Journals which refers to the
pages where the bill was considered by Congress. This leads to
the dates when Congress acted on the bill and then those dates
can be checked in the volume of debates listed below:

Annals of Congress (Sometimes cited as History of Congress)	1st Cong. to 18th Cong. 1st Sess.	1780-1824
Register of Debates	18th Cong., 2d Sess., to 25th Cong., 1st Sess.	1824-1837*
Congressional Globe	23d Cong., 1st Sess., to 42d Cong., 2d Sess.	1833-1873*
Congressional Record	43d Cong., 1st Sess., to	1873-

*Note that both the Register of Debates and the Congressional
Globe cover the years 1833-1837.

PUBLIC ACTS OF THE FIRST CONGRESS

Public Law/Resolution		Statutes at Large	Page	Date	Bill No.	
Chapter	Number					
1	1	1	23-24	6-01-89	HR	1
2	2	1	24-27	7-04-89	HR	2
3	3	1	27-28	7-20-89	HR	5
4	4	1	28-29	7-27-89	HR	8
5	5	1	29-49	7-31-89	HR	11
6	6	1	49	8-05-89	HR	13
7	7	1	49-50	8-07-89	HR	7
8	8	1	50-53	8-07-89	HR	14
9	9	1	53-54	8-07-89	HR	12
10	10	1	54	8-20-89	HR	20
11	11	1	55-65	9-01-89	HR	16
12	12	1	65-67	9-02-89	HR	9
13	13	1	67-68	9-11-89	HR	21
14	14	1	68-69	9-15-89	HR	18
15	15	1	69-70	9-16-89	HR	23
16	16	1	70	9-22-89	S	3
17	17	1	70-72	9-22-89	HR	19
18	18	1	72	9-23-89	HR	28
19	19	1	72	9-24-89	HR	15
20	20	1	73-93	9-24-89	S	1
21	21	1	93-94	9-29-89	S	4
22	22	1	94-95	9-29-89	HR	33
23	23	1	95	9-29-89	HR	32
24	24	1	95	9-29-89	HR	29
25	25	1	95-96	9-29-89	HR	27
27	26	1	96	9-29-89	HR	31

RESOLUTIONS OF THE FIRST CONGRESS

1	1	1	96	8-26-89	HJR	1
2	2	1	96-97	9-23-89	HJR	2
3	3	1	97-98	9-23-89	HJR	3

PUBLIC ACTS OF THE FIRST CONGRESS

Public Law/Resolution		Statutes at Large	Page	Date	Bill No.	
Chapter	Number					
1	1	1	99-101	2-08-90	HR	36
2	2	1	101-103	3-01-90	HR	34
3	3	1	103-104	3-26-90	HR	40
4	4	1	104-106	3-26-90	HR	47
5	5	1	106	4-02-90	HR	48
6	6	1	106-109	4-02-90	S	7
7	7	1	109-112	4-10-90	HR	41
8	8	1	112	4-15-90	HR	50
9	9	1	112-119	4-30-90	S	6
10	10	1	119-121	4-30-90	HR	55
11	11	1	122	5-26-90	HR	58
12	12	1	122-123	5-26-90	HR	57
13	13	1	123	5-26-90	S	9
14	14	1	123	5-26-90	S	8
15	15	1	124-126	5-31-90	HR	43
17	16	1	126	6-04-90	HR	68
18	17	1	126	6-04-90	HR	54
19	18	1	126-128	6-14-90	HR	71
21	19	1	128	6-23-90	HR	73
22	20	1	128-129	7-01-90	HR	52
25	21	1	129	7-05-90	HR	75
26	22	1	129	7-05-90	HR	76
27	23	1	129-130	7-16-90	HR	80
28	24	1	130	7-16-90	S	12
29	25	1	131-135	7-20-90	HR	61
30	26	1	135-136	7-20-90	HR	78
31	27	1	136	7-22-90	HR	87
32	28	1	137	7-22-90	HR	84
33	29	1	137-138	7-22-90	HR	65
34	30	1	138-144	8-04-90	HR	63
35	31	1	145-178	8-04-90	HR	82
36	32	1	178	8-04-90	HR	92
38	33	1	178-179	8-05-90	HR	77
39	34	1	180-182	8-10-90	HR	83
40	35	1	182-184	8-10-90	HR	85
41	36	1	184	8-10-90	HR	97
42	37	1	184	8-11-90	S	13
43	38	1	184-185	8-11-90	HR	93

PUBLIC ACTS OF THE FIRST CONGRESS

Public Law/Resolution		Statutes at Large	Page	Date	Bill No.	
Chapter	Number					
46	39	1	185–186	8–12–90	S	22
47	40	1	186–187	8–12–90	HR	100

RESOLUTIONS OF THE FIRST CONGRESS

1	1	1	187	6–07–90	HJR	1
2	2	1	187	6–14–90	HJR	2
3	3	1	187	8–02–90	HJR	3
4	4	1	187	8–02–90	HJR	4
5	5	1	187	8–12–90	HJR	5

PUBLIC ACTS OF THE FIRST CONGRESS

Public Law/Resolution		Statutes at Large	Page	Date	Bill No.	
Chapter	Number					
1	1	1	188	12-27-90	HR	129
2	2	1	188-189	1-07-91	HR	109
3	3	1	189	1-10-91	HR	103
4	4	1	189	2-04-91	S	16
5	5	1	190	2-09-91	HR	115
6	6	1	190	2-11-91	HR	120
7	7	1	191	2-18-91	S	19
8	8	1	191	2-18-91	HR	124
9	9	1	191	2-25-91	S	20
10	10	1	191-196	2-25-91	S	17
11	11	1	196-197	3-02-91	HR	125
12	12	1	197-198	3-02-91	HR	128
13	13	1	198	3-02-91	HR	129
14	14	1	198	3-02-91	HR	132
15	15	1	199-214	3-03-91	HR	110
16	16	1	214	3-03-91	S	22
17	17	1	214-215	3-03-91	S	21
18	18	1	215	3-03-91	HR	131
19	19	1	215-216	3-03-91	HR	134
20	20	1	216	3-03-91	HR	142
21	21	1	216	3-03-91	HR	135
22	22	1	216-217	3-03-91	HR	133
23	23	1	218	3-03-91	HR	137
24	24	1	218	3-03-91	S	23
25	25	1	218-219	3-03-91	HR	136
26	26	1	219-221	3-03-91	HR	130
27	27	1	221-222	3-03-91	S	15
28	28	1	222-224	3-03-91	HR	102

RESOLUTIONS OF THE FIRST CONGRESS

1	1	1	224	2-18-91	HJR	1
2	2	1	225	3-02-91	HJR	2
3	3	1	225	3-03-91	HJR	3
4	4	1	225	3-03-91	HJR	4
5	5	1	225	3-03-91	HJR	5

Public Law/Resolution		Statutes at Large	Page	Date	Bill No.	
Chapter	Number					
1	1	1	226	11-08-91	HR	144
3	2	1	226-229	12-23-91	HR	149
4	3	1	229	1-03-92	HR	157
5	4	1	229	1-23-92	HR	150
6	5	1	229-232	2-16-92	S	26
7	6	1	232-239	2-20-92	HR	154
8	7	1	239-241	3-01-92	S	25
9	8	1	241-243	3-05-92	S	32
10	9	1	243	3-19-92	HR	164
11	10	1	243-245	3-23-92	HR	152
12	11	1	245	3-27-92	HR	165
14	12	1	246	3-28-92	HR	162
15	13	1	246	4-02-92	HR	168
16	14	1	246-251	4-02-92	S	27
17	15	1	251	4-12-92	S	34
18	16	1	251	4-12-92	S	29
20	17	1	252	4-12-92	S	30
21	18	1	252-253	4-13-92	S	31
23	19	1	253	4-14-92	HR	179
24	20	1	254-257	4-14-92	S	24
25	21	1	257-258	4-21-92	HR	174
26	22	1	258	4-27-92	HR	177
27	23	1	259-263	5-02-92	HR	162
28	24	1	264-265	5-02-92	HR	185
29	25	1	265-266	5-05-92	S	33
30	26	1	266-267	5-05-92	HR	186
31	27	1	267	5-05-92	HR	187
32	28	1	267-271	5-08-92	HR	191
33	29	1	271-274	5-08-92	HR	148
34	30	1	274-275	5-08-92	HR	183
35	31	1	275	5-08-92	S	37
36	32	1	275-279	5-08-92	S	28
37	33	1	279-281	5-08-92	S	35
38	34	1	281-283	5-08-92	HR	178
39	35	1	283-284	5-08-92	HR	210
40	36	1	284	5-08-92	HR	194
41	37	1	284-285	5-08-92	HR	188
42	38	1	285-286	5-08-92	HR	175

RESOLUTION OF THE SECOND CONGRESS

Public Law/Resolution		Statutes at Large	Page	Date	Bill No.	
Chapter	Number					
1	1	1	286	5-08-92	HJR	1

PUBLIC ACTS OF THE SECOND CONGRESS

Public Law/Resolution		Statutes at Large	Page	Date	Bill No.	
Chapter	Number					
1	1	1	287-299	12-31-92	HR	195
2	2	1	299	1-14-93	HR	210
3	3	1	299	1-14-93	HR	208
4	4	1	299-300	2-09-93	HR	218
5	5	1	300-301	2-09-93	S	39
6	6	1	301-302	2-12-93	HR	211
7	7	1	302-305	2-12-93	S	42
8	8	1	305-318	2-18-93	HR	198
9	9	1	318	2-18-93	HR	227
10	10	1	318	2-21-93	HR	215
11	11	1	318-323	2-21-93	HR	204
15	12	1	324	2-27-93	HR	233
16	13	1	324	2-27-93	HR	220
17	14	1	324-325	2-28-93	HR	214
18	15	1	325-329	2-28-93	HR	216
19	16	1	329-332	3-01-93	HR	209
20	17	1	332-333	3-01-93	HR	197
21	18	1	333	3-02-93	HR	239
22	19	1	333-335	3-02-93	S	41
23	20	1	335-336	3-02-93	S	44
24	21	1	336-338	3-02-93	S	43
25	22	1	338	3-02-93	HR	207
26	23	1	338	3-02-93	HR	240
27	24	1	339	3-02-93	HR	241
30	25	1	339-340	3-02-93	HR	243
31	26	1	340	3-02-93	HR	245

Public Law/Resolution		Statutes at Large	Page	Date	Bill No.	
Chapter	Number					
1	1	1	341	1-13-94	S	1
4	2	1	341	3-03-94	S	2
5	3	1	342	3-07-94	HR	11
6	4	1	342-345	3-14-94	HR	5
7	5	1	345	3-20-94	HR	140
8	6	1	345	3-20-94	HR	18
9	7	1	345-346	3-20-94	HR	22
10	8	1	346-347	3-21-94	HR	20
11	9	1	347-349	3-22-94	HR	12
12	10	1	350-351	3-27-94	HR	14
13	11	1	351	3-27-94	S	5
14	12	1	352	4-02-94	HR	25
16	13	1	352-353	4-03-94	HR	15
17	14	1	353	4-03-94	S	7
18	15	1	353	4-05-94	HR	27
21	16	1	353-354	4-21-94	HR	3
23	17	1	354-366	5-08-94	HR	13
24	18	1	366-367	5-09-94	HR	34
25	19	1	367	5-09-94	HR	22
27	20	1	367-368	5-09-94	HR	33
28	21	1	368	5-13-94	S	3
31	22	1	368-369	5-19-94	HR	24
32	23	1	369	5-19-94	S	12
33	24	1	369-370	5-22-94	S	10
34	25	1	370	5-30-94	S	13
35	26	1	370	5-30-94	HR	52
36	27	1	370-371	5-30-94	S	14
37	28	1	371	5-31-94	HR	39
40	29	1	372	6-04-94	HR	17
41	30	1	372	6-04-94	HR	30
42	31	1	372-373	6-04-94	S	16*
43	32	1	373	6-04-94	HR	63
45	33	1	373-375	6-05-94	HR	55
46	34	1	376	6-05-94	S	15
47	35	1	376	6-05-94	S	16*
48	36	1	376-378	6-05-94	HR	56
49	37	1	378-381	6-05-94	HR	31
50	38	1	381-384	6-05-94	S	4

PUBLIC ACTS OF THE THIRD CONGRESS

Public Law/Resolution		Statutes at Large	Page	Date	Bill No.	
Chapter	Number					
51	39	1	384-390	6-05-94	HR	50
52	40	1	390	6-07-94	HR	49
53	41	1	390	6-07-94	S	6
54	42	1	390-392	6-07-94	HR	40
55	43	1	392	6-07-94	S	17
57	44	1	392-393	6-07-94	HR	62
58	45	1	393	6-07-94	HR	41
59	46	1	393	6-07-94	HR	65
61	47	1	393-394	6-09-94	HR	61
62	48	1	394	6-09-94	HR	26
63	49	1	394-395	6-09-94	HR	64
64	50	1	395-397	6-09-94	HR	23
65	51	1	397-400	6-09-94	HR	58

RESOLUTIONS OF THE THIRD CONGRESS

1	1	1	400	3-20-94	HJR	1
2	2	1	400	3-26-94	HJR	2
3	3	1	400-401	4-02-94	HJR	3
4	4	1	401	4-18-94	HJR	4
5	5	1	401	5-07-94	HJR	5
6	6	1	401	6-09-94	HJR	6
7	7	1	402	6-09-94	HJR	7
8	8	1	402	6-09-94	HJR	8

Public Law/Resolution		Statutes at Large	Page	Date	Bill No.	
Chapter	Number					
1	1	1	403	11-29-94	HR	73
2	2	1	403-404	12-03-94	HR	71
3	3	1	404	12-12-94	S	20
4	4	1	404	12-18-94	HR	85
6	5	1	404-405	12-31-94	HR	89
8	6	1	405-408	1-02-95	HR	816
9	7	1	408-409	1-02-95	HR	74
10	8	1	409	1-02-95	HR	87
11	9	1	409	1-08-95	HR	91
12	10	1	410	1-28-95	HR	97
13	11	1	410	1-28-95	S	22
14	12	1	410	1-28-95	HR	95
17	13	1	411	1-29-95	HR	77
18	14	1	411-413	1-29-95	HR	76
19	15	1	414	1-29-95	S	25
20	16	1	414-415	1-29-95	HR	83
21	17	1	415	2-13-95	HR	112
22	18	1	416	2-13-95	HR	102
23	19	1	416-417	2-14-95	HR	75
24	20	1	418	2-21-95	HR	98
25	21	1	418	2-21-95	HR	111
26	22	1	418-419	2-21-95	HR	103
27	23	1	419	2-23-95	S	21
28	24	1	419	2-25-95	HR	116
30	25	1	419-420	2-25-95	S	24
31	26	1	420-423	2-26-95	HR	79
33	27	1	423	2-27-95	HR	90
35	28	1	423	2-27-95	S	29
36	29	1	424-425	2-28-95	HR	99
37	30	1	425	3-02-95	S	27
40	31	1	426	3-02-95	HR	100
41	32	1	426	3-02-95	S	31
43	33	1	426-430	3-03-95	HR	107
44	34	1	430-432	3-03-95	HR	106
45	35	1	433-438	3-03-95	HR	110
46	36	1	438-439	3-03-95	HR	125
47	37	1	439-441	3-03-95	HR	123
48	38	1	441-442	3-03-95	HR	113

PUBLIC ACTS OF THE THIRD CONGRESS

Public Law/Resolution		Statutes at Large	Page	Date	Bill No.	
Chapter	Number					
49	39	1	442-443	3-03-95	S	34
50	40	1	443	3-03-95	HR	117
51	41	1	443	3-03-95	HR	124
52	42	1	443-444	3-03-95	S	32
53	43	1	444	3-03-95	S	10

RESOLUTION OF THE THIRD CONGRESS

1	1	1	444	3-03-95	HJR	1

PUBLIC ACTS OF THE FOURTH CONGRESS

Public Law/Resolution		Statutes at Large	Page	Date	Bill No.	
Chapter	Number					
1	1	1	445-448	2-05-96	HR	142
2	2	1	448	2-19-96	HR	139
4	3	1	448-449	3-10-96	HR	132
5	4	1	449-450	3-10-96	HR	151
7	5	1	450	3-12-96	HR	154
8	6	1	450	3-23-96	HR	145
10	7	1	450-451	3-31-96	S	39
11	8	1	451-452	3-31-96	HR	141
12	9	1	452	4-08-96	HR	159
13	10	1	452-453	4-18-96	HR	138
14	11	1	453-454	4-20-96	S	40
15	12	1	454-458	4-20-96	HR	156
16	13	1	458-459	4-28-96	HR	152
17	14	1	459	5-06-96	HR	178
18	15	1	459-460	5-06-96	HR	169
19	16	1	460	5-06-96	HR	171
20	17	1	460	5-06-96	HR	170
21	18	1	461	5-06-96	HR	144
22	19	1	461-462	5-06-96	HR	167
23	20	1	462	5-06-96	HR	177
24	21	1	463	5-12-96	HR	185
25	22	1	463	5-12-96	HR	173
26	23	1	463-464	5-12-96	HR	161
27	24	1	464	5-17-96	HR	179
29	25	1	464-469	5-18-96	HR	135
30	26	1	469-474	5-19-96	HR	137
31	27	1	474	5-27-96	HR	176
32	28	1	474-475	5-27-96	HR	189
33	29	1	475	5-27-96	S	45
34	30	1	475-476	5-27-96	HR	168
35	31	1	476-477	5-27-96	HR	182
36	32	1	477-478	5-28-96	HR	155
37	33	1	478-482	5-28-96	HR	133
38	34	1	482-483	5-28-96	S	37
39	35	1	483-486	5-30-96	HR	166
40	36	1	486-487	5-30-96	S	41
41	37	1	487-488	5-30-96	HR	140
43	38	1	488	5-30-96	S	43

PUBLIC ACTS OF THE FOURTH CONGRESS

Public Law/Resolution		Statutes at Large	Page	Date	Bill No.	
Chapter	Number					
44	39	1	488-489	5-31-96	HR	164
45	40	1	489-490	6-01-96	HR	196
46	41	1	490-491	6-01-96	HR	147
47	42	1	491-492	6-01-96	S	46
48	43	1	492	6-01-96	HR	193
49	44	1	492	6-01-96	HR	191
50	45	1	493	6-01-96	HR	203
51	46	1	493-494	6-01-96	HR	201
52	47	1	494	6-01-96	HR	172
53	48	1	495	6-01-96	HR	198

RESOLUTIONS OF THE FOURTH CONGRESS

1	1	1	495	4-18-96	HJR	1

PUBLIC ACTS OF THE FOURTH CONGRESS

Public Law/Resolution		Statutes at Large	Page	Date	Bill No.	
Chapter	Number					
1	1	1	496	12-21-96	HR	204
2	2	1	496-497	1-31-97	S	50
3	3	1	497	3-02-97	HR	220
5	4	1	497	3-02-97	S	49
6	5	1	497	3-02-97	S	52
7	6	1	498	3-02-97	HR	222
8	7	1	498-501	3-02-97	HR	223
9	8	1	502-503	3-03-97	HR	211
10	9	1	503-504	3-03-97	HR	233
11	10	1	504-505	3-03-97	HR	214
12	11	1	505-506	3-03-97	HR	234
13	12	1	506-507	3-03-97	HR	216
14	13	1	507	3-03-97	HR	235
15	14	1	507	3-03-97	S	54
16	15	1	507-508	3-03-97	HR	219
17	16	1	508-509	3-03-97	HR	236
18	17	1	509	3-03-97	HR	238
19	18	1	509-512	3-03-97	HR	205
20	19	1	512-516	3-03-97	HR	226
23	20	1	516	3-03-97	HR	237
24	21	1	516	3-03-97	HR	240
25	22	1	516-517	3-03-97	HR	241
26	23	1	517	3-03-97	HR	221
27	24	1	517-518	3-03-97	S	53

RESOLUTIONS OF THE FOURTH CONGRESS

1	1	1	519	3-02-97	HJR	1
2	2	1	519	3-03-97	HJR	2

PUBLIC ACTS OF THE FIFTH CONGRESS

Public Law/Resolution		Statutes at Large	Page	Date	Bill No.	
Chapter	Number					
1	1	1	520	6-14-97	S	2
2	2	1	520-521	6-14-97	S	1
3	3	1	521-522	6-23-97	HR	1
4	4	1	522	6-24-97	HR	9
5	5	1	523	6-27-97	HR	3
6	6	1	523	6-30-97	HR	6
7	7	1	523-525	7-01-97	S	4
8	8	1	525-526	7-01-97	S	5
9	9	1	526	7-05-97	HR	16
10	10	1	527	7-05-97	HR	13
11	11	1	527-532	7-06-97	HR	8
12	12	1	533	7-06-97	S	7
13	13	1	533	7-06-97	S	6
14	14	1	533	7-06-97	S	8
15	15	1	533-534	7-08-97	HR	17
16	16	1	534	7-08-97	HR	14
17	17	1	534-535	7-10-97	HR	15

Public Law/Resolution		Statutes at Large	Page	Date	Bill No.	
Chapter	Number					
1	1	1	536	12-15-97	HR	21
2	2	1	536-537	1-15-98	HR	34
6	3	1	537	1-20-98	S	10
8	4	1	537-539	1-23-98	HR	35
10	5	1	539	1-29-98	HR	32
11	6	1	539	2-01-98	HR	25
14	7	1	539-540	2-27-98	HR	44
15	8	1	540	3-14-98	HR	55
16	9	1	540	3-14-98	HR	50
17	10	1	541	3-19-98	HR	41
18	11	1	542-545	3-19-98	HR	43
20	12	1	545-546	3-19-98	HR	53
21	13	1	546	3-27-98	HR	58
22	14	1	546	3-27-98	HR	60
23	15	1	547	3-27-98	HR	64
24	16	1	547	3-28-98	HR	69
25	17	1	547	4-07-98	HR	68
26	18	1	547-549	4-07-98	HR	40
27	19	1	549	4-07-98	HR	62
28	20	1	549-550	4-07-98	S	12
29	21	1	551	4-18-98	HR	71
30	22	1	551	4-18-98	HR	65
31	23	1	552	4-27-98	HR	115
33	24	1	552-553	4-27-98	HR	80
34	25	1	553	4-27-98	HR	120
35	26	1	553-554	4-30-98	S	18
36	27	1	554	5-03-98	HR	74
37	28	1	554-555	5-03-98	HR	79
38	29	1	555-556	5-04-98	HR	81
39	30	1	556	5-04-98	HR	106
41	31	1	556	5-08-98	HR	85
42	32	1	556-557	5-08-98	HR	87
43	33	1	557	5-14-98	HR	66
46	34	1	557	5-22-98	S	21
47	35	1	558-561	5-28-98	HR	111
48	36	1	561	5-28-98	S	22
49	37	1	561-562	6-06-98	HR	98
50	38	1	562	6-06-98	HR	99

Public Law/Resolution		Statutes at Large	Page	Date	Bill No.	
Chapter	Number					
51	39	1	562-563	6-12-98	HR	83
52	40	1	563-564	6-12-98	HR	73
53	41	1	565-566	6-13-98	HR	102
54	42	1	566-569	6-18-98	HR	92
55	43	1	569	6-22-98	HR	106
56	44	1	569	6-22-98	S	27
57	45	1	569-570	6-22-98	HR	111
58	46	1	570-572	6-25-98	S	24
60	47	1	572-573	6-25-98	HR	109
61	48	1	573-574	6-27-98	S	28
62	49	1	574-575	6-28-98	S	26
63	50	1	575	6-28-98	HR	112
64	51	1	575-576	6-30-98	HR	115
65	52	1	576-577	7-06-98	HR	107
66	53	1	577-578	7-06-98	HR	108
67	54	1	578	7-07-98	S	29
68	55	1	578-580	7-09-98	HR	119
69	56	1	580	7-09-98	HR	61
70	57	1	580-591	7-09-98	HR	105
71	58	1	591-594	7-11-98	HR	100
72	59	1	594-596	7-11-98	HR	101
73	60	1	596	7-14-98	HR	122
74	61	1	596-597	7-14-98	S	31
75	62	1	597-604	7-14-98	HR	116
76	63	1	604-605	7-16-98	HR	125
77	64	1	605-606	7-16-98	HR	166
78	65	1	607	7-16-98	HR	120
79	66	1	607-608	7-16-98	HR	113
80	67	1	608	7-16-98	HR	121
81	68	1	608	7-16-98	HR	133
82	69	1	608-609	7-16-98	HR	123
83	70	1	609	7-16-98	HR	127
84	71	1	609-610	7-16-98	HR	129
85	72	1	610	7-16-98	HR	124
86	73	1	611	7-16-98	HR	126
88	74	1	611	7-16-98	S	36
89	75	1	612	7-16-98	HR	134

RESOLUTION OF THE FIFTH CONGRESS

Public Law/Resolution		Statutes at Large	Page	Date	Bill No.
Chapter	Number				
1	1	1	612	6-22-98	HJR 1

Public Law/Resolution		Statutes at Large	Page	Date	Bill No.	
Chapter	Number					
1	1	1	613	1-30-99	HR	141
2	2	1	613-616	2-09-99	HR	140
3	3	1	616-617	2-15-99	HR	136
6	4	1	617	2-19-99	HR	142
8	5	1	617-618	2-19-99	S	41
9	6	1	618	2-19-99	HR	161
10	7	1	618	2-25-99	HR	164
11	8	1	618-619	2-25-99	S	43
12	9	1	619-621	2-25-99	HR	145
13	10	1	621-622	2-25-99	HR	150
15	11	1	622	2-25-99	HR	151
16	12	1	622	2-25-99	HR	152
17	13	1	622-624	2-28-99	HR	138
18	14	1	624	2-28-99	S	50
19	15	1	624-626	2-28-99	HR	159
20	16	1	626-627	2-28-99	HR	143
21	17	1	627	2-28-99	S	51
22	18	1	627-704	3-02-99	HR	154
23	19	1	704-709	3-02-99	HR	162
24	20	1	709-717	3-02-99	HR	146
25	21	1	717-720	3-02-99	HR	147
26	22	1	720-721	3-02-99	HR	176
27	23	1	721-723	3-02-99	S	49
28	24	1	723-724	3-02-99	HR	173
29	25	1	724	3-02-99	HR	169
30	26	1	724-725	3-02-99	HR	178
31	27	1	725-727	3-02-99	S	45
32	28	1	727	3-02-99	S	47
33	29	1	727-728	3-02-99	HR	157
34	30	1	728-729	3-02-99	HR	175
36	31	1	729	3-02-99	HR	166
37	32	1	729	3-02-99	HR	171
38	33	1	729-730	3-02-99	HR	158
39	34	1	730	3-02-99	HR	167
40	35	1	730-731	3-02-99	HR	156
41	36	1	731-732	3-02-99	HR	174
42	37	1	732	3-02-99	HR	155
43	38	1	733-741	3-02-99	HR	160

PUBLIC ACTS OF THE FIFTH CONGRESS

Public Law/Resolution		Statutes at Large	Page	Date	Bill No.	
Chapter	Number					
44	39	1	741-743	3-02-99	HR	149
45	40	1	743	3-03-99	S	39
46	41	1	743-749	3-03-99	S	52
47	42	1	749	3-03-99	S	53
48	43	1	749-755	3-03-99	S	38

RESOLUTION OF THE FIFTH CONGRESS

1	1	1	755	3-02-99	HJR	1

PUBLIC ACTS OF THE SIXTH CONGRESS

Public Law/Resolution		Statutes at Large	Page	Date	Bill No.	
Chapter	Number					
1	1	2	3	12-24-99	S	55
2	2	2	4	1-02-00	HR	180
3	3	2	4	1-02-00	HR	181
4	4	2	4- 6	1-06-00	S	56
5	5	2	6- 7	1-17-00	HR	179
6	6	2	7	2-11-00	HR	187
8	7	2	7	2-11-00	HR	197
9	8	2	7	2-20-00	HR	188
10	9	2	7-11	2-27-00	HR	201
12	10	2	11-14	2-28-00	HR	182
13	11	2	14-16	3-01-00	HR	194
14	12	2	16-18	3-03-00	HR	183
15	13	2	18	3-17-00	HR	190
16	14	2	18-19	3-19-00	HR	214
18	15	2	19	4-03-00	HR	230
19	16	2	19-36	4-04-00	HR	186
21	17	2	36	4-05-00	HR	198
22	18	2	36-37	4-12-00	HR	193
23	19	2	37	4-12-00	HR	227
25	20	2	37-38	4-17-00	HR	205
26	21	2	38-39	4-22-00	HR	212
27	22	2	39	4-22-00	HR	237
28	23	2	39	4-22-00	HR	246
29	24	2	39	4-22-00	HR	226
30	25	2	39-40	4-22-00	HR	223
31	26	2	40-42	4-23-00	HR	196
32	27	2	42-45	4-23-00	HR	206
33	28	2	45-53	4-23-00	HR	211
34	29	2	53-54	4-24-00	HR	195
35	30	2	54	4-24-00	HR	236
36	31	2	54	4-24-00	HR	238
37	32	2	55-56	4-24-00	HR	228
38	33	2	56-57	4-28-00	HR	225
39	34	2	57-58	4-29-00	HR	234
40	35	2	58	5-02-00	HR	231
41	36	2	58-59	5-07-00	HR	224
42	37	2	60	5-07-00	HR	210
43	38	2	60-61	5-07-00	HR	248

Public Law/Resolution		Statutes at Large	Page	Date	Bill No.	
Chapter	Number					
45	39	2	61	5-07-00	HR	241
46	40	2	61-62	5-07-00	HR	219
47	41	2	62-66	5-07-00	HR	229
48	42	2	66-67	5-10-00	HR	235
49	43	2	68-69	5-10-00	HR	250
50	44	2	69-70	5-10-00	HR	218
51	45	2	70-71	5-10-00	S	62
53	46	2	71-72	5-10-00	HR	243
54	47	2	72	5-10-00	HR	256
55	48	2	73-78	5-10-00	HR	217
56	49	2	78-79	5-10-00	HR	216
57	50	2	79	5-10-00	HR	239
58	51	2	79-80	5-10-00	S	65
59	52	2	80	5-13-00	HR	251
60	53	2	80-81	5-13-00	HR	245
61	54	2	82	5-13-00	S	64
62	55	2	82	5-13-00	HR	259
63	56	2	82	5-13-00	HR	254
64	57	2	82-83	5-13-00	HR	266
65	58	2	83-84	5-13-00	HR	264
66	59	2	84-85	5-13-00	HR	267
67	60	2	85	5-13-00	S	67
68	61	2	85	5-13-00	HR	263
69	62	2	85-86	5-14-00	S	63
70	62	2	86	5-14-00	S	66

RESOLUTIONS OF THE SIXTH CONGRESS

1	1	2	86-87	12-24-99	HJR	1
2	2	2	87	1-06-00	HJR	2
3	3	2	87	2-03-00	HJR	3
4	4	2	87	3-29-00	HJR	4
5	5	2	87	4-16-00	HJR	5

PUBLIC ACTS OF THE SIXTH CONGRESS

Public Law/Resolution		Statutes at Large	Page	Date	Bill No.	
Chapter	Number					
1	1	2	88	12-15-00	HR	269
3	2	2	88-89	1-30-01	HR	282
4	3	2	89-100	2-13-01	HR	275
5	4	2	100-101	2-18-01	HR	280
6	5	2	101	2-18-01	HR	286
7	6	2	101-102	2-25-01	S	69
9	7	2	102	2-25-01	HR	303
11	8	2	102-103	2-25-01	HR	276
12	9	2	103	2-27-01	HR	312
13	10	2	103	2-27-01	HR	285
15	11	2	103-108	2-27-01	S	68
16	12	2	108	3-02-01	HR	300
17	13	2	108	3-02-01	HR	297
18	14	2	108-109	3-02-01	HR	298
19	15	2	109-110	3-03-01	HR	315
20	16	2	110-111	3-03-01	HR	306
21	17	2	111	3-03-01	HR	311
22	18	2	111-112	3-03-01	HR	316
23	19	2	112-114	3-03-01	HR	294
24	20	2	115-116	3-03-01	HR	321
25	21	2	116-117	3-03-01	HR	317
26	22	2	117	3-03-01	HR	320
27	23	2	117-121	3-03-01	HR	277
28	24	2	121	3-03-01	HR	319
29	25	2	121	3-03-01	HR	314
30	26	2	121-122	3-03-01	HR	324
31	27	2	122-123	3-03-01	HR	288
32	28	2	123-124	3-03-01	HR	322
33	29	2	124-125	2-27-01	HR	295
34	30	2	125	3-03-01	HR	305
35	31	2	125-127	3-03-01	HR	308

RESOLUTIONS OF THE SIXTH CONGRESS

1	1	2	127	3-02-01	HJR	1

Public Law/Resolution		Statutes at Large	Page	Date	Bill No.	
Chapter	Number					
1	1	2	128	1-14-02	HR	1
2	2	2	128-129	1-26-02	HR	5
4	3	2	129-130	2-06-02	HR	6
5	4	2	130-131	2-18-02	HR	4
6	5	2	131	2-23-02	HR	22
8	6	2	132	3-08-02	S	2
9	7	2	132-137	3-16-02	HR	7
11	8	2	137-138	3-16-02	HR	28
12	9	2	138-139	3-16-02	HR	24
13	10	2	139-146	3-30-02	S	5
15	11	2	147	4-02-02	HR	41
16	12	2	148	4-03-02	S	6
17	13	2	148	4-03-02	HR	36
19	14	2	148-150	4-06-02	HR	31
20	15	2	150-152	4-06-02	HR	30
21	16	2	152	4-06-02	HR	33
22	17	2	152	4-14-02	HR	9
23	18	2	152	4-14-02	HR	44
25	19	2	152	4-14-02	HR	26
26	20	2	153	4-14-02	HR	3
28	21	2	153-155	4-14-02	HR	18
30	22	2	155-156	4-26-02	HR	26
31	23	2	156-167	4-29-02	S	9
32	24	2	167-170	4-29-02	HR	56
33	25	2	170	4-29-02	HR	60
35	26	2	170-171	4-29-02	HR	42
36	27	2	171-172	4-29-02	S	8
37	28	2	172-173	4-30-02	HR	61
38	29	2	173	4-30-02	HR	13
39	30	2	173	4-30-02	HR	65
40	31	2	173-175	4-30-02	HR	46
41	32	2	175-178	5-01-02	HR	53
43	33	2	178-179	5-01-02	HR	58
44	34	2	179-180	5-01-02	S	10
45	35	2	181-182	5-01-02	HR	48
46	36	2	183-184	5-01-02	HR	63
47	37	2	184-188	5-01-02	HR	12
48	38	2	188-192	5-03-02	HR	43

PUBLIC ACTS OF THE SEVENTH CONGRESS

Public Law/Resolution		Statutes at Large	Page	Date	Bill No.	
Chapter	Number					
49	39	2	192	5-03-02	HR	67
51	40	2	192-193	5-03-02	HR	50
52	41	2	193-195	5-03-02	HR	66
53	42	2	195-197	5-03-02	HR	52

RESOLUTIONS OF THE SEVENTH CONGRESS

1	1	2	198	1-21-02	HJR	1
2	2	2	198	2-03-02	HJR	2

Public Law/Resolution		Statutes at Large	Page	Date	Bill No.	
Chapter	Number					
1	1	2	199	1-14-03	HR	71
4	2	2	199	2-10-03	HR	88
5	3	2	200-201	2-19-03	HR	95
6	4	2	201	2-19-03	HR	80
7	5	2	201-202	2-19-03	S	12
8	6	2	202	2-26-03	HR	126
9	7	2	203-205	2-28-03	HR	83
10	8	2	205-206	2-28-03	HR	101
11	9	2	206	2-28-03	HR	91
12	10	2	206	2-28-03	HR	127
13	11	2	206-207	2-28-03	HR	87
14	12	2	207	2-28-03	HR	108
15	13	2	207	3-02-03	HR	98
16	14	2	208	3-02-03	HR	96
17	15	2	208-209	3-02-03	HR	107
18	16	2	209-210	3-02-03	HR	106
19	17	2	210-215	3-02-03	HR	112
20	18	2	215-225	3-03-03	HR	124
21	19	2	225-227	3-03-03	HR	115
23	20	2	227	3-03-03	HR	104
24	21	2	227-228	3-03-03	HR	72
25	22	2	228	3-03-03	HR	109
26	23	2	228-229	3-03-03	HR	114
27	24	2	229-235	3-03-03	HR	119
28	25	2	235	3-03-03	HR	118
29	26	2	235-236	3-03-03	HR	131
30	27	2	236-237	3-03-03	HR	111
31	28	2	237-241	3-03-03	HR	75
32	29	2	241	3-03-03	S	16
33	30	2	242	3-03-03	S	14
34	31	2	242	3-03-03	S	15
35	32	2	242	3-03-03	HR	123
36	33	2	242	3-03-03	HR	92
37	34	2	242-243	3-03-03	HR	97
39	35	2	243-244	3-03-03	HR	122
40	36	2	244	3-03-03	HR	90

PUBLIC ACTS OF THE EIGHTH CONGRESS

Public Law/Resolution		Statutes at Large	Page	Date	Bill No.	
Chapter	Number					
1	1	2	245	10-31-03	S	17
2	2	2	245-247	11-10-03	HR	133
3	3	2	247-248	11-10-03	HR	134
4	4	2	248	11-16-03	HR	135
5	5	2	248	11-25-03	HR	137
6	6	2	248	12-19-03	HR	140
9	7	2	249	1-31-04	HR	152
11	8	2	249-250	2-10-04	HR	150
12	9	2	250	2-20-04	HR	168
13	10	2	251-254	2-24-04	HR	142
14	11	2	254-255	2-24-04	HR	166
15	12	2	255-259	2-25-04	HR	173
17	13	2	259-260	2-25-04	HR	155
18	14	2	260-261	3-03-04	HR	177
19	15	2	261	3-03-04	HR	149
20	16	2	262-264	3-03-04	HR	147
21	17	2	264-269	3-14-04	HR	165
22	18	2	269	3-16-04	HR	198
23	19	2	270	3-16-04	HR	189
24	20	2	270	3-16-04	HR	195
25	21	2	270-271	3-16-04	S	25
26	22	2	271-272	3-19-04	HR	175
27	23	2	272	3-19-04	HR	197
28	24	2	272	3-19-04	HR	204
29	25	2	273	3-19-04	HR	209
31	26	2	273-274	3-23-04	HR	187
32	27	2	274	3-23-04	HR	216
33	28	2	274-275	3-23-04	S	24
34	29	2	275-277	3-26-04	HR	176
35	30	2	277-283	3-26-04	HR	203
36	31	2	283	3-26-04	S	29
38	32	2	283-289	3-26-04	S	23
39	33	2	290	3-26-04	HR	206
40	34	2	290-291	3-26-04	S	20
43	35	2	291	3-26-04	S	30
44	36	2	291	3-26-04	HR	215
46	37	2	291-292	3-26-04	HR	219
47	38	2	292-293	3-26-04	HR	164

PUBLIC ACTS OF THE EIGHTH CONGRESS

Public Law/Resolution		Statutes at Large	Page	Date	Bill No.	
Chapter	Number					
48	39	2	293-294	3-26-04	S.	21
49	40	2	294	3-26-04	S	27
50	41	2	295-296	3-26-04	S	26
51	42	2	296	3-27-04	HR	208
52	43	2	296-297	3-27-04	HR	155
53	44	2	297	3-27-04	HR	185
54	45	2	297-298	3-27-04	HR	170
55	46	2	298	3-27-04	HR	214
56	47	2	298-299	3-27-04	HR	172
57	48	2	299-300	3-27-04	HR	211
58	49	2	300-301	3-27-04	HR	217
59	50	2	301-302	3-27-04	HR	199
60	51	2	302-303	3-27-04	S	35
61	52	2	303-306	3-27-04	HR	202

RESOLUTION OF THE EIGHTH CONGRESS

1	1	2	306	1804	HJR	1

PUBLIC ACTS OF THE EIGHTH CONGRESS

Public Law/Resolution		Statutes at Large	Page	Date	Bill No.	
Chapter	Number					
1	1	2	307	11-24-04	HR	1
2	2	2	307	12-06-04	HR	7
3	3	2	308	1-02-05	S	1
4	4	2	308-309	1-05-05	HR	6
5	5	2	309-310	1-11-05	S	2
6	6	2	310	1-11-05	HR	20
7	7	2	310	1-19-05	HR	8
9	8	2	310-311	1-25-05	HR	22
10	9	2	311	1-25-05	HR	31
11	10	2	311-313	1-30-05	HR	13
14	11	2	313-314	2-11-05	S	4
15	12	2	314	2-14-05	HR	23
16	13	2	315	2-14-05	HR	33
17	14	2	315	2-14-05	HR	34
18	15	2	315-316	2-22-05	HR	24
19	16	2	316	3-01-05	HR	42
20	17	2	316	3-01-05	S	9
21	18	2	316-321	3-01-05	HR	26
23	19	2	322-323	3-02-05	S	8
24	20	2	323-324	3-02-05	HR	30
26	21	2	324-329	3-02-05	S	7
27	22	2	329-330	3-02-05	HR	56
28	23	2	330	3-02-05	HR	17
29	24	2	330	3-02-05	HR	50
30	25	2	330	3-02-05	HR	45
31	26	2	331-332	3-03-05	S	11
32	27	2	332-336	3-03-05	HR	32
33	28	2	336	3-03-05	S	13
34	29	2	336-337	3-03-05	HR	36
35	30	2	337-338	3-03-05	HR	63
36	31	2	338	3-03-05	HR	70
38	32	2	338-339	3-03-05	S	5
40	33	2	339	3-03-05	S	3
41	34	2	339-342	3-03-05	HR	4
42	35	2	342-343	3-03-05	HR	5
43	36	2	343-345	3-03-05	HR	53
44	37	2	345-346	3-03-05	S	6
47	38	2	346	3-03-05	HR	69

RESOLUTIONS OF THE EIGHTH CONGRESS

Public Law/Resolution		Statutes at Large	Page	Date	Bill No.	
Chapter	Number					
1	1	2	346	11-27-04	HJR	1
2	2	2	346-347	3-03-05	SJR	1

PUBLIC ACTS OF THE NINTH CONGRESS

Public Law/Resolution		Statutes at Large	Page	Date	Bill No.	
Chapter	Number					
1	1	2	348	12-11-05	HR	71
2	2	2	348	12-31-05	HR	73
3	3	2	349	1-22-06	HR	90
4	4	2	349	1-22-06	HR	81
5	5	2	349-350	2-13-06	HR	144
6	6	2	350	2-21-06	S	18
7	7	2	350	2-21-06	S	19
8	8	2	350	2-21-06	HR	83
9	9	2	351-352	2-28-06	S	24
10	10	2	352	2-28-06	S	21
11	11	2	352-353	2-28-06	HR	82
12	12	2	353-354	2-28-06	HR	95
13	13	2	354	2-28-06	HR	96
14	14	2	354-355	3-08-06	HR	84
15	15	2	355	3-08-06	HR	100
16	16	2	356-357	3-28-06	HR	91
17	17	2	357	3-28-06	HR	87
19	18	2	357-359	3-29-06	S	16
20	19	2	359-372	4-10-06	HR	77
21	20	2	372-374	4-10-06	HR	88
22	21	2	374-375	4-10-06	HR	78
23	22	2	375	4-10-06	HR	93
24	23	2	375	4-10-06	HR	114
25	24	2	376-378	4-10-06	HR	74
26	25	2	378	4-15-06	HR	103
28	26	2	378-379	4-15-06	S	30
29	27	2	379-381	4-18-06	HR	117
30	28	2	381	4-18-06	HR	133
31	29	2	381-383	4-18-06	S	26
32	30	2	383-384	4-18-06	HR	85
33	31	2	384-389	4-18-06	HR	110
34	32	2	389-390	4-21-06	S	22
35	33	2	390	4-21-06	HR	89
36	34	2	390-391	4-21-06	S	32
38	35	2	391	4-21-06	HR	141
39	36	2	391-395	4-21-06	S	33
40	37	2	395-396	4-21-06	HR	137
41	38	2	396-397	4-21-06	S	31

PUBLIC ACTS OF THE NINTH CONGRESS

Public Law/Resolution		Statutes at Large	Page	Date	Bill No.	
Chapter	Number					
42	39	2	398	4-21-06	HR	125
43	40	2	398-399	4-21-06	HR	116
44	41	2	399	4-21-06	HR	120
45	42	2	399-400	4-21-06	HR	121
46	43	2	400-401	4-21-06	S	26
47	44	2	402	4-21-06	HR	128
48	45	2	402-404	4-21-06	HR	111
49	46	2	404-405	4-21-06	S	25
50	47	2	405-406	4-18-06	HR	86
51	48	2	406	4-21-06	HR	119
52	49	2	407	4-18-06	HR	131
53	50	2	407	4-21-06	HR	140
54	51	2	408	4-18-06	HR	124
55	52	2	408-410	4-21-06	HR	118

RESOLUTION OF THE NINTH CONGRESS

1	1	2	410	4-10-06	HJR	1

PUBLIC ACTS OF THE NINTH CONGRESS

Public Law/Resolution		Statutes at Large	Page	Date	Bill No.	
Chapter	Number					
1	1	2	411	12-19-06	HR	145
2	2	2	411-412	1-07-07	HR	155
3	3	2	412-413	1-10-07	HR	156
5	4	2	413	2-04-07	S	37
8	5	2	413-414	2-10-07	HR	164
9	6	2	414-415	2-10-07	HR	176
12	7	2	415-418	2-11-07	HR	158
13	8	2	418	2-13-07	HR	161
14	9	2	418-419	2-13-07	HR	169
15	10	2	419-420	2-24-07	HR	166
16	11	2	420-421	2-24-07	S	40
17	12	2	421-422	2-24-07	HR	168
18	13	2	422	2-24-07	HR	184
19	14	2	422-423	2-24-07	HR	194
20	15	2	423-424	2-24-07	S	46
21	16	2	424-426	3-02-07	HR	190
22	17	2	426-430	3-02-07	S	41
23	18	2	430-431	3-03-07	S	44
25	19	2	431	3-03-07	HR	173
28	20	2	432	3-03-07	HR	195
29	21	2	432-436	3-03-07	HR	204
30	22	2	436-437	3-03-07	HR	220
31	23	2	437	3-03-07	HR	199
34	24	2	437-439	3-03-07	S	47
35	25	2	440	3-03-07	HR	187
36	26	2	440-442	3-03-07	HR	191
37	27	2	443	3-03-07	HR	196
39	28	2	443	3-03-07	HR	152
40	29	2	443	3-03-07	HR	212
41	30	2	443-444	3-03-07	HR	217
43	31	2	444	3-03-07	HR	221
44	32	2	444	3-03-07	HR	214
45	33	2	444	3-03-07	HR	189
46	34	2	445-446	3-03-07	S	48
47	35	2	446-448	3-03-07	S	43
49	36	2	448-449	3-03-07	HR	175

RESOLUTION OF THE NINTH CONGRESS

1	1	2	449	3-02-07	HJR	1

PUBLIC ACTS OF THE TENTH CONGRESS

Public Law/Resolution		Statutes at Large	Page	Date	Bill No.	
Chapter	Number					
1	1	2	450	11-24-07	HR	1
2	2	2	450-451	12-05-07	HR	4
3	3	2	451	12-15-07	HR	8
4	4	2	451	12-18-07	S	2
5	5	2	451-453	12-22-07	HR	26
7	6	2	453	1-08-08	HR	10
8	7	2	453-454	1-09-08	HR	26*
9	8	2	455	1-09-08	HR	3
10	9	2	455-456	1-19-08	HR	13
11	10	2	456	1-19-08	HR	27
12	11	2	456	1-21-08	HR	14
14	12	2	456-457	1-27-08	HR	25
15	13	2	457-461	2-05-08	HR	2
16	14	2	462	2-10-08	HR	41
17	15	2	462-466	2-10-08	HR	23
18	16	2	466-467	2-10-08	HR	42
19	17	2	467	2-10-08	S	6
20	18	2	467-468	2-19-08	HR	54
21	19	2	468	2-19-08	S	5
22	20	2	468-469	2-25-08	HR	30
24	21	2	469	2-25-08	HR	36
25	22	2	469	2-27-08	HR	16
26	23	2	470	2-29-08	HR	17
27	24	2	470	3-03-08	HR	58
28	25	2	471	3-03-08	HR	44
29	26	2	471	3-09-08	HR	40
30	27	2	471-473	3-10-08	HR	55
31	28	2	473	3-11-08	HR	60
33	29	2	473-475	3-12-08	HR	56
34	30	2	476	3-13-08	HR	11
35	31	2	476	3-17-08	S	8
37	32	2	477	3-21-08	HR	49
38	33	2	477-478	3-22-08	S	10
39	34	2	478-479	3-30-08	HR	67
40	35	2	479-481	3-31-08	HR	57
41	36	2	481	4-01-08	HR	33
42	37	2	481	4-02-08	HR	66
43	38	2	481-483	4-12-08	S	11

PUBLIC ACTS OF THE TENTH CONGRESS

Public Law/Resolution		Statutes at Large	Page	Date	Bill No.	
Chapter	Number					
44	39	2	483-484	4-13-08	HR	86
46	40	2	484	4-19-08	S	17
47	41	2	484	4-20-08	S	15
48	42	2	484-485	4-21-08	HR	45
50	43	2	485-489	4-21-08	S	18
51	44	2	489-490	4-21-08	HR	65
52	46	2	490	4-22-08	S	19
53	47	2	490	4-22-08	S	23
55	48	2	490-491	4-23-08	HR	87
56	49	2	491	4-23-08	HR	97
57	50	2	491	4-23-08	HR	92
58	51	2	491-496	4-25-08	HR	78
60	52	2	496	4-25-08	HR	91
61	53	2	497	4-25-08	S	22
62	54	2	497-498	4-25-08	HR	95
63	55	2	498	4-25-08	S	16
65	56	2	499	4-25-08	HR	89
66	57	2	499-502	4-25-08	S	1*
67	58	2	502-504	4-25-08	HR	70

RESOLUTION OF THE TENTH CONGRESS

1	1	2	504	3-04-08	SJR	1

PUBLIC ACTS OF THE TENTH CONGRESS

Public Law/Resolution		Statutes at Large	Page	Date	Bill No.	
Chapter	Number					
1	1	2	505	11-18-08	HR	101
3	2	2	505	1-06-09	HR	104
4	3	2	505-506	1-07-09	HR	107
5	4	2	506-511	1-09-09	S	33
6	5	2	511	1-10-09	HR	126
8	6	2	511-513	1-12-09	HR	105
9	7	2	513	1-12-09	S	30
10	8	2	514	1-30-09	HR	140
11	9	2	514	1-31-09	S	32
13	10	2	514-516	2-03-09	HR	132
14	11	2	516	2-04-09	S	38
15	12	2	516-517	2-10-09	HR	148
16	13	2	517	2-15-09	HR	109
17	14	2	517-520	2-16-09	HR	108
18	15	2	520-525	2-17-09	HR	157
19	16	2	525-526	2-27-09	HR	124
20	17	2	526	2-28-09	S	50
22	18	2	526-527	2-28-09	HR	161
23	19	2	527	2-28-09	S	37
24	20	2	528-533	2-01-09	S	48
25	21	2	533	3-02-09	S	47
26	22	2	533-534	3-02-09	S	40
27	23	2	534-535	3-02-09	S	28
28	24	2	535-537	3-03-09	S	54
29	25	2	537	3-03-09	S	34
30	26	2	537-538	3-03-09	S	49
31	27	2	539-544	3-03-09	S	44
33	28	2	544	3-03-09	S	45
34	29	2	544-545	3-03-09	HR	166
36	30	2	545-546	3-03-09	HR	164

PUBLIC ACTS OF THE ELEVENTH CONGRESS

Public Law/Resolution		Statutes at Large	Page	Date	Bill No.	
Chapter	Number					
1	1	2	547	5-30-09	HR	1
2	2	2	547	6-14-09	S	2
3	3	2	548	6-15-09	HR	7
4	4	2	548	6-15-09	HR	3
5	5	2	549	6-15-09	HR	8
7	6	2	549	6-24-09	S	1
8	7	2	549-550	6-28-09	S	8
9	8	2	550-551	6-28-09	S	6
10	9	2	551	6-28-09	HR	11
11	10	2	552	6-28-09	S	7
12	11	2	552	6-28-09	S	3
14	12	2	552	6-28-09	S	10
15	13	2	552	6-28-09	HR	14
16	14	2	552-553	6-28-09	S	9
17	15	2	553	6-28-09	HR	22

Public Law/Resolution		Statutes at Large	Page	Date	Bill No.	
Chapter	Number					
1	1	2	554	12-09-09	HR	32
2	2	2	554-555	12-15-09	HR	33
3	3	2	555	12-19-09	HR	34
5	4	2	555	1-12-10	HR	58
8	5	2	555-556	2-14-10	S	13
11	6	2	556	2-24-10	HR	59
12	7	2	556-557	2-24-10	HR	35
13	8	2	557-562	2-26-10	HR	72
14	9	2	562-563	3-02-10	HR	71
15	10	2	563	3-02-10	HR	70
16	11	2	563-564	3-02-10	HR	63
17	12	2	564-568	3-26-10	HR	39
18	13	2	568	3-26-10	S	22
19	14	2	569	3-26-10	HR	68
20	15	2	569	3-30-10	S	18
21	16	2	569-570	3-30-10	HR	95
23	17	2	570	4-12-10	HR	126
26	18	2	570-577	4-20-10	S	21
27	19	2	577-578	4-25-10	HR	67
29	20	2	578	4-25-10	HR	116
30	21	2	579-589	4-28-10	HR	113
31	22	2	589	3-16-10	HR	53
33	23	2	589	4-27-10	HR	77
34	24	2	589-590	4-28-10	HR	122
35	25	2	590-591	4-30-10	HR	125
36	26	2	591-592	4-30-10	S	27
37	27	2	592-604	4-30-10	HR	90
38	28	2	605	5-01-10	HR	141
39	29	2	605-606	5-01-10	HR	129
40	30	2	607	5-01-10	HR	142
41	31	2	607	5-01-10	HR	60
43	32	2	607-608	5-01-10	HR	93
44	33	2	608-610	5-01-10	S	30
45	34	2	610-611	5-01-10	HR	128
47	35	2	611-612	5-01-10	S	32
50	36	2	612	5-01-10	S	38

RESOLUTIONS OF THE ELEVENTH CONGRESS

Public Law/Resolution		Statutes at Large	Page	Date	Bill No.	
Chapter	Number					
1	1	2	612	1-12-10	SJR	1
2	2	2	613	1-12-10	SJR	2

PUBLIC ACTS OF THE ELEVENTH CONGRESS

Public Law/Resolution		Statutes at Large	Page	Date	Bill No.	
Chapter	Number					
1	1	2	614	12-17-10	HR	144
2	2	2	614	1-07-11	HR	149
3	3	2	614-615	1-07-11	HR	150
4	4	2	615	1-17-11	HR	147
7	5	2	615	1-22-11	HR	151
9	6	2	615-616	2-06-11	HR	178
11	7	2	616-617	2-07-11	HR	179
12	8	2	617	2-13-11	S	56
14	9	2	617-621	2-15-11	HR	148
15	10	2	621-625	2-15-11	HR	161
16	11	2	625-629	2-15-11	S	49
17	12	2	629-633	2-16-11	S	47
18	13	2	633-636	2-16-11	S	48
19	14	2	636-640	2-18-11	S	52
20	15	2	641	2-18-11	S	57
21	16	2	641-643	2-20-11	HR	158
22	17	2	643-648	2-20-11	HR	177
23	18	2	648-649	2-22-11	S	61
24	19	2	649	2-25-11	HR	186
25	20	2	649-650	2-25-11	HR	156
26	21	2	650-651	2-26-11	HR	167
28	22	2	651	2-28-11	HR	202
29	23	2	651-652	3-02-11	HR	175
30	24	2	652-655	3-02-11	HR	180
31	25	2	655-656	3-02-11	S	60
32	26	2	656-657	3-02-11	HR	198
33	27	2	657-658	3-02-11	HR	210
34	28	2	658	3-02-11	HR	221
36	29	2	658	3-02-11	HR	220
37	30	2	659	3-02-11	HR	201
38	31	2	659-660	3-02-11	S	64
40	32	2	660	3-03-11	HR	193
41	33	2	660	3-03-11	HR	213
43	34	2	661	3-03-11	HR	219
44	35	2	661	3-03-11	HR	222
45	36	2	661-662	3-03-11	S	63
46	37	2	662-666	3-03-11	S	65

PUBLIC ACTS OF THE TWELFTH CONGRESS

Public Law/Resolution		Statutes at Large	Page	Date	Bill No.	
Chapter	Number					
1	1	2	667	11-18-11	HR	1
2	2	2	667	11-28-11	HR	5
3	3	2	667-668	12-06-11	S	2
4	4	2	668	12-12-11	HR	4
6	5	2	668	12-12-11	HR	13
8	6	2	668-669	12-12-11	S	1
9	7	2	669	12-21-11	HR	8
10	8	2	669-670	12-24-11	S	5
11	9	2	670	1-02-12	S	7
12	10	2	670-671	1-08-12	HR	7
14	11	2	671-674	1-11-12	S	6
15	12	2	674	1-14-12	HR	23
16	13	2	674-675	1-14-12	HR	22
17	14	2	675	1-23-12	HR	48
18	15	2	675-676	1-31-12	HR	17
20	16	2	676	2-06-12	HR	58
21	17	2	676-677	2-06-12	HR	32
22	18	2	677-678	2-20-12	HR	28
23	19	2	678	2-20-12	HR	43
24	20	2	679	2-20-12	HR	50
25	21	2	679-682	2-20-12	HR	11
26	22	2	682-683	2-21-12	HR	56
27	23	2	683-684	2-21-12	HR	57
29	24	2	684	2-21-12	HR	41
30	25	2	684-685	2-24-12	HR	59
31	26	2	685-686	2-21-12	HR	42
33	27	2	686-691	2-26-12	HR	54
34	28	2	691	3-02-12	HR	40
35	29	2	691-692	3-07-12	HR	66
36	30	2	692	3-10-12	HR	44
37	31	2	692	3-10-12	HR	25
38	32	2	692-693	3-10-12	HR	70
39	33	2	693	3-10-12	HR	73
40	34	2	694	3-12-12	S	11
41	35	2	694-695	3-14-12	HR	69
42	36	2	695	3-17-12	HR	75
43	37	2	695	3-19-12	HR	61
45	38	2	696	3-26-12	S	15

PUBLIC ACTS OF THE TWELFTH CONGRESS

Public Law/Resolution		Statutes at Large	Page	Date	Bill No.	
Chapter	Number					
46	39	2	696-699	3-28-12	S	12
47	40	2	699	3-30-12	HR	24
48	41	2	700	4-03-12	HR	84
49	42	2	700-701	4-04-12	HR	180
50	43	2	701-704	4-08-12	HR	88
53	44	2	704	4-08-12	HR	103
54	45	2	704-705	4-10-12	HR	76
55	46	2	705-707	4-10-12	HR	62
56	47	2	707-708	4-14-12	HR	183
57	48	2	708-709	4-14-12	S	22
58	49	2	709-710	4-14-12	S	21
62	50	2	710-711	4-23-12	HR	89
63	51	2	712	4-23-12	HR	85
64	52	2	712	4-23-12	HR	144
66	53	2	713	4-24-12	HR	16
67	54	2	713-716	4-25-12	HR	97
68	55	2	716-718	4-25-12	S	13
69	56	2	718-719	4-25-12	HR	77
70	57	2	719	4-27-12	HR	110
71	58	2	719-720	4-29-12	S	27
72	59	2	720-721	4-29-12	S	4
75	60	2	721-727	5-04-12	HR	33
76	61	2	728	5-06-12	S	14
77	62	2	728-730	5-06-12	S	20
78	63	2	730	5-06-12	S	28
79	64	2	730	5-08-12	HR	122
80	65	2	730-732	5-11-12	HR	51
83	66	2	732-734	5-14-12	HR	92
84	67	2	734	5-14-12	HR	123
85	68	2	734	5-16-12	HR	105
86	69	2	735	5-16-12	HR	175
87	70	2	735-741	5-16-12	S	23
88	71	2	741	5-20-12	S	17
90	72	2	741-742	5-20-12	HR	111
92	73	2	742-743	5-22-12	S	12
93	74	2	743	5-22-12	S	36
95	75	2	743-747	6-04-12	HR	4
97	76	2	748	6-10-12	HR	129

PUBLIC ACTS OF THE TWELFTH CONGRESS

Public Law/Resolution		Statutes at Large	Page	Date	Bill No.	
Chapter	Number					
98	77	2	748	6-10-12	HR	133
99	78	2	748-752	6-13-12	HR	113
100	79	2	752	6-17-12	HR	137
101	80	2	752-755	6-17-12	HR	86
102	81	2	755	6-18-12	HR	184
106	82	2	755-759	6-24-12	HR	49
107	83	2	759-764	6-26-12	HR	148
108	84	2	764	6-26-12	HR	132
109	85	2	764-765	6-26-12	HR	36
110	86	2	765-766	6-30-12	HR	135
111	87	2	766-768	6-30-12	HR	145
112	88	2	768-769	7-01-12	HR	128
113	89	2	769-771	7-01-12	S	39
115	90	2	771	7-01-12	HR	130
117	91	2	771-774	7-01-12	HR	99
118	92	2	774	7-01-12	HR	149
119	93	2	774-775	7-01-12	HR	139
120	94	2	775	7-01-12	S	43
121	95	2	775	7-05-12	HR	114
123	96	2	776	7-05-12	HR	134
124	97	2	776	7-05-12	S	34
125	98	2	776-777	7-05-12	HR	152
126	99	2	777	7-06-12	HR	101
127	100	2	777	7-06-12	HR	151
128	101	2	777	7-06-12	HR	179
129	102	2	778-781	7-06-12	HR	108
130	103	2	781	7-06-12	HR	173
131	104	2	781	7-06-12	HR	176
132	105	2	781-782	7-06-12	HR	174
133	106	2	782	7-06-12	S	44
134	107	2	782-783	7-06-12	HR	144
135	108	2	783-784	7-06-12	HR	172
136	109	2	784	7-06-12	HR	171
137	110	2	784-785	7-06-12	HR	175
138	111	2	785-786	7-06-12	HR	177

RESOLUTIONS OF THE TWELFTH CONGRESS

Public Law/Resolution		Statutes at Large	Page	Date	Bill No.	
Chapter	Number					
1	1	2	786	3-02-12	HJR	2
2	2	2	786	3-19-12	HJR	1
3	3	2	786	6-17-12	HJR	3
4	4	2	786	6-17-12	SJR	1

PUBLIC ACTS OF THE TWELFTH CONGRESS

Public Law/Resolution		Statutes at Large	Page	Date	Bill No.	
Chapter	Number					
1	1	2	787	11-12-12	HR	187
2	2	2	787	12-02-12	HR	188
3	3	2	787-788	12-12-12	HR	197
4	4	2	788	12-12-12	HR	193
5	5	2	788	12-18-12	HR	194
6	6	2	789	1-02-13	S	45
7	7	2	789-790	1-02-13	S	46
8	8	2	790	1-05-13	S	47
9	9	2	790	1-14-13	HR	208
10	10	2	790-791	1-20-13	HR	202
11	11	2	791	1-20-13	HR	224
12	12	2	791-792	1-20-13	HR	216
13	13	2	792-793	1-27-13	HR	189
14	14	2	794	1-27-13	S	48
16	15	2	794-796	1-29-13	HR	215
18	16	2	797	2-05-13	S	50
20	17	2	797-798	2-05-13	HR	217
21	18	2	798-799	2-08-13	HR	231
22	19	2	799-800	2-13-13	HR	213
23	20	2	800-801	2-13-13	HR	222
24	21	2	801	2-24-13	HR	195
27	22	2	801-804	2-25-13	HR	230
30	23	2	804	2-25-13	HR	227
31	24	2	804	2-25-13	HR	260
32	25	2	804	2-27-13	HR	272
33	26	2	804-805	2-27-13	S	61
34	27	2	805	2-27-13	HR	245
35	28	2	806	2-27-13	HR	241
36	29	2	806	2-27-13	S	66
37	30	2	806-807	2-27-13	HR	229
38	31	2	807-808	2-27-13	S	49
39	32	2	808	2-27-13	S	63
40	33	2	809	2-27-13	HR	268
42	34	2	809-811	3-03-13	HR	240
43	35	2	811-812	3-03-13	HR	243
44	36	2	812-815	3-03-13	HR	262
45	37	2	815	3-03-13	HR	253
47	38	2	816	3-03-13	S	62

PUBLIC ACTS OF THE TWELFTH CONGRESS

Public Law/Resolution		Statutes at Large	Page	Date	Bill No.	
Chapter	Number					
48	39	2	816-818	3-03-13	S	68
50	40	2	818	3-03-13	HR	264
51	41	2	818	3-03-13	HR	270
52	42	2	819-820	3-03-13	S	69
53	43	2	820	3-03-13	S	54
54	44	2	821	3-03-13	HR	248
55	45	2	821-822	3-03-13	HR	226
56	46	2	822	3-03-13	HR	277
57	47	2	822-823	3-03-13	HR	267
58	48	2	823-829	3-03-13	HR	255
60	49	2	829	3-03-13	HR	246
61	50	2	829-830	3-03-13	S	59

RESOLUTIONS OF THE TWELFTH CONGRESS

1	1	2	830	1-29-13	HJR	1
2	2	2	830	3-03-13	SJR	1
3	3	2	831	3-03-13	SJR	2

Public Law/Resolution		Statutes at Large	Page	Date	Bill No.	
Chapter	Number					
1	1	3	1	6-14-13	S	3
2	2	3	2-3	6-19-13	S	5
4	3	3	3	7-05-13	S	11
6	4	3	3	7-05-13	S	14
7	5	3	3-4	7-05-13	S	7
8	6	3	4	7-13-13	HR	21
9	7	3	4	7-13-13	HR	30
10	8	3	4-5	7-13-13	HR	49
11	9	3	5-12	7-13-13	HR	3
12	10	3	12-18	7-13-13	HR	2
13	11	3	18	7-16-13	S	19
14	12	3	19-21	7-22-13	S	24
16	13	3	22-34	7-22-13	HR	8
17	14	3	34-35	7-22-13	HR	42
18	15	3	35	7-22-13	HR	36
21	16	3	35-38	7-24-13	HR	16
22	17	3	39	7-24-13	HR	11
23	18	3	39-40	7-24-13	HR	26
24	19	3	40-41	7-24-13	HR	13
25	20	3	42-44	7-24-13	HR	14
26	21	3	44-47	7-25-13	HR	15
27	22	3	47-48	7-26-13	S	10
29	23	3	48	7-26-13	S	18
30	24	3	48	7-26-13	S	6
31	25	3	48	7-27-13	HR	45
33	26	3	48-49	7-28-13	HR	40
35	27	3	49-52	7-29-13	HR	10
36	28	3	53	7-30-13	S	2
37	29	3	53-72	8-02-13	HR	8
39	30	3	72-73	8-02-13	HR	12
40	31	3	73-74	8-02-13	HR	23
41	32	3	74	8-02-13	HR	26
45	33	3	74-75	8-02-13	HR	55
48	34	3	75	8-02-13	HR	41
49	35	3	75	8-02-13	HR	52
50	36	3	75	8-02-13	HR	27
51	37	3	75-77	8-02-13	HR	47
53	38	3	77-81	8-02-13	HR	17
54	39	3	81	8-02-13	HR	53
55	40	3	81	8-02-13	HR	46

PUBLIC ACTS OF THE THIRTEENTH CONGRESS

Public Law/Resolution		Statutes at Large	Page	Date	Bill No.	
Chapter	Number					
56	41	3	82-84	8-02-13	HR	18
57	42	3	84-86	8-02-13	S	22
58	43	3	86	8-02-13	HR	35
59	44	3	86-87	8-02-13	HR	37

Public Law/Resolution		Statutes at Large	Page	Date	Bill No.	
Chapter	Number					
1	1	3	88-93	12-17-13	HR	197*
2	2	3	93	1-11-14	HR	69
4	3	3	94	1-17-14	HR	70
5	4	3	94	1-25-14	S	28
7	5	3	94-95	1-27-14	HR	77
8	6	3	95	1-27-14	HR	61
9	7	3	96	1-28-14	S	26
11	8	3	96-97	2-10-14	HR	78
14	9	3	97-98	2-19-14	HR	64
15	10	3	98	2-24-14	HR	54
16	11	3	98	2-24-14	HR	96
17	12	3	98-99	3-04-14	HR	108
18	13	3	100-102	3-04-14	HR	100
19	14	3	103	3-04-14	HR	118
20	15	3	103-104	3-04-14	HR	82
21	16	3	104	3-09-14	S	14
25	17	3	104-105	3-19-14	HR	134
26	18	3	105	3-19-14	HR	135
27	19	3	105-106	3-19-14	S	32
28	20	3	106-111	3-24-14	HR	133
29	21	3	111-112	3-24-14	HR	99
31	22	3	112-113	3-24-14	HR	123
32	23	3	113	3-24-14	HR	141
36	24	3	113	3-28-14	HR	146
37	25	3	113-116	3-30-14	S	38
38	26	3	116	3-30-14	S	41
39	27	3	116-120	3-31-14	S	37
47	28	3	120	4-09-14	S	46
49	29	3	120-121	4-09-14	HR	114
52	30	3	121-123	4-12-14	HR	90
56	31	3	123	4-14-14	HR	179
57	32	3	123-124	4-14-14	HR	127
58	33	3	124-125	4-16-14	S	47
59	34	3	125	4-16-14	S	52
60	35	3	125	4-16-14	S	43
61	36	3	125-127	4-16-14	HR	122
62	37	3	127	4-18-14	S	48
65	38	3	127	4-18-14	HR	165
66	39	3	128	4-18-14	HR	185
67	40	3	128-129	4-18-14	S	50

PUBLIC ACTS OF THE THIRTEENTH CONGRESS

Public Law/Resolution		Statutes at Large	Page	Date	Bill No.	
Chapter	Number					
69	41	3	129-130	4-18-14	HR	94
70	42	3	130	4-18-14	HR	192
73	43	3	130	4-18-14	HR	154
75	44	3	130-133	4-18-14	HR	139
78	45	3	133	4-18-14	HR	109
79	46	3	133	4-18-14	S	56
80	47	3	134	4-18-14	S	55
82	48	3	134-136	4-18-14	HR	124
84	49	3	136-137	4-18-14	HR	167
85	50	3	137	4-18-14	HR	171
87	51	3	137	4-18-14	S	45
91	52	3	137-139	4-18-14	HR	189
92	53	3	139	4-18-14	HR	193
93	54	3	139-140	4-18-14	HR	171

RESOLUTIONS OF THE THIRTEENTH CONGRESS

1	1	3	140-141	12-27-13	HJR	1
2	2	3	141	1-06-14	SJR	3
3	3	3	141-142	1-06-14	SJR	2
4	4	3	142	1-11-14	HJR	3
5	5	3	142	2-19-14	HJR	4

PUBLIC ACTS OF THE THIRTEENTH CONGRESS

Public Law/Resolution		Statutes at Large	Page	Date	Bill No.	
Chapter	Number					
1	1	3	143	10-25-14	HR	198
2	2	3	143	11-03-14	S	59
3	3	3	144	11-15-14	S	60
4	4	3	144-145	11-15-14	HR	204
6	5	3	145-146	11-21-14	HR	226
7	6	3	146	11-22-14	HR	225
8	7	3	146	12-01-14	HR	209
10	8	3	146-147	12-10-14	S	61
11	9	3	148	12-10-14	S	63
12	10	3	148-151	12-15-14	HR	216
13	11	3	151-152	12-15-14	HR	200
14	12	3	152	12-15-14	HR	237
15	13	3	152-159	12-21-14	HR	214
16	14	3	159-161	12-23-14	HR	215
17	15	3	161-163	12-26-14	HR	236
18	16	3	163	12-26-14	HR	241
20	17	3	163-164	1-09-15	S	70
21	18	3	164-180	1-09-15	HR	219
22	19	3	180-186	1-18-15	HR	217
23	20	3	186-192	1-18-15	HR	218
24	21	3	192-193	1-23-15	S	70
25	22	3	193-195	1-27-15	HR	207
27	23	3	195	1-30-15	S	65
31	24	3	195-200	2-04-15	HR	238
32	25	3	201	2-04-15	HR	262
33	26	3	201	2-04-15	HR	247
34	27	3	201-202	2-04-15	HR	233
35	28	3	202-203	2-07-15	HR	254
38	29	3	203-205	2-08-15	HR	251
39	30	3	205	2-08-15	HR	271
40	31	3	205	2-08-15	HR	268
41	32	3	205	2-13-15	S	78
43	33	3	206	2-14-15	S	77
44	34	3	206-211	2-16-15	HR	274
45	35	3	211-212	2-17-15	HR	249
48	36	3	212	2-22-15	S	74
51	37	3	212-213	2-23-15	HR	279
54	38	3	213	2-24-15	HR	239
56	39	3	213-216	2-24-15	HR	275

PUBLIC ACTS OF THE THIRTEENTH CONGRESS

Public Law/Resolution		Statutes at Large	Page	Date	Bill No.	
Chapter	Number					
60	40	3	216	2-27-15	HR	221
61	41	3	217	2-27-15	HR	223
62	42	3	217-218	2-27-15	S	90
63	43	3	218-219	2-27-15	HR	272
64	44	3	219	2-27-15	S	86
65	45	3	220	2-27-15	HR	266
69	46	3	221-222	3-01-15	HR	282
72	47	3	222-223	3-03-15	HR	289
73	48	3	223	3-03-15	S	91
74	49	3	223-224	3-03-15	HR	288
77	50	3	224	3-03-15	S	87
79	51	3	224-225	3-03-15	HR	305
81	52	3	225-226	3-03-15	S	89
82	53	3	226	3-03-15	S	96
85	54	3	226	3-03-15	S	95
86	55	3	226	3-03-15	S	83
87	56	3	227-228	3-03-15	HR	307
88	57	3	228-229	3-03-15	S	94
89	58	3	229	3-03-15	HR	310
90	59	3	230	3-03-15	HR	315
91	60	3	230-231	3-03-15	HR	220
93	61	3	231	3-03-15	HR	313
94	62	3	231-235	3-03-15	S	98
95	63	3	235	3-03-15	HR	302
96	64	3	235	3-03-15	HR	314
97	65	3	235-237	3-03-15	S	88
98	66	3	237-239	3-03-15	HR	285
99	67	3	239	3-03-15	S	92
100	68	3	239-244	3-03-15	HR	276
101	69	3	244-245	3-03-15	HR	311

RESOLUTIONS OF THE THIRTEENTH CONGRESS

1	1	3	245-246	10-20-14	SJR	5
2	2	3	246	10-21-14	SJR	7
3	3	3	246	10-21-14	SJR	6
4	4	3	246-247	11-03-14	SJR	8
5	5	3	247	11-03-14	HJR	5
6	6	3	248	11-03-14	HJR	6
7	7	3	248	12-01-14	HJR	7

RESOLUTIONS OF THE THIRTEENTH CONGRESS

Public Law/Resolution		Statutes at Large	Page	Date	Bill No.	
Chapter	Number					
8	8	3	248	2-22-15	SJR	11
9	9	3	249	2-22-15	SJR	10
10	10	3	249	2-27-15	SJR	9
11	11	3	249-250	3-03-15	SJR	12
12	12	3	250	3-03-15	SJR	13
13	13	3	250	3-03-15	HJR	10

Public Law/Resolution		Statutes at Large	Page	Date	Bill No.	
Chapter	Number					
1	1	3	251	12-08-15	HR	59
2	2	3	251-252	12-21-15	HR	2
3	3	3	252	1-17-16	HR	11
7	4	3	252	2-01-16	HR	44
9	5	3	253	2-01-16	HR	45
10	6	3	253	2-05-16	HR	42
14	7	3	254	2-09-16	HR	43
16	8	3	254	2-15-16	S	21
18	9	3	254	2-22-16	HR	64
21	10	3	254-255	2-28-16	HR	10
22	11	3	255	3-01-16	HR	15
24	12	3	255-256	3-05-16	HR	72
25	13	3	256-257	3-05-16	HR	51
26	14	3	257	3-18-16	HR	57
30	15	3	257-258	3-19-16	S	6
31	16	3	258	3-22-16	S	60
32	17	3	258-259	3-22-16	S	2
33	18	3	259	3-25-16	S	26
35	19	3	260-261	3-25-16	S	34
39	20	3	261	4-02-16	S	32
40	21	3	261-264	4-09-16	HR	6
41	22	3	264	4-09-16	HR	120
43	23	3	264-266	4-09-16	HR	89
44	24	3	266-277	4-10-16	HR	25
45	25	3	277-283	4-16-16	HR	130
46	26	3	283-284	4-16-16	S	15
47	27	3	284	4-16-16	S	76
49	28	3	284-285	4-16-16	S	61
52	29	3	285	4-16-16	HR	41
53	30	3	285	4-16-16	S	66
55	31	3	285-287	4-16-16	HR	38
56	32	3	287-288	4-16-16	HR	85
57	33	3	289-291	4-19-16	HR	24
58	34	3	291-294	4-19-16	HR	121
63	35	3	294-295	4-20-16	HR	76
64	36	3	295	4-20-16	S	38
65	37	3	295-296	4-20-16	S	58
67	38	3	296	4-24-16	HR	29
68	39	3	296-297	4-24-16	HR	171

Public Law/Resolution		Statutes at Large	Page	Date	Bill No.	
Chapter	Number					
69	40	3	297–299	4–24–16	HR	68
71	41	3	299	4–24–16	S	79
73	42	3	300	4–24–16	HR	154
74	43	3	300	4–24–16	HR	127
75	44	3	300–301	4–24–16	HR	26
76	45	3	301	4–26–16	HR	81
77	46	3	301	4–26–16	HR	1
79	47	3	301	4–26–16	HR	71
81	48	3	302	4–26–16	S	70
82	49	3	302–306	4–26–16	HR	134
95	50	3	306	4–26–16	HR	62
98	51	3	306–307	4–26–16	S	23
101	52	3	307–308	4–27–16	HR	40
102	53	3	308–309	4–27–16	HR	102
103	54	3	309–310	4–27–16	HR	153
104	55	3	310	4–27–16	HR	17
107	56	3	310–314	4–27–16	S	97
110	57	3	315	4–27–16	HR	155
112	58	3	315	4–27–16	S	22
119	59	3	315–316	4–27–16	S	30
120	60	3	316	4–27–16	HR	166
121	61	3	316–317	4–27–16	S	78
123	62	3	317	4–27–16	HR	100
127	63	3	317–318	4–27–16	HR	114
129	64	3	318	4–27–16	S	48
130	65	3	318	4–27–16	HR	63
131	66	3	318	4–27–16	HR	180
132	67	3	319–320	4–27–16	HR	101
135	68	3	320	4–29–16	HR	185
137	69	3	320–321	4–29–16	HR	178
138	70	3	321	4–29–16	HR	94
139	71	3	322	4–29–16	HR	142
140	72	3	322	4–29–16	HR	196
141	73	3	323	4–29–16	HR	39
142	74	3	323	4–29–16	S	81
143	75	3	323	4–29–16	HR	19
145	76	3	323–324	4–29–16	S	14
149	77	3	324	4–29–16	S	87
150	78	3	324–325	4–29–16	HR	59

Public Law/Resolution		Statutes at Large	Page	Date	Bill No.	
Chapter	Number					
151	79	3	325-326	4-29-16	HR	146
152	80	3	326	4-29-16	HR	98
153	81	3	326-327	4-29-16	S	8
154	82	3	327-328	4-29-16	HR	36
155	83	3	328	4-29-16	HR	13
159	84	3	328-329	4-29-16	HR	176
160	85	3	330	4-29-16	HR	144
162	86	3	330-331	4-29-16	HR	70
163	87	3	331	4-29-16	S	40
164	88	3	332	4-29-16	HR	169
165	89	3	332-333	4-29=16	S	43
166	90	3	333	4-30-16	S	110
168	91	3	334	4-30-16	S	6
170	92	3	334	4-30-16	S	118
171	93	3	334-338	4-30-16	HR	157
172	94	3	338-340	4-30-16	HR	190
173	95	3	340	4-30-16	S	30

RESOLUTIONS OF THE FOURTEENTH CONGRESS

1	1	3	341	2-06-16	SJR	3
3	2	3	341	2-16-16	HJR	3
4	3	3	341	2-22-16	HJR	1
5	4	3	341-342	4-16-16	SJR	4
6	5	3	342	4-27-16	HJR	2
7	6	3	342	4-30-16	SJR	1
8	7	3	343	4-30-16	HJR	5

PUBLIC ACTS OF THE FOURTEENTH CONGRESS

Public Law/Resolution		Statutes at Large	Page	Date	Bill No.	
Chapter	Number					
3	1	3	344	1-14-17	HR	7
4	2	3	344-345	1-20-17	S	4
7	3	3	345	1-22-17	HR	42
9	4	3	345	2-06-17	HR	18
10	5	3	345	2-08-17	HR	49
13	6	3	345-346	2-22-17	S	26
15	7	3	346	2-22-17	S	20
18	8	3	346	2-24-17	S	13
21	9	3	347	3-01-17	S	47
22	10	3	347-348	3-01-17	S	44
23	11	3	348-349	3-01-17	S	16
24	12	3	350	3-01-17	HR	107
25	13	3	350	3-01-17	HR	145
29	14	3	350	3-01-17	HR	104
30	15	3	350	3-01-17	S	48
31	16	3	351-352	3-01-17	HR	32
33	17	3	352-358	3-03-17	HR	64
34	18	3	358	3-03-17	HR	142
35	19	3	359	3-03-17	HR	110
36	20	3	359-360	3-03-17	HR	124
37	21	3	360	3-03-17	HR	127
38	22	3	360-361	3-03-17	HR	122
39	23	3	361-362	3-03-17	HR	153
40	24	3	362	3-03-17	HR	74
41	25	3	362-363	3-03-17	HR	157
42	26	3	363	3-03-17	HR	56
43	27	3	363	3-03-17	S	53
44	28	3	363-366	3-03-17	HR	155
45	29	3	366-368	3-03-17	S	9
49	30	3	368-369	3-03-17	HR	112
50	31	3	369	3-03-17	HR	156
51	32	3	369	3-03-17	HR	7
55	33	3	369	3-03-17	HR	68
56	34	3	369-370	3-03-17	HR	72
57	35	3	370	3-03-17	HR	62
58	36	3	370-371	3-03-17	HR	55
59	37	3	371-373	3-03-17	S	15
60	38	3	373-374	3-03-17	S	31
61	39	3	374	3-03-17	S	46

PUBLIC ACTS OF THE FOURTEENTH CONGRESS

Public Law/Resolution		Statutes at Large	Page	Date	Bill No.	
Chapter	Number					
62	40	3	375-376	3-03-17	S	45
63	41	3	376	3-03-17	S	36
65	42	3	376-377	3-03-17	HR	140
67	43	3	377	3-03-17	HR	12
69	44	3	377	3-03-17	HR	115
85	45	3	377-378	3-03-17	HR	54
86	46	3	378	3-03-17	HR	111
87	47	3	379-380	3-03-17	HR	53
88	48	3	380-382	3-03-17	HR	43
91	49	3	382	3-03-17	HR	83
92	50	3	383	3-03-17	S	23
93	51	3	383-389	3-03-17	S	54
94	52	3	389-390	3-03-17	HR	159
96	53	3	390	3-03-17	HR	141
99	54	3	390	3-03-17	HR	66
100	55	3	390-391	3-03-17	S	41
101	56	3	391	3-03-17	HR	148
102	57	3	392	3-03-17	HR	152
103	58	3	392	3-03-17	HR	73
104	59	3	393	3-03-17	S	19
105	60	3	393	3-03-17	HR	63
106	61	3	393-394	3-03-17	HR	47
107	62	3	394-395	3-03-17	HR	48
108	63	3	395-396	3-03-17	HR	158
109	64	3	396-397	3-03-17	S	52
110	65	3	397-398	3-03-17	HR	13
111	66	3	398-399	3-03-17	S	59
112	67	3	399	3-03-17	S	67
114	68	3	399	3-03-17	HR	58

RESOLUTIONS OF THE FOURTEENTH CONGRESS

1	1	3	399-400	12-11-16	SJR	1
2	2	3	400	2-06-17	SJR	2
3	3	3	400	3-03-17	SJR	3

PUBLIC ACTS OF THE FIFTEENTH CONGRESS

Public Law/Resolution		Statutes at Large	Page	Date	Bill No.	
Chapter	Number					
1	1	3	401-403	12-23-17	HR	3
4	2	3	403	1-14-18	HR	4
5	3	3	404-405	1-22-18	HR	28
8	4	3	405	1-27-18	HR	33
9	5	3	405	2-06-18	S	8
10	6	3	405-406	2-16-18	HR	39
12	7	3	406-407	2-17-18	HR	13
13	8	3	407-408	2-19-18	HR	40
14	9	3	408	3-09-18	S	11
16	10	3	408-409	3-09-18	S	22
18	11	3	409-410	3-18-18	S	18
19	12	3	410-411	3-18-18	HR	8
21	13	3	411	3-18-18	HR	84
22	14	3	411	3-19-18	HR	95
23	15	3	411-412	3-27-18	S	31
24	16	3	412	3-27-18	S	6
26	17	3	412	4-03-18	S	37
29	18	3	413	4-03-18	HR	20
30	19	3	413	3-03-18	HR	118
32	20	3	413-415	4-03-18	HR	117
33	21	3	415	4-03-18	HR	23
34	22	3	415	4-04-18	HR	32
35	23	3	416	4-04-18	S	52
36	24	3	417	4-04-18	S	55
37	25	3	417	4-04-18	S	41
40	26	3	417	4-04-18	S	45
42	27	3	417	4-09-18	S	61
43	28	3	417-418	4-09-18	HR	156
45	29	3	418-423	4-11-18	HR	90
47	30	3	423-424	4-11-18	S	2
49	31	3	424	4-11-18	S	7
51	32	3	425	4-11-18	HR	174
56	33	3	425	4-13-18	HR	26
58	34	3	425	4-14-18	S	70
60	35	3	426	4-14-18	HR	139
61	36	3	426-427	4-14-18	S	29
64	37	3	427	4-16-18	S	30
65	38	3	427-428	4-16-18	S	14*

Public Law/Resolution		Statutes at Large	Page	Date	Bill No.	
Chapter	Number					
66	39	3	428	4-16-18	S	10
67	40	3	428-431	4-18-18	HR	53
68	41	3	431	4-18-18	HR	178
69	42	3	431-432	4-18-18	HR	87
70	43	3	432-433	4-18-18	S	64
71	44	3	433	4-18-18	HR	157
75	45	3	433	4-18-18	S	73
76	46	3	433	4-18-18	HR	175
79	47	3	433-438	4-20-18	HR	108
80	48	3	439-440	4-20-18	HR	43
82	49	3	441	4-20-18	HR	57
83	50	3	441-444	4-20-18	HR	116
84	51	3	444	4-20-18	S	39
86	52	3	444	4-20-18	HR	126
87	53	3	445-447	4-20-18	HR	127
88	54	3	447-450	4-20-18	HR	106
90	55	3	450	4-20-18	HR	58
91	56	3	450-453	4-20-18	S	65
92	57	3	453-457	4-20-18	HR	179
94	58	3	457	4-20-18	S	16
97	59	3	458	4-20-18	HR	122
98	60	3	458-459	4-20-18	HR	171
101	61	3	459	4-20-18	HR	180
102	62	3	460	4-20-18	HR	55
103	63	3	460-461	4-20-18	HR	73
104	64	3	461	4-20-18	S	77
107	65	3	461-462	4-20-18	HR	75
108	66	3	462-463	4-20-18	S	9
109	67	3	463-464	4-20-18	HR	190
110	68	3	464	4-20-18	S	76
112	69	3	464	4-20-18	S	75
113	70	3	464-465	4-20-18	HR	192
114	71	3	465	4-20-18	S	44
115	72	3	465-466	4-20-18	S	69
123	73	3	466	4-20-18	HR	120
124	74	3	466	4-20-18	HR	194
126	75	3	466-467	4-20-18	S	38
127	76	3	467	4-20-18	S	15

PUBLIC ACTS OF THE FIFTEENTH CONGRESS

Public Law/Resolution		Statutes at Large	Page	Date	Bill No.	
Chapter	Number					
128	77	3	468	4-20-18	S	35
129	78	3	469-470	4-20-18	HR	136

RESOLUTIONS OF THE FIFTEENTH CONGRESS

1	1	3	472	12-10-17	SJR	1
2	2	3	473	12-23-17	SJR	2
3	3	3	473	12-23-17	HJR	2
4	4	3	473	1-22-18	HJR	5
5	5	3	473	3-09-18	SJR	4
6	6	3	474	3-18-18	HJR	6
7	7	3	474-475	3-19-18	HJR	9
8	8	3	475	3-27-18	SJR	3
9	9	3	475	3-27-18	SJR	5
10	10	3	475	4-03-18	HJR	10
11	11	3	476	4-04-18	SJR	7
12	12	3	476	4-04-18	SJR	6
13	13	3	476	4-20-18	HJR	12

Public Law/Resolution		Statutes at Large	Page	Date	Bill No.	
Chapter	Number					
1	1	3	477	12-03-18	S	1
2	2	3	477	12-05-18	HR	199
3	3	3	478	12-16-18	S	67
4	4	3	478	12-16-18	HR	198
12	5	3	478-479	2-04-19	HR	97
13	6	3	479	2-04-19	HR	245
15	7	3	480	2-04-19	HR	112
18	8	3	480-481	2-15-19	HR	242
19	9	3	481-482	2-15-19	S	22
21	10	3	482	2-15-19	HR	256
22	11	3	482-483	2-16-19	HR	200
25	12	3	483-484	2-16-19	HR	235
27	13	3	484	2-20-19	S	2
28	14	3	484	2-20-19	S	49
31	15	3	485	2-20-19	S	28
35	16	3	485-486	2-20-19	S	24
36	17	3	486	2-20-19	HR	304
41	18	3	487	2-24-19	HR	287
43	19	3	487	2-24-19	HR	283
45	20	3	488	3-02-19	S	45
46	21	3	488-489	3-02-19	HR	128
47	22	3	489-492	3-02-19	S	16
48	23	3	492-493	3-02-19	S	25
49	24	3	493-496	3-02-19	HR	238
52	25	3	496	3-02-19	HR	288
54	26	3	496-502	3-03-19	HR	294
60	27	3	502-503	3-03-19	HR	205
70	28	3	503	3-03-19	S	15
71	29	3	503	3-03-19	HR	277
72	30	3	503-508	3-03-19	HR	316
73	31	3	508-509	3-03-19	HR	281
74	32	3	509-510	3-03-19	S	9
75	33	3	510	3-03-19	S	86
77	34	3	510-514	3-03-19	S	88
80	35	3	514	3-03-19	S	87
81	36	3	514-515	3-03-19	HR	129
82	37	3	515	3-03-19	HR	219
83	38	3	516	3-03-19	S	43

PUBLIC ACTS OF THE FIFTEENTH CONGRESS

Public Law/Resolution		Statutes at Large	Page	Date	Bill No.	
Chapter	Number					
84	39	3	516	3-03-19	HR	265
85	40	3	516-517	3-03-19	S	89
86	41	3	517	3-03-19	HR	221
87	42	3	517-519	3-03-19	S	67
88	43	3	520	3-03-19	HR	331
89	44	3	520	3-03-19	HR	311
90	45	3	521	3-03-19	HR	314
91	46	3	521	3-03-19	HR	307
92	47	3	521-523	3-03-19	S	54
93	48	3	523-524	3-03-19	HR	330
94	49	3	524	3-03-19	HR	317
95	50	3	525	3-03-19	S	90
96	51	3	525	3-03-19	S	68
97	52	3	525	3-03-19	S	42
98	53	3	526	3-03-19	S	77
99	54	3	526-528	3-03-19	HR	203
100	55	3	528-532	3-03-19	S	26
101	56	3	532-534	3-03-19	HR	272
102	57	3	534-536	3-03-19	HR	186
107	58	3	536	3-03-19	S	39

RESOLUTIONS OF THE FIFTEENTH CONGRESS

1	1	3	536	12-03-18	HJR	1
2	2	3	536	12-05-18	HJR	2
3	3	3	537	1-19-19	SJR	1
4	4	3	537	1-23-19	HJR	3
5	5	3	537	2-15-19	HJR	4
6	6	3	538	3-03-19	SJR	4
7	7	3	538	3-03-19	HJR	7

PUBLIC ACTS OF THE SIXTEENTH CONGRESS

Public Law/Resolution		Statutes at Large	Page	Date	Bill No.	
Chapter	Number					
1	1	3	539	12-14-19	S	1
2	2	3	539	1-14-20	HR	15
3	3	3	540	1-14-20	HR	13
5	4	3	540	1-14-20	HR	20
9	5	3	540	2-10-20	HR	45
10	6	3	541	2-10-20	HR	34
11	7	3	541-543	2-10-20	S	106
14	8	3	543	2-24-20	S	28
17	9	3	543	2-28-20	S	39
19	10	3	544	3-03-20	HR	17
20	11	3	544	3-04-20	HR	75
21	12	3	544-545	3-04-20	HR	85
22	13	3	545-548	3-06-20	HR	1
23	14	3	548	3-13-20	S	44
24	15	3	548-553	3-14-20	HR	22
25	16	3	553-554	3-17-20	HR	68
26	17	3	554	3-17-20	HR	87
27	18	3	554-555	3-30-20	S	8
28	19	3	555	3-30-20	S	37
39	20	3	555	4-07-20	S	67
40	21	3	555-561	4-11-20	HR	86
41	22	3	562	4-14-20	HR	78
45	23	3	562-563	4-18-20	HR	74
46	24	3	563-564	4-18-20	S	7
47	25	3	564-565	4-21-20	S	19
48	26	3	565	4-21-20	S	110
50	27	3	565	4-24-20	HR	106
51	28	3	566-567	4-24-20	S	18
52	29	3	567-569	5-01-20	HR	37
53	30	3	569-570	5-01-20	HR	122
54	31	3	570	5-01-20	S	52
62	32	3	570	5-04-20	HR	65
75	33	3	570-571	5-08-20	S	118
84	34	3	571	5-11-20	S	109
85	35	3	572	5-11-20	S	120
86	36	3	573	5-11-20	HR	46
87	37	3	573-575	5-11-20	S	26
88	38	3	575	5-11-20	S	38

PUBLIC ACTS OF THE SIXTEENTH CONGRESS

Public Law/Resolution		Statutes at Large	Page	Date	Bill No.	
Chapter	Number					
89	39	3	575	5-11-20	S	52
92	40	3	576	5-11-20	HR	110
93	41	3	576	5-11-20	HR	129
94	42	3	577	5-11-20	HR	134
97	43	3	577	5-12-20	HR	94
99	44	3	577-581	5-13-20	HR	116
101	45	3	581	5-13-20	HR	148
102	46	3	582	5-15-20	S	119
103	47	3	582-583	5-15-20	HR	138
104	48	3	583-592	5-15-20	S	34
107	49	3	592-596	5-15-20	S	15
108	50	3	596	5-15-20	S	88
109	51	3	596-597	5-15-20	HR	98
110	52	3	597-598	5-15-20	HR	89
111	53	3	598	5-15-20	S	20
112	54	3	598-600	5-15-20	S	60
113	55	3	600-601	5-15-20	S	106
117	56	3	601	5-15-20	HR	30
118	57	3	601-602	5-15-20	HR	149
119	58	3	602	5-15-20	S	101
121	59	3	602	5-15-20	HR	120
122	60	3	602-604	5-15-20	S	98
123	61	3	604	5-15-20	S	105
125	62	3	605	5-15-20	S	117
126	63	3	605	5-15-20	HR	77
127	64	3	606	5-15-20	S	112
131	65	3	606	5-15-20	S	17
132	66	3	606	5-15-20	HR	109
133	67	3	606-607	5-15-20	HR	115
134	68	3	607	5-15-20	HR	145*
135	69	3	607	5-15-20	S	81
136	70	3	607	5-15-20	HR	80
137	71	3	608	5-15-20	HR	143

RESOLUTIONS OF THE SIXTEENTH CONGRESS

1	1	3	608	12-14-19	SJR	1
2	2	3	609	1-19-20	HJR	1
3	3	3	609	4-21-20	HJR	2

RESOLUTIONS OF THE SIXTEENTH CONGRESS

Public Law/Resolution		Statutes at Large	Page	Date	Bill No.	
Chapter	Number					
4	4	3	609	5-08-20	HJR	4
5	5	3	609	5-12-20	HJR	3

PUBLIC ACTS OF THE SIXTEENTH CONGRESS

Public Law/Resolution		Statutes at Large	Page	Date	Bill No.	
Chapter	Number					
1	1	3	610	11-27-20	S	1
2	2	3	610-611	12-12-20	HR	81
3	3	3	611	12-29-20	HR	164
6	4	3	611	1-11-21	HR	161
8	5	3	612	1-17-21	HR	165
11	6	3	612	2-09-21	HR	163
12	7	3	612-614	3-02-21	S	16
13	8	3	615-616	3-02-21	HR	180
14	9	3	616-617	3-02-21	HR	171
15	10	3	617	3-02-21	HR	173
16	11	3	617	3-02-21	HR	170
17	12	3	618	3-02-21	HR	220
18	13	3	618-622	3-02-21	S	45
25	14	3	622	3-02-21	HR	210
31	15	3	622-623	3-02-21	HR	93
32	16	3	623	3-02-21	HR	211
33	17	3	623-628	3-03-21	HR	242
34	18	3	628-633	3-03-21	HR	227
35	19	3	633-634	3-03-21	HR	263
36	20	3	634-635	3-03-21	HR	255
37	21	3	635	3-03-21	HR	234
38	22	3	635-636	3-03-21	HR	264
39	23	3	637-639	3-03-21	HR	266
40	24	3	640	3-03-21	HR	245
41	25	3	640	3-03-21	HR	231
42	26	3	640	3-03-21	S	46
43	27	3	641	3-03-21	HR	269
44	28	3	641	3-03-21	HR	194
45	29	3	641	3-03-21	S	7
46	30	3	641-642	3-03-21	HR	162
47	31	3	642	3-03-21	HR	184
48	32	3	642	3-03-21	HR	179
49	33	3	643	3-03-21	S	75
50	34	3	643	3-03-21	S	42
51	35	3	643	3-03-21	HR	225
52	36	3	643-644	3-03-21	HR	257
53	37	3	645	3-03-21	HR	230
54	38	3	645	3-03-21	S	70

RESOLUTIONS OF THE SIXTEENTH CONGRESS

Public Law/Resolution		Statutes at Large	Page	Date	Bill No.	
Chapter	Number					
1	1	3	645	3-02-21	HJR	2
2	2	3	646-647	3-03-21	HJR	7
3	3	3	648	3-03-21	HJR	3

PUBLIC ACTS OF THE SEVENTEENTH CONGRESS

Public Law/Resolution		Statutes at Large	Page	Date	Bill No.	
Chapter	Number					
1	1	3	649	12-19-21	S	1
4	2	3	649	2-04-22	HR	2
6	3	3	650	2-04-22	HR	3
7	4	3	650-651	2-19-22	HR	64
8	5	3	651	2-19-22	S	20
9	6	3	651	2-23-22	HR	88
10	7	3	651-652	3-07-22	HR	26
11	8	3	652-653	3-15-22	HR	90
12	9	3	653-654	3-16-22	HR	13
13	10	3	654-659	3-30-22	S	39
14	11	3	659	3-30-22	S	26
15	12	3	660-661	3-30-22	S	61
16	13	3	661	3-30-22	S	33
18	14	3	661	3-30-22	S	64
23	15	3	662	4-17-22	S	25
24	16	3	662	4-17-22	HR	55
25	17	3	662	4-17-22	HR	98
26	18	3	662	4-17-22	HR	53
27	19	3	663	4-17-22	S	11
28	20	3	663-665	4-20-22	HR	15
29	21	3	665-666	4-20-22	HR	25
30	22	3	666	4-20-22	S	66
31	23	3	666-667	4-26-22	HR	63
32	24	3	667	4-26-22	HR	94
33	25	3	667	4-26-22	S	78
40	26	3	668	4-26-22	S	53
41	27	3	668-673	4-30-22	HR	79
45	28	3	673-674	5-01-22	HR	135
46	29	3	674-675	5-03-22	HR	4
47	30	3	675	5-03-22	HR	176
48	31	3	676	5-04-22	HR	152
49	32	3	676-677	5-04-22	HR	116
50	33	3	677	5-04-22	HR	172
51	34	3	678	5-04-22	S	76
52	35	3	678	5-04-22	HR	143
53	36	3	678	5-04-22	S	23
54	37	3	679-680	5-06-22	S	57
55	38	3	680-681	5-05-22	HR	29

PUBLIC ACTS OF THE SEVENTEENTH CONGRESS

Public Law/Resolution		Statutes at Large	Page	Date	Bill No.	
Chapter	Number					
56	39	3	681-682	5-04-22	S	89
57	40	3	682	5-06-22	HR	182
58	41	3	682-683	5-07-22	S	79
61	42	3	683	5-07-22	S	32
62	43	3	684-685	5-07-22	S	69
86	44	3	685-686	5-07-22	S	90
87	45	3	686	5-07-22	HR	158
88	46	3	686	5-07-22	S	74
89	47	3	686-688	5-07-22	HR	163
90	48	3	688-689	5-07-22	HR	113
91	49	3	689-690	5-07-22	HR	162
93	50	3	690	5-07-22	HR	181
96	51	3	691-693	5-07-22	S	80
107	52	3	693-696	5-07-22	S	9
108	53	3	696	5-07-22	HR	166
112	54	3	696-697	5-07-22	HR	12
118	55	3	697	5-07-22	HR	32
119	56	3	698-699	5-07-22	S	45
122	57	3	699-700	5-08-22	HR	170
124	58	3	700-701	5-08-22	S	48
126	59	3	701-702	5-08-22	S	35
127	60	3	702-707	5-08-22	HR	177
128	61	3	707-708	5-08-22	S	2
129	62	3	709-718	5-08-22	S	62

RESOLUTIONS OF THE SEVENTEENTH CONGRESS

1	1	3	718-719	1-11-22	HJR	1
2	2	3	719	2-04-22	HJR	4
3	3	3	719	3-30-22	HJR	5
4	4	3	719	4-26-22	HJR	16

Public Law/Resolution		Statutes at Large	Page	Date	Bill No.	
Chapter	Number					
1	1	3	720	12-20-22	HR	191
2	2	3	720	1-14-23	HR	202
3	3	3	721	1-14-23	HR	217
5	4	3	721	1-23-23	HR	197
6	5	3	721	1-23-23	HR	103
7	6	3	721	1-30-23	HR	147
8	7	3	722	1-30-23	HR	144
9	8	3	723-724	1-31-23	HR	174
10	9	3	724-725	2-21-23	HR	206
11	10	3	726	2-21-23	S	37
14	11	3	726	2-21-23	S	14
15	12	3	727	2-28-23	S	47
16	13	3	727-728	2-28-23	HR	112
17	14	3	728	2-28-23	S	16
18	15	3	729	2-28-23	S	49
19	16	3	729	2-28-23	S	38
21	17	3	729-739	3-01-23	HR	194
22	18	3	740-742	3-01-23	S	26
23	19	3	742	3-01-23	S	58
24	20	3	743-747	3-01-23	HR	39
25	21	3	747-748	3-03-23	HR	306
26	22	3	748-749	3-03-23	HR	265
27	23	3	749-750	3-03-23	HR	266
28	24	3	750-754	3-03-23	HR	242
29	25	3	754-756	3-03-23	HR	286
30	26	3	756-757	3-03-23	HR	123
31	27	3	757-763	3-03-23	HR	256
32	28	3	763-764	3-03-23	HR	257
33	29	3	764-768	3-03-23	HR	306
34	30	3	768	3-03-23	S	40
35	31	3	768	3-03-23	HR	297
36	32	3	769	3-03-23	HR	224
37	33	3	770-771	3-03-23	HR	215
38	34	3	771-772	3-03-23	S	48
39	35	3	772-773	3-03-23	S	59
40	36	3	773	3-03-23	S	25
41	37	3	773-774	3-03-23	HR	311
42	38	3	774	3-03-23	HR	86

PUBLIC ACTS OF THE SEVENTEENTH CONGRESS

Public Law/Resolution		Statutes at Large	Page	Date	Bill No.	
Chapter	Number					
43	39	3	774	3-03-23	HR	270
44	40	3	774-775	3-03-23	HR	231
45	41	3	776	3-03-23	HR	298
46	42	3	776	3-03-23	HR	211
47	43	3	776	3-03-23	HR	279
48	44	3	777	3-03-23	HR	282
49	45	3	777	3-03-23	S	41
50	46	3	777	3-03-23	HR	273
51	47	3	778	3-03-23	HR	229
52	48	3	778-779	3-03-23	HR	165
53	49	3	779	3-03-23	HR	277
54	50	3	779	3-03-23	S	61
55	51	3	779-780	3-03-23	HR	310
56	52	3	780-781	3-03-23	S	43
57	53	3	781	3-03-23	HR	271
58	54	3	781-782	3-03-23	HR	146
59	55	3	782-783	3-01-23	HR	207
60	56	3	783	3-03-23	S	63
61	57	3	783-784	3-03-23	HR	267
62	58	3	784	3-03-23	HR	294
63	59	3	784	3-03-23	HR	226
64	60	3	784-785	3-03-23	S	66
65	61	3	785	3-03-23	S	42
66	62	3	785-786	3-03-23	S	34
67	63	3	786	3-03-23	S	4
68	64	3	786-787	3-03-23	HR	167
69	65	3	787	3-03-23	S	2
70	66	3	788	3-03-23	HR	18
71	67	3	788	3-03-23	S	46
72	68	3	789	3-03-23	HR	315

RESOLUTIONS OF THE SEVENTEENTH CONGRESS

1	1	3	789	3-01-23	HJR	7
2	2	3	789	3-03-23	HJR	9

PUBLIC ACTS OF THE EIGHTEENTH CONGRESS

Public Law/Resolution		Statutes at Large	Page	Date	Bill No.	
Chapter	Number					
2	1	4	1	1-01-24	HR	4
3	2	4	1	1-07-24	S	1
4	3	4	2-3	1-07-24	S	2
9	4	4	3	1-19-24	HR	53
11	5	4	3	1-19-24	HR	26
15	6	4	4	1-22-24	HR	15
16	7	4	4-5	1-22-24	HR	41
17	8	4	5	1-31-24	HR	29
20	9	4	5	2-20-24	S	8
22	10	4	5-6	2-28-24	HR	30
23	11	4	6	2-28-24	HR	35
25	12	4	6-7	2-28-24	HR	43
26	13	4	8	3-08-24	HR	20
27	14	4	8-9	3-10-24	HR	78
28	15	4	9-10	3-10-24	HR	1
29	16	4	10	3-16-24	HR	106
30	17	4	11	3-24-24	S	51
31	18	4	11	3-24-24	S	44
32	19	4	11-17	4-02-24	HR	77
33	20	4	17	4-09-24	S	42
34	21	4	18	4-09-24	S	38
35	22	4	18	4-09-24	S	84
36	23	4	18-19	4-22-24	S	88
37	24	4	19	4-22-24	HR	122
38	25	4	19	4-22-24	HR	170
39	26	4	19-20	4-22-24	S	91
43	27	4	20-22	4-29-24	HR	83
44	28	4	22	4-29-24	HR	88
45	29	4	22	4-29-24	S	79
46	30	4	22-23	4-30-24	HR	5
47	31	4	23	5-04-24	S	20
65	32	4	23	5-13-24	S	45
66	33	4	23-24	5-13-24	S	89
88	34	4	24-25	5-18-24	HR	58
89	35	4	25	5-18-24	HR	68
136	36	4	25-30	5-22-24	HR	47
137	37	4	30-31	5-24-24	HR	74
138	38	4	31-32	5-24-24	HR	7
139	39	4	32-33	5-24-24	HR	139
140	40	4	33-34	5-24-24	HR	42

Public Law/Resolution		Statutes at Large	Page	Date	Bill No.	
Chapter	Number					
141	41	4	34	5-24-24	HR	166
145	42	4	34-35	5-25-24	HR	90
146	43	4	35-36	5-25-24	S	74
149	44	4	36-37	5-26-24	HR	82
150	45	4	37	5-26-24	HR	28
151	46	4	37-38	5-26-24	HR	237
152	47	4	38	5-26-24	HR	199
153	48	4	38	5-26-24	HR	209
154	49	4	39-40	5-26-24	HR	101
155	50	4	40-41	5-26-24	S	78
156	51	4	41	5-26-24	HR	64
157	52	4	41-43	5-26-24	HR	159
158	53	4	43	5-26-24	HR	80
159	54	4	43-44	5-26-24	HR	34
160	55	4	44	5-26-24	HR	223
161	56	4	44	5-26-24	HR	196
162	57	4	44-45	5-26-24	HR	126
163	58	4	45-47	5-26-24	HR	137
164	59	4	47	5-26-24	HR	94
165	60	4	47-48	5-26-24	HR	6
166	61	4	48	5-26-24	S	107
167	62	4	48-49	5-26-24	HR	154
168	63	4	49	5-26-24	HR	226
169	64	4	50	5-26-24	HR	167
170	65	4	50	5-26-24	HR	38
171	66	4	50-51	5-26-24	HR	147
172	67	4	51-52	5-26-24	HR	51
173	68	4	52-56	5-26-24	HR	65
174	69	4	56-59	5-26-24	HR	183
175	70	4	59-60	5-26-24	S	49
176	71	4	60	5-26-24	S	111
177	72	4	60	5-26-24	HR	144
178	73	4	60-61	5-26-24	HR	131
179	74	4	61-62	5-26-24	HR	202
181	75	4	62-64	5-26-24	HR	235
182	76	4	65	5-26-24	HR	165
183	77	4	65	5-26-24	S	109
184	78	4	65-66	5-26-24	S	86
185	79	4	66-69	5-26-24	HR	44
186	80	4	69	5-26-24	S	93

PUBLIC ACTS OF THE EIGHTEENTH CONGRESS

Public Law/Resolution		Statutes at Large	Page	Date	Bill No.	
Chapter	Number					
187	81	4	70	5-26-24	S	11
188	82	4	70	5-26-24	HR	220
189	83	4	71	5-26-24	HR	112
190	84	4	71	5-26-24	HR	228
191	85	4	71-73	5-26-24	HR	54
192	86	4	73-75	5-26-24	HR	172
194	87	4	75	5-26-24	HR	162
195	88	4	75	5-26-24	HR	178

RESOLUTIONS OF THE EIGHTEENTH CONGRESS

1	1	4	78	2-04-24	HJR	3
2	2	4	78	5-26-24	SJR	15

Public Law/Resolution		Statutes at Large	Page	Date	Bill No.	
Chapter	Number					
1	1	4	79	12-15-24	HR	239
3	2	4	79	12-28-24	HR	233
4	3	4	79-80	1-12-25	HR	175
5	4	4	80	1-12-25	HR	99
6	5	4	80-81	2-05-25	S	21
7	6	4	81	2-05-25	HR	164
9	7	4	81-82	2-11-25	HR	338
10	8	4	82	2-11-25	S	42
11	9	4	82-83	2-21-25	HR	277
12	10	4	83-85	2-21-25	HR	278
13	11	4	85-91	2-25-25	HR	274
14	12	4	92	2-25-25	HR	327
15	13	4	92	3-02-25	HR	280
16	14	4	92-94	3-03-25	HR	281
18	15	4	94	3-03-25	HR	331
20	16	4	94	3-03-25	HR	334
25	17	4	94	3-03-25	S	57
35	18	4	94-95	3-03-25	HR	268
45	19	4	95	3-03-25	HR	251
46	20	4	95-100	3-03-25	HR	272
50	21	4	100-101	3-03-25	S	23
51	22	4	101	3-03-25	HR	295
52	23	4	101-102	3-03-25	HR	316
57	24	4	102	3-03-25	HR	359
64	25	4	102-114	3-03-25	HR	247
65	26	4	115-123	3-03-25	HR	86
66	27	4	123	3-03-25	HR	187
74	28	4	123	3-03-25	HR	254
75	29	4	124	3-03-25	HR	338
76	30	4	124	3-03-25	HR	115
78	31	4	124	3-03-25	HR	363
80	32	4	125	3-03-25	HR	302
83	33	4	125-127	3-03-25	S	60
93	34	4	127	3-03-25	HR	150
95	35	4	127	3-03-25	S	46
96	36	4	127	3-03-25	HR	298
98	37	4	128	3-03-25	HR	14
99	38	4	129	3-03-25	HR	361

PUBLIC ACTS OF THE EIGHTEENTH CONGRESS

Public Law/Resolution		Statutes at Large	Page	Date	Bill No.	
Chapter	Number					
100	39	4	129-131	3-03-25	HR	266
101	40	4	131	3-03-25	S	19
102	41	4	131	3-03-25	HR	342
103	42	4	132	3-03-25	HR	269
106	43	4	132	3-03-25	HR	252
107	44	4	132-133	3-03-25	HR	369
111	45	4	133	3-03-25	HR	305
112	46	4	133	3-03-25	HR	367
113	47	4	133-135	3-03-25	HR	336
114	48	4	135	3-03-25	HR	270
120	49	4	135	3-03-25	HR	204

RESOLUTIONS OF THE EIGHTEENTH CONGRESS

1	1	4	136	3-03-25	HJR	4
2	2	4	136	3-03-25	SJR	2

Public Law/Resolution		Statutes at Large	Page	Date	Bill No.	
Chapter	Number					
1	1	4	137	12-23-25	HR	1
2	2	4	137	1-18-26	HR	3
3	3	4	138	2-01-26	S	3
4	4	4	138	2-01-26	S	18
5	5	4	138	2-01-26	S	25
6	6	4	138-139	2-01-26	HR	2
7	7	4	139	3-03-26	HR	96
8	8	4	139	3-03-26	S	6
9	9	4	139-140	3-03-26	S	22
10	10	4	140	3-03-26	HR	64
12	11	4	140-142	3-14-26	HR	46
13	12	4	142-149	3-14-26	HR	42
14	13	4	149	3-14-26	HR	10
15	14	4	149-150	3-14-26	S	40
16	15	4	150	3-25-26	HR	47
17	16	4	150-152	3-25-26	HR	45
18	17	4	152	3-31-26	S	45
21	18	4	152	4-05-26	HR	158
22	19	4	153	4-05-26	HR	59
23	20	4	153	4-05-26	S	51
25	21	4	153	4-14-26	S	70
26	22	4	154	4-20-26	S	117
27	23	4	154	4-20-26	S	41
28	24	4	154-155	4-22-26	HR	21
29	25	4	156-157	4-22-26	HR	39
30	26	4	157	5-04-26	S	57
31	27	4	157-158	5-04-26	S	96
32	28	4	158	5-04-26	HR	220
33	29	4	158	5-04-26	HR	180
34	30	4	158-159	5-04-26	HR	32
35	31	4	159	5-04-26	HR	162
36	32	4	160	5-04-26	HR	65
37	33	4	160-161	5-04-26	S	20
38	34	4	161	5-13-26	S	99
39	35	4	161-162	5-13-26	S	88
40	36	4	162	5-13-26	S	72
41	37	4	162	5-13-26	HR	245
45	38	4	162-164	5-13-26	HR	125
46	39	4	164-167	5-15-26	S	128

Public Law/Resolution		Statutes at Large	Page	Date	Bill No.	
Chapter	Number					
47	40	4	167	5-15-26	S	21
56	41	4	167-168	5-15-26	HR	63
59	42	4	168	5-16-26	HR	14
62	43	4	168	5-16-26	S	95
64	44	4	168-169	5-17-26	HR	270
65	45	4	169	5-18-26	HR	35
66	46	4	169-170	5-18-26	HR	148
67	47	4	170	5-18-26	HR	238
73	48	4	170-173	5-18-26	HR	185
74	49	4	173-174	5-18-26	HR	38
75	50	4	174	5-20-26	HR	121
76	51	4	175	5-20-26	HR	18
77	52	4	175	5-20-26	S	104
78	53	4	175-176	5-20-26	HR	192
79	54	4	177	5-20-26	S	134
80	55	4	177-178	5-20-26	HR	88
81	56	4	178	5-20-26	HR	28
82	57	4	178-179	5-20-26	HR	147
83	58	4	179	5-20-26	HR	150
88	59	4	179-180	5-20-26	HR	170
89	60	4	180	5-20-26	HR	202
90	61	4	180	5-20-26	HR	25
109	62	4	180-181	5-20-26	HR	191
110	63	4	181-183	5-20-26	HR	179
111	64	4	183	5-20-26	HR	49
112	65	4	184	5-20-26	HR	151
123	66	4	184	5-20-26	HR	196
124	67	4	184	5-20-26	S	155
125	68	4	184-185	5-20-26	S	82
126	69	4	185	5-20-26	S	157
127	70	4	185	5-20-26	S	50
128	71	4	185	5-20-26	HR	252
129	72	4	186	5-20-26	HR	216
130	73	4	186	5-20-26	HR	201
131	74	4	186	5-20-26	HR	259
132	75	4	187	5-20-26	HR	200
133	76	4	187-188	5-20-26	S	146
134	77	4	188	5-20-26	HR	109
135	78	4	188	5-20-26	S	71

PUBLIC ACTS OF THE NINETEENTH CONGRESS

Public Law/Resolution		Statutes at Large	Page	Date	Bill No.	
Chapter	Number					
136	79	4	188-189	5-20-26	S	154
137	80	4	189	5-20-26	HR	203
138	81	4	189-190	5-20-26	S	125
139	82	4	190	5-20-26	S	65
140	83	4	190	5-20-26	HR	29
147	84	4	190-191	5-20-26	HR	77
148	85	4	191	5-22-26	HR	232
149	86	4	192	5-22-26	HR	272
150	87	4	192	5-22-26	HR	257
151	88	4	192-193	5-22-26	S	140
152	89	4	193	5-22-26	S	24
153	90	4	193	5-22-26	S	90
154	91	4	194	5-22-26	HR	160
155	92	4	194	5-22-26	HR	146

RESOLUTIONS OF THE NINETEENTH CONGRESS

1	1	4	194	5-04-26	HJR	4
2	2	4	195	5-13-26	HJR	3
3	3	4	195	5-18-26	HJR	9
4	4	4	195	5-20-26	HJR	7
5	5	4	195-196	5-23-26	HJR	14

PUBLIC ACTS OF THE NINETEENTH CONGRESS

Public Law/Resolution		Statutes at Large	Page	Date	Bill No.	
Chapter	Number					
4	1	4	197-200	1-24-27	S	15
5	2	4	200	1-24-27	S	35
6	3	4	200-201	1-29-27	HR	384
7	4	4	201	1-29-27	HR	281
8	5	4	201-202	1-29-27	S	29
9	6	4	202-204	2-08-27	HR	308
14	7	4	205	2-22-27	S	84
18	8	4	205	2-22-27	S	19
19	9	4	205-206	2-22-27	HR	363
20	10	4	206	2-22-27	HR	423
21	11	4	206	2-22-27	HR	352
22	12	4	206-208	3-02-27	HR	413
23	13	4	208-214	3-02-27	HR	367
29	14	4	214-216	3-02-27	HR	372
30	15	4	216-217	3-02-27	HR	385
31	16	4	217	3-02-27	HR	394
32	17	4	217-218	3-02-27	HR	368
33	18	4	218-219	3-02-27	HR	428
34	19	4	219	3-02-27	S	11
35	20	4	219	3-02-27	S	91
36	21	4	219-221	3-02-27	S	68
37	22	4	221-226	3-02-27	HR	434
40	23	4	226	3-02-27	HR	440
41	24	4	226-227	3-02-27	HR	389
42	25	4	227	3-02-27	S	20
43	26	4	227-228	3-02-27	S	38
44	27	4	228	3-02-27	HR	290
45	28	4	228	3-02-27	HR	225
46	29	4	228-229	3-02-27	HR	438
47	30	4	229-231	3-02-27	HR	403
48	31	4	231-232	3-02-27	HR	293
49	32	4	232-233	3-02-27	HR	444
50	33	4	233-234	3-02-27	S	47
51	34	4	234	3-02-27	S	48
52	35	4	234-235	3-02-27	S	74
53	36	4	235	3-02-27	HR	304
55	37	4	235-236	3-02-27	HR	289
56	38	4	236	3-02-27	S	71
57	39	4	236-237	3-02-27	S	42
58	40	4	237	3-02-27	HR	429

PUBLIC ACTS OF THE NINETEENTH CONGRESS

Public Law/Resolution		Statutes at Large	Page	Date	Bill No.	
Chapter	Number					
59	41	4	237	3-02-27	S	101
60	42	4	237-238	3-02-27	HR	350
61	43	4	238-239	3-02-27	HR	409
62	44	4	239	3-02-27	S	53*
77	45	4	239	3-02-27	HR	381
78	46	4	239-240	3-02-27	S	16
79	47	4	240-241	3-02-27	S	36
80	48	4	241	3-02-27	S	57
91	49	4	241	3-02-27	HR	416
92	50	4	241-242	3-02-27	S	89
93	51	4	242	3-02-27	S	52*
94	52	4	242-243	3-02-27	S	50
95	53	4	243-244	3-02-27	S	49
96	54	4	244	3-02-27	HR	299
97	55	4	244	3-02-27	HR	411

RESOLUTION OF THE NINETEENTH CONGRESS

1	1	4	245	1-24-27	HJR	2

PUBLIC ACTS OF THE TWENTIETH CONGRESS

Public Law/Resolution		Statutes at Large	Page	Date	Bill No.	
Chapter	Number					
1	1	4	246	1-03-28	HR	23
2	2	4	246-247	1-25-28	HR	37
4	3	4	247	2-12-28	HR	85
6	4	4	247-253	2-02-28	HR	70
15	5	4	254	3-10-28	S	30
16	6	4	254	3-10-28	HR	26
17	7	4	254-256	3-10-28	HR	91
18	8	4	256	3-19-28	HR	96
19	9	4	256-257	3-19-28	HR	21
21	10	4	257-259	3-21-28	HR	142
22	11	4	259-260	3-21-28	HR	2
23	12	4	260	4-03-28	HR	76
28	13	4	260-261	4-17-28	HR	34
29	14	4	261-262	4-17-28	S	116
30	15	4	262-263	4-17-28	S	130
31	16	4	263	4-17-28	S	118
39	17	4	263	4-28-28	HR	212
40	18	4	264	4-28-28	S	100
41	19	4	264	4-28-28	HR	4
42	20	4	264-265	4-28-28	HR	257
44	21	4	265	5-02-28	HR	267
45	22	4	265-266	5-02-28	HR	158
46	23	4	267	5-09-28	S	61
47	24	4	267-268	5-09-28	HR	120
48	25	4	268-269	5-09-28	S	140
49	26	4	269	5-09-28	S	122
52	27	4	269	5-15-28	S	96
53	28	4	269-270	5-15-28	S	44
55	29	4	270-275	5-19-28	HR	132
56	30	4	275-276	5-19-28	HR	119
57	31	4	276	5-19-28	HR	290
58	32	4	276-277	5-19-28	HR	217
59	33	4	277	5-19-28	S	121
60	34	4	277	5-19-28	HR	24
67	35	4	277-278	5-19-28	HR	106
68	36	4	278-282	5-19-28	S	11
69	37	4	282-284	5-23-28	HR	177
70	38	4	284-286	5-23-28	S	49
71	39	4	286-288	5-23-28	HR	13
72	40	4	288	5-23-28	HR	270

Public Law/Resolution		Statutes at Large	Page	Date	Bill No.	
Chapter	Number					
73	41	4	288-289	5-23-28	HR	228
75	42	4	290	5-23-28	S	46
76	43	4	290-291	5-23-28	S	10
77	44	4	291-292	5-23-28	S	13
85	45	4	292-293	5-23-28	HR	40
86	46	4	293-294	5-24-28	HR	41
87	47	4	294-297	5-24-28	HR	128
89	48	4	297	5-24-28	S	39
90	49	4	298	5-24-28	S	134
91	50	4	298-299	5-24-28	S	2
93	51	4	299-300	5-24-28	S	79
94	52	4	300-301	5-24-28	HR	293
95	53	4	301	5-24-28	HR	291
96	54	4	301-302	5-24-28	S	32
97	55	4	302	5-24-28	HR	103
98	56	4	302	5-24-28	HR	190
99	57	4	303	5-24-28	HR	153
100	58	4	303	5-24-28	HR	234
101	59	4	303-304	5-24-28	S	113
102	60	4	304	5-24-28	S	36
103	61	4	304	5-24-28	S	22
104	62	4	304	5-24-28	S	45
105	63	4	304-305	5-24-28	S	55
107	64	4	305	5-24-28	S	12
108	65	4	305-307	5-24-28	HR	94
109	66	4	307-308	5-24-28	S	137
110	67	4	308	5-24-28	S	3
111	68	4	308-309	5-24-28	S	48
113	69	4	309	5-24-28	HR	130
114	70	4	310	5-24-28	HR	272
115	71	4	310	5-24-28	S	139
116	72	4	310-311	5-24-28	HR	121
117	73	4	311-312	5-24-28	HR	263
118	74	4	312	5-24-28	HR	285
119	75	4	312	5-24-28	HR	92
120	76	4	312-313	5-24-28	HR	135
121	77	4	313-314	5-24-28	S	72
122	78	4	314	5-24-28	HR	73
123	79	4	314	5-24-28	HR	264

PUBLIC ACTS OF THE TWENTIETH CONGRESS

Public Law/Resolution		Statutes at Large	Page	Date	Bill No.	
Chapter	Number					
124	80	4	315	5-24-28	S	126
125	81	4	315-320	5-24-28	S	133

RESOLUTIONS OF THE TWENTIETH CONGRESS

1	1	4	320	4-03-28	HJR	6
2	3	4	320	5-23-28	HJR	9
3	4	4	321	5-24-28	HJR	10
4	5	4	322	5-24-28	HJR	14
5	6	4	322	5-24-28	HJR	13
6	7	4	322	5-24-28	HJR	11

PUBLIC ACTS OF THE TWENTIETH CONGRESS

Public Law/Resolution		Statutes at Large	Page	Date	Bill No.	
Chapter	Number					
1	1	4	323-329	1-06-29	HR	284
2	2	4	329	1-06-29	S	18
3	3	4	329-330	1-06-29	HR	312
4	4	4	330	1-06-29	HR	28
5	5	4	330	1-06-29	S	17
7	6	4	330	1-21-29	S	31
8	7	4	331	1-21-29	S	43
9	8	4	331	1-21-29	S	34
10	9	4	331	1-21-29	HR	331
11	10	4	331-332	1-21-29	HR	47
12	11	4	332	1-21-29	S	63
13	12	4	332-333	1-21-29	HR	324
14	13	4	333-334	2-05-29	HR	344
15	14	4	334	2-05-29	S	37
18	15	4	334-335	2-24-29	S	16
19	16	4	335	2-24-29	S	83
20	17	4	335-336	2-24-29	HR	304
24	18	4	336-344	3-02-29	HR	433
25	19	4	345-348	3-02-29	HR	395
26	20	4	348-350	3-02-29	HR	388
27	21	4	350	3-02-29	S	91
28	22	4	350	3-02-29	S	67
29	23	4	351	3-02-29	S	98
30	24	4	351	3-02-29	S	57
31	25	4	351-352	3-02-29	S	1
32	26	4	352-353	3-02-29	HR	437
33	27	4	353	3-02-29	S	14
34	28	4	353-355	3-02-29	HR	420
35	29	4	355	3-02-29	HR	421
36	30	4	355-356	3-02-29	HR	424
37	31	4	356-357	3-02-29	HR	398
38	32	4	357	3-02-29	S	19
39	33	4	357-358	3-02-29	S	73
40	34	4	358-359	3-02-29	S	13
41	35	4	359-360	3-02-29	S	95
42	36	4	360	3-02-29	HR	39
43	37	4	360	3-02-29	HR	406
50	38	4	361-362	3-02-29	HR	459
51	39	4	362-363	3-03-29	HR	413
52	40	4	363	3-03-29	HR	434

PUBLIC ACTS OF THE TWENTIETH CONGRESS

Public Law/Resolution		Statutes at Large	Page	Date	Bill No.	
Chapter	Number					
53	41	4	363-364	3-03-29	HR	42
54	42	4	364	3-03-29	S	4
55	43	4	364	3-03-29	S	5
57	44	4	364-365	3-03-29	HR	127
65	45	4	365-369	3-03-29	HR	134

RESOLUTIONS OF THE TWENTIETH CONGRESS

1	1	4	369	2-05-29	SJR	1
2	2	4	369	3-02-29	SJR	3

PUBLIC ACTS OF THE TWENTY-FIRST CONGRESS

Public Law/Resolution		Statutes at Large	Page	Date	Bill No.	
Chapter	Number					
1	1	4	370	12-29-29	HR	16
2	2	4	370-371	1-13-30	S	13
3	3	4	371	1-13-30	S	11
5	4	4	371	1-30-30	HR	54
10	5	4	371-372	2-03-30	HR	90
11	6	4	372	2-11-30	HR	68
12	7	4	372	2-11-30	HR	8
14	8	4	372-373	2-11-30	HR	71
25	9	4	373	2-27-30	S	43
26	10	4	373	2-27-30	HR	162
27	11	4	374	2-27-30	HR	110
31	12	4	374-375	3-11-30	HR	144
32	13	4	375-376	3-11-30	HR	129
33	14	4	377-382	3-18-30	HR	102
35	15	4	382-383	3-23-30	HR	132
36	16	4	383	3-23-30	HR	99
40	17	4	383-389	3-23-30	HR	116
41	18	4	390	3-25-30	HR	278
48	19	4	390-392	3-31-30	S	28
49	20	4	392	3-31-30	S	81
50	21	4	392-393	3-31-30	S	82
52	22	4	393	4-02-30	HR	332
59	23	4	393	4-02-30	S	84
60	24	4	394	4-07-30	HR	299
68	25	4	394	4-15-30	HR	159
72	26	4	394-395	4-23-30	HR	242
73	27	4	395-396	4-23-30	HR	17
74	28	4	396	4-23-30	HR	143
78	29	4	396-397	4-24-30	S	45
79	30	4	397	4-24-30	S	97
84	31	4	397-398	4-30-30	HR	365
86	32	4	398	5-05-30	HR	260
87	33	4	399	5-05-30	S	66
89	34	4	399	5-05-30	S	172
90	35	4	390-401	5-08-30	HR	112
91	36	4	401	5-08-30	HR	380
92	37	4	401	5-10-30	HR	137
95	38	4	402-403	5-14-30	S	40
96	39	4	403	5-14-30	HR	101
98	40	4	403	5-20-30	HR	139

Public Law/Resolution		Statutes at Large	Page	Date	Bill No.	
Chapter	Number					
99	41	4	403	5-20-30	HR	369
101	42	4	403-404	5-20-30	HR	207
102	43	4	404	5-20-30	S	20
105	44	4	405	5-26-30	HR	141
106	45	4	405-406	5-26-30	HR	206
107	46	4	407	5-26-30	HR	471
146	47	4	408-409	5-28-30	HR	126
147	48	4	409-411	5-28-30	HR	164
148	49	4	411-412	5-28-30	S	102
149	50	4	413	5-28-30	HR	95
150	51	4	413	5-28-30	HR	234
151	52	4	413	5-28-30	HR	383
152	53	4	414	5-28-30	S	140
153	54	4	414-416	5-29-30	S	187
161	55	4	416	5-29-30	S	135
162	56	4	416-417	5-29-30	HR	443
163	57	4	417	5-29-30	HR	470
179	58	4	417-418	5-29-30	HR	259
180	59	4	418	5-29-30	HR	270
182	60	4	418	5-29-30	HR	271
183	61	4	418	5-29-30	HR	487
185	62	4	419	5-29-30	HR	479
189	63	4	419	5-29-30	HR	474
207	64	4	419-420	5-29-30	HR	495
208	65	4	420-421	5-29-30	S	19
211	66	4	421	5-29-30	S	192
213	67	4	422	5-29-30	S	51
215	68	4	422-424	5-30-30	S	134
217	69	4	424-425	5-31-30	HR	146
218	70	4	425	5-31-30	HR	466
219	71	4	425	5-31-30	S	2
220	72	4	425-426	5-31-30	HR	324
228	73	4	426	5-31-30	S	60
229	74	4	426-427	5-31-30	HR	233
232	75	4	427-428	5-31-30	HR	279
233	76	4	428	5-31-30	HR	496
234	77	4	428	5-31-30	S	31
235	78	4	428-429	5-31-30	S	18

RESOLUTIONS OF THE TWENTY-FIRST CONGRESS

Public Law/Resolution		Statutes at Large	Page	Date	Bill No.	
Chapter	Number					
1	1	4	429	12-29-29	HJR	1
2	2	4	429	1-13-30	HJR	2
3	3	4	429	4-30-30	SJR	3
4	4	4	430	5-28-30	HJR	9
5	5	4	430	5-29-30	HJR	8
6	6	4	430	5-29-30	HJR	7
7	7	4	430	5-29-30	HJR	5

PUBLIC ACTS OF THE TWENTY-FIRST CONGRESS

Public Law/Resolution		Statutes at Large	Page	Date	Bill No.	
Chapter	Number					
1	1	4	431	1-13-31	HR	502
2	2	4	431-432	1-13 31	S	25
3	3	4	432	1-13-31	S	24
6	4	4	432	1-19-31	S	51
8	5	4	433	1-27-31	HR	480
9	6	4	433-434	1-27-31	HR	538
10	7	4	434	1-27-31	HR	514
11	8	4	434-435	1-27-31	HR	533
12	9	4	435	1-27-31	S	41
14	10	4	435-436	2-03-31	S	78
15	11	4	436	2-03-31	HR	507
16	12	+	436-439	2-03-31	HR	145
17	13	4	439-440	2-03-31	HR	535
19	14	4	440	2-12-31	S	47
20	15	4	441	2-12-31	HR	590
22	16	4	441	2-12-31	S	17
23	17	4	441	2-12-31	S	89
24	18	4	442	2-02-31	S	35
26	19	4	442	2-19-31	HR	481
27	20	4	442-444	2-19-31	HR	210
28	21	4	444	2-19-31	S	142
30	22	4	444	2-19-31	S	68
31	23	4	445	2-25-31	HR	343
32	24	4	445	2-25-31	S	113
34	25	4	445-446	2-25-31	S	43
36	26	4	446-447	2-25-31	HR	523
37	27	4	448-450	3-02-31	HR	339
38	28	4	450-451	3-02-31	HR	545
39	29	4	451	3-02-31	HR	634
40	30	4	451	3-02-31	HR	588
41	31	4	451-452	3-02-31	HR	298
42	32	4	452	3-02-31	HR	542
55	33	4	452-459	3-02-31	HR	528
56	34	4	459-460	3-02-31	HR	566
57	35	4	460-462	3-02-31	HR	531
58	36	4	462-463	3-02-31	HR	584
59	37	4	463-464	3-02-31	S	145
60	38	4	464-465	3-02-31	HR	645
61	39	4	465-467	3-02-31	HR	539

PUBLIC ACTS OF THE TWENTY-FIRST CONGRESS

Public Law/Resolution		Statutes at Large	Page	Date	Bill No.	
Chapter	Number					
62	40	4	467-469	3-02-31	HR	336
63	41	4	469-470	3-02-31	S	100
64	42	4	470-471	3-02-31	HR	560
65	43	4	471	3-02-31	HR	652
66	44	4	472	3-02-31	HR	654
67	45	4	473	3-02-31	S	125
68	46	4	473	3-02-31	S	152
69	47	4	473-474	3-02-31	HR	513
70	48	4	474	3-02-31	HR	407
73	49	4	474-475	3-02-31	S	74
75	50	4	475	3-02-31	S	26
76	51	4	475-476	3-02-31	S	9
85	52	4	476-479	3-02-31	HR	517
86	53	4	479-480	3-02-31	HR	516
87	54	4	480-482	3-02-31	HR	520
88	55	4	482	3-02-31	S	138
91	56	4	482	3-02-31	S	2
92	57	4	482-483	3-02-31	S	70
97	58	4	483-486	3-02-31	S	165
98	59	4	487	3-02-31	HR	376
99	60	4	487-488	3-02-31	HR	620
103	61	4	488-491	3-02-31	HR	609
104	62	4	491-492	3-02-31	HR	541
114	63	4	492	3-02-31	S	136
115	64	4	492	3-02-31	S	131
116	65	4	492-494	3-02-31	S	137

RESOLUTIONS OF THE TWENTY-FIRST CONGRESS

1	1	4	495	1-13-31	HJR	3
2	2	4	495	3-02-31	SJR	2

PUBLIC ACTS OF THE TWENTY-SECOND CONGRESS

Public Law/Resolution		Statutes at Large	Page	Date	Bill No.	
Chapter	Number					
1	1	4	496	1-19-32	S	23
9	2	4	496	1-23-32	S	56
10	3	4	496-497	1-23-32	HR	103
15	4	4	497	2-10-32	HR	122
25	5	4	497	1-24-32	HR	85
26	7	4	497	1-24-32	HR	144
27	8	4	497-498	1-24-32	HR	174
28	9	4	498-499	1-24-32	HR	223
51	10	4	499-500	3-22-32	HR	4
52	11	4	500	3-22-32	HR	241
57	12	4	500-501	3-31-32	HR	124
58	13	4	501	3-31-32	HR	206
64	14	4	501-502	4-05-32	HR	164
65	15	4	503	4-05-32	S	22
66	16	4	503-504	4-05-32	S	79
67	17	4	504	4-05-32	S	4
69	18	4	504	4-20-32	HR	263
70	19	4	505	4-20-32	HR	274
71	20	4	505-506	4-20-32	HR	505
72	21	4	506	5-05-32	HR	518
74	22	4	506-514	5-05-32	HR	116
75	23	4	514-515	5-05-32	HR	526
77	24	4	515	5-19-32	HR	539
79	26	4	515-516	5-19-32	HR	320
80	27	4	516	5-19-32	HR	306
91	28	4	516	5-22-32	HR	208
92	29	4	516-517	5-22-32	HR	370
93	30	4	517	5-22-32	HR	418
104	31	4	517	5-25-32	S	178
105	32	4	517-518	5-25-32	HR	296
106	33	4	518	5-25-32	HR	376
107	34	4	518-519	5-25-32	HR	357
109	35	4	519-520	5-31-32	HR	173
110	36	4	520	5-31-32	HR	356
111	37	4	520	5-31-32	HR	519
112	38	4	520-521	5-31-32	HR	322
113	39	4	521-525	5-31-32	HR	492
114	40	4	525	5-31-32	HR	550
115	41	4	526	5-31-32	HR	364

Public Law/Resolution		Statutes at Large	Page	Date	Bill No.	
Chapter	Number					
123	42	4	526-528	6-04-32	HR	417
124	43	4	528-529	6-04-32	HR	566
126	44	4	529-530	6-04-32	S	1
127	45	4	530-531	6-15-32	HR	564
128	46	4	531	6-15-32	S	159
129	47	4	531	6-15-32	S	54
130	48	4	532	6-15-32	HR	525
131	49	4	533	6-15-32	S	6
140	50	4	534	6-15-32	S	34
141	51	4	534-549	6-15-32	HR	343
144	53	4	549	6-25-32	HR	541
150	54	4	550	6-28-32	S	120
151	55	4	550	6-28-32	HR	596
152	56	4	550-551	6-28-32	HR	405
153	57	4	551-557	7-03-32	HR	267
154	58	4	558	7-03-32	HR	318
155	59	4	558	7-03-32	S	105
161	64	4	558-559	7-03-32	S	209
162	65	4	559	7-03-32	HR	551
163	66	4	560	7-03-32	HR	502
164	60	4	560	7-04-32	HR	158
165	61	4	561	7-04-32	HR	165
166	62	4	561-562	7-04-32	HR	424
172	67	4	563	7-04-32	HR	549
173	63	4	563-564	7-05-32	S	88
174	68	4	564	7-09-32	S	125
175	69	4	564	7-09-32	S	11
180	71	4	565-567	7-09-32	S	114
181	72	4	567-568	7-09-32	S	158
182	73	4	568	7-09-32	S	112
184	74	4	569	7-09-32	S	194
186	75	4	569	7-10-32	HR	134
187	76	4	569	7-10-32	HR	91
188	77	4	570	7-10-32	HR	133
189	78	4	570	7-10-32	HR	58
190	79	4	570	7-10-32	HR	57
191	80	4	570-571	7-10-32	HR	74
192	81	4	571	7-10-32	HR	88
193	82	4	571-572	7-10-32	HR	556

PUBLIC ACTS OF THE TWENTY-SECOND CONGRESS

Public Law/Resolution		Statutes at Large	Page	Date	Bill No.	
Chapter	Number					
194	83	4	572-573	7-10-32	HR	387
196	84	4	573	7-13-32	HR	248
197	85	4	573-574	7-13-32	HR	517
198	86	4	574	7-13-32	HR	490
199	87	4	574-576	7-13-32	HR	415
200	88	4	576	7-13-32	HR	575
201	89	4	576-577	7-13-32	HR	586
202	90	4	577	7-13-32	HR	585
203	91	4	577	7-13-32	HR	222
204	92	4	577-578	7-13-32	HR	534
205	93	4	578	7-13-32	HR	594
206	94	4	578	7-13-32	HR	163
207	95	4	578-579	7-13-32	S	211
221	96	4	579	7-14-32	S	68
222	97	4	580	7-14-32	HR	90
223	98	4	580	7-14-32	S	151
224	99	4	580-582	7-14-32	HR	601
225	100	4	582-583	7-14-32	S	8
227	102	4	583-594	7-14-32	HR	584
228	103	4	594	7-14-32	HR	597
229	104	4	594-595	7-14-32	S	43
230	105	4	595	7-14-32	HR	313
231	106	4	595-596	7-14-32	HR	484
232	107	4	596	7-14-32	S	155
233	108	4	597-599	7-14-32	HR	442
234	109	4	599	7-14-32	HR	79
236	111	4	599	7-14-32	HR	225
237	112	4	600	7-14-32	HR	156
238	113	4	600	7-14-32	HR	569
239	114	4	600-601	7-14-32	HR	581
240	115	4	601	7-14-32	HR	583
241	116	4	601	7-14-32	HR	259
242	117	4	602	7-14-32	HR	554
243	118	4	602	7-14-32	HR	268
245	120	4	602	7-14-32	S	136
246	121	4	603	7-14-32	S	56
247	122	4	603	7-14-32	S	108
248	123	4	603-604	7-14-32	S	150

PUBLIC ACTS OF THE TWENTY-SECOND CONGRESS

Public Law/Resolution		Statutes at Large	Page	Date	Bill No.	
Chapter	Number					
250	125	4	604	7-14-32	S	131
301	126	4	604-605	7-16-32	S	201

RESOLUTIONS OF THE TWENTY-SECOND CONGRESS

1	1	4	605	2-10-32	HJR	3
2	2	4	605	3-07-32	HJR	2
3	3	4	605	5-25-32	HJR	6
4	4	4	605	6-28-32	HJR	7
5	5	4	606	7-03-32	HJR	5
6	6	4	606-607	7-10-32	HJR	8
7	7	4	607	7-13-32	SJR	10
8	8	4	607-608	7-14-32	HJR	1
9	9	4	608	7-14-32	HJR	11
10	10	4	608	7-14-32	HJR	14
11	11	4	608	7-14-32	HJR	12

PUBLIC ACTS OF THE TWENTY-SECOND CONGRESS

Public Law/Resolution		Statutes at Large	Page	Date	Bill No.	
Chapter	Number					
1	1	4	609	1-14-33	HR	621
2	2	4	610	1-14-33	HR	642
3	3	4	610	1-14-33	HR	625
12	4	4	610-611	1-30-33	HR	102
16	5	4	611	2-05-33	HR	591
23	6	4	611	2-09-33	HR	63
30	7	4	611-612	2-19-33	HR	350
31	8	4	612	2-19-33	HR	674
32	9	4	612-613	2-19-33	HR	631
33	10	4	613	2-19-33	S	20
34	11	4	613-614	2-19-33	HR	421
39	12	4	614-616	2-20-33	HR	657
40	13	4	616-618	2-20-33	HR	637
41	14	4	618	2-20-33	S	30
42	15	4	618-619	2-20-33	HR	653
43	16	4	619	2-20-33	HR	639
54	17	4	619-629	3-02-33	HR	669
55	18	4	629-631	3-02-33	HR	641
56	19	4	631-632	3-02-33	HR	630
57	20	4	632-635	3-02-33	S	82
58	21	4	635-636	3-02-33	S	48
59	22	4	636-641	3-02-33	S	128
60	23	4	641-642	3-02-33	HR	224
61	24	4	642-644	3-02-33	HR	686
62	25	4	644-645	3-02-33	HR	750
63	26	4	645	3-02-33	HR	663
64	27	4	645	3-02-33	S	103
65	28	4	646	3-02-33	HR	666
66	29	4	646	3-02-33	S	62
67	30	4	646-647	3-02-33	HR	622
68	31	4	647-648	3-02-33	HR	126
69	32	4	648-649	3-02-33	HR	714
70	33	4	649-650	3-02-33	HR	721
71	34	4	650	3-02-33	HR	560
72	35	4	650-651	3-02-33	HR	728
73	36	4	651	3-02-33	HR	706
74	37	4	651	3-02-33	S	120
75	38	4	652	3-02-33	HR	712
76	39	4	652	3-02-33	HR	646

PUBLIC ACTS OF THE TWENTY-SECOND CONGRESS

Public Law/Resolution		Statutes at Large	Page	Date	Bill No.	
Chapter	Number					
77	40	4	653-654	3-02-33	HR	635
78	41	4	654-655	3-02-33	S	81
79	42	4	655-659	3-02-33	S	102
80	43	4	659-660	3-02-33	HR	497
82	45	4	660	3-02-33	HR	723
83	46	4	661	3-02-33	HR	700
84	47	4	661-662	3-02-33	HR	652
85	48	4	662	3-02-33	HR	679
87	50	4	662	3-02-33	S	34
89	52	4	663	3-02-33	S	44
90	53	4	663	3-02-33	S	77
91	54	4	663	3-02-33	S	42
92	55	4	663-664	3-02-33	S	97
93	56	4	664-665	3-02-33	HR	716
94	57	4	665	3-02-33	HR	335
95	58	4	665	3-02-33	HR	746
96	59	4	666-667	3-02-33	HR	741
97	60	4	667-668	3-02-33	HR	732

RESOLUTIONS OF THE TWENTY-SECOND CONGRESS

1	1	4	668	2-19-33	SJR	2
2	2	4	668	3-02-33	HJR	15*
4	3	4	669	3-02-33	SJR	5
5	4	4	669	3-02-33	SJR	4
6	5	4	669	3-02-33	HJR	18

PUBLIC ACTS OF THE TWENTY-THIRD CONGRESS

Public Law/Resolution		Statutes at Large	Page	Date	Bill No.	
Chapter	Number					
1	1	4	670-671	1-24-34	HR	110
10	2	4	672	2-11-34	HR	36
11	3	4	672	2-26-34	S	48
15	4	4	672-673	2-27-34	HR	212
16	5	4	673	3-24-34	S	91
41	7	4	673-675	5-14-34	HR	246
45	8	4	676	6-07-34	HR	397
46	9	4	677	6-18-34	HR	457
47	10	4	677-678	6-18-34	HR	109
54	11	4	678	6-19-34	S	19
55	12	4	679	6-19-34	HR	49
56	13	4	679	6-19-34	HR	90
57	14	4	679	6-19-34	HR	330
58	15	4	680	6-19-34	HR	435
59	16	4	680	6-19-34	HR	486
60	17	4	680	6-19-34	HR	518
68	18	4	680-681	6-24-34	S	79
71	19	4	681-682	6-25-34	HR	255
72	20	4	682	6-25-34	HR	364
74	21	4	682-685	6-26-34	HR	182
75	22	4	685-686	6-26-34	S	77
76	23	4	686-687	6-26-34	S	76
77	24	4	687-688	6-26-34	HR	301
78	25	4	688	6-26-34	S	117
91	26	4	688-689	6-27-34	HR	134
92	27	4	689-699	6-27-34	HR	283
95	28	4	699-700	6-28-34	HR	313
96	29	4	700-701	6-28-34	HR	312
97	30	4	701	6-28-34	HR	549
98	31	4	701	6-28-34	HR	543
99	32	4	701	6-28-34	S	203
100	33	4	701-702	6-28-34	S	216
101	34	4	702	6-28-34	S	140
102	35	4	702	6-28-34	S	99
103	36	4	702-704	6-28-34	HR	269
104	37	4	704	6-28-34	HR	238
105	38	4	705-707	6-28-34	HR	541
106	39	4	707	6-28-34	HR	191
125	40	4	708	6-28-34	HR	167

PUBLIC ACTS OF THE TWENTY-THIRD CONGRESS

Public Law/Resolution		Statutes at Large	Page	Date	Bill No.	
Chapter	Number					
126	41	4	708-711	6-28-34	HR	504
128	42	4	711	6-30-34	S	85
129	43	4	712	6-30-34	HR	446
130	44	4	712	6-30-34	S	41
131	45	4	712	6-30-34	S	182
132	46	4	712-714	6-30-34	S	90
133	47	4	714	6-30-34	S	10
134	48	4	714-715	6-30-34	S	220
135	49	4	715-716	6-30-34	S	204
136	50	4	716	6-30-34	S	125
137	51	4	716-717	6-30-34	S	118
138	52	4	717	6-30-34	S	52
139	53	4	717-718	6-30-34	S	84
140	54	4	718	6-30-34	S	29
141	55	4	718	6-30-34	S	75
142	56	4	718-719	6-30-34	HR	47
143	57	4	719	6-30-34	HR	181
144	58	4	719-721	6-30-34	HR	240
145	59	4	721-722	6-30-34	HR	153
146	60	4	722-723	6-30-34	HR	207
147	61	4	723	6-30-34	HR	393
148	62	4	723	6-30-34	HR	274
149	63	4	724	6-30-34	HR	279
150	64	4	724	6-30-34	HR	159
151	65	4	724	6-30-34	HR	432
152	66	4	724-726	6-30-34	HR	164
153	67	4	726-727	6-30-34	HR	402
155	68	4	727	6-30-34	HR	303
156	69	4	727-728	6-30-34	HR	492
157	70	4	728	6-30-34	HR	419
158	71	4	728	6-30-34	HR	480
160	72	4	728-729	6-30-34	HR	452
161	73	4	729-735	6-30-34	HR	489
162	74	4	735-738	6-30-34	HR	488
163	75	4	739	6-30-34	S	165
164	76	4	739	6-30-34	HR	441
165	77	4	739-740	6-30-34	HR	404
166	78	4	740	6-30-34	HR	295
167	79	4	740	6-30-34	HR	409

PUBLIC ACTS OF THE TWENTY-THIRD CONGRESS

Public Law/Resolution		Statutes at Large	Page	Date	Bill No.	
Chapter	Number					
168	80	4	740-741	6-30-34	S	59
170	81	4	741	6-30-34	HR	482
171	82	4	742	6-30-34	HR	165
173	83	4	742	6-30-34	S	96
174	84	4	742-743	6-30-34	HR	511
247	85	4	743	6-30-34	S	158

RESOLUTIONS OF THE TWENTY-THIRD CONGRESS

1	1	4	743-744	6-19-34	HJR	6
2	2	4	744	6-19-34	HJR	4
3	3	4	744	6-25-34	HJR	3
4	4	4	745	6-26-34	HJR	9

PUBLIC ACTS OF THE TWENTY-THIRD CONGRESS

Public Law/Resolution		Statutes at Large	Page	Date	Bill No.	
Chapter	Number					
2	1	4	746	1-27-35	HR	581
3	2	4	746-747	1-27-35	S	56
4	3	4	747-748	1-27-35	HR	580
5	4	4	748-749	1-27-35	HR	566
6	5	4	749	1-27-35	HR	560
7	6	4	749	1-27-35	HR	570
17	7	4	749-750	2-06-35	HR	308
19	8	4	750-752	2-13-35	HR	599
21	9	4	752	2-24-35	S	33
22	10	4	752-753	2-24-35	S	53
23	11	4	753	2-24-35	S	63
24	12	4	753	2-24-35	S	82
25	13	4	753	2-24-35	S	131
26	14	4	753-755	3-03-35	HR	648
27	15	4	755-757	3-03-35	HR	334
28	16	4	757-758	3-03-35	HR	728
29	17	4	758-760	3-03-35	HR	660
30	18	4	760-771	3-03-35	HR	616
31	19	4	792	3-03-35	S	111
32	20	4	772	3-03-35	HR	682
33	21	4	773	3-03-35	HR	684
34	22	4	773	3-03-35	HR	619
35	23	4	773	3-03-35	HR	605
36	24	4	773	3-03-35	HR	708
37	25	4	774	3-03-35	HR	683
39	26	4	774-775	3-03-35	S	155
40	27	4	775-777	3-03-35	S	137
41	28	4	777	3-03-35	HR	632
43	29	4	778	3-03-35	S	173
44	30	4	778	3-03-35	S	170
45	31	4	778-779	3-03-35	S	78
46	32	4	779	3-03-35	S	104
47	33	4	779	3-03-35	HR	658
48	34	4	779-780	3-03-35	HR	290
49	35	4	780	3-03-35	HR	56
50	36	4	780-791	3-03-35	HR	664
76	37	4	791	3-03-35	HR	729

RESOLUTIONS OF THE TWENTY-THIRD CONGRESS

Public Law/Resolution		Statutes at Large	Page	Date	Bill No.	
Chapter	Number					
1	1	4	792	1-27-35	HJR	12
2	2	4	792	2-13-35	SJR	5
3	3	4	792	2-13-35	HJR	13

Public Law/Resolution		Statutes at Large	Page	Date	Bill No.	
Chapter	Number					
1	1	5	1	1-14-36	HR	69
3	2	5	1	1-29-36	HR	215
5	3*	5	1-2	2-09-36	HR	169
7	3	5	2	2-11-36	HR	51
38	35*	5	2-4	2-17-36	HR	79
40	37*	5	4-5	2-25-36	S	114
41	4	5	5	2-25-36	HR	300
42	5	5	6	3-19-36	S	65
43	6	5	6-7	3-19-36	HR	389
44	7	5	7-8	3-19-36	HR	338
46	8	5	8	4-01-36	HR	427
47	9	5	8	4-05-36	HR	533
48	10	5	8	4-09-36	HR	535
50	11	5	8-9	4-11-36	HR	303
52	12	5	9	4-14-36	HR	52
53	13	5	10	4-20-36	S	200
54	14	5	10-16	4-20-36	S	92
55	15	5	16	4-20-36	S	73
56	16	5	16	4-20-36	HR	304
57	17	5	17	4-29-36	HR	594
58	18	5	17	4-29-36	HR	566
59	19	5	17-25	5-09-36	HR	216
16	20	5	26-27	5-09-36	HR	454
61	21	5	27-29	5-14-36	HR	53
62	22	5	29-31	5-14-36	HR	55
76	23	5	31	5-20-36	S	79
77	24	5	31	5-20-36	S	191
79	55*	5	31-32	5-20-36	S	112
80	25	5	32-33	5-23-36	HR	264
81	26	5	33	5-23-36	HR	649
82	27	5	33-34	5-28-36	HR	590
85	58*	5	34	6-07-36	HR	450
86	28	5	34	6-07-36	S	248
87	29	5	34-36	6-07-36	HR	57
88	30	5	36-47	6-14-36	HR	70
89	31	5	47	6-14-36	HR	374
97	32	5	48	6-15-36	HR	342
98	33	5	48-49	6-15-36	S	14
99	34	5	49-50	6-15-36	S	177

PUBLIC ACTS OF THE TWENTY-FOURTH CONGRESS

Public Law/Resolution		Statutes at Large	Page	Date	Bill No.	
Chapter	Number					
100	35	5	50-52	6-15-36	S	178
115	36	5	52-56	6-23-36	S	42
116	37	5	56	6-23-36	HR	341
117	38	5	56-57	6-23-36	S	7
118	39	5	57	6-23-36	S	93
119	40	5	57-58	6-23-36	S	206
120	41	5	58-59	6-23-36	S	256
121	42	5	59-60	6-23-36	S	280
230	130*	5	60-61	6-28-36	HR	167
231	43	5	61	7-01-36	S	306
232	44	5	61	7-01-36	HR	410
233	45	5	61	7-01-36	S	285
234	46	5	61-62	7-01-36	S	281
235	189*	5	62	7-01-36	S	81
236	190*	5	63	7-01-36	S	254
248	202*	5	63	7-01-36	HR	463
249	203*	5	63-64	7-01-36	HR	552
252	47	5	64	7-01-36	S	308
253	66	5	65	7-02-36	HR	47
254	48	5	65	7-02-36	HR	733
255	49	5	65-66	7-02-36	HR	647
256	50	5	66	7-02-36	HR	524
257	51	5	66	7-02-36	HR	459
258	52	5	67	7-02-36	HR	406
259	53	5	67-69	7-02-36	HR	307
260	54	5	69	7-02-36	S	242
261	55	5	69-70	7-02-36	S	216
262	56	5	70-71	7-02-36	S	207
263	57	5	71	7-02-36	S	131
264	58	5	71-72	7-02-36	S	64
265	59	5	72	7-02-36	HR	259
266	60	5	73	7-02-36	S	311
267	61	5	73-77	7-02-36	HR	695
268	63	5	77-79	7-02-36	HR	54
269	64	5	79	7-02-36	S	208
270	65	5	80-90	7-02-36	HR	245
271	66	5	90-107	7-02-36	HR	604
290	224*	5	107	7-02-36	S	312
352	67	5	107-112	7-04-36	S	155

PUBLIC ACTS OF THE TWENTY-FOURTH CONGRESS

Public Law/Resolution		Statutes at Large	Page	Date	Bill No.	
Chapter	Number					
353	68	5	112-115	7-04-36	S	300
354	69	5	115-116	7-04-36	S	310
355	70	5	116	7-04-36	S	255
356	71	5	117	7-04-36	S	264
357	72	5	117-125	7-04-36	S	239
359	74	5	125-126	7-04-36	S	214
360	75	5	126	7-04-36	S	175
361	76	5	126-127	7-04-36	S	2
362	78	5	127-128	7-04-36	HR	426
363	79	5	128-131	7-04-36	HR	523
364	77	5	131	7-04-36	HR	545

RESOLUTIONS OF THE TWENTY-FOURTH CONGRESS

1	1	5	131	2-01-36	HJR	4
2	2	5	131	3-19-36	HJR	8
3	3	5	131-132	5-09-36	HJR	12
4	4	5	132	5-14-36	SJR	15
5	5	5	132	5-14-36	SJR	11
6	6	5	132	6-07-36	HJR	16
7	7	5	133	6-14-36	SJR	22
8	8	5	133	6-23-36	SJR	21
9	9	5	133-134	6-23-36	HJR	11
10	10	5	134	7-01-36	SJR	7

Public Law/Resolution		Statutes at Large	Page	Date	Bill No.	
Chapter	Number					
1	1	5	135	1-09-37	HR	751
2	2	5	135-136	1-09-37	HR	752
3	3	5	136-142	1-18-37	HR	529
4	4	5	142	1-18-37	HR	753
5	5	5	142-144	1-18-37	HR	744
6	6	5	144	1-26-37	S	81
9	3*	5	144-146	1-31-37	HR	784
12	7	5	146	2-09-37	S	121
13	8	5	146-147	2-13-37	HR	798
14	9	5	147	2-13-37	HR	750
15	10	5	147	3-01-37	S	41
16	11	5	147	3-01-37	S	129
17	12	5	148-151	3-01-37	HR	755
18	13	5	151-152	3-02-37	HR	801
19	14	5	152	3-02-37	HR	348
20	15	5	152-153	3-02-37	HR	922
21	16	5	153	3-02-37	S	39
22	17	5	153-154	3-02-37	S	249
23	18	5	154	3-02-37	S	72
25	7*	5	154-155	3-02-37	S	164
30	19	5	155-158	3-03-37	HR	754
31	20	5	158-163	3-03-37	HR	757
32	21	5	163	3-03-37	HR	226
33	22	5	163-176	3-03-37	HR	776
34	23	5	176-178	3-03-37	S	17
35	24	5	178	3-03-37	S	58
36	25	5	178-179	3-03-37	S	192
37	26	5	179	3-03-37	S	140
38	27	5	180	3-03-37	S	8
39	28	5	180-181	3-03-37	S	139
40	29	5	181-185	3-03-37	S	247
41	30	5	186	3-03-37	S	224
42	31	5	187	3-03-37	S	236
43	32	5	187	3-03-37	S	154
44	33	5	187-191	3-03-37	HR	895
45	34	5	191-195	3-03-37	S	107
46	35	5	195-196	3-03-37	HR	792
49	14*	5	196-197	3-03-37	HR	779
51	16*	5	197	3-03-37	HR	416

PUBLIC ACTS OF THE TWENTY-FOURTH CONGRESS

Public Law/Resolution		Statutes at Large	Page	Date	Bill No.	
Chapter	Number					
52	17	5	197-198	3-03-37	HR	482
95	40*	5	198	3-03-37	S	186

RESOLUTIONS OF THE TWENTY-FOURTH CONGRESS

1	1	5	198-199	3-02-37	SJR	7
2	2	5	199	3-03-37	HJR	6
4	4	5	200	3-03-37	HJR	20
5	5	5	200	3-03-37	SJR	11

PUBLIC ACTS OF THE TWENTY-FIFTH CONGRESS

Public Law/Resolution		Statutes at Large	Page	Date	Bill No.	
Chapter	Number					
1	1	5	201	10-02-37	S	1
2	2	5	201-204	10-12-37	HR	2
3	3	5	204	10-12-37	S	11
4	4	5	204	10-12-37	HR	10
5	5	5	204-205	10-14-37	HR	11
6	1*	5	205	10-14-37	S	12
7	7	5	205	10-16-37	HR	8
8	8	5	205-206	10-16-37	S	3
9	9	5	206	10-16-37	S	4
10	6	5	207	10-16-37	HR	9

RESOLUTIONS OF THE TWENTY-FIFTH CONGRESS

1	1	5	207	10-12-37	SJR	1

PUBLIC ACTS OF THE TWENTY-FIFTH CONGRESS

Public Law/Resolution		Statutes at Large	Page	Date	Bill No.	
Chapter	Number					
1	1	5	208	12-22-37.	S	12
2	2	5	208-209	1-16-38	S	42
3	3	5	209	1-16-38	S	137
4	4	5	209	1-30-38	HR	450
5	5	5	209-210	1-30-38	HR	393
12	6	5	210	2-22-38	S	205
13	7	5	211	2-22-38	S	189
14	8	5	211-212	3-02-38	S	204
15	9	5	212	3-02-38	HR	376
31	10	5	212-214	3-10-38	HR	595
32	11	5	214-215	3-10-38	HR	226
33	12	5	215	3-10-38	S	182
34	13	5	215	3-19-38	HR	232
46	14	5	215-216	3-28-38	HR	353
54	15	5	216-223	4-06-38	HR	224
55	16	5	224-225	4-06-38	HR	90
56	17	5	225-226	4-06-38	HR	645
57	18	5	226-228	4-20-38	S	161
59	20	5	228	4-20-38	S	106
82	21	5	228	5-21-38	HR	762
84	22	5	228	5-25-38	HR	230
85	23	5	229	5-25-38	S	212
88	65*	5	229-232	5-25-38	HR	521
91	68*	5	232	5-31-38	S	270
92	24	5	232-234	5-31-38	HR	225
93	25	5	234	5-31-38	S	140
96	26	5	235-241	6-12-38	S	269
97	27	5	241-242	6-12-38	HR	676
98	28	5	242-243	6-12-38	HR	413
99	29	5	243	6-12-38	S	30
100	30	5	243-244	6-12-38	S	39
101	31	5	244	6-12-38	S	11
110	79*	5	244	6-12-38	S	197
114	32	5	245-247	6-18-38	S	296
115	33	5	247-248	6-18-38	S	256
116	34	5	248-249	6-18-38	S	98
117	35	5	249	6-18-38	HR	822
118	36	5	249-250	6-18-38	HR	399

Public Law/Resolution		Statutes at Large	Page	Date	Bill No.	
Chapter	Number					
119	37	5	251-252	6-22-38	S	2
147	38	5	252-253	6-28-38	S	73
148	39	5	253	6-28-38	HR	282
150	41	5	253-254	6-28-38	HR	823
153	112*	5	254	6-28-38	HR	467
154	113*	5	254	7-05-38	S	297
157	116*	5	254-255	7-05-38	S	346
158	42	5	255	7-05-38	S	384
159	43	5	255	7-05-38	S	383
160	44	5	255-256	6-05-38	S	374
161	45	5	256	7-05-38	S	312
162	46	5	256-260	7-05-38	S	138
163	47	5	261	7-07-38	S	389
164	48	5	261	7-07-38	HR	829
165	49	5	261	7-07-38	HR	592
166	50	5	262	7-07-38	HR	836
167	51	5	262-263	7-07-38	HR	726
168	52	5	263-264	7-07-38	HR	828
169	53	5	264-267	7-07-38	HR	412
170	54	5	268	7-07-38	HR	869
171	55	5	268-270	7-07-38	HR	394
172	56	5	271-283	7-07-38	HR	839
173	57	5	284	7-07-38	HR	89
174	58	5	284-286	7-07-38	S	18
175	59	5	287	7-07-38	S	174
176	60	5	287-288	7-07-38	S	330
177	61	5	288	7-07-38	S	375
178	62	5	288	7-07-38	S	341
179	63	5	288	7-07-38	HR	733
180	64	5	289-294	7-07-38	S	380
181	65	5	294-295	7-07-38	HR	497
182	66	5	295-296	7-07-38	HR	861
183	67	5	296	7-07-38	HR	661
184	68	5	296-297	7-07-38	S	321
185	69	5	297	7-07-38	S	211
186	70	5	298-301	7-07-38	HR	269
187	71	5	302	7-07-38	S	252
188	72	5	302	7-07-38	S	241
189	73	5	303	7-07-38	S	150

PUBLIC ACTS OF THE TWENTY-FIFTH CONGRESS

Public Law/Resolution		Statutes at Large	Page	Date	Bill No.	
Chapter	Number					
190	74	5	303-304	7-07-38	S	29
191	75	5	304-306	7-07-38	S	1
192	76	5	306-308	7-07-38	S	160
193	77	5	308	7-07-38	S	368
194	78	5	308	7-07-38	S	387
212	135*	5	309	7-07-38	S	33
264	79	5	309-310	7-09-38	S	391

RESOLUTIONS OF THE TWENTY-FIFTH CONGRESS

1	1	5	310	3-19-38	HJR	9
2	2	5	310	4-04-38	SJR	8
4	4	5	310	5-31-38	SJR	11
5	5	5	310	6-12-38	SJR	6
6	6	5	311	6-18-38	HJR	3
7	7	5	311	7-07-38	SJR	18

Public Law/Resolution		Statutes at Large	Page	Date	Bill No.	
Chapter	Number					
1	1	5	312	12-22-38	HR	891
2	2	5	312-313	1-11-39	HR	975
3	3	5	313-314	1-18-39	S	26
4	4	5	314	1-25-39	S	80
20	5	5	315-316	2-06-39	HR	491
24	6	5	316	2-13-39	HR	1092
25	7	5	316-317	2-13-39	HR	893
26	8	5	317	2-16-39	HR	1091
27	9	5	317-318	2-16-39	HR	939
28	19*	5	318	2-16-39	S	35
30	21*	5	318-319	2-20-39	S	2
31	22*	5	319-321	2-20-39	S	78
33	24*	5	321	2-28-39	S	265
35	10	5	321	2-28-39	S	100
36	11	5	321-323	2-28-39	S	229
37	12	5	323	3-02-39	HR	982
70	13	5	323	3-03-39	HR	1081
71	14	5	323-328	3-03-39	HR	895
72	15	5	328-329	3-03-39	HR	1134
73	16	5	329	3-03-39	HR	1034
74	17	5	329	3-03-39	HR	669
75	18	5	329-330	3-03-39	HR	301
76	19	5	330	3-03-39	HR	1097
77	20	5	330-331	3-03-39	HR	1103
78	21	5	331	3-03-39	HR	1136
79	22	5	331	3-03-39	HR	1135
80	23	5	331-337	3-03-39	HR	1138
81	24	5	337-339	3-03-39	S	281
82	25	5	339-349	3-03-39	HR	981
83	26	5	349-351	3-03-39	HR	1112
84	27	5	351-352	3-03-39	HR	892
85	28	5	352	3-03-39	HR	481
86	29	5	352-353	3-03-39	HR	1061
87	30	5	353	3-03-39	HR	1031
88	31	5	353-355	3-03-39	S	256
89	32	5	355-356	3-03-39	HR	1176
90	33	5	356-357	3-03-39	HR	1115
91	34	5	357	3-03-39	HR	1028
92	35	5	357	3-03-39	HR	1058

PUBLIC ACTS OF THE TWENTY-FIFTH CONGRESS

Public Law/Resolution		Statutes at Large	Page	Date	Bill No.	
Chapter	Number					
93	36	5	357-359	3-03-39	HR	1090
94	37	5	359-362	3-03-39	HR	897
95	38	5	362-364	3-03-39	HR	896
226	188*	5	364	3-03-39	HR	1146
229	191*	5	364-365	3-03-39	S	101

RESOLUTIONS OF THE TWENTY-FIFTH CONGRESS

1	1	5	365	1-18-39	HJR	29
2	1	5	365	2-13-39	SJR	9
3	2	5	365-366	2-16-39	SJR	3
4	2	5	366	2-28-39	SJR	11
9	3	5	366	3-03-39	SJR	6

PUBLIC ACTS OF THE TWENTY-SIXTH CONGRESS

Public Law/Resolution		Statutes at Large	Page	Date	Bill No.	
Chapter	Number					
1	1	5	367	1-08-40	HR	2
2	2	5	367-368	2-22-40	HR	3
3	3	5	368-369	2-26-40	S	154
4	4	5	369-370	3-04-40	S	179
5	5	5	370	3-31-40	HR	18
6	6	5	370-371	4-04-40	S	25
22	7	5	371-380	5-08-40	HR	8
23	8	5	380	5-08-40	S	314
25	9	5	380	5-27-40	S	73
26	10	5	381	5-27-40	S	250
27	11	5	381	5-27-40	S	341
32	12	5	382	6-01-40	S	12
34	13	5	383-384	6-12-40	HR	403
35	14	5	384	6-12-40	S	176
36	15	5	384-385	6-12-40	S	92
37	16	5	385	6-12-40	S	358
39	17	5	385	6-19-40	S	353
41	18	5	385-392	7-04-40	S	127
42	19	5	392	7-04-40	S	300
43	20	5	392-393	7-04-40	S	315
44	21	5	393	7-04-40	HR	72
47	22	5	394	7-20-40	S	375
48	23	5	394-397	7-20-40	S	367
49	24	5	397	7-20-40	HR	68
50	25	5	397-398	7-20-40	HR	26
51	26	5	398-402	7-20-40	HR	6
52	27	5	402	7-20-40	HR	467
53	28	5	402-404	7-20-40	HR	4
54	29	5	404-407	7-20-40	HR	5
98	30	5	407-408	7-21-40	HR	260

RESOLUTIONS OF THE TWENTY-SIXTH CONGRESS

1	1	5	409	5-02-40	HJR	8
3	3	5	409	5-27-40	SJR	8
4	4	5	409	7-20-40	SJR	16
5	5	5	409	7-20-40	HJR	14

PUBLIC ACTS OF THE TWENTY-SIXTH CONGRESS

Public Law/Resolution		Statutes at Large	Page	Date	Bill No.	
Chapter	Number					
1	1	5	410	12-18-40	HR	525
2	2	5	410	1-14-41	S	7
3	3	5	411	1-14-41	S	101
5	4	5	411-412	2-15-41	HR	598
6	5	5	412	2-18-41	HR	529
7	6	5	412-413	2-18-41	HR	607
11	7	5	413-414	2-27-41	HR	637
12	8	5	414	2-27-41	S	65
13	9	5	414	2-27-41	HR	679
21	10	5	414-415	3-02-41	HR	684
24	11	5	415	3-03-41	HR	612
25	12	5	415-416	3-03-41	HR	676
26	13	5	416-417	3-03-41	HR	682
33	14	5	417-419	3-03-41	HR	543
34	15	5	419-420	3-03-41	HR	544
35	16	5	421-433	3-03-41	HR	601
36	17	5	433-435	3-03-41	HR	580
37	18	5	435	3-03-41	HR	685
38	19	5	436	3-03-41	S	264
40	20	5	436	3-03-41	S	194

RESOLUTION OF THE TWENTY-SIXTH CONGRESS

1	1	5	436	1-14-41	HJR	19

Public Law/Resolution		Statutes at Large	Page	Date	Bill No.	
Chapter	Number					
1	1	5	437	6-25-41	HR	2
2	1*	5	437-438	6-30-41	HR	1
3	2	5	438	7-21-41	HR	5
4	3	5	438-439	8-01-41	HR	10
5	2*	5	439	8-03-41	HR	7
7	4	5	439-440	8-13-41	S	1
8	5	5	440	8-16-41	HR	6
9	6	5	440-449	8-16-41	S	3
10	7	5	449	8-19-41	HR	21
11	4*	5	449	8-19-41	HR	28
12	5*	5	449-451	8-25-41	S	4
13	6*	5	451-452	9-01-41	HR	31
14	8	5	452	9-01-41	S	8
15	9	5	452-453	9-01-41	S	7
16	10	5	453-458	9-04-41	HR	4
17	11	5	458-460	9-09-41	HR	8
18	12	5	460-461	9-09-41	HR	29
19	13	5	461	9-09-41	HR	36
20	14	5	461	9-09-41	HR	30
21	15	5	461	9-11-41	HR	9
22	16	5	461-462	9-11-41	HR	17
23	7*	5	462	9-11-41	HR	22
24	17	5	463-465	9-11-41	HR	12
25	18	5	465	9-11-41	HR	34

RESOLUTIONS OF THE TWENTY-SEVENTH CONGRESS

1	1	5	466	6-14-41	SJR	1
2	2	5	466	8-25-41	SJR	4
3	3	5	466-467	9-01-41	SJR	2
4	4	5	467	9-01-41	SJR	5
5	5	5	467-468	9-11-41	SJR	3
6	6	5	468	9-11-41	HJR	3

PUBLIC ACTS OF THE TWENTY-SEVENTH CONGRESS

Public Law/Resolution		Statutes at Large	Page	Date	Bill No.	
Chapter	Number					
1	1	5	469	12-22-41	HR	38
2	2	5	469	1-31-42	HR	67
3	3	5	470	2-12-42	HR	79
4	4	5	470	2-12-42	HR	78
5	5	5	470	3-04-42	S	1
6	6	5	470-471	3-19-42	HR	300
7	7	5	471	3-19-42	HR	299
8	8	5	471	3-19-42	S	113
20	9	5	471-472	4-14-42	HR	307
21	10	5	472	4-14-42	S	211
22	11	5	472	4-14-42	S	175
23	12	5	473	4-14-42	S	208
24	13	5	473	4-14-42	S	11
25	14	5	473	4-14-42	S	120
26	15	5	473-475	4-15-42	HR	39
29	16	5	475-488	5-18-42	HR	74
30	17	5	488	5-18-42	HR	405
31	18	5	488-489	6-01-42	HR	113
32	19	5	489	6-01-42	S	71
38	20	5	489-490	6-04-42	HR	411
39	21	5	490	6-13-42	S	4
40	22	5	490-491	6-13-42	HR	434
47	24	5	491	6-25-42	HR	73
50	25	5	491-493	7-06-42	S	76
64	26	5	493-496	7-17-42	HR	77
66	28	5	496	7-27-42	S	177
67	29	5	496	7-27-42	HR	100
68	30	5	496	7-27-42	HR	523
69	31	5	497	7-27-42	HR	26
82	51*	5	497	7-27-42	HR	232
96	65*	5	498	7-27-42	HR	467
106	75*	5	498	7-27-42	HR	423
107	32	5	498	7-30-42	S	264
108	33	5	498-499	8-01-42	HR	504
109	34	5	499	8-01-42	S	259
120	38	5	499-500	8-03-42	HR	409
121	39	5	500-502	8-04-42	HR	76
122	40	5	502-504	8-04-42	S	257

Public Law/Resolution		Statutes at Large	Page	Date	Bill No.	
Chapter	Number					
123	41	5	504	8-04-42	S	273
126	42	5	504	8-09-42	S	193
127	43	5	504-505	8-11-42	S	17
128	44	5	505	8-11-42	S	35
129	45	5	505	8-11-42	HR	566
130	46	5	506	8-11-42	HR	565
177	47	5	506	8-16-42	HR	572
178	48	5	506-507	8-16-42	S	53
179	49	5	507	8-16-42	HR	542
180	50	5	507	8-16-42	S	157
181	51	5	507	8-16-42	HR	569
182	52	5	507-508	8-16-42	HR	517
183	53	5	508-510	8-23-42	HR	75
184	54	5	511	8-23-42	HR	468
185	55	5	511-512	8-23-42	S	269
186	56	5	512-513	8-23-42	S	283
187	57	5	513-516	8-23-42	S	216
188	58	5	516-518	8-23-42	S	142
189	59	5	519-521	8-23-42	HR	402
190	60	5	521	8-23-42	HR	510
191	61	5	521	8-23-42	HR	132
192	62	5	522	8-23-42	HR	516
194	132*	5	522	8-23-42	HR	507
202	63	5	523-533	8-26-42	HR	539
203	64	5	534	8-26-42	HR	570
204	65	5	534	8-26-42	S	257
205	66	5	534-535	8-26-42	HR	331
206	67	5	535-536	8-26-42	S	201
207	68	5	536-537	8-26-42	S	286
227	159*	5	537	8-29-42	HR	446
228	160*	5	537-538	8-29-42	S	88
255	69	5	538	8-29-42	S	226
256	70	5	538-539	8-29-42	S	45
257	71	5	539-540	8-29-42	S	181
258	72	5	540	8-29-42	S	282
259	73	5	540-541	8-29-42	S	251
260	74	5	541-542	8-29-42	S	31
261	75	5	542	8-29-42	S	57
262	76	5	542-543	8-29-42	S	59

PUBLIC ACTS OF THE TWENTY-SEVENTH CONGRESS

Public Law/Resolution		Statutes at Large	Page	Date	Bill No.	
Chapter	Number					
263	77	5	543-545	8-29-42	S	220
264	78	5	545	8-29-42	S	186
265	79	5	545-546	8-29-42	HR	512
266	80	5	546	8-29-42	HR	418
267	81	5	546-547	8-29-42	S	207
268	82	5	547	8-29-42	S	225
269	83	5	547-548	8-29-42	HR	556
270	84	5	548-567	8-30-42	HR	547
271	85	5	567	8-30-42	HR	329
272	187*	5	567-568	8-30-42	HR	202
274	86	5	568-575	8-31-42	HR	564
275	87	5	576	8-31-42	S	315
276	88	5	576	8-31-42	S	291
277	89	5	576	8-31-42	S	285
279	91	5	577	8-31-42	S	262
280	92	5	578	8-31-42	HR	606
281	93	5	578	8-31-42	HR	229
282	189*	5	578-579	8-31-42	HR	470
283	190*	5	579	8-31-42	HR	557
286	94	5	579-581	8-31-42	S	280
287	95	5	581-582	8-31-42	HR	607
288	96	5	582	8-31-42	HR	80

RESOLUTIONS OF THE TWENTY-SEVENTH CONGRESS

2	1	5	583	4-14-42	HJR	5
3	2	5	583	4-15-42	SJR	5
4	3	5	583	5-18-42	HJR	6
5	4	5	583	6-01-42	SJR	9
7	5	5	584	8-11-42	HJR	14
8	6	5	584	8-16-42	SJR	18
10	7	5	584	8-30-42	HJR	18
12	8	5	584-585	8-31-42	HJR	19
13	9	5	585	8-31-42	SJR	22
14	10	5	585	8-31-42	SJR	12

Public Law/Resolution		Statutes at Large	Page	Date	Bill No.	
Chapter	Number					
1	1	5	586-597	12-24-42	HR	615
3	2	5	597	1-20-43	HR	631
4	3	5	597	1-20-43	S	36
20	4	5	597-598	1-28-43	S	60
26	22*	5	598	2-04-43	HR	380
27	5	5	598-599	2-14-43	HR	661
30	25*	5	599	2-15-43	S	69
31	6	5	600	2-15-43	HR	544
32	7	5	600	2-15-43	HR	199
33	8	5	600-601	2-15-43	S	33
34	26*	5	601	2-18-43	HR	483
44	9	5	601	2-24-43	S	95
45	10	5	602	2-24-43	HR	773
46	11	5	602	2-27-43	HR	767
47	12	5	602	2-27-43	HR	762
49	13	5	602	3-01-43	HR	816
50	14	5	603	3-01-43	S	19
51	15	5	603	3-01-43	S	101
52	16	5	604-606	3-01-43	HR	645
53	17	5	606-607	3-01-43	HR	788
69	18	5	607	3-03-43	S	31
70	19	5	607-609	3-03-43	HR	670
71	20	5	609	3-03-43	S	88
72	21	5	609	3-03-43	S	137
73	22	5	610	3-03-43	HR	774
74	123*	5	610	3-03-43	HR	824
75	24	5	610	3-03-43	HR	768
76	25	5	610-611	3-03-43	HR	748
77	26	5	611	3-03-43	HR	717
78	27	5	611	3-03-43	HR	212
79	28	5	612	3-03-43	HR	775
80	29	5	612-613	3-03-43	HR	660
81	30	5	614	3-03-43	HR	782
82	31	5	614	3-03-43	HR	614
83	32	5	615-618	3-03-43	HR	659
84	33	5	618-619	3-03-43	HR	641
85	34	5	619	3-03-43	HR	678
86	35	5	619-621	3-03-43	HR	740
87	36	5	621-622	3-03-43	HR	393

PUBLIC ACTS OF THE TWENTY-SEVENTH CONGRESS

Public Law/Resolution		Statutes at Large	Page	Date	Bill No.	
Chapter	Number					
88	37	5	622-623	3-03-43	HR	806
89	38	5	623	3-03-43	HR	697
90	39	5	624	3-03-43	HR	720
91	40	5	624-625	3-03-43	HR	752
92	41	5	625	3-03-43	S	134
93	42	5	626	3-03-43	HR	738
94	43	5	626-627	3-03-43	HR	602
95	44	5	627-628	3-03-43	HR	334
96	45	5	628	3-03-43	HR	693
97	46	5	628	3-03-43	S	140
98	47	5	629	3-03-43	S	127
99	48	5	630	3-03-43	HR	668
100	49	5	630-645	3-03-43	HR	804
101	50	5	645-647	3-03-43	HR	559
102	51	5	647	3-03-43	HR	655
103	52	5	648	3-03-43	HR	671

RESOLUTIONS OF THE TWENTY-SEVENTH CONGRESS

1	1	5	648	1-20-43	HJR	22
2	2	5	648	2-18-43	HJR	29
3	3	5	648-649	2-24-43	SJR	3
4	4	5	649	3-03-43	HJR	23
5	5	5	649	3-03-43	HJR	40
6	6	5	650	3-03-43	HJR	30
7	7	5	650	3-03-43	HJR	39

PUBLIC ACTS OF THE TWENTY-EIGHTH CONGRESS

Public Law/Resolution		Statutes at Large	Page	Date	Bill No.	
Chapter	Number					
1	1	5	651	1-22-44	HR	50
2	1*	5	651	2-16-44	HR	1
3	2	5	651-652	2-23-44	HR	4
4	3	5	652	3-04-44	S	65
5	4	5	652	3-26-44	S	37
7	5	5	652	4-02-44	S	98
8	6	5	653-654	4-02-44	S	55
10	7	5	654	4-04-44	S	52
11	8	5	654-655	4-04-44	S	59
12	9	5	655	2-12-44	HR	225
13	10	5	655-656	4-12-44	HR	30
14	11	5	656	4-22-44	HR	188
15	12	5	656-657	4-30-44	HR	60
16	13	5	657	4-30-44	HR	30
17	14	5	657	5-23-44	S	77
18	15	5	657-658	5-23-44	HR	192
30	16	5	658	5-31-44	S	160
31	17	5	658	5-31-44	S	70
32	18	5	658-660	5-31-44	HR	61
37	19	5	660	6-03-44	HR	375
38	20	5	660-661	6-04-44	HR	191
39	21	5	662	6-04-44	S	81
44	22	5	661-662	6-11-44	HR	126
45	23	5	662	6-12-44	S	94
46	24	5	662-663	6-12-44	S	120
47	25	5	663	6-12-44	S	177
49	26	5	663	6-15-44	HR	354
50	27	5	663-664	6-15-44	HR	288
51	28	5	664	6-15-44	S	144
52	29	5	665	6-15-44	S	18
53	30	5	665-666	6-15-44	HR	36
54	31	5	666	6-15-44	S	127
55	32	5	666	6-15-44	HR	131
56	33	5	666-667	6-15-44	HR	253
57	34	5	667	6-15-44	HR	299
58	35	5	667	6-15-44	HR	395
59	36	5	667	6-15-44	HR	368
60	37	5	668	6-15-44	HR	241
61	38	5	668	6-15-44	HR	240
62	39	5	668	6-15-44	HR	337

Public Law/Resolution		Statutes at Large	Page	Date	Bill No.	
Chapter	Number					
63	40	5	669	6-15-44	HR	394
64	41	5	669	6-15-44	HR	396
65	42	5	669	6-15-44	HR	293
66	43	5	670	6-15-44	HR	242
67	44	5	670	6-15-44	HR	243
68	45	5	670	6-15-44	HR	303
69	46	5	670-671	6-15-44	HR	297
70	47	5	671	6-15-44	HR	247
71	48	5	671-672	6-15-44	HR	302
72	49	5	672	6-15-44	S	10
73	50	5	673	6-15-44	HR	19
74	51	5	673	6-15-44	HR	304
75	52	5	674	6-15-44	S	171
94	53	5	674-675	6-17-44	HR	262
95	54	5	676	6-17-44	S	20
96	55	5	676-677	6-17-44	S	32
97	56	5	677	6-17-44	S	115
98	57	5	677-678	6-17-44	S	86
99	58	5	678	6-17-44	HR	309
100	59	5	678-679	6-17-44	HR	158
101	60	5	679-680	6-17-44	HR	150
102	61	5	680	6-17-44	HR	7
103	62	5	680	6-17-44	S	165
104	63	5	680-681	6-17-44	HR	51
105	64	5	681-696	6-17-44	HR	32
106	65	5	696-698	6-17-44	HR	31
107	66	5	699-703	6-17-44	HR	62
108	67	5	704-715	6-17-44	HR	29
117	50*	5	715-716	6-17-44	S	35

RESOLUTIONS OF THE TWENTY-EIGHTH CONGRESS

1	1	5	716	3-04-44	HJR	9
2	2	5	716	4-30-44	HJR	28
3	3	5	716	4-30-44	HJR	27
4	4	5	716-717	4-30-44	HJR	22
5	5	5	717	4-30-44	HJR	25
6	6	5	717	5-23-44	HJR	26
9	9	5	717	6-03-44	HJR	32

Public Law/Resolution		Statutes at Large	Page	Date	Bill No.	
Chapter	Number					
10	10	5	718	6-12-44	SJR	10
11	11	5	718	6-12-44	SJR	7
12	12	5	718	6-12-44	SJR	18
14	14	5	718-719	6-15-44	HJR	43
15	15	5	719	6-15-44	SJR	24
16	16	5	719	6-15-44	HJR	29
17	17	5	719-720	6-15-44	SJR	20
18	18	5	720	6-17-44	HJR	16

Public Law/Resolution		Statutes at Large	Page	Date	Bill No.	
Chapter	Number					
1	1	5	721	1-23-45	HR	432
2	2	5	721-722	2-04-45	HR	521
4	3	5	722	2-07-45	S	24
5	4	5	722	2-13-45	S	64
13	5	5	722-723	2-20-45	HR	440
14	6	5	723-724	2-20-45	HR	492
15	7	5	724	2-20-45	S	114
16	8	5	724-725	2-20-45	S	53
17	9	5	725	2-20-45	S	91
18	10	5	725-726	2-20-45	S	39
19	11	5	726	2-26-45	S	137
20	12	5	726-727	2-26-45	S	36
22	14	5	727	2-26-45	S	101
24	16	5	727	2-26-45	S	127
25	17	5	727-729	2-26-45	S	56
26	18	5	729	2-26-45	S	100
28	10*	5	729	2-26-45	S	102
35	20	5	729-730	3-01-45	HR	503
36	21	5	730	3-01-45	HR	629
37	22	5	730	3-01-45	HR	607
38	23	5	730	3-01-45	HR	520
39	24	5	730-731	3-01-45	S	1
41	25	5	731	3-03-45	S	40
42	26	5	731-732	3-03-45	S	3
43	27	5	732-739	3-03-45	S	46
44	28	5	739-740	3-03-45	HR	494
45	29	5	740	3-03-45	S	144
46	30	5	740-741	3-03-45	S	4
47	31	5	742	3-03-45	HR	493
48	32	5	742-743	3-03-45	HR	497
63	33	5	743-745	3-03-45	HR	524
64	34	5	745	3-03-45	HR	592
65	35	5	745-747	3-03-45	HR	501
66	36	5	748	3-03-45	HR	637
67	37	5	748	3-03-45	HR	564
68	38	5	748	3-03-45	HR	563
69	39	5	748-750	3-03-45	S	72
70	40	5	750-752	3-03-45	S	68
71	41	5	752-765	3-03-45	HR	498

PUBLIC ACTS OF THE TWENTY-EIGHTH CONGRESS

Public Law/Resolution		Statutes at Large	Page	Date	Bill No.	
Chapter	Number					
72	42	5	766-777	3-03-45	HR	491
73	43	5	778	3-03-45	HR	598
74	44	5	778-787	3-03-45	HR	426
75	45	5	788	3-03-45	HR	639
76	46	5	789-790	3-03-45	HR	640
77	47	5	790-795	3-03-45	HR	502
78	48	5	795-796	3-03-45	S	66

RESOLUTIONS OF THE TWENTY-EIGHTH CONGRESS

1	1	5	796	1-23-45	SJR	3
3	2	5	796	2-13-45	SJR	14
4	3	5	796	2-20-45	HJR	63
5	4	5	797	2-20-45	SJR	11
7	5	5	797	3-01-45	SJR	12
8	6	5	797-798	3-01-45	HJR	46
9	3*	5	798	3-03-45	SJR	23
10	7*	5	798-800	3-03-45	SJR	6
11	8	5	800	3-03-45	HJR	40
13	9	5	800	3-03-45	HJR	78
14	10	5	801	3-03-45	HJR	71
15	11	5	801	3-03-45	SJR	16

PUBLIC ACTS OF THE TWENTY-NINTH CONGRESS

Public Law/Resolution		Statutes at Large	Page	Date	Bill No.	
Chapter	Number					
1	1	9	1-2	12-29-45	S	11
2	2	9	2	12-31-45	S	27
3	3	9	3	1-12-46	S	22
4	4	9	3	1-14-46	S	26
6	5	9	3	2-06-46	S	34
7	6	9	3-4	2-11-46	HR	128
8	7	9	4-5	2-20-46	HR	192
10	8	9	5	3-24-46	HR	260
11	9	9	5	3-30-46	S	132
13	10	9	5-6	5-07-46	HR	65
14	11	9	6-9	5-08-46	HR	179
15	12	9	9	5-08-46	S	42
16	13	9	9-10	5-13-46	HR	145
17	14	9	11	5-13-46	HR	38
20	15	9	11-12	5-15-46	HR	47
21	16	9	12-13	5-15-46	S	21
22	17	9	13-14	5-19-46	S	29
23	18	9	14	5-22-46	HR	232
25	19	9	15-16	5-29-46	S	148
26	20	9	16	5-29-46	S	196
28	21	9	17	6-17-46	S	120
29	22	9	17-18	6-18-46	S	185
31	24	9	19	6-19-46	HR	286
33	25	9	20	6-26-46	S	211
34	26	9	20-35	6-27-46	HR	48
35	27	9	35-37	7-09-46	HR	259
36	28	9	37	7-11-46	HR	8
37	29	9	37-38	7-15-46	HR	20
38	30	9	38	7-15-46	HR	272
56	31	9	38	7-16-46	HR	6
60	32	9	38-39	7-20-46	HR	15
61	33	9	39	7-20-46	HR	491
64	34	9	39-40	7-22-46	HR	492
65	35	9	40-41	7-23-46	HR	515
66	36	9	41	7-29-46	HR	459
67	37	9	41	7-29-46	HR	454
68	38	9	42	7-29-46	S	56
74	39	9	42-49	7-30-46	HR	384
75	40	9	49-50	8-03-46	HR	121

PUBLIC ACTS OF THE TWENTY-NINTH CONGRESS

Public Law/Resolution		Statutes at Large	Page	Date	Bill No.	
Chapter	Number					
76	41	9	50	8-03-46	S	243
77	42	9	50-51	8-03-46	HR	235
78	43	9	51-52	8-03-46	S	28
82	44	9	52-53	8-04-46	HR	14
84	45	9	53-55	8-06-46	S	57
85	46	9	55-56	8-06-46	HR	321
89	47	9	56-58	8-06-46	HR	105
90	48	9	59-66	8-06-46	HR	1
91	49	9	66	8-06-46	S	79
92	50	9	66-67	8-07-46	S	127
94	51	9	67	8-08-46	HR	92
95	52	9	68-70	8-08-46	HR	49
96	53	9	70-71	8-08-46	HR	116
97	54	9	71-72	8-08-46	HR	526
98	55	9	72-75	8-08-46	HR	174
99	56	9	75	8-08-46	HR	80
100	57	9	75-76	8-08-46	HR	457
101	58	9	76-77	8-08-46	S	64
102	59	9	77	8-08-46	HR	450
103	60	9	77-78	8-08-46	HR	106
104	61	9	78	8-08-46	HR	68
105	62	9	78-79	8-08-46	HR	297
106	63	9	79-80	8-08-46	HR	373
107	64	9	80	8-08-46	HR	449
108	65	9	80-81	8-08-46	HR	109
109	66	9	82	8-08-46	HR	445
110	67	9	82	8-08-46	HR	215
169	68	9	82	8-08-46	HR	93
170	69	9	83	8-08-46	HR	374
174	85*	9	84	8-08-46	S	170
175	73	9	85-97	8-10-46	HR	50
176	74	9	97-101	8-10-46	HR	51
177	75	9	101-102	8-10-46	HR	66
178	76	9	102-106	8-10-46	HR	5
179	77	9	106	8-10-46	HR	129
180	78	9	106-107	8-10-46	S	51

RESOLUTIONS OF THE TWENTY-NINTH CONGRESS

Public Law/Resolution		Statutes at Large	Page	Date	Bill No.
Chapter	Number				
1	1	9	108	12-29-45	H Res. 2
2	2	9	108	1-07-46	H Res. 4
3	3	9	109	3-04-46	S Res. 12
4	4	9	109-110	4-27-46	H Res. 5
5	5	9	110	5-15-46	H Res. 31
6	6	9	110	5-20-46	S Res. 11
9	9	9	110	6-26-46	S Res. 6
10	8	9	111	7-15-46	S Res. 31
11	9	9	111	7-16-46	H Res. 34
12	10	9	111	7-16-46	H Res. 37
14	11	9	112	7-23-46	S Res. 3
15	12	9	113	7-23-46	S Res. 33
16	13	9	113-114	8-03-46	H Res. 42
17	14	9	114	8-03-46	H Res. 46
20	15	9	115	8-08-46	H Res. 47
23	16	9	115	8-10-46	S Res. 37
24	17	9	115-116	8-10-46	S Res. 29

PUBLIC ACTS OF THE TWENTY-NINTH CONGRESS

Public Law/Resolution		Statutes at Large	Page	Date	Bill No.	
Chapter	Number					
1	1	9	117	12-28-46	HR	557
2	2	9	117-118	1-12-47	S	73
3	3	9	118	1-26-47	S	23
5	4	9	118-122	1-28-47	HR	600
6	5	9	122-123	2-02-47	HR	602
7	6	9	123	2-09-47	HR	645
8	7	9	123-126	2-11-47	HR	576
9	8	9	126	2-15-47	S	151
13	10	9	126-127	2-20-47	HR	604
16	11	9	127-128	2-22-47	HR	637
17	12	9	128-131	2-22-47	S	114
20	14	9	131-132	2-23-47	S	147
21	15	9	132	2-23-47	S	166
31	17	9	132-145	3-01-47	HR	595
32	18	9	146-147	3-01-47	S	10
33	19	9	147-148	3-01-47	HR	691
34	20	9	149	3-02-47	S	177
35	21	9	149-152	3-02-47	HR	597
36	22	9	152	3-02-47	HR	605
37	23	9	152-153	3-02-47	HR	635
38	24	9	153-154	3-02-47	HR	612
39	25	9	154	3-02-47	HR	234
40	26	9	154-155	3-02-47	HR	646
47	27	9	155-168	3-03-47	HR	599
48	28	9	168-173	3-03-47	HR	596
49	29	9	174	3-03-47	HR	655
50	30	9	174	3-03-47	S	105
51	31	9	175	3-03-47	S	190
52	32	9	175-178	3-03-47	HR	636
53	33	9	178-179	3-03-47	HR	648
54	34	9	179-181	3-03-47	HR	569
55	35	9	181	3-03-47	HR	575
56	36	9	181-182	3-03-47	HR	657
57	37	9	182-183	3-03-47	HR	676
59	39	9	183	3-03-47	S	188
60	40	9	183-184	3-03-47	HR	369
61	41	9	184-186	3-03-47	S	160
62	42	9	187-188	3-03-47	S	128
63	43	9	188-202	3-03-47	HR	638

PUBLIC ACTS OF THE TWENTY-NINTH CONGRESS

Public Law/Resolution		Statutes at Large	Page	Date	Bill No.	
Chapter	Number					
64	44	9	202	3-03-47	HR	684
66	46	9	203-204	3-03-47	HR	649
67	47	9	204-205	3-03-47	S	104

RESOLUTIONS OF THE TWENTY-NINTH CONGRESS

4	1	9	206	3-01-47	S Res.	10
5	2	9	206	3-02-47	H Res.	55
7	3	9	206-207	3-03-47	S Res.	13
8	4	9	207	3-03-47	S Res.	16
9	5	9	207	3-03-47	S Res.	5
10	6	9	207	3-03-47	S Res.	14
11	7	9	208	3-03-47	H Res.	53
12	8	9	208	3-03-47	H Res.	61

PUBLIC ACTS OF THE THIRTIETH CONGRESS

Public Law/Resolution		Statutes at Large	Page	Date	Bill No.	
Chapter	Number					
1	1	9	209	1-04-48	HR	6
4	4	9	209	1-26-48	HR	91
5	5	9	209-210	1-26-48	S	5
6	6	9	210	1-26-48	S	38
7	7	9	210	1-31-48	S	54
8	8	9	210-211	2-02-48	HR	18
10	10	9	211	2-15-48	HR	142
12	11	9	211-212	2-22-48	S	27
13	12	9	212	2-22-48	S	105
15	14	9	213	3-09-48	S	12
16	15	9	213	3-09-48	HR	231
17	16	9	213	3-09-48	HR	182
18	17	9	213-214	3-14-48	S	89
19	18	9	214	3-14-48	S	144
22	19	9	214	3-21-48	S	1
23	20	9	215-217	3-27-48	HR	135
24	21	9	217	3-29-48	S	159
26	22	9	217-219	3-31-48	HR	104
28	23	9	219	4-08-48	HR	175
32	44	9	219	4-14-48	HR	8
35	26	9	219	5-09-48	HR	146
36	27	9	219-220	5-09-48	HR	418
40	28	9	220	5-09-48	HR	390
41	29	9	220-223	5-17-48	HR	292
42	30	9	223-230	5-17-48	HR	422
43	31	9	230	5-17-48	S	119
44	32	9	231	5-17-48	S	100
47	34	9	231-232	5-27-48	S	39
48	35	9	232	5-27-48	S	228
49	36	9	232-233	5-27-48	S	188
50	37	9	233-235	5-29-48	HR	397
52	38	9	235	5-31-48	S	31
54	39	9	235-236	5-31-48	HR	107
55	40	9	236	5-31-48	S	270
60	41	9	236	6-02-48	HR	430
61	42	9	237	6-13-48	HR	179
67	43	9	237	6-16-48	HR	490
68	44	9	237	6-16-48	HR	370
70	45	9	237-239	6-26-48	HR	524

Public Law/Resolution		Statutes at Large	Page	Date	Bill No.	
Chapter	Number					
71	46	9	239-240	6-26-48	HR	108
72	47	9	240	6-26-48	S	7
73	48	9	240	6-26-48	HR	469
74	49	9	240	6-26-48	HR	50
79	50	9	241-242	6-27-48	HR	180
82	53	9	242	6-28-48	HR	546
83	54	9	242-243	6-28-48	S	216
90	55	9	243-244	7-01-48	S	202
92	56	9	244	7-05-48	S	84
93	57	9	244-245	7-05-48	HR	81
94	58	9	245	7-05-48	HR	491
98	60	9	245-246	7-10-48	HR	394
99	61	9	246	7-10-48	S	124
100	62	9	246	7-10-48	HR	114
101	63	9	246-247	7-17-48	S	305
102	64	9	247	7-17-48	HR	257
104	65	9	247-248	7-19-48	HR	429
105	66	9	248-249	7-20-48	HR	154
108	67	9	249-250	7-21-48	S	62
109	68	9	250-251	7-25-48	S	141
110	69	9	251	7-25-48	S	300
111	70	9	251	7-25-48	S	281
118	72	9	252-265	7-29-48	HR	136
119	73	9	265	7-29-48	S	315
120	74	9	265-266	7-29-48	HR	612
121	75	9	266-273	8-03-48	HR	219
122	76	9	273-274	8-05-48	HR	350
141	78	9	274	8-07-48	HR	178
143	79	9	274-275	8-07-48	HR	352
144	80	9	275	8-07-48	HR	482
145	81	9	275	8-07-48	HR	592
147	83	9	275	8-07-48	HR	398
150	84	9	276-280	8-11-48	S	128
151	85	9	280-281	8-11-48	HR	152
152	86	9	281-282	8-11-48	HR	634
153	87	9	282	8-11-48	S	320
154	88	9	282	8-11-48	S	36
155	89	9	282-283	8-11-48	S	246
156	90	9	283	8-12-48	HR	581

PUBLIC ACTS OF THE THIRTIETH CONGRESS

Public Law/Resolution		Statutes at Large	Page	Date	Bill No.	
Chapter	Number					
166	91	9	284-302	8-12-48	HR	298
167	92	9	302-303	8-12-48	S	136
168	93	9	303	8-12-48	S	308
169	94	9	303-304	8-12-48	S	203
173	95	9	304-306	8-14-48	HR	618
175	97	9	306-320	8-14-48	HR	599
176	98	9	321-323	8-14-48	S	294
177	99	9	323-331	8-14-48	HR	201
178	100	9	331	8-14-48	S	190
179	101	9	331-332	8-14-48	S	110
180	102	9	332	8-14-48	HR	419

RESOLUTIONS OF THE THIRTIETH CONGRESS

1	1	9	333	1-31-48	S Res.	2
2	2	9	333	3-09-48	H Res.	11
4	3	9	334	3-24-48	H Res.	21
5	4	9	334	4-13-48	S Res.	15
6	5	9	334	5-09-48	S Res.	14
7	6	9	334-335	5-09-48	H Res.	12
8	7	9	335	6-16-48	H Res.	30
9	8	9	335-336	6-16-48	H Res.	9
12	9	9	336	6-30-48	S Res.	26
13	10	9	336	7-01-48	H Res.	27
15	11	9	336	7-10-48	H Res.	32
16	12	9	337	7-10-48	H Res.	33
17	13	9	337	7-25-48	H Res.	10
18	14	9	337	7-25-48	H Res.	34
19	15	9	337-339	7-25-48	S Res.	16
20	16	9	339	7-29-48	S Res.	35
21	5*	9	339	8-07-48	S Res.	33
22	17	9	339	8-07-48	H Res.	38
23	18	9	339-340	8-07-48	H Res.	29
24	19	9	340	8-10-48	H Res.	37
25	20	9	340	8-11-48	S Res.	37
26	21	9	340	8-11-48	H Res.	34

Public Law/Resolution		Statutes at Large	Page	Date	Bill No.	
Chapter	Number					
14	1	9	341	1-10-49	HR	405
19	2	9	341	1-19-49	HR	196
20	3	9	341-342	1-19-49	S	373
24	4	9	342-344	1-26-49	HR	665
25	5	9	344	2-01-49	S	351
37	7	9	344	2-19-49	S	81
52	8	9	345	2-19-49	HR	696
53	9	9	345-346	2-19-49	HR	697
55	45*	9	346	2-19-49	S	163
61	11	9	346-347	2-22-49	S	20
62	12	9	347	2-22-49	HR	765
70	13	9	347-348	2-26-49	HR	525
71	14	9	348	2-26-49	HR	684
72	15	9	348-349	2-26-49	S	470
77	18	9	349	3-02-49	HR	698
78	19	9	349	3-02-49	S	413
79	20	9	349-350	3-02-49	S	295
80	21	9	350	3-02-49	S	258
81	22	9	350	3-02-49	S	473
82	23	9	350-351	3-02-49	S	484
83	24	9	351	3-02-49	S	393
84	25	9	351-352	3-02-49	S	411
86	27	9	352	3-02-49	HR	797
87	28	9	352-353	3-02-49	HR	635
88	29	9	353	3-02-49	HR	15
89	30	9	353	3-02-49	S	399
100	31	9	354-370	3-03-49	HR	692
101	32	9	370-373	3-03-49	HR	695
102	33	9	373-374	3-03-49	HR	686
103	34	9	374-379	3-03-49	HR	699
104	35	9	379-380	3-03-49	HR	754
105	36	9	380-382	3-03-49	S	485
106	37	9	382-393	3-03-49	HR	691
107	38	9	393-394	3-03-49	S	313
108	39	9	395-397	3-03-49	HR	764
109	40	9	397-398	3-03-49	HR	746
110	41	9	398-399	3-03-49	HR	291
111	42	9	399-400	3-03-49	HR	738
112	43	9	400	3-03-49	HR	734

PUBLIC ACTS OF THE THIRTIETH CONGRESS

Public Law/Resolution		Statutes at Large	Page	Date	Bill No.	
Chapter	Number					
113	44	9	400-401	3-03-49	HR	487
114	45	9	401-402	3-03-49	S	282
115	46	9	402-403	3-03-49	HR	813
118	49	9	403	3-03-49	HR	804
120	51	9	403	3-03-49	HR	805
121	52	9	403-409	3-03-49	S	152
122	53	9	409-410	3-03-49	S	299
123	54	9	410	3-03-49	S	367
124	55	9	410-412	3-03-49	HR	700
125	56	9	412	3-03-49	HR	344
126	57	9	412-414	3-03-49	HR	747
127	58	9	414	3-03-49	HR	791
129	60	9	414-416	3-03-49	HR	659
179	119*	9	416	3-03-49	HR	779

RESOLUTIONS OF THE THIRTIETH CONGRESS

1	1	9	417	12-19-48	S Res.	41
2	2	9	417	1-06-49	S Res.	47
10	4	9	417	3-02-49	H Res.	43
11	5	9	418	3-02-49	H Res.	54
12	6	9	418	3-02-49	S Res.	56
14	7	9	418	3-03-49	H Res.	52
15	8	9	419	3-03-49	H Res.	61
16	9	9	419	3-03-49	H Res.	58
17	10	9	419	3-03-49	H Res.	51
18	11	9	420	3-03-49	S Res.	70
19	12	9	420	3-03-49	H Res.	47
20	13	9	420	3-03-49	S Res.	71

Public Law/Resolution		Statutes at Large	Page	Date	Bill No.	
Chapter	Number					
1	1*	9	421	1-10-50	HR	1
3	1	9	421	2-20-50	HR	22
6	2	9	422-423	3-29-50	S	87
10	3	9	423-428	5-15-50	HR	154
11	4	9	428-436	5-23-50	S	76
12	5	9	436-437	5-23-50	HR	118
16	6	9	437	6-05-50	S	90
17	7	9	438	6-05-50	HR	97
19	8	9	438	6-11-50	HR	148
20	9	9	438-439	6-17-50	S	124
22	10	9	439	6-21-50	HR	332
23	11	9	439-440	7-18-50	HR	21
24	12	9	440	7-18-50	HR	319
25	13	9	440	7-18-50	HR	336
27	14	9	440-441	7-29-50	HR	87
28	15	9	441-442	7-29-50	S	69
29	16	9	442	7-29-50	S	172
30	17	9	442-443	7-29-50	S	212
31	18	9	443-444	7-29-50	S	244
39	19	9	444	8-17-50	HR	279
40	20	9	444	8-17-50	HR	280
43	21	9	445	8-30-50	S	262
44	22	9	445	8-30-50	S	300
47	25*	9	446	8-30-50	S	28
49	23	9	446-452	9-09-50	S	307
50	24	9	452-453	9-09-50	S	169
51	25	9	453-458	9-09-50	S	225
52	26	9	458	9-16-50	S	47
53	27	9	458	9-16-50	S	318
54	28	9	459	9-16-50	HR	214
55	29	9	459-460	9-16-50	S	199
56	30	9	460-461	9-16-50	HR	330
60	31	9	462-465	9-18-50	S	23
61	32	9	466-467	9-20-50	S	22
62	33	9	467	9-20-50	S	191
63	34	9	467-468	9-20-50	S	226
64	35	9	468	9-20-50	HR	387
65	36	9	468-469	9-20-50	S	338
69	37	9	469	9-26-50	S	308

PUBLIC ACTS OF THE THIRTY-FIRST CONGRESS

Public Law/Resolution		Statutes at Large	Page	Date	Bill No.	
Chapter	Number					
70	38	9	469	9-26-50	S	126
71	39	9	469-472	9-26-50	S	44
72	40	9	472	9-26-50	S	27
73	41	9	473	9-26-50	HR	388
75	42	9	473-496	9-27-50	HR	385
76	43	9	496-500	9-27-50	HR	250
77	44	9	500-504	9-27-50	S	359
78	45	9	504-508	9-28-50	HR	234
79	46	9	508-513	9-28-50	S	315
80	47	9	513-517	9-28-50	HR	235
81	48	9	517-518	9-28-50	HR	155
82	49	9	519	9-28-50	S	332
83	50	9	519	9-28-50	HR	6
84	51	9	519-520	9-28-50	S	3
85	52	9	520-521	9-28-50	HR	244
86	53	9	521-523	9-28-50	S	330
90	54	9	523-544	9-30-50	HR	334
91	55	9	544-559	9-30-50	HR	331

RESOLUTIONS OF THE THIRTY-FIRST CONGRESS

1	2	9	560	2-12-50	S Res.	5
2	1	9	560	2-12-50	S Res.	3
4	3	9	560-561	2-14-50	S Res.	1
5	2	9	561	2-20-50	H Res.	2
7	4	9	561	5-02-50	H Res.	16
8	5	9	562	7-18-50	S Res.	24
9	6	9	562	7-29-50	S Res.	7
10	4*	9	562	7-29-50	H Res.	21
11	7	9	562-563	8-10-50	S Res.	13
13	8	9	563	9-09-50	H Res.	20
15	7*	9	563	9-20-50	H Res.	23
16	9	9	563	9-26-50	S Res.	29
17	10	9	564	9-26-50	S Res.	34
19	12	9	564	9-28-50	S Res.	42
20	11	9	564	9-28-50	H Res.	10

PUBLIC ACTS OF THE THIRTY-FIRST CONGRESS

Public Law/Resolution		Statutes at Large	Page	Date	Bill No.	
Chapter	Number					
2	1	9	565-566	1-27-51	S	68
6	3	9	566	2-14-51	S	357
7	4	9	566	2-14-51	S	405
8	5	9	566-567	2-14-51	S	407
9	6	9	567	2-19-51	HR	421
10	7	9	568	2-19-51	HR	430
11	8	9	568-570	2-19-51	HR	402
12	9	9	570-574	2-27-51	HR	433
13	10	9	574	2-27-51	HR	435
14	11	9	574-587	2-27-51	HR	437
20	12	9	587-591	3-03-51	HR	351
21	13	9	591-593	3-03-51	HR	438
22	14	9	593-594	3-03-51	HR	434
23	15	9	594	3-03-51	HR	436
24	20	9	594-595	3-03-51	S	18
25	21	9	595-597	3-03-51	S	392
26	22	9	597-598	3-03-51	S	156
32	16	9	598-618	3-03-51	HR	461
33	17	9	618-621	3-03-51	HR	462
34	18	9	621-626	3-03-51	HR	474
35	27	9	626	3-03-51	S	210
36	28	9	626-627	3-03-51	S	232
37	19	9	627-629	3-03-51	HR	297
38	24	9	629-630	3-03-51	S	412
39	25	9	630-631	3-03-51	S	448
40	26	9	631	3-03-51	S	380
41	27	9	631-634	3-03-51	S	346
42	30	9	635	3-03-51	S	483
43	31	9	635-636	3-03-51	S	251
44	33	9	636-637	3-03-51	S	14
48	32	9	637-645	3-03-51	HR	475

RESOLUTIONS OF THE THIRTY-FIRST CONGRESS

1	1	9	646	12-24-50	S Res.	41
2	2	9	646-647	2-27-51	S Res.	46
4	3	9	647	3-03-51	S Res.	58
5	4	9	647	3-03-51	S Res.	52
6	5	9	647-648	3-03-51	H Res.	9
8	6	9	648	3-03-51	S Res.	59

PUBLIC ACTS OF THE THIRTY-SECOND CONGRESS

Public Law/Resolution		Statutes at Large	Page	Date	Bill No.	
Chapter	Number					
1	1	10	1	1-13-52	HR	40
2	2	10	1	1-23-52	S	99
5	3	10	1-2	1-27-52	HR	4
8	4	10	2	2-10-52	HR	46
9	5	10	2	2-10-52	HR	63
11	6	10	2-3	3-03-52	S	139
15	8	10	3	3-19-52	S	184
19	9	10	3-4	3-22-52	S	146
20	10	10	5	4-02-52	S	78
24	11	10	5	5-04-52	S	19
25	12	10	5	5-04-52	S	209
33	13	10	5-6	5-10-52	S	136
35	14	10	6	5-19-52	HR	219
36	15	10	7	5-19-52	HR	205
37	16	10	7	5-26-52	HR	217
42	17	10	7	5-27-52	S	55
43	18	10	7-8	5-27-52	S	331
44	19	10	8	5-27-52	S	403
45	20	10	8-10	6-10-52	S	3
46	21	10	10	6-10-52	HR	266
49	22	10	10	6-15-52	S	175
51	23	10	10	6-19-52	HR	45
53	24	10	11	7-03-52	S	451
54	25	10	11-13	7-03-52	S	6
55	26	10	13	7-03-52	HR	21
57	27	10	13	7-12-52	HR	44
58	28	10	14	7-12-52	HR	239
59	29	10	14	7-12-52	HR	238
60	30	10	15	7-12-52	HR	226
61	31	10	15	7-12-52	HR	270
62	32	10	15	7-12-52	HR	48
66	33	10	15-24	7-21-52	HR	207
67	34	10	24	7-21-52	S	241
68	35	10	24-25	7-21-52	HR	262
74	36	10	25	7-30-52	S	281
75	37	10	25-26	7-30-52	HR	288
77	38	10	26-27	8-02-52	S	478
78	39	10	27-28	8-02-52	HR	3
80	41	10	28-29	8-04-52	HR	284
81	42	10	29	8-06-52	HR	87
85	43	10	30	8-21-52	HR	257

PUBLIC ACTS OF THE THIRTY-SECOND CONGRESS

Public Law/Resolution		Statutes at Large	Page	Date	Bill No.	
Chapter	Number					
87	44	10	30	8-25-52	S	30
91	45	10	30-35	8-26-52	HR	299
92	46	10	35-36	8-26-52	S	28
95	47	10	36-37	8-26-52	HR	258
96	48	10	37-38	8-30-52	S	415
97	49	10	38	8-30-52	S	191
98	50	10	38-40	8-30-52	HR	144
101	51	10	40	8-30-52	S	447
102	52	10	40-41	8-30-52	S	540
103	57	10	41-56	8-30-52	HR	43
104	58	10	56-60	8-30-52	HR	282
105	59	10	61	8-30-52	HR	242
106	62	10	61-75	8-30-52	S	223
107	64	10	75-76	8-30-52	HR	322
108	53	10	76-100	8-31-52	HR	196
109	54	10	100-105	8-31-52	HR	240
110	55	10	105-110	8-31-52	HR	220
111	56	10	110-112	8-31-52	HR	241
112	60	10	112-121	8-31-52	HR	312
113	61	10	121-142	8-31-52	HR	314
114	63	10	143	8-31-52	HR	273
115	65	10	143-144	8-31-52	S	486

RESOLUTIONS OF THE THIRTY-SECOND CONGRESS

1	1	10	145	12-15-51	S Res.	4
2	2	10	145	12-23-51	H Res.	7
3	3	10	145	1-13-52	H Res.	6
4	4	10	145	1-27-52	H Res.	5
5	5	10	146	2-27-52	S Res.	20
7	6	10	146	4-14-52	S Res.	17
8	7	10	146	5-04-52	H Res.	17
9	8	10	147	5-10-52	S Res.	15
12	11	10	147	6-19-52	H Res.	18
13	12	10	147	7-03-52	H Res.	20
14	13	10	147	7-12-52	S Res.	9
16	14	10	147	8-06-52	H Res.	24
17	15	10	148	8-31-52	S Res.	61

Public Law/Resolution		Statutes at Large	Page	Date	Bill No.	
Chapter	Number					
1	1	10	149	12-16-52	HR	327
3	2	10	149	12-23-52	S	553
4	3	10	149-150	12-23-52	S	448
6	4	10	150	1-07-53	HR	260
7	6	10	150	1-07-53	HR	255
8	7	10	150-151	1-07-53	HR	120
9	8	10	151	1-07-53	HR	187
18	9	10	151	1-20-53	HR	330
19	10	10	152	1-20-53	HR	243
20	11	10	152	1-20-53	HR	329
24	12	10	152	1-22-53	HR	291
29	15	10	153	1-25-53	HR	283
30	13	10	153	1-25-53	HR	343
31	14	10	153	1-25-53	S	369
40	16	10	153-154	2-03-53	S	582
41	17	10	154	2-03-53	S	477
58	41*	10	154-155	2- -53	HR	351
59	18	10	155-156	2-09-53	HR	233
66	19	10	157	2-11-53	S	97
67	20	10	157	2-14-53	S	316
69	22	10	158-160	2-14-53	HR	224
76	23	10	160	2-16-53	S	624
79	26	10	160-161	2-21-53	S	271
80	25	10	161-169	2-26-53	HR	146
81	26	10	170-171	2-26-53	HR	326
82	27	10	171-172	2-26-53	S	242
89	29	10	172	3-02-53	S	59
90	30	10	172-179	3-02-53	HR	348
91	28	10	179-180	3-02-53	HR	332
93	32	10	180	3-02-53	S	539
94	33	10	180	3-02-53	HR	357
96	34	10	181-189	3-03-53	HR	335
97	35	10	189-214	3-03-53	HR	337
98	36	10	214-219	3-03-53	HR	336
102	37	10	220-224	3-03-53	HR	342
103	38	10	225	3-03-53	HR	350
104	41	10	226-239	3-03-53	HR	333
139	40	10	239-240	3-03-53	HR	349
140	39	10	240-243	3-03-53	HR	362
142	43	10	243-244	3-03-53	HR	253

PUBLIC ACTS OF THE THIRTY-SECOND CONGRESS

Public Law/Resolution		Statutes at Large	Page	Date	Bill No.	
Chapter	Number					
143	44	10	244	3-03-53	S	586
144	45	10	244	3-03-53	S	622
145	46	10	244-248	3-03-53	S	7
146	47	10	249-256	3-03-53	HR	364
147	48	10	256-257	3-03-53	S	399
148	49	10	257	3-03-53	HR	263
149	50	10	257-258	3-03-53	HR	264
150	51	10	258	3-03-53	HR	134
152	53	10	258	3-03-53	S	75
153	54	10	259	3-03-53	S	123

RESOLUTIONS OF THE THIRTY-SECOND CONGRESS

1	1	10	260	12-23-52	S Res.	54
2	1*	10	260	12-23-52	H Res.	29
3	2	10	260	1-07-53	S Res.	65
4	3	10	261	1-07-53	S Res.	66
5	4	10	261	1-07-53	S Res.	67
6	5	10	261	1-13-53	S Res.	64
8	7	10	261	1-20-53	S Res.	68
12	8	10	262	3-02-53	S Res.	23
13	9	10	262	3-03-53	S Res.	79
14	10	10	262-263	3-03-53	S Res.	44
15	11	10	263-264	3-03-53	H Res.	31

PUBLIC ACTS OF THE THIRTY-THIRD CONGRESS

Public Law/Resolution		Statutes at Large	Page	Date	Bill No.	
Chapter	Number					
1	1	10	265	1-18-54	S	28
2	2	10	265	1-18-54	S	65
7	3	10	266	2-02-54	S	159
8	4	10	266	2-02-54	HR	187
9	5	10	266	2-02-54	HR	5
10	6	10	267	2-08-54	HR	198
11	7	10	267	2-10-54	S	12
12	8	10	267-268	2-23-54	S	2
13	9	10	268	2-23-54	S	55
14	10	10	268	2-23-54	HR	197
17	11	10	268	3-01-54	S	124
24	12	10	269	3-27-54	HR	135
25	13	10	269	3-27-54	S	228
26	14	10	269-270	3-27-54	HR	14
30	15	10	270-273	3-28-54	S	39
32	16	10	273	4-06-54	HR	52
33	17	10	273-274	4-06-54	S	92
35	18	10	274-275	4-12-54	HR	166
46	19	10	275	4-20-54	HR	284
47	20	10	275	4-20-54	HR	32
52	21	10	276	4-22-54	S	122
54	22	10	276-277	5-10-54	HR	47
59	23	10	277-290	5-30-54	HR	236
60	24	10	290-298	5-31-54	HR	271
61	25	10	298-299	6-22-54	HR	311
62	26	10	299	6-22-54	HR	318
68	27	10	299-300	6-22-54	S	23
69	28	10	300	6-29-54	S	17
70	29	10	300-301	6-29-54	S	180
71	30	10	301	6-29-54	HR	405
72	31	10	302-303	6-29-54	HR	342
79	32	10	303	7-17-54	HR	291
80	33	10	303	7-17-54	HR	294
81	34	10	303	7-17-54	HR	119
82	35	10	304	7-17-54	HR	340
83	36	10	304	7-17-54	HR	338
84	37	10	305-306	7-17-54	HR	316
85	38	10	306-307	7-17-54	HR	164
86	39	10	307	7-17-54	HR	341
87	40	10	307	7-17-54	HR	339

Public Law/Resolution		Statutes at Large	Page	Date	Bill No.	
Chapter	Number					
99	42	10	307	7-20-54	S	377
102	43	10	307-308	7-22-54	S	202
103	44	10	308-310	7-22-54	HR	315
105	46	10	310-311	7-27-54	HR	109
106	47	10	311	7-27-54	HR	232
107	48	10	311-312	7-27-54	HR	162
108	49	10	312	7-27-54	HR	50
109	50	10	312-313	7-27-54	HR	344
110	51	10	313-315	7-27-54	S	373
159	53	10	315	7-29-54	S	320
167	54	10	315-333	7-31-54	HR	46
188	56	10	333	8-02-54	S	38
189	57	10	333-334	8-02-54	S	243
191	59	10	334	8-02-54	S	413
192	60	10	334-335	8-02-54	S	425
193	61	10	335	8-03-54	S	418
194	62	10	335-344	8-03-54	HR	351
195	63	10	344	8-03-54	S	19
196	64	10	344-345	8-03-54	S	245
198	66	10	345	8-03-54	S	219
199	67	10	345	8-03-54	S	200
200	68	10	345-346	8-03-54	S	259
201	69	10	346	8-03-54	S	432
202	70	10	346-347	8-03-54	S	179
204	76	10	347	8-03-54	HR	220
227	74	10	347-348	8-03-54	HR	116
230	72	10	349-546	8-03-54	HR	490
242	76½	10	546-574	8-04-54	HR	48
244	81	10	547	8-04-54	HR	30
245	82	10	575	8-04-54	HR	511
246	83	10	575	8-04-54	HR	383
247	77	10	575-576	8-04-54	HR	508
248	78	10	576	8-04-54	HR	8
249	80	10	576	8-04-54	HR	335
267	84	10	576-583	8-05-54	HR	95
268	85	10	583-587	8-05-54	HR	97
269	87	10	587-588	8-05-54	HR	513
270	86	10	588-589	8-05-54	HR	336
271	88	10	589	8-05-54	S	485
273	90	10	589	8-05-54	HR	8

PUBLIC ACTS OF THE THIRTY-THIRD CONGRESS

Public Law/Resolution		Statutes at Large	Page	Date	Bill No.	
Chapter	Number					
274	91	10	590	8-05-54	HR	110
276	93	10	590	8-05-54	S	93

RESOLUTIONS OF THE THIRTY-THIRD CONGRESS

1	1	10	591	1-14-54	H Res.	4
3	2	10	591	2-10-54	S Res.	7
4	3	10	591	2-23-54	S Res.	6
5	4	10	591	3-01-54	H Res.	15
6	5	10	592	3-27-54	S Res.	12
7	6	10	592	3-27-54	H Res.	18
8	7	10	592	3-27-54	H Res.	14
10	8	10	592-593	4-06-54	S Res.	1
11	9	10	593	5-03-54	H Res.	9
12	10	10	593	5-03-54	S Res.	11
13	11	10	593	6-29-54	H Res.	22
16	12	10	593-594	7-17-54	H Res.	21
17	13	10	594	7-20-54	S Res.	22
18	14	10	594	7-20-54	H Res.	30
24	15	10	594-595	8-04-54	H Res.	7
25	16	10	595	8-05-54	H Res.	33

Public Law/Resolution		Statutes at Large	Page	Date	Bill No.	
Chapter	Number					
1	1	10	597	12-14-54	S	993
5	2	10	597-598	12-15-54	S	126
6	3	10	598	12-19-54	HR	514
7	4	10	598-599	12-19-54	HR	293
10	5	10	599	12-22-54	S	238
15	6	10	599-601	12-27-54	S	16
18	7	10	601-602	12-29-54	HR	443
19	8	10	602	12-30-54	S	528
20	9	10	602	1-03-55	HR	601
21	10	10	602	1-03-55	HR	583
23	12	10	603	1-03-55	HR	354
25	13	10	603	1-10-55	HR	547
55	18	10	603-604	2-06-55	S	435
70	21	10	604	2-10-55	S	550
71	22	10	604	2-10-55	HR	133
73	27	10	604-606	2-10-55	S	47
96	24	10	606-607	2-13-55	HR	285
97	25	10	607	2-13-55	S	587
98	26	10	607	2-14-55	HR	499
103	29	10	608	2-14-55	S	67
104	30	10	608	2-17-55	HR	543
105	31	10	608	2-17-55	HR	691
106	32	10	608	2-17-55	HR	477
107	33	10	608-609	2-17-55	HR	337
108	34	10	609	2-17-55	HR	542
109	35	10	609-610	2-17-55	HR	612
110	36	10	610	2-17-55	HR	680
111	37	10	610	2-17-55	HR	588
112	38	10	610-611	2-17-55	S	60
117	40	10	611	2-21-55	HR	689
118	41	10	611-612	2-21-55	S	286
122	42	10	612-614	2-24-55	S	523
123	43	10	614	2-24-55	HR	534
124	44	10	615	2-24-55	HR	538
125	45	10	615	2-24-55	HR	592
126	46	10	615-616	2-28-55	HR	554
127	47	10	616-617	2-28-55	S	568
128	48	10	617	2-28-55	HR	747
129	49	10	617-619	2-28-55	S	96
133	78	10	619-626	3-01-55	HR	353

Public Law/Resolution		Statutes at Large	Page	Date	Bill No.	
Chapter	Number					
134	51	10	626	3-02-55	S	352
135	52	10	627	3-02-55	HR	688
136	53	10	627-629	3-02-55	HR	563
137	54	10	629	3-02-55	S	534
138	55	10	629-630	3-02-55	S	679
139	56	10	630	3-02-55	S	543
140	57	10	630	3-02-55	S	683
141	58	10	630	3-02-55	HR	242
142	59	10	631-632	3-02-55	S	589
143	60	10	632	3-02-55	HR	736
144	61	10	632-633	3-02-55	S	560
145	62	10	633-634	3-02-55	HR	517
146	50	10	634	3-02-55	S	6
147	79	10	634-635	3-02-55	S	519
166	64	10	635	3-03-55	S	515
167	67	10	635	3-03-55	HR	605
168	68	10	635	3-03-55	HR	681
169	69	10	635-640	3-03-55	HR	562
170	70	10	640	3-03-55	S	549
171	71	10	640-641	3-03-55	HR	580
172	74	10	641	3-03-55	HR	690
173	76	10	641-642	3-03-55	HR	406
174	77	10	642-643	3-03-55	HR	445
175	63	10	643-675	3-03-55	HR	569
198	65	10	675-682	3-03-55	HR	579
199	75	10	682-683	3-03-55	HR	755
200	72	10	683	3-03-55	HR	665
201	66	10	683-685	3-03-55	HR	594
202	73	10	686	3-03-55	HR	794
203	85	10	686	3-03-55	HR	857
204	88	10	686-701	3-03-55	HR	555
206	80	10	701	3-03-55	HR	650
207	81	10	701-702	3-03-55	S	511
208	86	10	703	3-03-55	HR	561
209	87	10	703	3-03-55	HR	750
210	89	10	703-704	3-03-55	HR	790
211	84	10	704-714	3-03-55	HR	865
212	82	10	714-715	3-03-55	S	621
213	85	10	715-721	3-03-55	HR	752

RESOLUTIONS OF THE THIRTY-THIRD CONGRESS

Public Law/Resolution		Statutes at Large	Page	Date	Bill No.
Chapter	Number				
2	1	10	722	12-19-54	H Res. 39
4	2	10	722	12-27-54	S Res. 28
5	3	10	722	1-18-55	S Res. 32
6	4	10	723	2-03-55	S Res. 30
7	5	10	723	2-03-55	S Res. 33
9	6	10	723	2-15-55	S Res. 4
13	8	10	723	2-28-55	S Res. 49
14	9	10	724	3-02-55	S Res. 39
23	10	10	724	3-03-55	H Res. 22
24	11	10	724	3-03-55	S Res. 48
25	12	10	724	3-03-55	H Res. 63

PUBLIC ACTS OF THE THIRTY-FOURTH CONGRESS

Public Law/Resolution		Statutes at Large	Page	Date	Bill No.	
Chapter	Number					
1	1	11	1	2-20-56	S	57
4	2	11	1	3-05-56	S	106
8	3	11	1	3-19-56	HR	156
9	4	11	2	3-28-56	S	6
11	5	11	2	4-05-56	S	97
12	6	11	2-3	4-05-56	HR	64
13	7	11	3	4-05-56	HR	203
14	8	11	3-4	4-05-56	HR	70
18	9	11	4	4-23-56	HR	78
19	10	11	5	4-23-56	HR	69
20	11	11	5	4-23-56	HR	129
21	12	11	6	4-23-56	S	80
23	13	11	6-7	4-30-56	S	33
24	14	11	7	5-09-56	HR	303
25	15	11	7	5-09-56	HR	121
26	16	11	8-9	5-14-56	HR	8
28	17	11	9-10	5-15-56	HR	56
29	18	11	10-15	5-15-56	HR	68
30	19	11	15	5-16-56	S	125
31	20	11	15-16	5-17-56	HR	322
36	22	11	17	6-02-56	S	263
41	24	11	17-18	6-03-56	HR	31
42	25	11	18-19	6-03-56	HR	36
43	26	11	20-21	6-03-56	HR	326
44	27	11	21-22	6-03-56	HR	172
45	28	11	22	6-14-56	S	232
47	29	11	22-23	6-26-56	HR	311
48	30	11	23	6-26-56	S	156
50	31	11	23	7-03-56	HR	421
51	32	11	23-24	7-03-56	HR	409
54	33	11	24	7-08-56	S	14
55	34	11	25	7-08-56	S	2
56	35	11	25-26	7-08-56	S	1
57	37	11	26	7-08-56	HR	185
58	38	11	26-27	7-08-56	HR	67
59	39	11	27	7-08-56	HR	197
65	40	11	27	7-22-56	HR	417
72	41	11	27-29	8-01-56	HR	152
73	42	11	29	8-01-56	S	76

PUBLIC ACTS OF THE THIRTY-FOURTH CONGRESS

Public Law/Resolution		Statutes at Large	Page	Date	Bill No.	
Chapter	Number					
81	43	11	30	8-06-56	S	117
82	51	11	30	8-07-56	HR	261
83	44	11	30-32	8-11-56	HR	553
84	46	11	32-33	8-11-56	S	353
85	47	11	33	8-11-56	HR	352
86	49	11	33-42	8-11-56	S	341
87	50	11	42	8-11-56	HR	73
118	52	11	43	8-16-56	S	53
119	53	11	43	8-16-56	S	419
120	6	11	43-44	8-16-56	HR	3
121	64	11	44	8-16-56	S	53
122	66	11	44-48	8-16-56	HR	189
123	67	11	48-49	8-16-56	S	398
124	68	11	49-51	8-16-56	S	381
125	72	11	51	8-16-56	S	111
126	74	11	51-52	8-16-56	HR	12
127	59	11	52-65	8-18-56	HR	549
128	71	11	65-81	8-18-56	HR	71
129	55	11	81-94	8-18-56	HR	201
130	56	11	94-95	8-18-56	HR	315
160	57	11	95-101	8-18-56	HR	451
161	58	11	101-102	8-18-56	HR	316
162	54	11	102-118	8-18-56	HR	202
163	60	11	118-119	8-18-56	HR	215
164	61	11	119-120	8-18-56	S	339
165	62	11	120	8-18-56	HR	214
166	65	11	120-121	8-18-56	S	204
167	69	11	121-122	8-18-56	HR	180
168	77	11	122-138	8-18-56	HR	568
169	73	11	138-139	8-18-56	S	234
170	75	11	139	8-18-56	S	264
171	76	11	139-140	8-18-56	HR	574
172	70	11	140-141	8-18-56	HR	123

RESOLUTIONS OF THE THIRTY-FOURTH CONGRESS

1	1	11	142	2-27-56	S Res.	4
2	2	11	142	2-27-56	S Res.	5
3	3	11	142	3-13-56	S Res.	10
4	4	11	142-143	4-05-56	H Res.	6

RESOLUTIONS OF THE THIRTY-FOURTH CONGRESS

Public Law/Resolution		Statutes at Large	Page	Date	Bill No.
Chapter	Number				
5	5	11	143	4-23-56	H Res. 5
7	7	11	143-144	5-09-56	H Res. 12
8	8	11	144	5-12-56	H Res. 3
9	9	11	144	5-14-56	H Res. 13
10	10	11	144	5-15-56	H Res. 15
14	14	11	145	8-01-56	S Res. 21
17	17	11	145	8-18-56	H Res. 27
18	18	11	145-146	8-18-56	H Res. 26

PUBLIC ACTS OF THE THIRTY-FOURTH CONGRESS

Public Law/Resolution		Statutes at Large	Page	Date	Bill No.	
Chapter	Number					
28	1	11	147	8-28-56	S	463
29	2	11	147-150	8-30-56	HR	153
30	3	11	150	8-30-56	S	465

RESOLUTIONS OF THE THIRTY-FOURTH CONGRESS

1	1	11	151	8-28-56	S Res.	22
2	2	11	151	8-30-56	S Res.	31
3	3	11	152	8-30-56	S Res.	12
4	4	11	152	8-30-56	S Res.	34

PUBLIC ACTS OF THE THIRTY-FOURTH CONGRESS

Public Law/Resolution		Statutes at Large	Page	Date	Bill No.	
Chapter	Number					
2	1	11	153	1-02-57	S	391
12	3	11	153-154	1-16-57	S	113
13	2	11	155	1-17-57	HR	582
18	15*	11	155	1-21-57	S	363
19	4	11	155-156	1-24-57	HR	757
24	20*	11	156	1-26-57	S	211
25	15	11	156	1-28-57	HR	301
32	6	11	157	2-05-57	HR	251
36	7	11	157-158	2-07-57	S	447
37	8	11	158	2-07-57	S	129
38	9	11	159-160	2-07-57	HR	607
45	10	11	160-161	2-16-57	HR	581
46	36*	11	161-162	2-16-57	HR	806
50	11	11	162-163	2-17-57	HR	710
55	12	11	163	2-21-57	HR	782
56	15	11	163-164	2-21-57	S	190
57	14	11	164-166	2-21-57	HR	400
60	15	11	166-167	2-26-57	HR	642
61	16	11	168	3-02-57	HR	2
62	17	11	168	3-02-57	HR	803
63	18	11	168-169	3-02-57	HR	617
90	19	11	169-185	3-03-57	HR	614
91	20	11	185-186	3-03-57	S	253
92	21	11	186	3-03-57	HR	804
93	22	11	186-187	3-03-57	HR	212
94	23	11	187	3-03-57	HR	613
95	24	11	187-188	3-03-57	S	493
96	25	11	188-190	3-03-57	HR	636
97	26	11	191-192	3-03-57	HR	634
98	27	11	192-195	3-03-57	HR	566
99	28	11	195-197	3-03-57	S	576
100	29	11	197-199	3-03-57	S	593
101	30	11	199	3-03-57	S	586
102	31	11	199	3-03-57	S	556
103	32	11	200	3-03-57	S	502
104	33	11	200	3-03-57	S	4
105	34	11	200	3-03-57	S	84
106	35	11	200-205	3-03-57	HR	616
107	36	11	206-221	3-03-57	HR	606

PUBLIC ACTS OF THE THIRTY-FOURTH CONGRESS

Public Law/Resolution		Statutes at Large	Page	Date	Bill No.	
Chapter	Number					
108	37	11	221-230	3-03-57	HR	615
109	38	11	230-240	3-03-57	HR	852
110	39	11	240-243	3-03-57	HR	635
111	40	11	243-248	3-03-57	HR	633
112	41	11	248	3-03-57	S	330
113	42	11	248-249	3-03-57	HR	637
114	43	11	249	3-03-57	S	528
115	44	11	249-250	3-03-57	HR	684
116	45	11	250-251	3-03-57	S	474
117	46	11	251	3-03-57	S	110
118	47	11	251	3-03-57	HR	293
119	48	11	252	3-03-57	HR	853
120	49	11	252	3-03-57	HR	422
121	50	11	252	3-03-57	HR	641

RESOLUTIONS OF THE THIRTY-FOURTH CONGRESS

1	1	11	252	12-26-56	S Res.	44
2	1*	11	253	1-13-57	S Res.	40
5	2	11	253	1-28-57	S Res.	38
6	4*	11	253	1-28-57	S Res.	46
7	5*	11	254	2-16-57	H Res.	37
8	3	11	254	2-26-57	S Res.	42
9	4	11	254	2-26-57	S Res.	53
12	5	11	254-255	3-03-57	S Res.	39
13	6	11	255	3-03-57	S Res.	30
14	8*	11	255	3-03-57	S Res.	59
15	9*	11	255	3-03-57	H Res.	11
16	10	11	255-256	3-03-57	S Res.	56
17	12*	11	256	3-03-57	S Res.	52
18	13	11	256	3-03-57	H Res.	38

PUBLIC ACTS OF THE THIRTY-FIFTH CONGRESS

Public Law/Resolution		Statutes at Large	Page	Date	Bill No.	
Chapter	Number					
1	1	11	257-260	12-23-57	S	13
3	2	11	260	1-27-58	S	27
4	3	11	260	2-04-58	HR	63
5	4	11	260	2-10-58	HR	22
6	5	11	260-261	2-10-58	HR	3
8	6	11	261	3-04-58	HR	271
9	7	11	261-262	3-11-58	HR	307
12	8	11	262	3-29-58	S	210
13	9	11	262-263	4-07-58	HR	313
14	10	11	263-265	4-08-58	S	176
23	11	11	265-266	5-04-58	S	76
24	12	11	266	5-04-58	S	97
25	13	11	266-269	5-04-58	HR	306
26	14	11	269-272	5-04-58	S	161
27	15	11	272	5-04-58	S	36
28	16	11	272	5-04-58	S	111
29	17	11	273-285	5-04-58	HR	5
31	18	11	285	5-11-58	S	86
32	19	11	285-286	5-11-58	S	296
33	20	11	286	5-11-58	S	289
34	21	11	286-287	5-11-58	HR	62
35	22	11	287	5-11-58	S	313
36	23	11	287-288	5-11-58	S	300
37	24	11	288	5-11-58	S	307
38	25	11	289	5-18-58	HR	542
39	26	11	289-290	5-18-58	S	312
40	27	11	290-291	5-18-58	S	314
43	28	11	292	5-19-58	S	82
44	29	11	292	5-24-58	HR	564
45	30	11	293	5-24-58	HR	578
46	31	11	293	5-24-58	HR	207
58	32	11	293	5-29-58	HR	170
59	33	11	293-294	5-29-58	S	99
81	34	11	294-295	6-02-58	S	41
82	35	11	295-308	6-03-58	HR	201
84	36	11	308-309	6-03-58	HR	300
85	37	11	309	6-03-58	S	297
86	38	11	309	6-03-58	S	47
91	39	11	310	6-05-58	HR	169

PUBLIC ACTS OF THE THIRTY-FIFTH CONGRESS

Public Law/Resolution		Statutes at Large	Page	Date	Bill No.	
Chapter	Number					
92	40	11	310	6-05-58	HR	152
93	41	11	310-312	6-05-58	HR	6
122	42	11	312	6-08-58	S	323
133	43	11	313	6-09-58	HR	246
145	44	11	313	6-11-58	S	127
146	45	11	313-314	6-11-58	HR	538
147	46	11	314	6-11-58	HR	647
148	47	11	314	6-11-58	HR	399
153	48	11	314-319	6-12-58	HR	199
154	49	11	319-328	6-12-58	HR	200
155	50	11	329-332	6-12-58	HR	557
156	51	11	332-336	6-12-58	HR	243
160	52	11	337	6-14-58	HR	466
161	53	11	337	6-14-58	HR	56
162	54	11	337-362	6-14-58	HR	585
163	55	11	362-363	6-14-58	HR	555
164	56	11	364-365	6-14-58	HR	558
165	57	11	365-366	6-14-58	HR	582
166	58	11	366	6-14-58	HR	59
167	59	11	366	6-14-58	HR	556

RESOLUTIONS OF THE THIRTY-FIFTH CONGRESS

1	1	11	367	12-23-57	H Res.	2
2	2	11	367	2-18-58	H Res.	12
3	3	11	367-368	5-10-58	S Res.	3
4	4	11	368	5-16-58	S Res.	5
5	5	11	368	5-29-58	H Res.	14
6	6	11	368	4-07-58	S Res.	24
7	7	11	368	5-04-58	S Res.	22
8	8	11	369	5-11-58	S Res.	4
9	9	11	369	5-11-58	S Res.	30
10	10	11	369-370	5-11-58	S Res.	33
11	11	11	370	5-18-58	S Res.	2
12	12	11	370	5-24-58	S Res.	30
13	13	11	370	5-29-58	H Res.	32
15	14	11	370	6-02-58	S Res.	28
16	15	11	370-371	6-02-58	S Res.	47
17	16	11	371	6-03-58	H Res.	26
20	17	11	371	6-05-58	H Res.	31
23	18	11	371	6-09-58	S Res.	31

PUBLIC ACTS OF THE THIRTY-FIFTH CONGRESS

Public Law/Resolution		Statutes at Large	Page	Date	Bill No.	
Chapter	Number					
1	1	11	373	12-21-58	HR	302
5	2	11	374	12-22-58	HR	365
6	3	11	374-375	1-12-59	HR	663
8	4	11	375	1-17-59	S	32
10	5	11	375	1-19-59	S	476
11	6	11	376	1-19-59	S	493
13	7	11	376	1-25-59	S	478
17	8	11	376-378	2-02-59	S	182
18	9	11	378	2-02-59	HR	540
19	10	11	378	2-02-59	HR	801
20	11	11	379	2-02-59	HR	788
21	12	11	379	2-05-59	HR	820
22	13	11	379-381	2-05-59	HR	583
23	14	11	381	2-05-59	HR	830
26	15	11	381-382	2-08-59	S	263
27	16	11	382	2-09-59	S	380
28	17	11	382-383	2-09-59	S	554
33	18	11	383-384	2-14-59	S	239
35	19	11	384-385	2-18-59	HR	659
58	20	11	385	2-26-59	HR	804
59	21	11	385	2-26-59	HR	551
60	22	11	386-387	2-26-59	S	554
64	25	11	387-388	2-28-59	HR	803
65	24	11	388	2-28-59	HR	303
66	25	11	388-402	2-28-59	HR	664
68	26	11	402	3-01-59	S	596
74	27	11	402	3-03-59	S	412
75	28	11	402-404	3-03-59	HR	666
76	29	11	404-407	3-03-59	HR	712
77	30	11	408	3-03-59	S	606
78	31	11	408	3-03-59	HR	886
79	32	11	409-410	3-03-59	HR	888
80	33	11	410-422	3-03-59	HR	711
81	34	11	423-425	3-03-59	HR	550
82	35	11	425-431	3-03-59	HR	713
83	36	11	431-435	3-03-59	HR	667
84	37	11	435-437	3-03-59	HR	889
85	38	11	437-438	3-03-59	S	593
86	39	11	438	3-03-59	HR	489

PUBLIC ACTS OF THE THIRTY-FIFTH CONGRESS

Public Law/Resolution		Statutes at Large	Page	Date	Bill No.	
Chapter	Number					
87	40	11	438-439	3-03-59	HR	890
88	41	11	439	3-03-59	HR	662

RESOLUTIONS OF THE THIRTY-FIFTH CONGRESS

1	1	11	440	1-17-59	S Res.	67
2	2	11	440	1-25-59	H Res.	45
4	3	11	440	2-05-59	S Res.	65
6	4	11	440-441	2-09-59	S Res.	48
7	5	11	441	2-09-59	S Res.	54
8	6	11	441	2-09-59	H Res.	52
9	7	11	441-442	2-14-59	H Res.	38
10	8	11	442	2-18-59	H Res.	39
12	9	11	442	3-02-59	S Res.	69
13	10	11	442	3-03-59	S Res.	88
14	11	11	442-443	3-03-59	H Res.	34

PUBLIC ACTS OF THE THIRTY-SIXTH CONGRESS

Public Law/Resolution		Statutes at Large	Page	Date	Bill No.	
Chapter	Number					
1	1	12	1-2	2-15-60	HR	1
2	2	12	2	3-02-60	HR	3
3	3	12	2	3-02-60	S	146
5	4	12	3	3-12-60	S	26
7	5	12	3	3-24-60	HR	331
8	6	12	3-4	3-24-60	HR	19
9	7	12	4	3-27-60	HR	326
10	8	12	4-11	3-29-60	HR	216
11	9	12	11	4-03-60	HR	241
13	10	12	11	4-06-60	S	302
27	11	12	11-12	4-13-60	S	306
31	12	12	12-13	4-19-60	HR	213
35	13	12	13-14	4-20-60	S	344
37	14	12	14	5-05-60	HR	660
39	15	12	14-15	5-09-60	S	192
40	16	12	15	5-09-60	HR	368
48	17	12	15-16	5-16-60	S	340
49	18	12	16	5-16-60	HR	661
50	19	12	16-17	5-16-60	S	90
51	20	12	17	5-22-60	S	62
56	21	12	17-19	5-24-60	HR	499
57	22	12	19	5-25-60	HR	702
60	23	12	19-21	5-26-60	HR	4
61	24	12	21-22	5-26-60	HR	637
62	25	12	22	5-26-60	HR	706
64	26	12	22	6-01-60	S	106
65	27	12	23	6-01-60	HR	5
66	28	12	23	6-01-60	S	468
67	29	12	23-27	6-01-60	S	299
77	30	12	27	6-05-60	HR	520
79	31	12	28	6-07-60	S	371
83	52*	12	28	6-07-60	HR	284
84	32	12	28	6-09-60	HR	130
85	33	12	28-29	6-09-60	HR	764
114	34	12	29	6-12-60	HR	89
115	35	12	29	6-12-60	S	261
116	36	12	29-30	6-12-60	S	202
117	40	12	30	6-13-60	S	252
120	37	12	30-31	6-13-60	S	426
121	38	12	31	6-13-60	HR	523
122	39	12	32-33	6-13-60	S	385

PUBLIC ACTS OF THE THIRTY-SIXTH CONGRESS

Public Law/Resolution		Statutes at Large	Page	Date	Bill No.	
Chapter	Number					
128	41	12	33-35	6-14-60	S	168
129	42	12	35-36	6-15-60	S	287
130	43	12	36-37	6-15-60	HR	819
131	44	12	37-39	6-15-60	HR	564
132	45	12	39	6-15-60	HR	324
134	46	12	39-40	6-16-60	S	450
135	47	12	40	6-16-60	HR	699
136	48	12	40-41	6-16-60	S	464
137	49	12	41-42	6-16-60	S	84
138	50	12	42	6-16-60	HR	703
139	51	12	43	6-16-60	S	378
140	52	12	43	6-16-60	HR	838
141	53	12	43	6-16-60	HR	288
142	54	12	43	6-16-60	HR	839
143	56	12	44	6-16-60	HR	235
144	55	12	44	6-16-60	HR	374
157	57	12	44-59	6-19-60	HR	215
158	58	12	59-61	6-19-60	HR	663
162	60	12	61-63	6-20-60	HR	350
163	61	12	64-69	6-21-60	HR	305
164	62	12	69	6-21-60	HR	804
165	63	12	69-70	6-21-60	HR	715
166	64	12	70-71	6-21-60	HR	44
167	65	12	71-72	6-21-60	HR	195
179	66	12	72-79	6-22-60	S	448
180	67	12	79-80	6-22-60	HR	847
181	68	12	80-83	6-22-60	HR	500
182	69	12	83-84	6-22-60	S	509
183	70	12	84	6-22-60	S	347
184	71	12	84	6-22-60	S	497
185	73	12	84-85	6-22-60	HR	424
186	74	12	85	6-22-60	S	9
187	75	12	85	6-22-60	S	444
188	76	12	85-88	6-22-60	S	104
189	77	12	88	6-22-60	S	190
190	78	12	88-89	6-22-60	S	488
200	79	12	89-90	6-23-60	HR	814
201	80	12	90	6-23-60	HR	848
202	81	12	90	6-23-60	S	199
203	82	12	90-91	6-23-60	HR	807

PUBLIC ACTS OF THE THIRTY-SIXTH CONGRESS

Public Law/Resolution		Statutes at Large	Page	Date	Bill No.	
Chapter	Number					
204	83	12	91	6-23-60	HR	622
205	84	12	91-104	6-23-60	HR	339
211	85	12	104-112	6-25-60	HR	501
212	86	12	112-113	6-25-60	HR	503
213	88	12	113	6-25-60	HR	557
214	89	12	113	6-25-60	S	258

RESOLUTIONS OF THE THIRTY-SIXTH CONGRESS

1	1	12	114	2-24-60	S Res.	12
2	2	12	114	2-24-60	H Res.	8
4	3	12	114	3-28-60	H Res.	21
5	4	12	114-115	4-06-60	H Res.	26
6	5	12	115	4-19-60	S Res.	23
7	6	12	115-116	4-19-60	S Res.	4
9	7	12	116	5-09-60	S Res.	16
12	8	12	116	5-24-60	S Res.	6
18	9	12	116	6-15-60	S Res.	5
19	10	12	116-117	6-15-60	S Res.	34
20	11	12	117	6-15-60	S Res.	35
25	12	12	117-120	6-23-60	H Res.	22
26	13	12	120	6-25-60	S Res.	31
27	14	12	120	6-25-60	H Res.	41

PUBLIC ACTS OF THE THIRTY-SIXTH CONGRESS

Public Law/Resolution		Statutes at Large	Page	Date	Bill No.	
Chapter	Number					
1	1	12	121-124	12-17-60	HR	863
2	2	12	124	12-17-60	S	82
3	3	12	124	12-21-60	HR	861
5	4	12	124-125	1-05-61	HR	862
11	5	12	125	1-19-61	S	539
19	14*	12	125-126	1-26-61	S	97
20	6	12	126-128	1-29-61	HR	23
25	7	12	128	2-05-61	S	64
29	8	12	129-130	2-08-61	HR	972
30	9	12	130	2-08-61	HR	181
33	10	12	130	2-13-61	S	531
37	11	12	130-131	2-18-61	HR	554
38	12	12	131	2-18-61	HR	841
42	13	12	131-133	2-19-61	HR	866
44	14	12	133-144	2-20-61	HR	892
45	15	12	145-146	2-20-61	S	543
49	16	12	147-151	2-21-61	HR	914
56	17	12	151	2-27-61	HR	435
57	18	12	151-170	2-27-61	HR	714
58	19	12	170-172	2-28-61	HR	864
59	20	12	172-177	2-28-61	S	366
60	21	12	177	2-28-61	HR	999
61	21½	12	177-178	2-28-61	HR	950
68	22	12	178-198	3-02-61	HR	338
69	23	12	198	3-02-61	HR	943
70	24	12	198-199	3-02-61	S	11
71	25	12	199-200	3-02-61	HR	299
72	26	12	200-204	3-02-61	HR	899
73	27	12	204-207	3-02-61	HR	971
74	28	12	207	3-02-61	HR	852
75	29	12	207	3-02-61	HR	1007
76	30	12	207	3-02-61	S	149
77	31	12	208	3-02-61	S	524
78	32	12	208	3-02-61	HR	200
79	33	12	208	3-02-61	S	567
80	34	12	208-209	3-02-61	HR	132
81	35	12	209	3-02-61	S	215
82	36	12	209	3-02-61	S	19
83	37	12	209-214	3-02-61	S	563
84	38	12	214-220	3-02-61	HR	895

PUBLIC ACTS OF THE THIRTY-SIXTH CONGRESS

Public Law/Resolution		Statutes at Large	Page	Date	Bill No.	
Chapter	Number					
85	39	12	221-239	3-02-61	HR	865
86	40	12	239-244	3-02-61	S	562
87	41	12	244-246	3-02-61	HR	665
88	42	12	246-249	3-02-61	S	10

RESOLUTIONS OF THE THIRTY-SIXTH CONGRESS

1	1	12	250	1-19-61	S Res.	57
2	2	12	250	1-19-61	H Res.	53
5	3	12	250	2-13-61	S Res.	58
9	4	12	250-251	2-21-61	H Res.	43
11	5	12	251	3-02-61	H Res.	70
12	6	12	251	3-02-61	S Res.	64
13	7	12	251	3-02-61	H Res.	80
14	8	12	252	3-02-61	S Res.	45
15	9	12	252	3-02-61	S Res.	42
16	10	12	252	3-02-61	H Res.	59
17	11	12	252	3-02-61	S Res.	65
18	12	12	252-253	3-02-61	S Res.	67

PUBLIC ACTS OF THE THIRTY-SEVENTH CONGRESS

Public Law/Resolution		Statutes at Large	Page	Date	Bill No.	
Chapter	Number					
1	1	12	255	7-10-61	S	6
2	2	12	255	7-13-61	HR	15
3	3	12	255-258	7-13-61	HR	16
4	4	12	258-259	7-13-61	S	13
5	5	12	259-261	7-17-61	HR	14
6	6	12	261-264	7-17-61	HR	18
7	7	12	264-265	7-18-61	S	9
8	8	12	265-268	7-18-61	HR	19
9	13	12	268-271	7-22-61	S	1
10	9	12	271	7-24-61	HR	17
11	10	12	271-272	7-24-61	HR	26
12	11	12	272	7-24-61	HR	56
13	12	12	272-273	7-24-61	S	32
14	1*	12	273	7-24-61	S	21
15	2*	12	273-274	7-24-61	HR	23
16	3*	12	274	7-24-61	HR	57
17	14	12	274	7-25-61	S	42
18	15	12	274	7-25-61	HR	64
19	16	12	275	7-25-61	S	14
20	17	12	275-276	7-25-61	HR	53
21	18	12	276	7-27-61	HR	69
22	19	12	276-279	7-27-61	HR	25
23	20	12	279	7-27-61	HR	70
24	21	12	279-281	7-29-61	S	2
25	22	12	281-282	7-29-61	HR	20
27	23	12	282-283	7-31-61	S	20
28	24	12	283	7-31-61	S	38
29	25	12	283	7-31-61	HR	81
30	26	12	283-284	7-31-61	S	48
31	27	12	284	7-31-61	S	31
32	28	12	284	7-31-61	S	51
33	29	12	284	7-31-61	HR	45
34	30	12	284-285	7-31-61	S	24
35	31	12	285	8-02-61	HR	74
36	32	12	285	8-02-61	HR	78
37	33	12	285-286	8-02-61	S	16
38	34	12	286	8-03-61	S	36
39	35	12	286	8-03-61	S	61
40	36	12	286	8-03-61	S	52

PUBLIC ACTS OF THE THIRTY-SEVENTH CONGRESS

Public Law/Resolution		Statutes at Large	Page	Date	Bill No.	
Chapter	Number					
41	37	12	286	8-03-61	HR	100
42	38	12	287-291	8-03-61	S	3
44	39	12	291-292	8-05-61	S	53
45	40	12	292-313	8-05-61	HR	54
46	41	12	313-314	8-05-61	S	41
47	42	12	314	8-05-61	S	58
48	43	12	314-315	8-05-61	HR	55
49	44	12	315	8-05-61	S	64
50	45	12	315	8-05-61	HR	87
51	46	12	315-316	8-05-61	HR	96
52	47	12	316	8-05-61	HR	99
53	48	12	316	8-05-61	HR	80
54	49	12	316-317	8-05-61	S	63
55	50	12	317	8-06-61	S	59
56	51	12	317	8-06-61	HR	86
57	52	12	317-318	8-06-61	HR	101
58	53	12	318	8-06-61	S	65
59	54	12	318-319	8-06-61	S	39
60	55	12	319	8-06-61	S	25
61	56	12	319-320	8-06-61	S	60
62	57	12	320-326	8-06-61	S	49
63	58	12	326	8-06-61	S	72
64	59	12	326-327	8-06-61	S	54
65	60	12	327	8-06-61	S	67
66	61	12	327	8-06-61	S	46
67	6*	12	327	8-06-61	HR	103

RESOLUTIONS OF THE THIRTY-SEVENTH CONGRESS

1	1	12	328	7-24-61	H Res.	1
2	2	12	328	7-27-61	S Res.	9
3	3	12	328	8-05-61	S Res.	15
5	5	12	328	8-06-61	S Res.	16

PUBLIC ACTS OF THE THIRTY-SEVENTH CONGRESS

Public Law/Resolution		Statutes at Large	Page	Date	Bill No.	
Chapter	Number					
1	1	12	329-330	12-21-61	S	82
2	2	12	330	12-24-61	HR	176
3	3	12	330-331	12-24-61	S	83
4	4	12	331	12-24-61	S	84
5	5	12	331	12-24-61	HR	155
6	6	12	331-332	1-08-62	HR	149
8	7	12	332	1-21-62	HR	160
9	8	12	332	1-21-62	HR	193
10	9	12	332	1-22-62	S	164
11	10	12	333	1-24-62	HR	219
12	11	12	333	1-27-62	S	107
13	12	12	333	1-27-62	S	99
14	13	12	334	1-31-62	HR	238
15	14	12	334-335	1-31-62	S	169
17	15	12	335-337	2-04-62	HR	150
18	16	12	337	2-04-62	HR	139
19	17	12	337	2-10-62	HR	224
20	18	12	338	2-12-62	S	190
21	19	12	338	2-12-62	S	180
22	20	12	338	2-13-62	HR	255
23	21	12	338	2-13-62	HR	153
24	22	12	338-339	2-13-62	HR	186
25	23	12	339-340	2-13-62	HR	165
27	24	12	340-341	2-19-62	HR	109
28	25	12	341-343	2-20-62	HR	156
29	26	12	343	2-20-62	HR	286
30	27	12	344	2-22-62	S	112
31	28	12	344	2-22-62	S	141
32	29	12	344-345	2-25-62	HR	209
33	30	12	345-348	2-25-62	HR	240
34	31	12	348-352	3-01-62	HR	154
35	32	12	352-353	3-01-62	S	212
36	33	12	353	3-04-62	HR	104
37	34	12	353	3-06-62	HR	302
38	35	12	354	3-06-62	HR	294
39	36	12	354	3-13-62	HR	326
40	37	12	354	3-13-62	HR	299
41	38	12	355-369	3-14-62	HR	208
43	39	12	369	3-15-62	S	150

Public Law/Resolution		Statutes at Large	Page	Date	Bill No.	
Chapter	Number					
44	40	12	369-370	3-15-62	S	80
45	41	12	370	3-17-62	HR	341
46	42	12	371	3-17-62	HR	114
47	43	12	371-373	3-19-62	S	136
48	44	12	373	3-19-62	HR	353
49	45	12	374	3-25-62	HR	148
50	46	12	374-375	3-25-62	HR	279
51	47	12	375	4-02-62	S	120
52	48	12	375-376	4-02-62	S	244
53	49	12	376	4-02-62	HR	318
54	50	12	376-378	4-16-62	S	108
55	51	12	378-379	4-16-62	S	188
56	52	12	379-380	4-16-62	HR	118
57	53	12	380-381	4-17-62	HR	242
58	54	12	381-382	4-17-62	HR	259
59	55	12	382-383	4-21-62	HR	287
63	56	12	383-384	5-03-62	S	124
66	57	12	384-385	5-13-62	HR	444
67	58	12	385	5-13-62	HR	460
69	59	12	385	5-14-62	HR	404
70	60	12	385-386	5-14-62	S	289
71	61	12	386-387	5-15-62	HR	258
72	62	12	387-388	5-15-62	HR	269
73	63	12	388-392	5-17-62	S	178
75	64	12	392-393	5-20-62	HR	125
76	65	12	394	5-20-62	HR	388
77	66	12	394-403	5-20-62	S	240
78	67	12	403	5-20-62	S	271
79	68	12	403	5-20-62	S	222
80	69	12	403-404	5-20-62	S	304
81	70	12	404-405	5-20-62	HR	446
82	71	12	405-407	5-21-62	S	211
83	72	12	407	5-21-62	S	290
84	73	12	408	5-26-62	HR	183
85	74	12	408-409	5-26-62	HR	479
86	75	12	409-410	5-30-62	S	187
90	76	12	410-411	6-02-62	HR	189
91	77	12	411	6-02-62	HR	459
92	78	12	411	6-02-62	HR	476
93	79	12	411-412	6-02-62	S	43
94	80	12	413	6-02-62	S	272

Public Law/Resolution		Statutes at Large	Page	Date	Bill No.	
Chapter	Number					
95	81	12	413-421	6-02-62	HR	389
96	82	12	421	6-05-62	S	184
97	83	12	422	6-05-62	HR	281
98	84	12	422-426	6-07-62	S	292
99	85	12	426-427	6-10-62	S	265
101	86	12	427-428	6-14-62	S	302
102	87	12	428-430	6-16-62	S	279
103	88	12	430-431	6-17-62	S	281
104	89	12	431	6-17-62	S	339
105	90	12	431	6-17-62	HR	475
108	91	12	431	6-18-62	HR	474
109	92	12	431	6-18-62	HR	495
110	93	12	431-432	6-18-62	HR	499
111	94	12	432	6-19-62	HR	374
112	95	12	432	6-19-62	S	241
116	96	12	432	6-20-62	HR	507
119	97	12	432-489	7-11-62	HR	312
120	98	12	489-498	7-01-62	HR	364
121	99	12	498	7-01-62	S	243
122	100	12	498	7-01-62	S	242
123	101	12	498-499	7-01-62	HR	515
124	102	12	499	7-01-62	HR	521
125	103	12	499-501	7-01-62	HR	425
126	104	12	501-502	7-01-62	HR	39
127	105	12	502	7-02-62	S	370
128	106	12	502-503	7-02-62	HR	371
129	107	12	503	7-02-62	HR	442
130	108	12	503-505	7-02-62	S	298
133	109	12	505-510	7-05-62	HR	450
134	110	12	510-512	7-05-62	S	171
135	111	12	512-530	7-05-62	HR	260
138	112	12	530	7-11-62	S	307
139	113	12	530-531	7-11-62	S	362
140	114	12	531	7-11-62	S	352
141	115	12	531	7-11-62	S	256
142	116	12	532-533	7-11-62	HR	187
143	117	12	533-535	7-11-62	HR	393
144	118	12	535	7-11-62	HR	540
145	119	12	536	7-11-62	S	102
146	120	12	536	7-11-62	HR	529

Public Law/Resolution		Statutes at Large	Page	Date	Bill No.	
Chapter	Number					
147	121	12	537	7-11-62	HR	549
148	122	12	537	7-11-62	S	342
149	123	12	537	7-11-62	HR	556
150	124	12	537	7-11-62	HR	545
151	125	12	537-538	7-11-62	HR	543
154	126	12	538	7-12-62	S	379
155	127	12	538-539	7-11-62	S	351
156	128	12	539	7-12-62	HR	554
157	129	12	540-541	7-12-62	HR	377
158	130	12	542	7-12-62	S	316
159	131	12	542	7-12-62	HR	454
160	29*	12	542-543	7-12-62	S	318
161	132	12	543	7-12-62	S	119
163	134	12	543-561	7-14-62	HR	531
164	135	12	561-565	7-14-62	HR	423
165	136	12	566	7-14-62	HR	84
166	137	12	566-569	7-14-62	HR	438
167	133	12	569-571	7-14-62	HR	392
168	138	12	571	7-14-62	S	98
169	139	12	571-572	7-14-62	HR	550
170	140	12	572	7-14-62	HR	525
171	141	12	572-574	7-14-62	HR	553
172	142	12	574	7-14-62	S	270
173	143	12	575	7-14-62	HR	437
174	144	12	575	7-14-62	S	93
175	150	12	575	7-14-62	S	380
177	145	12	575-576	7-14-62	S	363
178	146	12	576-577	7-15-62	S	89
179	147	12	577	7-15-62	S	123
180	148	12	577-578	7-16-62	S	358
181	149	12	578-582	7-16-62	S	250
182	151	12	582-583	7-16-62	HR	572
183	152	12	583-587	7-16-62	HR	280
184	153	12	587	7-16-62	HR	355
185	154	12	587	7-16-62	HR	518
186	155	12	587-588	7-16-62	HR	496
187	156	12	588	7-16-62	HR	573
188	157	12	588	7-16-62	HR	571
189	158	12	588-589	7-16-62	HR	390
190	159	12	589	7-16-62	HR	524

Public Law/Resolution		Statutes at Large	Page	Date	Bill No.	
Chapter	Number					
195	160	12	589-592	7-17-62	HR	471
196	161	12	592	7-17-62	HR	579
197	162	12	592-593	7-17-62	S	385
198	163	12	593	7-17-62	HR	548
199	164	12	593-594	7-17-62	HR	511
200	165	12	594-597	7-17-62	S	383
201	166	12	597-600	7-17-62	S	394
202	167	12	600	7-17-62	S	376
203	168	12	600	7-17-62	S	350
204	169	12	600-610	7-17-62	S	348
205	170	12	610	7-17-62	S	202

RESOLUTIONS OF THE THIRTY-SEVENTH CONGRESS

1	1	12	611	12-24-61	H Res.	20	
2	2	12	611	1-11-62	H Res.	26	
3	3	12	611	1-11-62	H Res.	22	
4	4	12	612	1-18-62	H Res.	25	
5	5	12	612	1-21-62	H Res.	29	
6	6	12	612	1-21-62	H Res.	32	
7	7	12	612	1-25-62	S Res.	34	
8	8	12	613	1-27-62	S Res.	35	
9	9	12	613	2-06-62	S Res.	41	
10	10	12	613	2-22-62	S Res.	37	
11	11	12	613	2-22-62	S Res.	44	
12	12	12	613-614	2-22-62	S Res.	51	
13	13	12	614	2-22-62	S Res.	49	
14	14	12	614	2-22-62	S Res.	39	
15	15	12	614-615	3-06-62	H Res.	37	
16	16	12	615	3-08-62	S Res.	46	
18	17	12	615	3-11-62	S.Res.	22	
19	18	12	615-616	3-15-62	S Res.	54	
20	19	12	616	3-15-62	S Res.	57	
21	20	12	616	3-17-62	H Res.	57	
22	21	12	616	3-19-62	S Res.	65	
23	22	12	616	3-19-62	S Res.	64	
24	23	12	617	4-02-62	H Res.	49	
25	24	12	617	4-04-62	S Res.	68	
26	25	12	617	4-10-62	H Res.	48	
27	26	12	617	4-10-62	H Res.	59	

RESOLUTIONS OF THE THIRTY-SEVENTH CONGRESS

Public Law/Resolution		Statutes at Large	Page	Date	Bill No.
Chapter	Number				
28	27	12	617	4-16-62	S Res. 50
29	28	12	618	4-24-62	H Res. 67
30	29	12	618-619	4-25-62	S Res. 26
32	30	12	619	5-21-62	H Res. 73
34	31	12	619	6-14-62	H Res. 68
35	32	12	619	6-17-62	H Res. 77
36	33	12	620	6-18-62	H Res. 72
37	34	12	620	6-21-62	S Res. 88
38	35	12	620-621	7-05-62	H Res. 83
39	36	12	621-622	7-11-62	S Res. 61
40	37	12	622	7-11-62	S Res. 66
41	38	12	622	7-11-62	S Res. 83
42	39	12	622	7-11-62	S Res. 77
43	40	12	622-623	7-11-62	S Res. 85
44	41	12	623	7-11-62	H Res. 71
51	42	12	623	7-12-62	S Res. 78
52	43	12	623-624	7-12-62	S Res. 82
53	44	12	624	7-12-62	S Res. 93
54	45	12	624	7-12-62	S Res. 76
55	46	12	624	7-12-62	S Res. 98
56	47	12	624-625	7-12-62	S Res. 80
57	48	12	625	7-14-62	S Res. 94
58	49	12	625	7-14-62	H Res. 39
59	50	12	625-626	7-16-62	H Res.105
60	51	12	626	7-16-62	H Res.102
61	52	12	626	7-16-62	H Res.108
62	53	12	626	7-17-62	S Res. 86
63	54	12	627	7-17-62	H Res.110
64	55	12	627	7-17-62	H Res.109
65	56	12	627-628	7-17-62	S Res. 97
66	57	12	628	7-17-62	S Res. 99
67	58	12	628	7-17-62	S Res. 98
68	59	12	628	7-17-62	H Res.107
69	60	12	628-629	7-17-62	H Res. 81
70	61	12	629	7-17-62	S Res. 58
71	62	12	629	7-17-62	S Res.101
72	63	12	630	7-17-62	S Res.100

PUBLIC ACTS OF THE THIRTY-SEVENTH CONGRESS

Public Law/Resolution		Statutes at Large	Page	Date	Bill No.	
Chapter	Number					
1	1	12	631	12-15-62	S	405
3	2	12	631-632	12-19-62	HR	598
4	3	12	632-633	12-25-62	HR	592
5	5	12	633	12-27-62	S	420
6	4	12	633-634	12-31-62	S	365
7	6	12	634	1-06-63	S	419
9	7	12	634-635	1-13-63	HR	608
10	8	12	635-636	1-16-63	HR	587
11	9	12	636	1-23-63	HR	611
13	10	12	637	1-28-63	S	437
14	11	12	637	1-30-63	HR	568
17	12	12	637-638	2-03-63	HR	616
19	13	12	638-639	2-04-63	HR	649
20	14	12	639-640	2-04-63	HR	561
21	15	12	640-641	2-06-63	S	458
22	16	12	641	2-07-63	S	463
23	17	12	641-642	2-07-63	HR	137
24	18	12	642	2-07-63	S	430
25	19	12	642-646	2-09-63	HR	610
26	20	12	646-647	2-09-63	HR	665
27	21	12	648	2-09-63	HR	636
28	22	12	648	2-09-63	HR	720
29	23	12	648	2-09-63	HR	658
32	24	12	648-650	2-12-63	HR	617
33	25	12	650-651	2-14-63	S	505
34	26	12	651-652	2-14-63	S	482
36	27	12	652	2-16-63	HR	737
37	28	12	652-654	2-16-63	HR	582
43	29	12	654-656	2-20-63	HR	707
44	30	12	656	2-20-63	HR	695
45	31	12	656	2-20-63	S	468
46	32	12	656-654	2-20-63	S	440
47	33	12	657	2-20-63	HR	762
49	34	12	657	2-21-63	S	488
50	35	12	657-658	2-21-63	S	516
51	36	12	658	2-21-63	S	337
52	37	12	658	2-21-63	S	519
53	38	12	658-660	2-21-63	S	417
54	39	12	660-662	2-24-63	HR	267
55	40	12	662-664	2-24-63	HR	722

PUBLIC ACTS OF THE THIRTY-SEVENTH CONGRESS

Public Law/Resolution		Statutes at Large	Page	Date	Bill No.	
Chapter	Number					
56	41	12	664-665	2-24-63	HR	357
58	42	12	665-682	2-25-63	S	486
59	43	12	682-696	2-25-63	HR	635
60	44	12	696	2-25-63	S	451
61	45	12	696	2-25-63	S	473
67	46	12	696-699	3-02-63	S	467
68	47	12	699	3-02-63	S	515
69	48	12	699-700	3-02-63	S	407
70	49	12	700-701	3-02-63	S	311
71	50	12	701-709	3-02-63	S	492
72	51	12	709	3-03-63	S	512
73	52	12	709-713	3-03-63	HR	659
74	53	12	713-731	3-03-63	HR	770
75	54	12	731-737	3-03-63	S	511
76	55	12	737-742	3-03-63	S	506
77	56	12	742-743	3-03-63	HR	779
78	57	12	743-744	3-03-63	HR	523
79	58	12	744-754	3-03-63	HR	732
80	59	12	754-755	3-03-63	S	355
81	60	12	755-758	3-03-63	HR	591
82	61	12	758	3-03-63	S	540
83	62	12	758	3-03-63	HR	753
84	63	12	758	3-03-63	S	564
85	64	12	758	3-03-63	S	393
86	65	12	759-760	3-03-63	S	577
87	66	12	760-761	3-03-63	HR	551
88	67	12	761	3-03-63	HR	711
89	68	12	761-762	3-03-63	S	526
90	69	12	762	3-03-63	HR	615
91	70	12	762-765	3-03-63	S	359
92	71	12	765-768	3-03-63	HR	226
93	72	12	768	3-03-63	S	494
94	73	12	769	3-03-63	S	545
95	74	12	769-770	3-03-63	S	562
96	75	12	770-771	3-03-63	HR	663
97	76	12	771-772	3-03-63	S	543
98	77	12	772-774	3-03-63	S	435
99	78	12	774-794	3-03-63	HR	731
100	79	12	794-795	3-03-63	S	548
101	80	12	795-796	3-03-63	S	554
102	81	12	796	3-03-63	HR	365
103	82	12	796-797	3-03-63	S	536

PUBLIC ACTS OF THE THIRTY-SEVENTH CONGRESS

Public Law/Resolution		Statutes at Large	Page	Date	Bill No.	
Chapter	Number					
104	83	12	797-798	3-03-63	S	208
105	84	12	798-799	3-03-63	HR	712
106	85	12	799-803	3-03-63	S	532
107	86	12	803-804	3-03-63	S	574
108	87	12	804	3-03-63	HR	780
109	88	12	804-805	3-03-63	S	231
110	89	12	805-806	3-03-63	HR	468
111	90	12	806-807	3-03-63	S	555
112	91	12	807	3-03-63	S	483
113	92	12	807	3-03-63	HR	678
114	93	12	807	3-03-63	S	557
115	94	12	807	3-03-63	HR	599
116	95	12	808	3-03-63	S	537
117	96	12	808-814	3-03-63	HR	738
118	97	12	814-818	3-03-63	HR	708
119	98	12	819-820	3-03-63	S	565
120	99	12	820-821	3-03-63	S	544

RESOLUTIONS OF THE THIRTY-SEVENTH CONGRESS

1	1	12	822	12-18-62	S	Res.108
2	2	12	822	1-06-63	S	Res.110
3	3	12	822	1-13-63	H	Res.125
9	4	12	822-823	1-17-63	H	Res.133
10	5	12	823	1-28-63	S	Res.125
11	6	12	823	2-03-63	H	Res.117
13	7	12	823-824	2-07-63	H	Res.112
18	8	12	824	2-13-63	H	Res.144
19	9	12	824	2-16-63	H	Res.118
20	10	12	824-825	2-20-63	S	Res.127
21	11	12	825	2-21-63	S	Res.126
24	12	12	825	3-03-63	H	Res.143
25	13	12	825	3-03-63	H	Res.145
26	14	12	825	3-03-63	S	Res.131
27	15	12	825-826	3-03-63	S	Res.123
28	16	12	826-827	3-03-63	H	Res. 63
29	17	12	827	3-03-63	S	Res.117
30	18	12	827	3-03-63	H	Res.150
31	19	12	827-828	3-03-63	S	Res.132
32	20	12	828-829	3-03-63	H	Res.115

Public Law/Resolution		Statutes at Large	Page	Date	Bill No.
Chapter	Number				
33	21	12	829	3-03-63	H Res.154
34	22	12	829	3-03-63	H Res.155
35	23	12	830	3-03-63	S Res.129
36	24	12	830	3-03-63	S Res.133
37	25	12	830	3-03-63	S Res.130
38	26	12	830-831	3-03-63	S Res.137

PUBLIC ACTS OF THE THIRTY-EIGHTH CONGRESS

Public Law/Resolution		Statutes at Large	Page	Date	Bill No.	
Chapter	Number					
1	1	13	1	1-16-64	S	57
2	2	13	1	1-19-64	S	50
3	3	13	1-2	1-22-64	HR	35
4	4	13	2	1-22-64	HR	143
5	5	13	2	1-26-64	HR	65
6	6	13	3	1-28-64	S	49
7	7	13	3	1-29-64	HR	33
8	8	13	3	2-12-64	S	100
9	9	13	3	2-13-64	HR	225
11	10	13	4-5	2-19-64	S	51
13	11	13	6-11	2-24-64	S	36
14	12	13	11-12	2-29-64	HR	26
15	13	13	12	2-29-64	HR	230
16	14	13	12-13	2-29-64	S	86
17	15	13	13	3-03-64	HR	265
18	16	13	14	3-03-64	S	140
20	17	13	14-17	3-07-64	HR	122
21	18	13	17-18	3-08-64	S	15
22	19	13	18-19	3-08-64	HR	42
23	20	13	19	3-08-64	S	81
24	21	13	19	3-08-64	S	39
27	22	13	20-22	3-11-64	S	30
28	23	13	22	3-11-64	S	69
30	24	13	22-28	3-14-64	HR	156
31	25	13	28	3-14-64	HR	116
33	27	13	29	3-15-64	S	120
34	28	13	29-30	3-16-64	HR	50
35	29	13	30	3-16-64	S	158
36	30	13	30-32	3-21-64	S	96
37	31	13	32-35	3-21-64	S	97
38	32	13	35-36	3-21-64	S	60
40	33	13	36-37	3-25-64	HR	299
41	34	13	37	3-25-64	S	25
42	35	13	37-38	3-28-64	HR	341
45	36	13	38-39	4-01-64	HR	34
46	37	13	39	4-01-64	HR	312
47	38	13	39	4-01-64	S	108
48	39	13	39-41	4-08-64	S	80
49	40	13	41-43	4-08-64	S	155
50	41	13	43-44	4-08-64	S	79

PUBLIC ACTS OF THE THIRTY-EIGHTH CONGRESS

Public Law/Resolution		Statutes at Large	Page	Date	Bill No.	
Chapter	Number					
51	42	13	44-45	4-08-64	S	82
52	43	13	45	4-08-64	S	163
53	44	13	46	4-09-64	HR	302
54	45	13	46-47	4-09-64	HR	373
58	46	13	47	4-14-64	S	12
59	47	13	47-50	4-19-64	HR	14½
60	48	13	50-52	4-19-64	HR	206
61	49	13	52-53	4-19-64	HR	297
63	50	13	53-54	4-21-64	HR	303
64	51	13	54	4-21-64	HR	301
65	52	13	54	4-21-64	HR	287
66	53	13	54-55	4-22-64	S	183
67	54	13	55-57	4-26-64	S	130
68	55	13	57-58	4-26-64	S	249
69	56	13	58-61	4-29-64	HR	62
70	57	13	61	4-19-64	HR	367
71	58	13	61-62	4-19-64	S	66
72	59	13	62	4-29-64	S	181
73	59	13	62	4-29-64	HR	408
74	61	13	62	5-03-64	S	198
77	62	13	63	5-05-64	HR	220
78	63	13	63-64	5-05-64	HR	360
79	64	13	64-65	5-05-64	S	31
80	65	13	66-68	5-05-64	S	160
81	66	13	68-69	5-05-64	S	126
83	67	13	69-72	5-06-64	HR	119
84	68	13	72-74	5-12-64	HR	159
85	69	13	74-75	5-12-64	S	172
86	70	13	75	5-16-64	S	76
87	71	13	76-79	5-17-64	HR	185
89	72	13	79-80	5-17-64	HR	370
92	73	13	80	5-20-64	HR	251
93	74	13	80-85	5-21-64	HR	151
94	75	13	85	5-21-64	S	267
95	76	13	85-92	5-26-64	HR	15
96	77	13	92	5-26-64	HR	300
97	78	13	92-93	5-28-64	HR	377
98	79	13	93-94	5-28-64	HR	407
99	80	13	94-95	5-28-64	HR	432
101	81	13	95	6-01-64	S	65

PUBLIC ACTS OF THE THIRTY-EIGHTH CONGRESS

Public Law/Resolution		Statutes at Large	Page	Date	Bill No.	
Chapter	Number					
102	82	13	95	6-01-64	S	248
103	83	13	95-99	6-02-64	HR	381
104	84	13	99	6-02-64	HR	484
106	85	13	99-118	6-03-64	HR	395
107	86	13	118	6-03-64	HR	474
108	87	13	119	6-03-64	S	218
109	88	13	119	6-03-64	HR	120
110	89	13	119	6-07-64	S	250
111	90	13	120	6-07-64	S	236
113	91	13	120	6-08-64	HR	426
114	92	13	120-121	6-08-64	HR	455
115	93	13	121	6-08-64	HR	293
116	94	13	121-122	6-11-64	HR	487
117	95	13	122-123	6-11-64	HR	355
118	96	13	123	6-11-64	S	42
119	97	13	123	6-11-64	S	28
120	98	13	124	6-11-64	S	256
121	99	13	124-125	6-11-64	S	52
122	100	13	125	6-11-64	S	283
124	101	13	126-130	6-15-64	HR	198
125	102	13	130-131	6-15-64	HR	383
126	103	13	132	6-15-64	HR	149
127	104	13	132-133	6-17-64	S	106
128	105	13	133	6-17-64	S	282
129	106	13	133-134	6-17-64	S	129
130	107	13	134	6-17-64	S	223
131	108	13	135	6-17-64	S	285
132	109	13	135-136	6-17-64	S	293
133	110	13	136	6-17-64	S	216
134	111	13	137	6-18-64	HR	469
135	112	13	137	6-18-64	S	291
136	113	13	137-140	6-20-64	HR	40
137	114	13	140-141	6-20-64	HR	227
138	115	13	141-142	6-20-64	HR	521
139	116	13	142	6-20-64	HR	356
140	117	13	142	6-20-64	HR	504
141	118	13	142-143	6-20-64	HR	486
142	119	13	143	6-20-64	HR	217
143	120	13	143	6-20-64	HR	513
144	121	13	143-144	6-20-64	HR	179

PUBLIC ACTS OF THE THIRTY-EIGHTH CONGRESS

Public Law/Resolution		Statutes at Large	Page	Date	Bill No.	
Chapter	Number					
145	122	13	144-145	6-20-64	S	145
147	123	13	145-161	6-25-64	HR	192
148	124	13	161-181	6-25-64	HR	240
149	125	13	181-182	6-25-64	S	85
150	126	13	182	6-25-64	HR	545
151	127	13	182	6-25-64	S	270
152	128	13	183	6-25-64	S	253
153	129	13	183-184	6-25-64	HR	247
154	130	13	184	6-25-64	S	279
155	131	13	184-186	6-25-64	S	265
156	132	13	187-193	6-25-64	S	26
157	133	13	193-194	6-25-64	S	115
158	134	13	194	6-25-64	HR	434
159	135	13	194	6-25-64	S	162
160	136	13	194-195	6-25-64	S	306
162	137	13	195	6-27-64	S	187
163	138	13	195-196	6-27-64	S	296
164	139	13	197-199	6-27-64	S	266
165	140	13	199-200	6-27-64	S	55
166	141	13	200	6-28-64	HR	512
167	142	13	200	6-28-64	HR	554
168	143	13	200-201	6-28-64	HR	450
169	144	13	201	6-28-64	HR	551
170	145	13	201-202	6-28-64	HR	519
171	146	13	202-218	6-30-64	HR	494
172	147	13	218-222	6-30-64	HR	540
173	148	13	223-306	6-30-64	HR	405
174	149	13	306-316	6-30-64	HR	446
175	150	13	316-322	6-30-64	HR	532
176	151	13	322	6-30-64	HR	522
177	152	13	323	6-30-64	S	226
178	153	13	323	6-30-64	S	335
179	154	13	323	6-30-64	S	190
180	155	13	324	6-30-64	HR	255
181	156	13	324	6-30-64	HR	442
182	157	13	324-325	6-30-64	HR	497
183	158	13	325	6-30-64	S	199
184	159	13	325	6-30-64	S	203
185	160	13	326	6-30-64	HR	205
189	161	13	326	7-01-64	S	272

PUBLIC ACTS OF THE THIRTY-EIGHTH CONGRESS

Public Law/Resolution		Statutes at Large	Page	Date	Bill No.	
Chapter	Number					
190	162	13	326-331	7-01-64	S	54
191	163	13	331	7-01-64	S	298
192	164	13	331-332	7-01-64	S	299
193	165	13	332	7-01-64	S	321
194	166	13	332-334	7-01-64	S	109
195	167	13	334-335	7-01-64	S	301
196	168	13	335	7-01-64	S	312
197	169	13	335-339	7-01-64	S	332
198	170	13	339-340	7-01-64	S	233
199	171	13	340-341	7-01-64	S	302
200	172	13	341	7-01-64	S	308
201	173	13	342	7-01-64	S	292
202	174	13	342	7-01-64	S	242
203	175	13	342-343	7-01-64	S	273
204	176	13	343	7-01-64	S	324
205	177	13	343-344	7-01-64	S	264
209	178	13	344	7-02-64	S	325
210	179	13	344-353	7-02-64	HR	527
211	180	13	353-354	7-02-64	HR	207
212	181	13	354-355	7-02-64	HR	561
213	182	13	355	7-02-64	S	23
214	183	13	355	7-02-64	HR	550
215	184	13	356	7-02-64	HR	511
216	185	13	356-365	7-02-64	HR	438
217	186	13	365-372	7-02-64	HR	483
218	187	13	372-373	7-02-64	HR	559
219	188	13	373 ·	7-02-64	HR	470
220	189	13	373-374	7-02-64	S	290
221	190	13	374	7-02-64	S	315
222	191	13	374-375	7-02-64	S	271
223	192	13	375	7-02-64	S	176
224	193	13	375	7-02-64	S	278
225	194	13	375-378	7-02-64	S	232
226	195	13	378-379	7-02-64	S	228
237	196	13	379-380	7-04-64	HR	549
238	197	13	381	7-04-64	S	339
239	198	13	381	7-04-64	HR	573
240	199	13	381-382	7-04-64	HR	305
241	200	13	382	7-04-64	HR	575
242	201	13	382-383	7-04-64	S	185

PUBLIC ACTS OF THE THIRTY-EIGHTH CONGRESS

Public Law/Resolution		Statutes at Large	Page	Date	Bill No.	
Chapter	Number					
243	202	13	383-384	7-04-64	S	138
244	203	13	384	7-04-64	S	348
245	204	13	385	7-04-64	HR	32
246	205	13	385-387	7-04-64	HR	411
247	206	13	387-389	7-04-64	HR	406
248	207	13	389-390	7-04-64	S	246
249	208	13	390-392	7-04-64	HR	510
250	209	13	392	7-04-64	HR	421
251	210	13	392-393	7-04-64	S	343
252	211	13	393-394	7-04-64	HR	534
253	212	13	394-398	7-04-64	S	154

RESOLUTIONS OF THE THIRTY-EIGHTH CONGRESS

1	1	13	399	12-17-63	H Res.	1
2	2	13	399	12-23-63	H Res.	12
3	3	13	399-300	12-23-63	H Res.	14
4	4	13	400	1-13-64	H Res.	15
5	5	13	400	1-13-64	H Res.	16
6	6	13	400	1-16-64	S Res.	15
7	7	13	401	1-28-64	S Res.	2
8	8	13	401	1-28-64	S Res.	5
9	9	13	401	1-28-64	S Res.	3
10	10	13	401-402	1-28-64	S Res.	14
11	11	13	402	2-03-64	S Res.	18
12	12	13	402	2-19-64	H Res.	30
13	14	13	402	2-22-64	H Res.	31
14	15	13	402-403	2-24-64	S Res.	27
15	16	13	403	3-03-64	H Res.	35
16	17	13	403	3-03-64	H Res.	41
17	18	13	403-404	3-07-64	S Res.	19
18	20	13	404	3-17-64	H Res.	37
19	21	13	404	3-25-64	S Res.	31
20	22	13	404	4-19-64	H Res.	13
21	23	13	404	4-19-64	H Res.	54
22	24	13	404-405	4-19-64	H Res.	21
23	25	13	405	4-21-64	H Res.	65
24	26	13	405	4-22-64	S Res.	39
25	27	13	405	4-29-64	H Res.	67
26	28	13	405	4-29-64	H Res.	69

RESOLUTIONS OF THE THIRTY-EIGHTH CONGRESS

Public Law/Resolution		Statutes at Large	Page	Date	Bill No.
Chapter	Number				
27	29	13	406	5-19-64	S Res. 21
28	30	13	406	5-19-64	S Res. 37
29	31	13	406-407	5-20-64	H Res. 72
30	32	13	407	5-20-64	H Res. 78
31	35	13	407	6-01-64	S Res. 57
32	38	13	408	6-07-64	S Res. 35
33	39	13	408	6-07-64	S Res. 51
34	40	13	408	6-11-64	S Res. 60
35	41	13	408	6-15-64	H Res. 55
36	42	13	408-409	6-18-64	S Res. 59
37	43	13	409	6-18-64	S Res. 64
38	45	13	409-410	6-25-64	H Res. 95
39	46	13	410	6-25-64	H Res. 87
40	47	13	410	6-25-64	S Res. 44
41	49	13	411	6-27-64	H Res.115
42	50	13	411	6-28-64	H Res.109
44	53	13	411-412	6-30-64	H Res. 93
45	54	13	412	6-30-64	H Res.101
46	55	13	412	6-30-64	H Res. 68
47	56	13	412-413	6-30-64	H Res.111
48	57	13	413	6-30-64	H Res. 23
49	59	13	413-414	7-01-64	S Res. 8
50	60	13	414	7-01-64	S Res. 38
51	61	13	414	7-01-64	S Res. 70
52	62	13	414-415	7-01-64	S Res. 69
53	63	13	415	7-01-64	H Res. 32
54	66	13	415-416	7-02-64	S Res. 74
55	67	13	416	7-02-64	S Res. 58
56	68	13	416	7-02-64	S Res. 77
57	75	13	416	7-04-64	S Res. 79
58	76	13	416-417	7-04-64	H Res.118
59	77	13	417	7-04-64	H Res.120
60	78	13	417	7-04-64	H Res.119

PUBLIC ACTS OF THE THIRTY-EIGHTH CONGRESS

Public Law/Resolution		Statutes at Large	Page	Date	Bill No.	
Chapter	Number					
1	1	13	419	12-15-64	HR	563
2	2	13	419	12-20-64	S	352
3	3	13	419	12-21-64	S	350
6	4	13	420	12-21-64	S	358
8	5	13	420	12-22-64	HR	618
9	6	13	420	12-22-64	HR	603
11	7	13	420	1-10-65	S	367
12	8	13	421	1-11-65	HR	597
13	9	13	421	1-13-65	HR	595
16	10	13	421-422	1-20-65	HR	623
18	11	13	422-424	1-24-65	HR	598
19	12	13	424	1-24-65	HR	607
20	13	13	424	1-24-65	S	72
22	14	13	425	1-28-65	HR	677
23	15	13	425-426	1-28-65	HR	659
24	16	13	426	1-30-65	S	363
25	17	13	426	1-30-65	HR	622
26	18	13	426	1-30-65	S	384
29	19	13	427	2-09-65	S	225
30	20	13	427	2-09-65	HR	644
32	21	13	427	2-13-65	HR	689
34	22	13	428-429	2-14-65	HR	517
35	23	13	429-430	2-14-65	HR	705
37	24	13	430	2-17-65	S	407
38	25	13	431	2-17-65	S	392
39	26	13	431	2-17-65	S	413
41	27	13	431	2-20-65	S	385
42	28	13	431	2-20-65	S	410
43	29	13	432	2-20-65	S	402
45	30	13	432	2-23-65	HR	222
46	31	13	432	2-23-65	HR	624
47	32	13	432-434	2-23-65	S	424
48	33	13	434-435	2-23-65	S	376
49	34	13	435-436	2-23-65	S	368
50	35	13	436	2-23-65	S	421
52	36	13	437	2-25-65	S	37
53	37	13	437-438	2-25-65	HR	543
54	38	13	438	2-25-65	HR	184
55	39	13	438-439	2-25-65	S	454
56	40	13	439	2-25-65	S	393

Public Law/Resolution		Statutes at Large	Page	Date	Bill No.	
Chapter	Number					
57	41	13	439	2-25-65	HR	364
58	42	13	439	2-25-65	HR	692
59	43	13	440	2-25-65	HR	664
64	44	13	440-441	2-27-65	HR	640
67	45	13	441-442	2-28-65	HR	690
68	46	13	442-444	2-28-65	HR	688
69	47	13	444	2-28-65	HR	738
70	48	13	444	2-28-65	HR	784
71	49	13	444-445	2-28-65	HR	783
72	50	13	445	2-28-65	HR	781
73	51	13	445-462	3-02-65	HR	649
74	52	13	462-467	3-02-65	HR	676
75	53	13	467	3-02-65	HR	621
76	54	13	468	3-02-65	HR	800
77	55	13	468-469	3-03-65	HR	772
78	56	13	469-487	3-03-65	HR	744
79	57	13	487-491	3-03-65	H Res.170*	
80	58	13	491-495	3-03-65	HR	195
81	59	13	495-498	3-03-65	HR	683
82	60	13	498	3-03-65	HR	703
83	61	13	498-499	3-03-65	HR	798
84	62	13	499-500	3-03-65	HR	756
85	63	13	500	3-03-65	S	476
86	64	13	500-501	3-03-65	S	88
87	65	13	501-504	3-03-65	S	171
88	66	13	504	3-03-65	HR	763
89	67	13	504-507	3-03-65	S	390
90	68	13	507-509	3-03-65	HR	51
91	69	13	509-510	3-03-65	S	479
92	70	13	510-513	3-03-65	S	443
93	71	13	513-514	3-03-65	HR	600
94	72	13	514	3-03-65	HR	667
95	73	13	514-515	3-03-65	HR	707
96	74	13	515	3-03-65	S	62
97	75	13	515-516	3-03-65	S	389
98	76	13	516	3-03-65	HR	758
99	77	13	516-517	3-03-65	S	472
100	78	13	517-518	3-03-65	HR	807
101	79	13	518-519	3-03-65	HR	739
102	80	13	519-520	3-03-65	HR	745

PUBLIC ACTS OF THE THIRTY-EIGHTH CONGRESS

Public Law/Resolution		Statutes at Large	Page	Date	Bill No.	
Chapter	Number					
103	81	13	520-522	3-03-65	HR	710
104	82	13	522-526	3-03-65	HR	774
105	83	13	526-528	3-03-65	HR	761
106	84	13	528-529	3-03-65	HR	779
107	85	13	529-530	3-03-65	S	380
108	86	13	530	3-03-65	S	463
109	87	13	530-531	3-03-65	HR	558
110	88	13	531-532	3-03-65	S	91
111	89	13	532-533	3-03-65	HR	697
112	90	13	533	3-03-65	S	387
113	91	13	533	3-03-65	HR	657
114	92	13	533-534	3-03-65	S	478
115	93	13	534	3-03-65	HR	775
116	94	13	535	3-03-65	S	70
117	95	13	535	3-03-65	HR	780
118	96	13	535-536	3-03-65	S	451
119	97	13	536-537	3-03-65	S	411
120	98	13	537-538	3-03-65	HR	764
121	99	13	538	3-03-65	HR	749
122	100	13	538-539	3-03-65	S	370
123	101	13	539	3-03-65	S	318
124	102	13	539	3-03-65	HR	605
125	103	13	539-540	3-03-65	S	452
126	104	13	540-541	3-03-65	S	468
127	105	13	541-563	3-03-65	HR	682

RESOLUTIONS OF THE THIRTY-EIGHTH CONGRESS

1	1	13	565	12-15-64	H Res.	114
3	2	13	565	12-20-64	S Res.	83
4	3	13	565	12-20-64	S Res.	84
5	4	13	565-566	1-10-65	H Res.	131
6	5	13	566	1-18-65	H Res.	56
7	6	13	566	1-24-65	S Res.	98
8	7	13	566-567	1-24-65	S Res.	99
9	8	13	567	1-25-65	H Res.	140
10	9	13	567	1-30-65	H Res.	99
11	10	13	567	2-01-65	S Res.	16
12	11	13	567-568	2-08-65	H Res.	126

RESOLUTIONS OF THE THIRTY-EIGHTH CONGRESS

Public Law/Resolution		Statutes at Large	Page	Date	Bill No.
Chapter	Number				
13	12	13	568	2-09-65	H Res. 91
14	13	13	568	2-09-65	H Res.142
15	14	13	568	2-14-65	S Res.106
16	15	13	569	2-14-65	S Res. 91
17	16	13	569	2-17-65	S Res, 42
18	17	13	569	2-23-65	H Res. 45
19	18	13	569	2-23-65	H Res.143
20	19	13	570	2-25-65	H Res.173
23	20	13	570	2-28-65	H Res. 82
24	21	13	570	3-02-65	H Res.169
25	22	13	570	3-02-65	H Res.164
27	23	13	571	3-03-65	S Res.111
28	24	13	571	3-03-65	H Res.139
29	25	13	571	3-03-65	S Res. 82
30	26	13	571-572	3-03-65	S Res. 90
31	27	13	572	3-03-65	S Res.122
32	28	13	572	3-03-65	H Res.174
33	29	13	572-573	3-03-65	S Res. 89
34	30	13	573	3-03-65	S Res.123
35	31	13	573	3-03-65	S Res.125
36	32	13	573	3-03-65	S Res.105
37	33	13	574	3-03-65	S Res.121

PUBLIC ACTS OF THE THIRTY-NINTH CONGRESS

Public Law/Resolution		Statutes at Large	Page	Date	Bill No.	
Chapter	Number					
1	1	14	1	12-18-65	HR	24
2	2	14	1-2	12-18-65	HR	23
3	3	14	2	12-18-65	HR	35
5	4	14	2	1-15-66	HR	58
6	5	14	2-3	2-07-66	HR	36
8	6	14	3	2-10-66	HR	204
9	7	14	3	2-10-66	S	86
10	8	14	3	2-16-66	S	96
12	9	14	3-4	3-06-66	HR	321
13	10	14	4	3-08-66	S	93
15	11	14	4-5	3-10-66	HR	201
16	12	14	5-8	3-14-66	HR	61
17	13	14	8	3-14-66	HR	135
18	14	14	9	3-16-66	HR	154
19	15	14	9	3-17-66	S	33
20	16	14	9	3-17-66	HR	358
21	17	14	10-11	3-21-66	S	54
22	18	14	12	3-21-66	S	36
24	19	14	12-13	4-05-66	S	165
25	20	14	13	4-05-66	S	216
26	21	14	14	4-05-66	S	107
27	22	14	14	4-06-66	S	94
28	23	14	14-26	4-07-66	HR	86
29	24	14	26	4-07-66	HR	420
31	25	14	27-30	4-09-66	S	61
32	26	14	30-31	4-10-66	S	85
33	27	14	31	4-10-66	S	105
39	28	14	31-32	4-12-66	HR	207
40	29	14	32	4-12-66	HR	360
41	30	14	32	4-12-66	HR	223
44	31	14	32-33	4-13-66	S	199
45	32	14	33-38	4-17-66	HR	122
46	33	14	38-39	4-17-66	S	31
47	34	14	39-40	4-17-66	S	229
48	35	14	40	4-17-66	HR	471
63	36	14	40	4-20-66	HR	184
65	37	14	40-41	4-25-66	S	891
68	38	14	41	4-26-66	HR	500
70	39	14	41-42	5-02-66	S	158
71	40	14	42-43	5-02-66	S	255
72	41	14	43	5-03-66	HR	197
73	42	14	43	5-03-66	S	155

PUBLIC ACTS OF THE THIRTY-NINTH CONGRESS

Public Law/Resolution		Statutes at Large	Page	Date	Bill No.	
Chapter	Number					
74	43	14	44	5-05-66	S	26
75	44	14	44	5-09-66	HR	473
76	45	14	45	5-09-66	S	90
79	46	14	45	5-10-66	HR	352
80	47	14	46-47	5-11-66	HR	238
81	48	14	47-48	5-16-66	HR	397
82	49	14	48	5-16-66	HR	511
83	50	14	48	5-16-66	S	310
84	51	14	48	5-16-66	HR	567
85	52	14	48-50	5-18-66	HR	280
86	53	14	50	5-21-66	S	132
87	54	14	51	5-21-66	S	316
88	55	14	51	5-21-66	S	186
89	56	14	51-52	5-22-66	HR	563
96	57	14	52-53	5-24-66	HR	510
97	58	14	53	5-24-66	HR	558
100	59	14	54	5-24-66	S	318
102	60	14	54	5-26-66	HR	568
103	61	14	54-55	5-30-66	S	184
104	62	14	55-56	6-01-66	S	167
105	63	14	56	6-01-66	S	208
106	64	14	56-58	6-01-66	HR	363
110	65	14	58-59	6-06-66	HR	37
111	66	14	59	6-08-66	HR	654
114	67	14	59-61	6-08-66	HR	281
115	68	14	61-62	6-12-66	HR	255
116	69	14	62-63	6-12-66	HR	15
117	70	14	64	6-12-66	S	140
122	71	14	64-65	6-14-66	HR	621
123	72	14	65-66	6-15-66	HR	406
124	73	14	66	6-15-66	HR	11
126	74	14	66	6-18-66	S	350
127	75	14	66-67	6-21-66	HR	85
128	76	14	68	6-21-66	S	230
129	77	14	69	6-21-66	S	774
130	78	14	69-70	6-21-66	HR	482
131	79	14	70	6-21-66	S	360
132	80	14	70	6-21-66	S	307
138	81	14	70-74	6-23-66	HR	492
140	82	14	74-75	6-27-66	S	59

PUBLIC ACTS OF THE THIRTY-NINTH CONGRESS

Public Law/Resolution		Statutes at Large	Page	Date	Bill No.	
Chapter	Number					
141	83	14	75-76	6-27-66	S	330
142	84	14	76	6-27-66	S	381
143	85	14	76-77	6-27-66	HR	342
144	86	14	77	6-27-66	HR	249
155	87	14	77	6-29-66	HR	179
156	88	14	77	6-29-66	HR	391
158	89	14	78-79	7-03-66	S	243
159	90	14	79-80	7-03-66	S	317
160	91	14	80-81	7-03-66	S	219
161	92	14	81	7-03-66	S	193
162	93	14	81-82	7-03-66	S	313
163	94	14	82	7-03-66	HR	18
164	95	14	82-83	7-03-66	S	30
165	96	14	83-85	7-04-66	S	37
166	97	14	85-86	7-04-66	S	215
167	98	14	86-87	7-04-66	S	58
168	99	14	87-88	7-04-66	S	156
169	100	14	88-89	7-04-66	S	168
174	101	14	89	7-05-66	S	99
175	102	14	90	7-05-66	HR	725
176	103	14	90-93	7-13-66	HR	127
177	104	14	93	7-13-66	HR	730
178	105	14	93	7-13-66	HR	191
179	106	14	93-94	7-13-66	HR	726
180	107	14	94	7-13-66	HR	611
181	108	14	94	7-13-66	HR	456
182	109	14	94-97	7-13-66	S	125
183	110	14	97	7-13-66	S	221
184	111	14	98-173	7-13-66	HR	513
200	112	14	173-177	7-16-66	HR	613
201	113	14	178-188	7-18-66	S	222
202	114	14	189-191	7-18-66	S	369
208	115	14	191-208	7-23-66	HR	213
209	116	14	208-209	7-23-66	HR	50
210	117	14	209	7-23-66	HR	334
211	118	14	209-210	7-23-66	HR	557
212	119	14	210-212	7-23-66	S	145
213	120	14	212	7-23-66	HR	727
214	121	14	212	7-23-66	HR	448
215	122	14	212-215	7-23-66	S	137

Public Law/Resolution		Statutes at Large	Page	Date	Bill No.	
Chapter	Number					
216	123	14	215-216	7-23-66	S	325
217	124	14	216	7-23-66	S	246
218	125	14	217-218	7-23-66	S	178
219	126	14	218-221	7-23-66	S	343
230	127	14	221-222	7-24-66	S	357
231	128	14	222-223	7-25-66	S	269
232	129	14	223	7-25-66	HR	3
233	130	14	224-226	7-25-66	HR	261
234	131	14	227-229	7-25-66	HR	447
235	132	14	230-231	7-25-66	HR	692
236	133	14	231-232	7-25-66	HR	124
237	134	14	232	7-25-66	HR	564
238	135	14	232-235	7-25-66	HR	379
239	136	14	235	7-25-66	HR	587
240	137	14	236	7-25-66	HR	615
241	138	14	236-239	7-25-66	S	285
242	139	14	239-242	7-25-66	S	123
243	140	14	242	7-25-66	S	382
244	141	14	242-243	7-25-66	S	352
245	142	14	243-244	7-25-66	S	414
246	143	14	244-246	7-25-66	S	236
247	144	14	246	7-25-66	S	361
248	145	14	247	7-25-66	HR	93
249	146	14	247-248	7-25-66	HR	779
250	147	14	248-249	7-25-66	HR	230
251	148	14	250	7-25-66	HR	559
252	149	14	250	7-25-66	HR	729
253	150	14	251	7-25-66	HR	601
254	151	14	251	7-25-66	HR	776
255	152	14	251	7-25-66	HR	795
262	153	14	251-253	7-26-66	HR	365
263	154	14	253-255	7-26-66	S	281
264	155	14	255	7-26-66	HR	798
265	156	14	255	7-26-66	HR	772
266	157	14	255-280	7-26-66	HR	387
267	158	14	280-288	7-26-66	HR	775
268	159	14	288	7-26-66	HR	438
269	160	14	289	7-26-66	HR	480
270	161	14	289-291	7-26-66	S	224

PUBLIC ACTS OF THE THIRTY-NINTH CONGRESS

Public Law/Resolution		Statutes at Large	Page	Date	Bill No.	
Chapter	Number					
277	162	14	291-292	7-27-66	S	424
278	163	14	292-299	7-27-66	S	20
279	164	14	299-300	7-27-66	S	214
280	165	14	300-301	7-27-66	S	179
281	166	14	301	7-27-66	HR	597
282	167	14	301	7-27-66	HR	759
283	168	14	301-302	7-27-66	HR	810
284	169	14	302-304	7-27-66	S	39
285	170	14	304	7-27-66	HR	814
286	171	14	304	7-27-66	S	334
287	172	14	305-306	7-27-66	HR	809
288	173	14	306-307	7-27-66	S	406
289	174	14	307-308	7-27-66	HR	761
293	175	14	308-309	7-28-66	S	400
294	176	14	309	7-28-66	S	43
295	177	14	309-310	7-28-66	S	353
296	178	14	310-323	7-28-66	HR	767
297	179	14	324-327	7-28-66	HR	791
298	180	14	328-331	7-28-66	HR	780
299	181	14	332-338	7-28-66	S	138
300	182	14	338-339	7-28-66	S	223
301	183	14	339-340	7-28-66	HR	596
302	184	14	341	7-28-66	HR	612
303	185	14	341-342	7-28-66	HR	801
304	186	14	342	7-28-66	HR	62
305	187	14	342	7-28-66	HR	792
306	188	14	342-343	7-28-66	HR	815
307	189	14	343	7-28-66	S	265
308	190	14	343	7-28-66	S	247
309	191	14	343	7-28-66	HR	32
310	192	14	344	7-28-66	HR	468
311	193	14	344	7-28-66	HR	491
312	194	14	344-345	7-28-66	HR	667

RESOLUTIONS OF THE THIRTY-NINTH CONGRESS

1	1	14	347	12-21-65	S Res.	6
2	2	14	347	1-12-66	S Res.	7
3	3	14	347-348	1-15-66	H Res.	28
4	4	14	348	1-22-66	H Res.	18
5	5	14	348	1-31-66	H Res.	53
6	6	14	348	2-07-66	S Res.	17

RESOLUTIONS OF THE THIRTY-NINTH CONGRESS

Public Law/Resolution		Statutes at Large	Page	Date	Bill No.
Chapter	Number				
7	7	14	349	2-10-66	S Res. 20
8	8	14	349	2-10-66	S Res. 25
9	9	14	349	2-10-66	S Res. 26
10	10	14	350	2-26-66	H Res. 75
11	11	14	350	3-10-66	S Res. 36
12	12	14	350	3-10-66	H Res. 17
13	13	14	351	3-10-66	H Res. 76
14	14	14	351	3-17-66	H Res. 84
15	15	14	351	3-22-66	H Res. 45
16	16	14	351	3-24-66	H Res. 57
17	17	14	352	3-31-66	S Res. 50
18	18	14	352	4-04-66	H Res. 96
19	19	14	352	4-05-66	S Res. 2
20	20	14	352	4-12-66	H Res.105
21	21	14	353	4-13-66	S Res. 58
24	22	14	353	4-17-66	S Res. 45
25	23	14	353	4-17-66	S Res. 49
26	24	14	353	4-21-66	H Res.108
27	25	14	354	4-21-66	H Res. 88
29	26	14	354	4-25-66	S Res. 29
31	27	14	354	5-03-66	S Res. 75
32	28	14	354-355	5-03-66	S Res. 34
34	29	14	355	5-07-66	S Res. 80
35	30	14	355	5-09-66	H Res.137
37	31	14	355	5-09-66	H Res.133
38	32	14	356	5-16-66	H Res. 66
39	33	14	356	5-16-66	S Res. 88
40	34	14	356	5-21-66	S Res. 61
41	35	14	356	5-26-66	S Res. 97
42	36	14	357	5-26-66	H Res.116
43	37	14	357	5-26-66	S Res. 74
44	38	14	357	6-01-66	S Res. 92
45	39	14	357	6-06-66	H Res.142
46	40	14	357-358	6-15-66	S Res. 51
47	41	14	358	6-15-66	S Res. 69
48	41½	14	358-359	6-16-66	H Res.127
49	42	14	359-360	6-16-66	H Res.134
50	43	14	360	6-18-66	H Res.120
51	44	14	360	6-18-66	H Res.143
52	45	14	360	6-21-66	S Res. 87

Public Law/Resolution		Statutes at Large	Page	Date	Bill No.
Chapter	Number				
53	46	14	360-361	6-22-66	S Res. 85
55	47	14	361	6-23-66	S Res.100
57	48	14	361	6-23-66	H Res.148
58	49	14	361-362	7-03-66	H Res.166
62	50	14	362	7-03-66	S Res.113
63	51	14	362	7-03-66	S Res.110
66	52	14	362-363	7-05-66	H Res. 52
67	53	14	363	7-13-66	H Res.149
69	54	14	364	7-14-66	S Res.129
73	55	14	364	7-24-66	H Res. 83
74	56	14	364	7-25-66	H Res.190
75	57	14	365	7-25-66	H Res.178
76	58	14	365	7-25-66	H Res.159
77	59	14	365	7-25-66	S Res. 79
79	60	14	365-366	7-26-66	S Res. 31
80	61	14	366	7-26-66	S Res.126
81	62	14	366	7-26-66	S Res.139
82	63	14	366	7-26-66	S Res. 84
83	64	14	367	7-26-66	S Res. 82
84	65	14	367	7-26-66	S Res.121
85	66	14	367	7-26-66	S Res.125
86	67	14	367-368	7-26-66	H Res.176
87	68	14	368	7-26-66	H Res.101
90	69	14	369	7-27-66	S Res.133
91	70	14	369	7-27-66	S Res. 86
92	71	14	369	7-27-66	S Res.131
93	72	14	369	7-27-66	H Res.140
96	73	14	370	7-28-66	H Res.208
97	74	14	370	7-28-66	H Res.199
98	75	14	370	7-28-66	H Res.197
99	76	14	370-371	7-28-66	H Res.195
100	77	14	371	7-28-66	H Res.193
101	78	14	371	7-28-66	H Res.200
102	79	14	371	7-28-66	H Res.155

PUBLIC ACTS OF THE THIRTY-NINTH CONGRESS

Public Law/Resolution		Statutes at Large	Page	Date	Bill No.	
Chapter	Number					
4	1	14	373-374	12-20-66	HR	876
5	2	14	374-375	12-26-66	S	62
6	3	14	375-376	1-08-67	S	1
7	4	14	376-377	1-14-67	S	459
8	5	14	377	1-21-67	HR	828
9	6	14	377	1-22-67	HR	715
10	7	14	378	1-22-67	HR	830
11	8	14	378	1-22-67	HR	964
12	9	14	378-379	1-22-67	S	177
15	10	14	379-380	1-25-67	HR	508
16	11	14	380-382	1-31-67	S	380
17	12	14	382-383	1-31-67	S	253
26	13	14	383-385	2-05-67	HR	719
27	14	14	385	2-05-67	HR	755
28	15	14	385-387	2-05-67	HR	605
29	16	14	387-389	2-05-67	HR	388
30	17	14	389-390	2-05-67	S	218
31	18	14	390	2-05-67	S	479
32	19	14	391	2-05-67	S	69
34	20	14	391	2-08-67	HR	1090
36	21	14	391-392	2-09-67	S	456
37	22	14	393	2-12-67	HR	1144
38	23	14	393	2-12-67	HR	1127
41	24	14	393-394	2-18-67	HR	918
42	25	14	394	2-18-67	S	525
43	26	14	395	2-18-67	S	491
44	27	14	395	2-18-67	HR	1128
45	28	14	395	2-18-67	HR	1141
46	29	14	396	2-18-67	HR	452
47	30	14	396	2-18-67	S	506
48	31	14	397	2-18-67	HR	183
56	32	14	397	2-21-67	HR	874
57	33	14	397-398	2-21-67	HR	902
58	34	14	398	2-22-67	HR	903
59	35	14	398-399	2-22-67	HR	1099
60	36	14	399	2-22-67	HR	643
61	37	14	399-401	2-22-67	HR	788
62	38	14	401	2-22-67	HR	848
63	39	14	401-403	2-22-67	HR	571

PUBLIC ACTS OF THE THIRTY-NINTH CONGRESS

Public Law/Resolution		Statutes at Large	Page	Date	Bill No.	
Chapter	Number					
64	40	14	403-406	2-22-67	HR	907
65	41	14	406-408	2-22-67	HR	431
66	42	14	408	2-22-67	HR	140
67	43	14	408	2-22-67	HR	356
76	44	14	408-409	2-25-67	S	421
77	45	14	409	2-25-67	HR	910
78	46	14	410	2-25-67	S	605
79	47	14	410	2-25-67	HR	1130
80	48	14	410	2-25-67	HR	607
81	49	14	410-411	2-25-67	S	347
82	50	14	411	2-25-67	S	399
83	51	14	411-412	2-25-67	S	467
98	52	14	412	2-27-67	HR	965
99	53	14	412-415	2-28-67	HR	904
100	54	14	415-416	2-28-67	HR	912
101	55	14	416	2-28-67	HR	900
102	56	14	417	2-28-67	HR	811
103	57	14	417-418	2-28-67	HR	1062
143	58	14	418	3-01-67	HR	878
144	59	14	418-422	3-02-67	HR	1154
145	60	14	422-423	3-02-67	S	592
146	61	14	424	3-02-67	S	460
147	62	14	424	3-02-67	S	220
148	63	14	425	3-02-67	S	547
149	64	14	425-426	3-02-67	HR	1166
150	65	14	426-427	3-02-67	S	501
151	66	14	427	3-02-67	S	490
152	67	14	428	3-02-67	S	550
153	68	14	428-430	3-02-67	HR	1143
154	69	14	430-432	3-02-67	S	453
155	70	14	432-433	3-02-67	HR	859
156	71	14	433	3-02-67	S	534
157	72	14	433-434	3-02-67	S	477
158	73	14	434	3-02-67	HR	276
159	74	14	434-435	3-02-67	HR	1134
160	75	14	435	3-02-67	S	264
161	76	14	435-438	3-02-67	S	124
162	77	14	438-439	3-02-67	S	529
163	78	14	439-440	3-02-67	S	493
164	79	14	440	3-02-67	S	589

PUBLIC ACTS OF THE THIRTY-NINTH CONGRESS

Public Law/Resolution		Statutes at Large	Page	Date	Bill No.	
Chapter	Number					
165	80	14	440	3-02-67	S	570
166	81	14	440-457	3-02-67	HR	896
167	82	14	457-468	3-02-67	HR	1173
168	83	14	468-471	3-02-67	HR	1227
169	84	14	471-485	3-02-67	HR	1161
170	85	14	485-487	3-02-67	HR	1126
171	86	14	487-489	3-02-67	HR	1184
172	87	14	489-492	3-02-67	HR	1176
173	88	14	492-515	3-02-67	HR	1039
174	89	14	515-517	3-02-67	S	509
175	90	14	517	3-02-67	S	634
176	91	14	517-541	3-02-67	HR	598
177	92	14	541-542	3-02-67	S	532
178	93	14	542	3-02-67	S	609
179	94	14	542-543	3-02-67	HR	746
180	95	14	543	3-02-67	S	563
181	96	14	543	3-02-67	S	614
182	97	14	543-544	3-02-67	S	603
183	98	14	544	3-02-67	S	625
184	99	14	544	3-02-67	S	578
185	100	14	545	3-02-67	S	576
186	101	14	545	3-02-67	S	595
187	102	14	546	3-02-67	S	543
188	103	14	546-547	3-02-67	S	577
189	104	14	548-550	3-02-67	HR	865
190	105	14	550-551	3-02-67	HR	1234
191	106	14	551-556	3-02-67	HR	1182
192	107	14	556-557	3-02-67	HR	234
193	108	14	557	3-02-67	HR	604
194	109	14	558	3-02-67	HR	1220
195	110	14	558	3-02-67	HR	710
196	111	14	558-559	3-02-67	S	606
197	112	14	559-562	3-02-67	HR	793

RESOLUTIONS OF THE THIRTY-NINTH CONGRESS

1	1	14	563	12-07-66	H Res.	212
3	2	14	563	1-11-67	S Res.	154
4	3	14	563	1-14-67	H Res.	221
5	4	14	563-564	1-22-67	H Res.	229

RESOLUTIONS OF THE THIRTY-NINTH CONGRESS

Public Law/Resolution		Statutes at Large	Page	Date	Bill No.
Chapter	Number				
6	5	14	564	1-22-67	S Res.151
7	6	14	564	1-29-67	H Res.227
8	7	14	564-565	1-29-67	S Res.156
11	8	14	565	2-05-67	H Res.244
12	9	14	565	2-08-67	S Res. 94
14	10	14	565-566	2-18-67	S Res.163
15	11	14	566	2-18-67	S Res.157
16	12	14	566	2-18-67	H Res.206
17	13	14	566	2-18-67	H Res.263
21	14	14	567	2-22-67	H Res.251
22	15	14	567	2-22-67	H Res.216
23	16	14	567	2-22-67	H Res.293
26	17	14	567	2-25-67	S Res.149
27	18	14	567-568	2-25-67	S Res.159
28	19	14	568	2-25-67	S Res. 90
30	20	14	569	2-28-67	H Rés.224
31	21	14	569	2-28-67	H Res.213
32	22	14	569-570	2-28-67	H Res.275
33	23	14	570	2-28-67	H Res.290
42	24	14	570	3-01-67	H Res. 92
44	25	14	570	3-02-67	S Res.182
45	26	14	571	3-02-67	H Res.205
46	27	14	571	3-02-67	H Res.222
47	28	14	571	3-02-67	H Res.305
48	29	14	571-572	3-02-67	S Res.173
49	30	14	572	3-02-67	S Res.178
50	31	14	572	3-02-67	H Res.226
51	32	14	572	3-02-67	S Res.181
52	33	14	572-573	3-02-67	S Res.183
53	34	14	573	3-02-67	S Res.176
54	35	14	573	3-02-67	H Res.303
55	36	14	573	3-02-67	S Res.179
56	37	14	573-574	3-02-67	H Res.267
57	38	14	574	3-02-67	S Res.148
58	39	14	574	3-02-67	H Res.297
59	40	14	575	3-02-67	H Res.283
60	41	14	575	3-02-67	H Res.304

PUBLIC ACTS OF THE FORTIETH CONGRESS

Public Law/Resolution		Statutes at Large	Page	Date	Bill No.	
Chapter	Number					
1	1	15	1	3-12-67	S	31
2	2	15	1	3-14-67	HR	1
3	3	15	1	3-16-67	S	49
4	4	15	1-2	3-22-67	HR	19
5	5	15	2	3-22-67	S	22
6	6	15	2-5	3-23-67	HR	33
7	7	15	5-6	3-25-67	S	61
8	8	15	6	3-26-67	HR	72
9	9	15	6	3-26-67	S	38
10	10	15	6	3-26-67	S	77
11	11	15	7	3-28-67	S	63
12	12	15	7	3-28-67	S	80
13	13	15	7-9	3-29-67	S	83
14	14	15	9-10	3-29-67	S	105
15	15	15	10	3-29-67	S	28
16	16	15	10	3-29-67	S	96
17	17	15	10-11	3-29-67	HR	28
18	18	15	11	3-29-67	S	112
20	19	15	11-12	3-30-67	HR	79
21	20	15	12-13	3-30-67	S	114
22	21	15	13	3-30-67	S	122
23	22	15	13	3-30-67	S	86
24	23	15	13	3-30-67	S	64
27	24	15	13	7-19-67	HR	130
28	25	15	14	7-19-67	HR	108
29	26	15	14	7-19-67	HR	107
30	27	15	14-16	7-19-67	HR	123
32	28	15	17-18	7-20-67	S	136
33	29	15	18	7-20-67	S	138
34	30	15	18	7-20-67	HR	137

RESOLUTIONS OF THE FORTIETH CONGRESS

1	1	15	19-20	3-12-67	S Res.	2
2	2	15	20	3-12-67	S Res.	6
3	3	15	20	3-16-67	S Res.	1
4	4	15	20	3-16-67	S Res.	15
5	5	15	21	3-22-67	H Res.	2
6	6	15	21	3-22-67	H Res.	10
7	7	15	21	3-22-67	H Res.	17
8	8	15	21	3-22-67	H Res.	20
9	9	15	21-22	3-22-67	S Res.	26

RESOLUTIONS OF THE FORTIETH CONGRESS

Public Law/Resolution		Statutes at Large	Page	Date	Bill No.
Chapter	Number				
10	10	15	22	3-22-67	S Res. 30
11	11	15	22	3-25-67	H Res. 16
12	12	15	22-23	3-26-67	S Res. 29
13	13	15	23	3-26-67	H Res. 25
14	14	15	23	3-26-67	S Res. 25
15	15	15	23	3-27-67	S Res. 39
16	16	15	24	3-28-67	S Res. 22
17	17	15	24	3-29-67	H Res. 50
18	18	15	24	3-29-67	H Res. 39
19	19	15	24	3-29-67	H Res. 47
20	20	15	25	3-27-67	H Res. 41
21	21	15	25	3-29-67	H Res. 37
22	22	15	25	3-29-67	H Res. 26
23	23	15	25-26	3-29-67	H Res. 21
24	24	15	26	3-29-67	S Res. 43
25	25	15	26-27	3-29-67	S Res. 21
26	26	15	27	3-29-67	S Res. 24
27	27	15	28	3-29-67	S Res. 48
28	28	15	28	3-30-67	S Res. 16
29	29	15	28	3-30-67	S Res. 51
30	30	15	28	3-30-67	S Res. 19
31	31	15	29	3-30-67	H Res. 15
32	32	15	29	3-30-67	H Res. 7
33	33	15	29	3-30-67	S Res. 35
34	34	15	29	3-30-67	S Res. 41
38	35	15	30	7-19-67	H Res. 69
39	36	15	30	7-19-67	H Res. 71
40	37	15	30-31	7-20-67	H Res. 78
41	38	15	31	7-20-67	S Res. 63

PUBLIC ACTS OF THE FORTIETH CONGRESS

Public Law/Resolution		Statutes at Large	Page	Date	Bill No.	
Chapter	Number					
1	1	15	33	12-14-67	HR	155
2	2	15	33	12-20-67	S	143
3	3	15	34	1-11-68	HR	369
5	4	15	34	2-03-68	HR	207
6	5	15	34	2-04-68	HR	213
7	6	15	34	2-10-68	HR	512
8	7	15	35-36	2-12-68	HR	320
9	8	15	36-37	2-21-68	HR	510
10	9	15	37	2-21-68	HR	96
11	10	15	37	2-21-68	HR	127
13	11	15	37	2-25-68	S	306
15	12	15	38	3-02-68	HR	296
16	13	15	38	3-02-68	HR	208
17	14	15	39	3-02-68	HR	223
19	15	15	39	3-04-68	HR	368
20	16	15	39	3-06-68	HR	660
21	17	15	39	3-06-68	HR	358
22	18	15	40-41	3-09-68	S	237
24	19	15	41	3-10-68	S	270
25	20	15	41	3-11-68	HR	214
26	21	15	42	3-12-68	HR	785
27	22	15	42	3-12-68	HR	274
29	23	15	42	3-16-68	S	376
30	24	15	42-43	3-16-68	HR	599
31	25	15	43-44	3-19-68	HR	331
34	26	15	44	3-27-68	S	213
35	27	15	45-54	3-30-68	HR	328
36	28	15	54	3-30-68	S	350
37	29	15	55-56	3-30-68	HR	832
38	30	15	56-58	3-30-68	HR	718
41	31	15	58-60	3-31-68	HR	900
43	32	15	60	5-19-68	S	462
46	33	15	60-61	5-20-68	HR	1062
48	34	15	61-62	5-28-68	S	475
49	35	15	63	5-30-68	HR	1045
50	36	15	63	6-05-68	HR	786
51	37	15	63-64	6-08-68	HR	1117
52	38	15	64-66	6-08-68	HR	658
53	39	15	67	6-08-68	S	188
54	40	15	67	6-08-68	S	331
55	41	15	67-68	6-08-68	S	190

PUBLIC ACTS OF THE FORTIETH CONGRESS

Public Law/Resolution		Statutes at Large	Page	Date	Bill No.	
Chapter	Number					
61	42	15	68-72	6-17-68	HR	601
69	43	15	72-73	6-22-68	HR	1039
70	44	15	73-74	6-25-68	HR	1058
71	45	15	75-77	6-25-68	S	164
72	46	15	77	6-25-68	HR	365
73	47	15	78	6-25-68	HR	764
74	48	15	78	6-25-68	HR	198
75	49	15	78	6-25-68	HR	538
76	50	15	79	6-25-68	HR	176
77	51	15	79	6-25-68	S	450
78	52	15	80	6-25-68	HR	1218
79	53	15	80	6-25-68	S	377
80	54	15	80	6-25-68	S	216
81	55	15	80	6-25-68	HR	861
82	56	15	81	6-25-68	HR	1120
117	57	15	81-82	6-27-68	S	534
118	58	15	82	7-03-68	HR	347
131	59	15	82	7-04-68	S	469
134	60	15	82	7-06-68	HR	1027
135	63	15	83-84	7-06-68	HR	598
136	61	15	84	7-07-68	HR	502
137	62	15	84	7-07-68	S	505
139	64	15	85	7-11-68	HR	869
140	65	15	85-88	7-13-68	HR	420
141	66	15	88-89	7-13-68	HR	366
142	67	15	89-90	7-13-68	HR	650
143	79	15	90-91	7-13-68	HR	1068
175	68	15	91-92	7-16-68	HR	202
176	69	15	92-110	7-20-68	HR	605
177	70	15	110-120	7-20-68	HR	818
178	71	15	120-121	7-20-68	S	486
179	72	15	121-122	7-20-68	S	355
180	73	15	122	7-20-68	HR	1119
181	74	15	123	7-20-68	S	564
182	75	15	123	7-20-68	HR	631
183	76	15	123-124	7-20-68	HR	550
184	77	15	124	7-20-68	HR	485
185	78	15	125	7-20-68	HR	201
186	79	15	125-168	7-20-68	HR	1284
226	80	15	168	7-23-68	HR	761
227	81	15	168-169	7-23-68	S	352

Public Law/Resolution		Statutes at Large	Page	Date	Bill No.	
Chapter	Number					
228	82	15	169	7-23-68	HR	554
229	83	15	170	7-23-68	HR	678
230	84	15	170-171	7-23-68	HR	344
233	85	15	171-177	7-25-68	HR	1341
234	86	15	177-178	7-25-68	HR	1376
235	87	15	178-183	7-25-68	S	357
236	88	15	183	7-25-68	S	509
237	89	15	183	7-25-68	S	543
238	90	15	184	7-25-68	S	252
239	91	15	184-186	7-25-68	S	286
240	92	15	186	7-25-68	S	481
241	93	15	186-187	7-25-68	S	433
242	94	15	187	7-25-68	S	492
243	95	15	187-188	7-25-68	HR	451
244	96	15	188-193	7-25-68	HR	1427
245	97	15	193-194	7-25-68	S	567
246	98	15	194-197	7-27-68	HR	1205
247	99	15	198	7-27-68	HR	1096
248	100	15	198-223	7-27-68	HR	1073
249	101	15	223-224	7-27-68	HR	76
250	102	15	224	7-27-68	S	579
251	103	15	225	7-27-68	S	540
252	104	15	225	7-27-68	S	209
253	105	15	226	7-27-68	S	637
254	106	15	226	7-27-68	S	442
255	107	15	226-227	7-27-68	S	472
256	108	15	227	7-27-68	HR	23
257	109	15	227	7-27-68	HR	1444
258	110	15	227-228	7-27-68	HR	1021
259	111	15	228	7-27-68	HR	1375
260	112	15	229-231	7-27-68	HR	939
261	113	15	231-232	7-27-68	HR	1275
262	114	15	232-234	7-27-68	HR	541
263	115	15	234	7-27-68	HR	1448
264	116	15	235-237	7-27-68	HR	1010
265	117	15	237	7-27-68	HR	1457
266	118	15	238	7-27-68	HR	1455
267	119	15	238	7-27-68	HR	1052
268	120	15	238	7-27-68	HR	1447
269	121	15	238-239	7-27-68	S	16

PUBLIC ACTS OF THE FORTIETH CONGRESS

Public Law/Resolution		Statutes at Large	Page	Date	Bill No.	
Chapter	Number					
270	122	15	239	7-27-68	S	604
271	123	15	239	7-27-68	S	487
272	124	15	239-240	7-27-68	S	417
273	125	15	240-242	7-27-68	S	619
274	126	15	242	7-27-68	S	621
275	127	15	242	7-27-68	S	576
276	128	15	243-244	7-27-68	HR	1131

RESOLUTIONS OF THE FORTIETH CONGRESS

1	1	15	245	12-20-67	H Res.119
2	2	15	245	12-20-67	H Res.112
3	3	15	245	1-11-68	S Res. 80
4	4	15	246	1-11-68	H Res.130
5	5	15	246	1-11-68	S Res. 83
7	6	15	246	1-31-68	H Res.171
8	7	15	246	1-31-68	S Res. 85
9	8	15	246-247	2-03-68	H Res.140
10	9	15	247	2-03-68	H Res.136
11	10	15	247-248	2-21-68	H Res.203
12	11	15	248	2-22-68	S Res. 99
13	12	15	248	2-28-68	S Res.114
14	13	15	248	3-02-68	H Res.104
15	14	15	248-249	3-02-68	H Res.105
16	15	15	249	3-02-68	S Res. 95
17	16	15	249	3-02-68	S Res.108
18	17	15	249	3-12-68	S Res. 89
19	18	15	250	3-12-68	S Res.111
20	19	15	250	3-12-68	H Res.228
23	20	15	250	3-16-68	S Res.117
24	21	15	250-251	3-24-68	H Res.226
25	22	15	251	3-30-68	H Res. 19
28	23	15	251-252	5-19-68	S Res.118
30	24	15	252	5-20-68	H Res. 91
31	25	15	252	6-05-68	H Res.279
32	26	15	253	6-08-68	H Res.278
33	27	15	253	6-10-68	H Res.284
34	28	15	253	6-11-68	H Res.251
37	29	15	254	6-19-68	H Res.137
38	30	15	254	6-25-68	H Res.262

Public Law/Resolution		Statutes at Large	Page	Date	Bill No.
Chapter	Number				
39	31	15	254	6-25-68	S Res.134
40	32	15	254	6-25-68	H Res.264
41	33	15	254-255	6-25-68	H Res.246
42	34	15	255	6-25-68	H Res.216
43	35	15	255	6-25-68	H Res.294
47	36	15	255	7-01-68	H Res.316
48	37	15	256	7-03-68	S Res.129
49	38	15	256	7-03-68	H Res.312
51	39	15	256	7-06-68	H Res.318
52	40	15	256	7-07-68	H Res.321
54	41	15	256	7-13-68	S Res. 81
55	42	15	257	7-13-68	S Res.107
56	43	15	257	7-13-68	H Res.324
58	44	15	257-258	. 7-20-68	S Res.139
59	45	15	258	7-20-68	S Res.113
60	46	15	258-259	7-20-68	H Res.201
61	47	15	259	7-20-68	H Res.292
62	48	15	259	7-20-68	H Res.281
63	49	15	259-260	7-20-68	H Res.331
64	50	15	260	7-20-68	H Res.338
67	51	15	260	7-23-68	H Res.343
68	52	15	260	7-23-68	H Res.354
69	53	15	260	7-23-68	H Res.329
72	54	15	260-261	7-25-68	S Res.121
73	55	15	261	7-25-68	S Res. 93
74	56	15	261	7-27-68	S Res.154
75	57	15	261-262	7-27-68	S Res. 57
76	58	15	262	7-27-68	H Res.323
77	59	15	262	7-27-68	H Res.345
78	60	15	262	7-27-68	H Res.328
79	61	15	263	7-27-68	H Res.358
80	62	15	263	7-27-68	H Res.296
81	63	15	263	7-27-68	S Res.151
82	64	15	263-264	7-27-68	S Res.169
83	65	15	264	7-27-68	H Res.362
84	66	15	264	7-27-68	H Res.325

PUBLIC ACTS OF THE FORTIETH CONGRESS

Public Law/Resolution		Statutes at Large	Page	Date	Bill No.	
Chapter	Number					
2	1	15	265–266	12–15–68	S	186
4	2	15	266	12–22–68	HR	1555
7	3	15	266	1–08–69	HR	1428
9	4	15	266	1–14–69	HR	1537
13	5	15	267	1–22–69	HR	1261
15	6	15	267	1–23–69	HR	1558
16	7	15	267	1–30–69	HR	1751
19	8	15	268	2–02–69	HR	1596
20	9	15	268	2–02–69	HR	1564
21	10	15	269	2–02–69	S	730
23	11	15	269	2–09–69	HR	1809
24	12	15	269	2–09–69	S	644
31	13	15	269	2–18–69	S	693
32	14	15	270	2–19–69	HR	1974
33	15	15	270–271	2–19–69	HR	264
34	16	15	271	2–19–69	S	765
35	17	15	271	2–19–69	HR	1456
36	18	15	272	2–19–69	S	667
37	19	15	272	2–19–69	HR	1856
38	20	15	273	2–19–69	HR	1861
42	21	15	273	2–22–69	HR	1906
43	22	15	274	2–22–69	S	935
45	23	15	274–275	2–24–69	HR	1460
46	24	15	275	2–25–69	HR	1858
47	23	15	275–276	2–25–69	HR	1345
48	25	15	276–280	3–01–69	HR	1599
49	26	15	280–281	3–01–69	HR	1549
50	27	15	281	3–01–69	HR	2004
51	28	15	281	3–01–69	HR	1489
52	29	15	281	3–01–69	HR	273
53	30	15	281–282	3–01–69	S	968
54	31	15	282	3–01–69	HR	1864
55	32	15	282	3–01–69	HR	2003
56	33	15	282	3–01–69	HR	424
57	34	15	282–283	3–01–69	HR	1812
121	35	15	283–301	3–03–69	HR	1672
122	36	15	301–311	3–03–69	HR	2007
123	37	15	311–315	3–03–69	HR	1911
124	38	15	315–318	3–03–69	HR	1803
125	39	15	319–322	3–03–69	HR	1570

PUBLIC ACTS OF THE FORTIETH CONGRESS

Public Law/Resolution		Statutes at Large	Page	Date	Bill No.	
Chapter	Number					
126	40	15	323	3-03-69	HR	1808
127	41	15	324	3-03-69	S	871
128	42	15	324-325	3-03-69	S	729
129	43	15	325-326	3-03-69	HR	1041
130	44	15	326-327	3-03-69	HR	1881
131	45	15	327-334	3-03-69	HR	2006
132	46	15	334	3-03-69	HR	2009
133	47	15	334	3-03-69	HR	1279
134	48	15	334-335	3-03-69	HR	1758
135	49	15	335-336	3-03-69	HR	1973
136	50	15	336	3-03-69	HR	1327
137	51	15	336	3-03-69	HR	112
138	52	15	336	3-03-69	HR	568
139	53	15	336-337	3-03-69	HR	1804
140	54	15	337	3-03-69	S	665
141	55	15	337-338	3-03-69	S	705
142	56	15	338	3-03-69	S	753
143	57	15	338	3-03-69	S	679
144	58	15	339	3-03-69	S	862
145	59	15	339	3-03-69	S	722
146	60	15	339	3-03-69	S	711
147	61	15	339	3-03-69	S	810
148	62	15	340	3-03-69	S	584
149	63	15	340	3-03-69	S	612
150	64	15	340-341	3-03-69	S	167
151	65	15	341-342	3-03-69	S	712
152	93	15	342	3-03-69	HR	1344

RESOLUTIONS OF THE FORTIETH CONGRESS

1	1	15	343	12-15-68	S Res.170
2	2	15	343	12-21-68	H Res.375
3	3	15	343	1-14-69	H Res.388
5	4	15	343-344	2-09-69	S Res.194
7	5	15	344	2-18-69	S Res.175
8	6	15	344	2-18-69	S Res.173
9	7	15	345	2-19-69	H Res.372
10	8	15	345	2-19-69	H Res.459
11	9	15	345-346	2-19-69	S Res.171
14	10	15	346	2-27-69	S Res. 8

RESOLUTIONS OF THE FORTIETH CONGRESS

Public Law/Resolution		Statutes at Large	Page	Date	Bill No.
Chapter	Number				
15	11	15	346	3-01-69	H Res.458
16	12	15	346	3-01-69	H Res.460
17	13	15	347	3-01-69	H Res.120
19	14	15	347	3-03-69	S Res.231
20	15	15	347	3-03-69	S Res.217
21	16	15	347-348	3-03-69	S Res.219
22	17	15	348	3-03-69	S Res.239
23	18	15	348	3-03-69	H Res.468
24	19	15	348	3-03-69	H Res.438
25	20	15	349	3-03-69	S Res.195
26	21	15	349	3-03-69	H Res.466
27	22	15	349	3-03-69	S Res.238
28	23	15	349	3-03-69	S Res.200
29	24	15	349	3-03-69	H Res.327

PUBLIC ACTS OF THE FORTY-FIRST CONGRESS

Public Law/Resolution		Statutes at Large	Page	Date	Bill No.	
Chapter	Number					
1	1	16	1	3-18-69	HR	7
2	2	16	1-3	3-18-69	S	25
3	3	16	3	3-18-69	S	23
5	4	16	3-6	3-29-69	S	62
9	5	16	6	4-03-69	HR	237
10	6	16	6-7	4-05-69	HR	3
11	7	16	7	4-06-69	S	190
12	8	16	7-8	4-07-69	S	195
13	9	16	8	4-07-69	S	185
14	10	16	8-9	4-07-69	S	200
15	11	16	9-13	4-10-69	HR	354
16	12	16	13-40	4-10-69	HR	123
17	13	16	40-41	4-10-69	HR	405
18	14	16	41-44	4-10-69	HR	140
19	15	16	44	4-10-69	HR	367
20	16	16	44	4-10-69	HR	124
21	17	16	44	4-10-69	HR	404
22	18	16	44-45	4-10-69	S	44
23	19	16	45	4-10-69	S	75
24	20	16	45-46	4-10-69	S	11
25	21	16	46	4-10-69	HR	243
26	22	16	46-47	4-10-69	S	236
27	23	16	47	4-10-69	S	94
28	24	16	47	4-10-69	HR	92
29	25	16	47	4-10-69	HR	421
30	26	16	48-50	4-10-69	HR	403

RESOLUTIONS OF THE FORTY-FIRST CONGRESS

1	1	16	51	3-23-69	S Res.	21
2	2	16	51	3-24-69	H Res.	1
3	3	16	51	3-26-69	S Res.	22
4	4	16	51	3-26-69	S Res.	20
5	5	16	52	3-29-69	H Res.	30
6	6	16	52	4-03-69	H Res.	65
7	7	16	52	4-06-69	S Res.	33
8	8	16	52	4-06-69	S Res.	42
9	9	16	53	4-07-69	S Res.	8
10	10	16	53	4-07-69	H Res.	64
11	11	16	53-54	4-10-69	H Res.	43
12	12	16	54	4-10-69	H Res.	51

RESOLUTIONS OF THE FORTY-FIRST CONGRESS

Public Law/Resolution		Statutes at Large	Page	Date	Bill No.
Chapter	Number				
13	13	16	54	4-10-69	S Res. 29
14	14	16	54	4-10-69	S Res. 36
15	15	16	54-55	4-10-69	S Res. 58
16	16	16	55	4-10-69	S Res. 61
17	17	16	55	4-10-69	S Res. 59
18	18	16	55-56	4-10-69	S Res. 19
19	19	16	56-57	4-10-69	H Res. 6
20	20	16	57	4-10-69	H Res. 48

PUBLIC ACTS OF THE FORTY-FIRST CONGRESS

Public Law/Resolution		Statutes at Large	Page	Date	Bill No.	
Chapter	Number					
3	1	16	59-60	12-22-69	S	281
4	2	16	61	12-23-69	HR	695
5	3	16	61	12-23-69	HR	679
6	4	16	61	1-15-70	S	92
7	5	16	61-62	1-20-70	HR	790
8	6	16	62	1-20-70	HR	861
9	7	16	62	1-21-70	HR	238
10	8	16	62-63	1-26-70	HR	783
11	9	16	63	2-01-70	HR	804
12	10	16	63-64	2-01-70	HR	985
13	11	16	64	2-02-70	S	305
14	12	16	64-65	2-05-70	HR	134
17	13	16	65	2-15-70	S	435
18	14	16	66-67	2-21-70	HR	782
19	15	16	67-68	2-23-70	HR	1096
20	16	16	68	2-24-70	HR	1097
21	17	16	69	2-24-70	HR	1264
22	18	16	69-75	3-05-70	HR	1007
23	19	16	75	3-07-70	S	266
25	20	16	76	3-08-70	S	374
26	21	16	76	3-09-70	HR	195
28	22	16	76	3-18-70	HR	207
29	23	16	76-77	3-23-70	HR	866
30	24	16	77	3-25-70	S	444
31	25	16	77-78	3-25-70	S	234
32	26	16	78	3-25-70	S	425
33	27	16	78-79	3-25-70	S	430
34	28	16	79	3-25-70	S	133
35	29	16	80	3-25-70	HR	1138
34	30	16	80	3-25-70	S	383
39	31	16	80-81	3-30-70	HR	1536
44	14*	16	81	4-05-70	HR	1598
46	32	16	81-82	4-06-70	S	302
47	33	16	82	4-06-70	S	745
54	34	16	83	4-13-70	HR	601
55	35	16	83	4-13-70	HR	1713
56	36	16	83-90	4-20-70	HR	1346
57	37	16	90-91	4-20-70	HR	1542
59	38	16	91	4-22-70	S	215
60	39	16	91-92	4-22-70	S	226

Public Law/Resolution		Statutes at Large	Page	Date	Bill No.	
Chapter	Number					
61	40	16	92	4-22-70	S	589
62	41	16	93	4-22-70	S	414
64	42	16	93	4-28-70	HR	779
69	43	16	94-95	5-04-70	S	396
70	44	16	95	5-04-70	HR	1635
71	45	16	96	5-04-70	HR	1912
72	46	16	96	5-04-70	HR	9
73	47	16	96	5-04-70	HR	840
74	48	16	96	5-04-70	HR	869
75	49	16	97	5-04-70	HR	897
76	50	16	97-98	5-04-70	HR	945
80	51	16	98-116	5-05-70	HR	1427
81	52	16	116	5-05-70	S	93
82	53	16	116-117	5-05-70	S	746
83	54	16	117	5-05-70	S	684
84	55	16	117-118	5-05-70	S	579
87	56	16	118	5-06-70	HR	1575
88	57	16	118-119	5-06-70	S	774
89	58	16	119	5-06-70	HR	983
90	59	16	119	5-06-70	HR	1594
91	60	16	119-121	5-06-70	HR	1025½
92	61	16	121	5-06-70	HR	1766
93	62	16	121	5-06-70	HR	486
94	63	16	121-122	5-06-70	S	580
98	64	16	122	5-11-70	S	369
102	65	16	122-123	5-12-70	HR	902
106	66	16	123-124	5-18-70	S	788
108	67	16	124-133	5-20-70	HR	1084
109	68	16	133-137	5-24-70	S	227
110	69	16	137-139	5-24-70	S	550
111	70	16	139	5-24-70	S	492
113	71	16	139-140	5-27-70	S	177
114	72	16	140-146	5-31-70	HR	1293
115	73	16	146-147	6-01-70	HR	2065
116	74	16	147	6-01-70	S	76
117	75	16	148	6-01-70	HR	2064
118	76	16	148	6-01-70	HR	2063
123	77	16	148	6-06-70	HR	1977
124	78	16	148	6-07-70	S	97
125	79	16	149	6-08-70	S	263
126	80	16	149-150	6-11-70	S	95
127	81	16	150-151	6-14-70	S	395
128	82	16	151	6-14-70	S	554

Public Law/Resolution		Statutes at Large	Page	Date	Bill No.	
Chapter	Number					
129	83	16	151-152	6-15-70	HR	2115
130	84	16	152	6-17-70	HR	1258
131	85	16	153	6-17-70	HR	2005
132	86	16	153	6-17-70	HR	785
133	87	16	153-157	6-17-70	HR	38
134	88	16	157-158	6-21-70	S	754
135	89	16	158-159	6-21-70	S	785
136	90	16	159	6-21-70	S	948
137	91	16	159	6-21-70	S	399
138	92	16	160	6-21-70	S	891
139	93	16	160	6-21-70	S	927
140	94	16	160	6-21-70	S	781
141	95	16	160-161	6-21-70	S	491
142	96	16	161-162	6-21-70	HR	2218
150	97	16	162-165	6-22-70	HR	1328
151	98	16	165	6-22-70	HR	1956
152	99	16	165-166	6-23-70	HR	1697
153	100	16	166-167	6-23-70	S	459
164	101	16	167	6-24-70	S	99
165	102	16	167-168	6-28-70	HR	572
166	103	16	168	6-28-70	HR	2044
167	104	16	168	6-28-70	HR	2224
168	105	16	168-169	6-29-70	S	558
169	106	16	169-170	6-29-70	S	489
170	107	16	170-171	6-29-70	S	237
171	108	16	171	6-29-70	S	742
175	109	16	171-173	6-29-70	S	722
176	110	16	173	6-30-70	HR	489
177	111	16	173-174	6-30-70	HR	386
178	112	16	174	6-30-70	HR	249
179	113	16	174	6-30-70	HR	2277
180	114	16	175-176	6-30-70	HR	230
181	115	16	176	6-30-70	S	339
185	116	16	176-179	7-01-70	S	613
186	117	16	179	7-01-70	S	723
187	118	16	179	7-01-70	S	517
188	119	16	180	7-01-70	S	677
189	120	16	180-182	7-01-70	S	32
190	121	16	182	7-01-70	S	834
191	122	16	182-183	7-01-70	S	495

PUBLIC ACTS OF THE FORTY-FIRST CONGRESS

Public Law/Resolution		Statutes at Large	Page	Date	Bill No.	
Chapter	Number					
192	123	16	183	7-01-70	S	616
193	124	16	183	7-01-70	S	509
194	125	16	183-184	7-01-70	S	632
195	126	16	185-186	7-01-70	S	949
196	127	16	186	7-01-70	S	167
197	128	16	186-187	7-01-70	S	241
198	129	16	187	7-01-70	S	351
199	130	16	187-188	7-01-70	S	471
200	131	16	188	7-01-70	S	474
207	132	16	188	7-07-70	S	713
208	133	16	188	7-07-70	S	1040
209	134	16	189	7-07-70	S	893
210	135	16	189-190	7-07-70	S	947
211	136	16	190	7-07-70	S	297
212	137	16	190-191	7-07-70	HR	2106
213	138	16	191-192	7-07-70	HR	1467
214	139	16	192	7-07-70	HR	2351
224	140	16	192-193	7-08-70	HR	2363
225	141	16	193-195	7-08-70	HR	1987
226	142	16	195	7-08-70	HR	2000
227	143	16	196	7-08-70	HR	253
228	144	16	196-199	7-08-70	HR	2275
229	145	16	197-198	7-08-70	HR	2104
230	146	16	198-217	7-08-70	HR	1714
235	147	16	217-218	7-09-70	HR	562
236	148	16	218	7-09-70	S	602
237	149	16	218-221	7-11-70	HR	1604
238	150	16	221-222	7-11-70	HR	781
239	151	16	222-223	7-11-70	HR	1883
240	152	16	223-227	7-11-70	HR	2092
241	153	16	227-228	7-11-70	HR	1828
242	154	16	228	7-11-70	HR	2213
243	155	16	229	7-11-70	HR	2226
244	156	16	229	7-11-70	HR	2180
245	157	16	230	7-11-70	HR	1545
246	158	16	230	7-11-70	HR	686
247	159	16	230	7-11-70	HR	2353
251	160	16	230-251	7-12-70	HR	974
252	161	16	251-254	7-12-70	S	378
253	162	16	254	7-13-70	S	319
254	163	16	254-256	7-14-70	HR	2201

Public Law/Resolution		Statutes at Large	Page	Date	Bill No.	
Chapter	Number					
255	164	16	256-272	7-14-70	HR	2045
256	165	16	272-274	7-14-70	S	380
257	166	16	274	7-14-70	HR	2062
258	167	16	274	7-14-70	HR	2244
259	168	16	274-275	7-14-70	S	296
260	169	16	275	7-14-70	HR	1149
261	170	16	275	7-14-70	HR	569
262	171	16	276	7-14-70	S	1021
263	172	16	276	7-14-70	S	1018
264	173	16	277	7-14-70	S	881
265	174	16	277	7-14-70	HR	2404
266	175	16	277	7-14-70	HR	2359
267	176	16	277-278	7-14-70	HR	2350
268	177	16	278	7-14-70	HR	2169
269	178	16	278	7-14-70	HR	2160
270	179	16	278-279	7-14-70	HR	2090
271	180	16	279	7-14-70	HR	2111
272	181	16	279	7-14-70	HR	1986
273	182	16	279-291	7-14-70	HR	2370
292	183	16	291-310	7-15-70	HR	2165
293	184	16	311-315	7-15-70	HR	2369
294	185	16	315-321	7-15-70	HR	2082
295	186	16	321-335	7-15-70	HR	1533
296	187	16	335-363	7-15-70	HR	2413
297	188	16	363	7-15-70	S	952
298	189	16	363	7-15-70	HR	936
299	190	16	363-364	7-15-70	HR	1335
300	191	16	364	7-15-70	HR	1898
301	192	16	364-365	7-15-70	HR	363
302	193	16	365	7-15-70	HR	1300
303	194	16	365	7-15-70	HR	1224
304	195	16	365-366	7-15-70	HR	2408
305	196	16	366	7-15-70	HR	1803

RESOLUTIONS OF THE FORTY-FIRST CONGRESS

1	1	16	367	12-14-69	S Res. 62
2	2	16	367	12-14-69	S Res. 64
3	3	16	367	12-22-69	H Res. 77
4	4	16	367	12-22-69	S Res. 88
5	5	16	368	12-23-69	H Res. 4

Public Law/Resolution		Statutes at Large	Page	Date	Bill No.
Chapter	Number				
6	6	16	368	12-23-69	H Res. 96
7	7	16	368	2-02-70	S Res. 74
8	8	16	368-369	2-03-70	S Res.105
12	9	16	369	2-09-70	H Res.143
13	10	16	369	2-12-70	S Res. 41
15	11	16	369	2-21-70	H Res.117
16	12	16	369-370	2-24-70	H Res. 34
18	13	16	370	3-01-70	S Res.117
21	14	16	370	3-14-70	S Res.109
22	15	16	370	3-16-70	H Res.182
23	16	16	370-371	3-18-70	H Res.115
26	17	16	371	3-23-70	H Res.194
28	18	16	371	3-24-70	S Res.150
29	19	16	371	3-25-70	H Res.151
30	20	16	371	4-05-70	H Res.218
31	21	16	372	4-06-70	S Res.135
32	22	16	372	4-06-70	S Res.167
33	23	16	372	4-07-70	H Res.234
36	24	16	372	4-16-70	S Res. 75
37	25	16	373	4-28-70	H Res.122
38	113*	16	373	4-28-70	H Res.116
39	26	16	373	5-04-70	H Res.271
40	27	16	373	5-04-70	H Res.215
41	28	16	374	5-04-70	H Res.156
42	29	16	374	5-04-70	H Res.146
43	30	16	374	5-04-70	H Res.245
47	31	16	374-375	5-05-70	S Res.159
48	32	16	375	5-05-70	S Res.141
49	33	16	375	5-05-70	S Res.169
50	34	16	376	5-05-70	S Res. 78
53	35	16	376	5-06-70	S Res.165
54	36	16	376	5-06-70	H Res.131
55	37	16	376	5-06-70	H Res.222
57	38	16	376	5-07-70	S Res. 23
59	39	16	377	5-11-70	H Res.273
60	40	16	377	5-11-70	H Res.269
62	41	16	377-378	5-15-70	H Res. 85
63	42	16	378	5-23-70	S Res.198
66	43	16	378	5-27-70	S Res.120
67	44	16	378-379	5-31-70	S Res.121

RESOLUTIONS OF THE FORTY-FIRST CONGRESS

Public Law/Resolution		Statutes at Large	Page	Date	Bill No.
Chapter	Number				
69	45	16	379	6-06-70	H Res.301
70	46	16	379-380	6-07-70	S Res. 98
72	47	16	380	6-09-70	S Res.212
73	48	16	380	6-09-70	S Res.140
75	49	16	380	6-21-70	H Res.173
76	50	16	381	6-21-70	S Res. 77
77	51	16	381	6-22-70	H Res.227
78	52	16	381	6-22-70	H Res.324
79	53	16	381	6-23-70	H Res.304
80	54	16	381	6-23-70	H Res.327
87	55	16	382	6-28-70	H Res. 86
88	56	16	382	6-28-70	H Res.306
89	57	16	382	6-28-70	H Res.302
90	58	16	382	6-29-70	H Res.354
91	59	16	383	6-30-70	H Res.216
93	60	16	383	7-01-70	S Res.163
94	61	16	383	7-01-70	S Res.199
95	62	16	383	7-01-70	S Res.197
96	63	16	384	7-01-70	S Res.134
97	64	16	384	7-01-70	S Res.133
98	65	16	384	7-01-70	S Res.116
99	66	16	384-385	7-01-70	S Res.218
100	67	16	385	7-01-70	S Res.230
101	68	16	385	7-07-70	H Res.355
102	69	16	385-386	7-11-70	H Res.109
103	70	16	386	7-11-70	H Res.286
104	71	16	386	7-11-70	H Res.290
105	72	16	386-387	7-11-70	H Res.305
106	73	16	387	7-11-70	H Res.359
108	74	16	387	7-12-70	S Res. 96
109	75	16	387	7-13-70	S Res.205
110	76	16	387	7-13-70	S Res.217
111	77	16	388	7-14-70	H Res.231
112	78	16	388	7-14-70	H Res.358
113	79	16	389	7-14-70	S Res.248
114	80	16	389	7-14-70	S Res.247
115	81	16	389	7-14-70	S Res.243
116	82	16	389	7-14-70	S Res.215
117	83	16	390	7-14-70	S Res. 40
118	84	16	390	7-14-70	S Res. 34

Public Law/Resolution		Statutes at Large	Page	Date	Bill No.
Chapter	Number				
119	85	16	390	7-14-70	H Res.322
120	86	16	390-391	7-14-70	H Res.236
128	87	16	391	7-15-70	H Res.323
129	88	16	391	7-15-70	H Res.384
130	89	16	391	7-15-70	H Res.382
131	90	16	391-392	7-15-70	H Res.383
132	91	16	392	7-15-70	H Res.381
133	92	16	392	7-15-70	H Res.376
134	93	16	392	7-15-70	H Res.378
135	94	16	392	7-15-70	H Res.380
136	95	16	393	7-15-70	H Res.372

Public Law/Resolution		Statutes at Large	Page	Date	Bill No.	
Chapter	Number					
1	1	16	395	12-13-70	HR	228
2	2	16	395-396	12-15-70	HR	871
3	1*	16	396	12-22-70	HR	2416
6	3	16	397	12-22-70	HR	2530
7	2*	16	397	12-22-70	HR	2527
8	3*	16	397-398	12-22-70	HR	2431
15	4	16	398	1-10-71	S	1100
16	4*	16	398	1-10-71	S	1119
21	5*	16	399	1-10-71	HR	2616
23	5	16	399	1-20-71	S	1149
24	6	16	399	1-21-71	HR	2414
28	7	16	399-400	1-25-71	HR	2355
29	8	16	400	1-30-71	HR	2529
30	9	16	401	1-30-71	HR	1549
31	10	16	401	1-31-71	HR	2360
32	11	16	401	2-02-71	S	53
33	6*	16	402	2-02-71	S	874
34	7*	16	402	2-02-71	S	1257
35	12	16	403-404	2-03-71	S	698
38	14	16	404-407	2-06-71	S	610
39	13	16	407	2-08-71	HR	666
40	8*	16	408	2-09-71	HR	2793
45	15	16	408-409	2-10-71	HR	2287
46	16	16	409	2-10-71	S	1190
48	17	16	410-411	2-13-71	S	849
49	18	16	411	2-13-71	HR	2914
50	19	16	411-412	2-14-71	HR	1829
51	20	16	412	2-14-71	HR	2911
53	21	16	412-413	2-15-71	S	218
54	22	16	413-415	2-18-71	HR	2536
55	23	16	415-416	2-18-71	HR	2372
56	24	16	416	2-18-71	HR	175
57	25	16	416	2-18-71	HR	2921
58	9*	16	416	2-18-71	HR	2490
59	10*	16	416	2-18-71	HR	1521
61	26	16	417-419	2-21-71	HR	2689
62	27	16	419-429	2-21-71	S	594
63	28	16	429	2-21-71	HR	2792
64	11*	16	429	2-21-71	HR	2504
65	12*	16	429-430	2-21-71	HR	2691

PUBLIC ACTS OF THE FORTY-FIRST CONGRESS

Public Law/Resolution		Statutes at Large	Page	Date	Bill No.	
Chapter	Number					
67	29	16	430	2-24-71	HR	1227
68	30	16	430-431	2-24-71	S	569
71	31	16	431-432	2-25-71	HR	1351
72	32	16	432	2-25-71	HR	2805
73	33	16	432	2-27-71	HR	2909
74	13*	16	432	2-27-71	HR	2996
99	34	16	433-440	2-28-71	HR	2634
100	35	16	440-459	2028-71	S	716
101	36	16	460-470	2-28-71	HR	2998
102	14*	16	470	3-02-71	HR	2933
105	37	16	470-471	3-03-71	HR	1478
106	38	16	471-472	3-03-71	HR	1582
107	39	16	472-473	3-03-71	S	1266
108	40	16	473	3-03-71	HR	2925
109	41	16	473	3-03-71	HR	996
110	42	16	473-474	3-03-71	HR	3033
111	43	16	474-475	3-03-71	S	141
112	44	16	475	3-03-71	S	1134
113	45	16	475-495	3-03-71	HR	2524
114	46	16	495-515	3-03-71	HR	3064
115	47	16	515-521	3-03-71	HR	2995
116	48	16	521-525	3-03-71	HR	2816
117	49	16	526-538	3-03-71	HR	2789
118	50	16	538-543	3-03-71	HR	3036
119	51	16	543-544	3-03-71	HR	2860
120	52	16	544-571	3-03-71	HR	2615
121	53	16	571-573	3-03-71	HR	2579
122	54	16	573-579	3-03-71	S	647
123	55	16	580	3-03-71	S	140
124	56	16	580	3-03-71	S	1181
125	57	16	580-581	3-03-71	S	829
126	58	16	581	3-03-71	S	325
127	59	16	581-582	3-03-71	HR	2173
128	60	16	582	3-03-71	S	574
129	61	16	582-583	3-03-71	S	1202
130	62	16	583	3-03-71	S	1327
131	63	16	583	3-03-71	S	1137
132	64	16	583-584	3-03-71	S	1356
133	85	16	584	3-03-71	S	1204
134	66	16	584	3-03-71	HR	1619
135	67	16	584	3-03-71	S	1271

PUBLIC ACTS OF THE FORTY-FIRST CONGRESS

Public Law/Resolution		Statutes at Large	Page	Date	Bill No.	
Chapter	Number					
136	15*	16	584-585	3-03-71	S	1241
137	16*	16	585	3-03-71	HR	3014
138	17*	16	585	3-03-71	HR	2959
139	18*	16	586	3-03-71	HR	3048
140	19*	16	586-587	3-03-71	HR	3035
141	20*	16	587-588	3-03-71	S	892
142	21*	16	588	3-03-71	S	913
143	22*	16	588	3-03-71	HR	2906
144	23*	16	588	3-03-71	S	381

RESOLUTIONS OF THE FORTY-FIRST CONGRESS

1	1*	16	589	12-20-70	H	Res.428
2	1	16	589	12-20-70	H	Res.419
3	2	16	589	12-22-70	S	Res.191
4	2*	16	589-590	1-10-71	S	Res.118
5	3	16	590	1-10-71	H	Res.188
6	3*	16	590-591	1-10-71	H	Res.440
7	4	16	591	1-12-71	S	Res.262
8	4*	16	591	1-18-71	H	Res.377
9	5	16	592	1-20-71	H	Res. 80
14	5*	16	592	1-25-71	S	Res. 72
15	6*	16	592	1-25-71	S	Res.270
17	7*	16	592	1-26-71	H	Res.434
18	6	16	592-593	1-30-71	H	Res.460
19	8*	16	593	1-30-71	S	Res.246
20	9*	16	593	2-02-71	S	Res.302
21	7	16	593	2-03-71	S	Res. 10
22	8	16	593-594	2-09-71	H	Res.468
23	9	16	594-595	2-09-71	H	Res.170
24	10*	16	595	2-09-71	H	Res.487
25	11*	16	595	2-09-71	H	Res.417
27	10	16	595-596	2-09-71	H	Res.449
28	11	16	596	2-10-71	S	Res.308
29	12*	16	596	2-10-71	S	Res.293
30	13*	16	596-597	2-14-71	S	Res. 17
31	12	16	597	2-14-71	H	Res.285
33	13	16	597	2-16-71	S	Res.238
34	14	16	597	2-16-71	S	Res.108

RESOLUTIONS OF THE FORTY-FIRST CONGRESS

Public Law/Resolution		Statutes at Large	Page	Date	Bill No.
Chapter	Number				
36	14*	16	597-598	2-17-71	H Res.484
39	15*	16	598	2-18-71	H Res.499
40	16*	16	598	2-21-71	S Res.179
42	15	16	598-599	2-24-71	H Res.503
45	16	16	599	2-28-71	H Res.447
47	17*	16	599	3-02-71	H Res.519
48	17	16	599-600	3-03-71	H Res.469
49	18	16	600	3-03-71	H Res.488
50	19	16	600	3-03-71	S Res.292
51	20	16	600-601	3-03-71	S Res.209
52	21	16	601	3-03-71	S Res.277
53	22	16	601	3-03-71	H Res.520
54	23	16	601	3-03-71	S Res.313
55	18*	16	601	3-03-71	S Res.315

PUBLIC ACTS OF THE FORTY-SECOND CONGRESS

Public Law/Resolution		Statutes at Large	Page	Date	Bill No.	
Chapter	Number					
1	1*	17	1	3-20-71	S	179
2	1	17	1-2	3-24-71	S	74
3	2*	17	2	3-24-71	S	244
4	3*	17	2	3-24-71	HR	285
5	4*	17	2-3	3-24-71	S	119
6	2	17	3	3-27-71	S	202
7	3	17	3	3-30-71	S	130
8	4	17	3	4-04-71	S	88
9	5*	17	3-4	4-04-71	S	220
14	5	17	4	4-15-71	HR	381
15	6*	17	4	4-15-71	S	295
16	6	17	4	4-19-71	S	137
17	7	17	4-5	4-19-71	S	89
18	8	17	5	4-19-71	S	53
19	7*	17	5	4-19-71	S	45
21	9	17	5-12	4-20-71	HR	19
22	10	17	13-15	4-20-71	HR	320
23	11	17	16	4-20-71	HR	426
24	12	17	16	4-20-71	S	116
25	13	17	16	4-20-71	S	29
26	14	17	16	4-20-71	S	257
27	15	17	17	4-20-71	HR	428
28	16	17	17-18	4-20-71	HR	181
29	8*	17	18	4-20-71	HR	386
30	9*	17	19	4-20-71	HR	425
31	10*	17	19	4-20-71	S	273
32	11*	17	19	4-20-71	HR	322
33	12*	17	19-20	4-20-71	S	242

RESOLUTIONS OF THE FORTY-SECOND CONGRESS

1	1	17	21	3-30-71	S Res.	1
2	1*	17	21	3-20-71	H Res.	4
3	2*	17	21	3-24-71	H Res.	31

Public Law/Resolution		Statutes at Large	Page	Date	Bill No.	
Chapter	Number					
1	1*	17	23	12-16-71	HR	612
2	1	17	23	12-20-71	HR	65
3	2*	17	24	12-21-71	HR	489
4	3*	17	24	12-21-71	HR	487
5	4*	17	24-25	12-21-71	HR	459
6	2	17	25-27	1-16-72	HR	774
7	3	17	27	1-16-72	HR	777
8	5*	17	27	1-16-72	HR	484
10	4	17	27-28	2-01-72	HR	1051
11	5	17	28-29	2-02-72	HR	243
12	6	17	29	2-02-72	HR	1061
13	7	17	29	2-02-72	HR	1062
14	8	17	30	2-02-72	HR	434
15	6*	17	30	2-02-72	HR	1186
16	9	17	30	2-06-72	S	487
18	10	17	30	2-12-72	HR	1076
19	11	17	30-31	2-20-72	HR	1340
20	12	17	31	2-20-72	HR	625
21	13	17	31-32	2-20-72	HR	1071
22	14	17	32	3-01-72	S	187
23	15	17	32	3-01-72	S	384
24	16	17	32-33	3-01-72	S	392
25	17	17	33	3-01-72	S	550
28	18	17	33-34	3-05-72	HR	383
29	19	17	35	3-05-72	HR	1260
30	20	17	35	3-05-72	S	570
31	21	17	35	3-05-72	HR	1342
32	22	17	36	3-05-72	S	644
33	23	17	36	3-05-72	HR	1760
34	24	17	36	3-05-72	HR	1333
35	7*	17	36	3-05-72	S	445
36	8*	17	36-37	3-05-72	HR	1074
37	9*	17	37	3-05-72	HR	213
38	10*	17	37	3-05-72	HR	1669
39	11*	17	37	3-05-72	S	533
40	25	17	37-38	3-11-72	HR	1417
42	26	17	38	3-12-72	HR	436
43	27	17	38	3-12-72	HR	1324
44	12*	17	38-39	3-12-72	HR	1663
45	13*	17	39	3-12-72	HR	1540
46	14*	17	39	3-12-72	HR	1534

PUBLIC ACTS OF THE FORTY-SECOND CONGRESS

Public Law/Resolution		Statutes at Large	Page	Date	Bill No.	
Chapter	Number					
47	15*	17	40	3-12-72	HR	1745
49	16*	17	40	3-14-72	S	475
53	16½*	17	40	3-15-72	HR	330
54	28	17	40	3-16-72	HR	437
55	17*	17	40	3-16-72	S	528
56	29	17	40-41	3-18-72	S	353
57	30	17	41	3-08-72	S	742
58	18*	17	41-42	3-18-72	S	442
59	19*	17	42	3-18-72	HR	1538
60	20*	17	42-43	3-18-72	HR	1539
62	31	17	43	3-19-72	HR	1056
63	21*	17	43	3-22-72	HR	1021
65	22*	17	43-44	3-27-72	HR	619
66	23*	17	44	3-27-72	HR	1761
72	32	17	44	3-30-72	S	792
73	33	17	44-46	4-01-72	S	547
74	34	17	46	4-01-72	S	320
75	24*	17	46-47	4-01-72	HR	635
78	35	17	47	4-02-72	HR	435
79	36	17	47	4-02-72	S	681
80	37	17	47-48	4-02-72	HR	1049
81	38	17	48	4-02-72	HR	166
82	25*	17	48-49	4-02-72	HR	2047
83	26*	17	49	4-02-72	HR	2043
85	39	17	49-50	4-04-72	S	447
86	40	17	50	4-05-72	HR	1330
87	27*	17	51	4-05-72	HR	1664
88	28*	17	51	4-05-72	HR	555
90	41	17	51-52	4-09-72	HR	1213
91	29*	17	52	4-09-72	HR	48
96	30*	17	52	4-12-72	HR	2124
99	42	17	52-53	4-13-72	HR	1588
102	43	17	53	4-17-72	HR	2205
103	44	17	53	4-17-72	HR	131
104	45	17	53-54	4-17-72	HR	1337
111	46	17	54	4-22-72	S	770
112	47	17	54	4-22-72	HR	1180
113	31*	17	54	4-22-72	HR	1781
114	48	17	55	4-22-72	HR	1782
115	32*	17	55	4-23-72	HR	1862
118	49	17	55	4-24-72	HR	1638

PUBLIC ACTS OF THE FORTY-SECOND CONGRESS

Public Law/Resolution		Statutes at Large	Page	Date	Bill No.	
Chapter	Number					
119	33*	17	56	4-24-72	HR	578
125	50	17	56-57	4-27-72	HR	1930
126	34*	17	57-58	4-29-72	HR	1303
129	51	17	58	4-30-72	HR	1657
130	52	17	58-59	5-01-72	S	1014
131	53	17	59	5-01-72	HR	174
132	54	17	59-61	5-02-72	S	724
139	55	17	61	5-03-72	S	793
140	56	17	61-85	5-08-72	HR	1060
141	57	17	85-86	5-08-72	HR	2624
142	35*	17	86-88	5-08-72	S	973
143	58	17	88	5-09-72	HR	859
144	59	17	88-89	5-09-72	HR	864
145	60	17	89	5-09-72	HR	106
146	61	17	89-90	5-09-72	HR	286
147	36*	17	90	5-09-72	HR	1030
148	37*	17	90	5-09-72	HR	501
149	38*	17	90-91	5-09-72	HR	873
152	62	17	91-96	5-10-72	HR	1016
153	39*	17	96	5-10-72	S	869
156	63	17	97-98	5-11-72	HR	1149
157	40*	17	98-99	5-11-72	HR	1496
158	41*	17	99-100	5-11-72	S	696
159	64	17	100-116	5-14-72	HR	1666
160	65	17	116-117	5-15-72	S	607
161	66	17	117	5-15-72	S	448
162	67	17	117-118	5-15-72	HR	838
163	42*	17	118	5-15-72	S	671
164	43*	17	118-119	5-15-72	S	354
165	44*	17	120	5-15-72	HR	1776
169	68	17	120	5-17-72	HR	1055
170	69	17	120-121	5-17-72	S	845
171	45*	17	121-122	5-17-72	HR	2616
172	70	17	122-134	5-18-72	HR	1654
173	71	17	135	5-18-72	S	446
174	46*	17	135	5-18-72	S	807
175	47*	17	135	5-18-72	HR	2341
176	72	17	135-136	5-21-72	HR	1072
177	73	17	136-137	5-21-72	HR	2290
178	74	17	137-138	5-21-72	S	309

PUBLIC ACTS OF THE FORTY-SECOND CONGRESS

Public Law/Resolution		Statutes at Large	Page	Date	Bill No.	
Chapter	Number					
179	75	17	138	5-21-72	HR	2685
180	76	17	138	5-21-72	HR	1182
181	48*	17	138	5-21-72	HR	2567
182	49*	17	139	5-21-72	S	609
183	50*	17	139	5-21-72	S	936
184	51*	17	139	5-21-72	HR	2313
185	52*	17	139	5-21-72	HR	2093
186	53*	17	139-140	5-21-72	HR	1958
187	54*	17	140	5-21-72	HR	2627
188	55*	17	140	5-21-72	HR	2682
189	56*	17	140-141	5-21-72	HR	2187
193	77	17	141	5-22-72	HR	2761
194	78	17	142-145	5-22-72	HR	1323
195	79	17	145-154	5-23-72	HR	1191
196	80	17	154-156	5-23-72	HR	1661
197	81	17	156-157	5-23-72	HR	2690
198	82	17	157	5-23-72	S	816
199	83	17	157	5-23-72	S	327
200	84	17	157	5-23-72	S	877
201	85	17	157-158	5-23-72	HR	534
202	86	17	158	5-23-72	S	468
203	57*	17	158	5-23-72	S	691
204	58*	17	158-159	5-23-72	HR	2631
205	59*	17	159	5-23-72	HR	2195
206	60*	17	159-160	5-23-72	S	988
207	61*	17	160	5-23-72	HR	1766
213	87	17	160-162	5-23-72	HR	2207
218	88	17	162	5-27-72	S	881
219	62*	17	162	5-27-72	S	677
220	63*	17	162-163	5-27-72	S	617
221	64*	17	163	5-27-72	S	1062
226	89	17	163-164	5-28-72	S	854
227	90	17	164	5-28-72	S	1027
228	65*	17	164	5-28-72	S	812
229	65½*	17	164	5-28-72	S	934
233	91	17	165-191	5-29-72	HR	1192
234	66*	17	191-192	5-29-72	HR	1416
235	67*	17	192	5-29-72	HR	2833
239	93	17	192	5-30-72	HR	1343
240	94	17	192	5-31-72	S	417

Public Law/Resolution		Statutes at Large	Page	Date	Bill No.	
Chapter	Number					
241	95	17	192-193	5-31-72	S	998
242	68*	17	193-194	5-31-72	S	931
243	69*	17	194	5-31-72	S	376
244	70*	17	194-195	5-31-72	S	1086
245	71*	17	195	5-31-72	S	159
246	71½*	17	195	6-01-72	S	908
253	96	17	195	6-01-72	S	58
254	97	17	196	6-01-72	HR	2565
255	98	17	196-199	6-01-72	S	473
256	99	17	199-202	6-01-72	HR	1070
257	100	17	202	6-01-72	HR	2699
258	72*	17	202-203	6-01-72	HR	2592
259	73*	17	203-211	6-01-72	HR	2708
260	74*	17	211-212	6-01-72	HR	1552
261	75*	17	212-213	6-01-72	HR	2938
262	76*	17	213-214	6-01-72	HR	183
263	77*	17	214	6-01-72	HR	1914
279	78*	17	214	6-03-72	S	757
280	101	17	214-215	6-04-72	S	659
281	102	17	215	6-04-72	HR	2866
282	103	17	215-217	6-04-72	HR	2192
283	104	17	217-218	6-04-72	HR	1297
284	105	17	218-219	6-04-72	HR	1422
285	106	17	219	6-04-72	S	429
286	107	17	219-220	6-04-72	S	463
287	79*	17	220	6-04-72	S	910
288	80*	17	220-221	6-04-72	HR	1672
289	81*	17	221	6-04-72	S	298
290	82*	17	221	6-04-72	S	299
291	83*	17	222-223	6-04-72	S	828
292	84*	17	223-224	6-04-72	S	631
293	85*	17	224-225	6-04-72	S	754
294	86*	17	225	6-04-72	S	790
295	87*	17	225	6-04-72	S	837
296	88*	17	225-226	6-04-72	S	855
305	108	17	226	6-05-72	S	608
306	109	17	226	6-05-72	S	897
307	110	17	226	6-05-72	S	595
308	89*	17	226-227	6-05-72	HR	2623
309	90*	17	228	6-05-72	HR	757

Public Law/Resolution		Statutes at Large	Page	Date	Bill No.	
Chapter	Number					
310	91*	17	228–229	6-05-72	HR	2334
311	92*	17	229–230	6-05-72	HR	2851
312	93*	17	230	6-05-72	HR	903
313	94*	17	230	6-05-72	HR	2937
315	111	17	230–258	6-06-72	HR	2322
316	112	17	258–261	6-06-72	HR	1541
321	113	17	262	6-07-72	S	611
322	114	17	262–280	6-07-72	HR	2044
323	95*	17	280	6-07-72	S	1036
324	96*	17	280–281	6-07-72	S	382
325	97*	17	281	6-07-72	S	1045
326	98*	17	281	6-07-72	S	745
327	99*	17	281–282	6-07-72	HR	2848
332	115	17	282	6-08-72	HR	837
333	116	17	282	6-08-72	HR	631
334	117	17	282–283	6-08-72	HR	1982
335	118	17	283–330	6-08-72	HR	1
336	119	17	330	6-08-72	HR	1758
337	120	17	330–332	6-08-72	S	780
338	121	17	333–334	6-08-72	S	1153
339	122	17	334	6-08-72	S	399
340	123	17	334	6-08-72	S	774
341	124	17	334	6-08-72	S	480
342	125	17	335	6-08-72	S	1073
343	126	17	335	6-08-72	S	218
344	127	17	335	6-08-72	HR	2632
345	128	17	335–336	6-08-72	HR	2706
346	129	17	336	6-08-72	HR	1869
347	130	17	336	6-08-72	HR	2773
348	131	17	337	6-08-72	HR	2975
349	100*	17	337	6-08-72	S	546
350	101*	17	337–338	6-08-72	S	699
351	102*	17	338	6-08-72	HR	2136
352	103*	17	338	6-08-72	S	1182
353	104*	17	338–339	6-08-72	HR	471
354	105*	17	339	6-08-72	S	984
355	106*	17	339	6-08-72	S	1099
356	107*	17	339–340	6-08-72	S	527
357	108*	17	340	6-08-72	S	995
358	109*	17	340	6-08-72	S	562

Public Law/Resolution		Statutes at Large	Page	Date	Bill No.	
Chapter	Number					
359	110*	17	340-341	6-08-72	S	1002
360	111*	17	341	6-08-72	HR	2750
361	112*	17	341-342	6-08-72	HR	2709
362	113*	17	342	6-08-72	HR	2850
363	114*	17	342-343	6-08-72	HR	2847
364	115*	17	343-344	6-08-72	HR	2956
365	116*	17	344	6-08-72	HR	1513
366	117*	17	344-345	6-08-72	HR	1063
367	118*	17	345	6-08-72	HR	2838
368	119*	17	345	6-08-72	HR	12
369	120*	17	346	6-08-72	S	1054
414	132	17	346	6-10-72	HR	224
415	133	17	347-369	6-10-72	HR	2705
416	134	17	370-376	6-10-72	HR	2208
417	135	17	376-377	6-10-72	HR	1671
418	136	17	378	6-10-72	HR	2876
419	137	17	378	6-10-72	HR	2697
420	138	17	378	6-10-72	HR	1017
421	139	17	378-379	6-10-72	S	324
422	140	17	379-380	6-10-72	S	842
423	141	17	380	6-10-72	S	626
424	142	17	381	6-10-72	HR	2977
425	143	17	381-382	6-10-72	HR	2973
426	144	17	382	6-10-72	S	996
427	145	17	382-387	6-10-72	HR	2935
428	121*	17	387	6-10-72	HR	2942
429	122*	17	388	6-10-72	S	1164
430	123*	17	388-389	6-10-72	S	1175
431	124*	17	389	6-10-72	HR	2800
432	125*	17	389-390	6-10-72	S	624
433	126*	17	390	6-10-72	S	467
434	127*	17	390-391	6-10-72	HR	2633
435	128*	17	391	6-10-72	S	1089
436	129*	17	391-393	6-10-72	S	508
437	130*	17	393	6-10-72	HR	1842

RESOLUTIONS OF THE FORTY-SECOND CONGRESS

Public Law/Resolution		Statutes at Large	Page	Date	Bill No.
Chapter	Number				
1	1*	17	395	1-16-72	H Res. 56
2	2*	17	395	4-16-72	H Res.117
3	3*	17	395	4-22-72	H Res.108
4	4*	17	395-396	5-07-72	H Res.136
6	1	17	396	6-06-72	H Res. 82

Public Law/Resolution		Statutes at Large	Page	Date	Bill No.	
Chapter	Number					
1	1*	17	397	12-10-72	HR	902
2	2*	17	397-398	12-13-72	HR	2109
4	1	17	398-400	12-17-72	HR	827
5	3*	17	400	12-17-72	HR	2332
8	4*	17	400	12-19-72	HR	3123
12	2	17	400-401	12-24-72	S	819
13	3	17	401-403	12-24-72	HR	2994
14	4	17	404	12-24-72	HR	1735
15	5*	17	404	12-24-72	S	1211
17	6*	17	404-405	12-29-72	HR	845
18	5	17	405-406	1-08-73	HR	3131
19	7*	17	406	1-18-73	HR	3124
20	8*	17	406	1-08-73	HR	3257
21	6	17	406-407	1-09-73	HR	3248
22	9*	17	407	1-09-73	HR	3259
23	7	17	407-408	1-10-73	HR	2990
24	8	17	408-409	1-10-73	HR	1048
25	10*	17	409	1-10-73	HR	3005
32	11*	17	409	1-11-73	S	616
33	12*	17	409-410	1-11-73	S	1272
34	13*	17	410	1-11-73	HR	3122
35	9	17	410	1-15-73	HR	3365
36	10	17	411	1-16-73	HR	2774
37	11	17	411	1-16-73	HR	1028
38	14*	17	411	1-16-73	HR	2987
39	12	17	411	1-17-73	HR	2865
43	13	17	412	1-20-73	HR	3183
45	15*	17	412-413	1-21-73	HR	772
46	16*	17	413-415	1-22-73	HR	1916
47	17*	17	416	1-22-73	HR	2340
48	14	17	416	1-23-73	HR	3364
49	15	17	416	1-23-73	HR	3350
50	16	17	416-417	1-23-73	S	964
51	17	17	417	1-23-73	HR	1952
52	18*	17	417	1-23-73	HR	1841
53	19*	17	417-418	1-23-73	HR	1812
54	20*	17	418	1-23-73	HR	3497
62	18	17	418	1-24-73	HR	2871
63	19	17	418-419	1-24-73	HR	3362
64	20	17	419	1-24-73	S	1220

Public Law/Resolution		Statutes at Large	Page	Date	Bill No.	
Chapter	Number					
65	21*	17	419	1-24-73	HR	2943
66	22*	17	419	1-24-73	HR	2878
67	23*	17	420	1-24-73	S	1144
68	24*	17	420	1-24-73	HR	171
70	21	17	420	1-27-73	HR	2870
72	25*	17	420-421	1-28-73	HR	2764
82	22	17	421	1-31-73	HR	2982
83	26*	17	421	1-31-73	S	1015
84	27*	17	422	1-31-73	HR	2333
88	23	17	422	2-01-73	HR	2227
105	24	17	422	2-05-73	HR	3617
120	25	17	422-423	2-07-73	S	1317
122	28*	17	423	2-08-73	S	1441
126	26	17	423	2-10-73	HR	3010
131	27	17	424-436	2-12-73	HR	2934
132	29*	17	436	2-12-73	HR	2880
133	30*	17	436	2-12-73	HR	3476
135	28	17	436-437	2-12-73	HR	3496
136	29	17	437	2-14-73	HR	3253
137	30	17	437	2-14-73	HR	3789
138	31	17	437-464	2-14-73	HR	2989
147	32	17	464	2-17-73	HR	2593
148	33	17	464	2-17-73	HR	3482
149	31*	17	464-465	2-17-73	HR	1626
150	32*	17	465	2-17-73	S	1206
159	34	17	465	2-18-73	S	1354
160	35	17	465-466	2-18-73	HR	2689
166	36	17	460	2-19-73	HR	3399
167	33*	17	466-467	2-19-73	HR	872
168	34*	17	467	2-19-73	HR	3534
169	35*	17	467	2-19-73	HR	2698
173	37	17	468	2-21-73	HR	3620
174	38	17	468	2-21-73	HR	2053
175	39	17	468-469	2-21-73	HR	3352
176	36*	17	469-470	2-21-73	HR	2763
177	37*	17	470	2-21-73	S	1296
178	38*	17	470	2-21-73	S	1199
179	39*	17	471	2-21-73	S	714
184	40	17	471-474	2-22-73	HR	3258
185	40*	17	475	2-22-73	HR	2629

Public Law/Resolution		Statutes at Large	Page	Date	Bill No.	
Chapter	Number					
186	41*	17	475	2-22-73	HR	3628
188	42*	17	475	2-24-73	HR	3326
198	41	17	475-476	2-25-73	S	1156
199	42	17	476	2-25-73	HR	2704
200	43	17	476-477	2-25-73	HR	3021
201	44	17	477	2-25-73	HR	2252
2029	43*	17	477	2-25-73	S	1325
207	44*	17	477-479	2-27-73	S	1499
208	45*	17	479	2-27-73	S	1602
210	45	17	479-481	2-28-73	HR	3737
211	46*	17	481-482	2-28-73	S	530
213	46	17	482-483	3-01-73	HR	488
214	47	17	483	3-01-73	S	1482
215	48	17	484	3-01-73	S	1597
216	49	17	484	3-01-73	HR	2873
217	50	17	484	3-01-73	S	1439
218	47*	17	484	3-01-73	S	1645
223	51	17	484-485	3-03-73	S	1596
224	52	17	485	3-03-73	HR	3452
225	53	17	485	3-03-73	HR	446
226	54	17	485-509	3-03-73	HR	2991
227	55	17	510-530	3-03-73	HR	3921
228	56	17	530-543	3-03-73	HR	4051
229	57	17	543-547	3-03-73	HR	3850
230	58	17	547-556	3-03-73	HR	3351
231	59	17	556-559	3-03-73	HR	3498
232	60	17	559-560	3-03-73	HR	4057
233	61	17	560-566	3-03-73	HR	3922
234	62	17	566-577	3-03-73	HR	2312
235	63	17	577	3-03-73	HR	3702
236	64	17	577	3-03-73	HR	3088
237	65	17	578	3-03-73	HR	3999
238	66	17	578	3-03-73	HR	1891
239	67	17	578-579	3-03-73	HR	3324
240	68	17	579	3-03-73	HR	3045
241	69	17	579-580	3-03-73	HR	4061
242	70	17	580	3-03-73	HR	3949
243	71	17	580	3-03-73	HR	3735
244	72	17	580-581	3-03-73	HR	187
245	73	17	581	3-03-73	HR	2959
246	74	17	581	3-03-73	HR	2874

PUBLIC ACTS OF THE FORTY-SECOND CONGRESS

Public Law/Resolution		Statutes at Large	Page	Date	Bill No.	
Chapter	Number					
247	75	17	582	3-03-73	HR	2797
248	76	17	582	3-03-73	HR	2703
249	77	17	582-584	3-03-73	HR	2692
250	78	17	584	3-03-73	HR	882
251	79	17	584	3-03-73	HR	862
252	80	17	584-585	3-03-73	HR	694
253	81	17	585-586	3-03-73	HR	1907
254	82	17	586	3-03-73	HR	4054
255	83	17	586-598	3-03-73	HR	3274
256	84	17	598	3-03-73	S	1580
257	85	17	598	3-03-73	S	1425
258	86	17	598-600	3-03-73	S	1572
259	87	17	600	3-03-73	S	1575
260	88	17	600-601	3-03-73	S	1527
261	89	17	601	3-03-73	S	1203
262	90	17	601	3-03-73	S	627
263	91	17	601	3-03-73	S	1497
264	92	17	601-602	3-03-73	S	1483
265	93	17	602	3-03-73	S	1438
266	94	17	602	3-03-73	S	1434
267	95	17	602	3-03-73	S	1429
268	96	17	602-603	3-03-73	S	1427
269	97	17	603-604	3-03-73	S	1378
270	98	17	604	3-03-73	S	1344
271	99	17	604	3-03-73	S	1312
272	100	17	604	3-03-73	S	1318
273	101	17	604-605	3-03-73	S	1279
274	102	17	605	3-03-73	S	1299
275	103	17	605	3-03-73	S	1283
276	104	17	605	3-03-73	S	968
277	105	17	605-606	3-03-73	S	680
278	106	17	606-607	3-03-73	S	693
279	107	17	607-608	3-03-73	S	522
280	108	17	608	3-03-73	S	1224
281	109	17	608	3-03-73	HR	3687
282	110	17	608	3-03-73	HR	2969
283	111	17	609	3-03-73	HR	2202
284	48*	17	609	3-03-73	HR	3794
285	49*	17	609	3-03-73	HR	3970

PUBLIC ACTS OF THE FORTY-SECOND CONGRESS

Public Law/Resolution		Statutes at Large	Page	Date	Bill No.	
Chapter	Number					
286	50*	17	610	3-03-73	HR	3972
287	51*	17	610	3-03-73	HR	4050
288	52*	17	610-611	3-03-73	HR	4034
289	53*	17	611	3-03-73	S	363
290	54*	17	611	3-03-73	HR	3310
291	55*	17	612	3-03-73	HR	1158
292	56*	17	612	3-03-73	HR	3622
293	57*	17	613	3-03-73	HR	3470
294	58*	17	613	3-03-73	HR	4068
295	59*	17	613-614	3-03-73	HR	4071
296	60*	17	614	3-03-73	HR	1130
297	61*	17	614-615	3-03-73	HR	239
298	62*	17	615	3-03-73	HR	3279
299	63*	17	615	3-03-73	HR	3302
300	64*	17	615	3-03-73	HR	4059
301	65*	17	615	3-03-73	HR	4049
302	66*	17	616-617	3-03-73	HR	4033
303	67*	17	617	3-03-73	HR	4019
304	68*	17	617-618	3-03-73	HR	4008
305	69*	17	618	3-03-73	HR	3946
306	70*	17	618-619	3-03-73	HR	3919
307	71*	17	619	3-03-73	HR	3710
308	72*	17	619-620	3-03-73	HR	3625
309	73*	17	620	3-03-73	HR	3615
310	74*	17	620-621	3-03-73	HR	119
311	75*	17	621	3-03-73	HR	2984
312	76*	17	621	3-03-73	HR	2747
313	77*	17	621-622	3-03-73	S	420
314	78*	17	622	3-03-73	S	1636
315	79*	17	622	3-03-73	S	950
316	80*	17	622-623	3-03-73	S	1584
317	81*	17	623	3-03-73	S	1514
318	82*	17	623	3-03-73	S	1464
319	83*	17	623-625	3-03-73	S	1391
320	84*	17	625-626	3-03-73	S	1384
321	85*	17	626	3-03-73	S	1282
322	86*	17	626	3-03-73	S	1274
323	87*	17	627	3-03-73	S	1267
324	88*	17	627	3-03-73	S	1183

PUBLIC ACTS OF THE FORTY-SECOND CONGRESS

Public Law/Resolution		Statutes at Large	Page	Date	Bill No.	
Chapter	Number					
325	89*	17	627-629	3-03-73	S	1079
326	90*	17	629	3-03-73	S	1016
327	91*	17	629	3-03-73	S	999
328	92*	17	629	3-03-73	S	957
329	93*	17	630-631	3-03-73	S	597
330	94*	17	631	3-03-73	S	1607
331	95*	17	631	3-03-73	S	1305
332	96*	17	631-633	3-03-73	HR	1535
333	97*	17	633-634	3-03-73	HR	4058
334	98*	17	634-635	3-03-73	S	1025

RESOLUTIONS OF THE FORTY-SECOND CONGRESS

1	1*	17	637	12-24-72	S Res.	9
2	1	17	637	1-24-73	H Res.	184
3	2	17	637-638	2-14-73	H Res.	170
4	2*	17	638	2-24-73	H Res.	196
5	3	17	638	3-03-73	H Res.	202
6	4	17	638-639	3-03-73	S Res.	14
7	3*	17	639	3-03-73	H Res.	203
8	4*	17	639	3-03-73	H Res.	200

PUBLIC ACTS OF THE FORTY-THIRD CONGRESS

Public Law/Resolution		Statutes at Large	Page	Date	Bill No.	
Chapter	Number					
1	1	18	1	12-17-73	HR	478
3	2	18	1-2	12-31-73	HR	481
5	3	18	2	1-05-74	HR	474
6	4	18	2	1-06-74	HR	470
7	5	18	2-3	1-08-74	HR	614
8	1*	18	3	1-08-74	HR	418
9	2*	18	4	1-09-74	HR	34
10	6	18	4	1-14-74	HR	434
11	7	18	4	1-20-74	HR	793
14	8	18	5	1-22-74	HR	718
15	3*	18	5	1-23-74	S	215
16	9	18	5	1-28-74	HR	795
17	4*	18	6	1-28-74	HR	1218
18	10	18	6	1-29-74	HR	1231
19	5*	18	6	1-29-74	HR	1382
20	6*	18	6	1-29-74	S	61
21	11	18	7-14	2-04-74	HR	798
22	7*	18	14	2-04-74	S	89
23	8*	18	15	2-07-74	S	216
24	12	18	15	2-09-74	HR	223
25	9*	18	15	2-11-74	HR	1168
26	10*	18	15	2-11-74	S	194
29	11*	18	16	2-14-74	HR	1221
30	12*	18	16-17	2-19-74	HR	1761
31	13	18	17	2-19-74	S	367
32	14	18	17	2-20-74	S	29
35	15	18	17	2-24-74	S	269
36	16	18	18	2-24-74	S	438
39	17	18	18	2-25-74	HR	1906
40	13*	18	18	2-27-74	S	493
42	18	18	18	2-27-74	S	437
43	14*	18	18-19	3-03-74	HR	429
44	19	18	19	3-04-74	HR	1284
45	20	18	19	3-04-74	HR	2201
46	15*	18	19-20	3-05-74	HR	1920
47	21	18	20	3-05-74	HR	2076
50	22	18	20	3-07-74	HR	2224
51	23	18	20	3-07-74	HR	447

Public Law/Resolution		Statutes at Large	Page	Date	Bill No.	
Chapter	Number					
55	16	18	21-22	3-13-74	HR	1558
56	24	18	22	3-16-74	HR	1365
57	25	18	23	3-18-74	HR	919
58	26	18	23	3-21-74	S	360
61	27	18	23	3-23-74	HR	2228
62	28	18	23-24	3-23-74	HR	1015
64	17	18	24	3-24-74	HR	2225
65	18	18	24	3-24-74	HR	476
69	29	18	24	3-26-74	S	583
70	30	18	25	3-26-74	HR	1756
72	31	18	25	3-28-74	HR	2422
74	19*	18	25-26	4-03-74	HR	1037
75	32	18	26	4-03-74	HR	2451
76	33	18	26	4-03-74	HR	485
77	34	18	27	4-03-74	HR	2651
80	20*	18	27-28	4-07-74	HR	1762
82	35	18	28	4-09-74	S	512
93	36	18	28	4-14-74	HR	519
96	37	18	28-29	4-15-74	HR	1922
97	38	18	29	4-15-74	HR	1923
98	39	18	29	4-15-74	S	254
99	40	18	29	4-15-74	HR	971
100	41	18	30	4-15-74	HR	1892
106	21*	18	30	4-17-74	S	191
107	22*	18	30	4-17-74	S	580
108	42	18	30-31	4-17-74	HR	1942
110	23*	18	31	4-18-74	HR	2549
111	43	18	31	4-18-74	HR	1930
112	44	18	31	4-18-74	HR	2867
113	45	18	32	4-18-74	HR	2550
114	46	18	32	4-18-74	HR	2124
115	47	18	32	4-18-74	HR	1600
116	48	18	32	4-18-74	HR	2186
117	49	18	33	4-20-74	HR	912
118	50	18	33	4-21-74	HR	911
122	51	18	33-34	4-22-74	HR	2667
123	52	18	34	4-22-74	HR	2907
125	53	18	34	4-23-74	HR	3029

PUBLIC ACTS OF THE FORTY-THIRD CONGRESS

Public Law/Resolution		Statutes at Large	Page	Date	Bill No.	
Chapter	Number					
127	24*	18	34	4-24-74	HR	994
132	54	18	35	4-25-74	HR	2350
135	25*	18	35-36	4-29-74	HR	668
136	55	18	36-41	4-29-74	HR	2193
137	56	18	41	4-29-74	HR	200
141	57	18	41-42	5-01-74	HR	1573
142	58	18	42	5-01-74	HR	2868
145	59	18	42	5-06-74	HR	2206
149	26*	18	42-43	5-07-74	HR	1364
154	27*	18	43	5-08-74	HR	1933
163	28*	18	43	5-09-74	HR	2191
165	60	18	43-45	5-11-74	S	350
166	61	18	45	5-11-74	HR	3085
168	29*	18	45	5-12-74	HR	3255
170	62	18	45-46	5-13-74	HR	3161
175	63	18	46	5-15-74	HR	83
176	64	18	46	5-15-74	HR	3028
180	65	18	46-47	5-16-74	S	347
181	66	18	47	5-16-74	HR	420
182	67	18	47-48	5-18-74	S	149
184	68	18	48	5-20-74	HR	3139
186	30*	18	48	5-21-74	HR	2074
187	31*	18	48	5-21-74	HR	2846
194	69	18	48-49	5-27-74	S	253
195	70	18	49	5-28-74	HR	2989
200	32*	18	50	6-01-74	HR	2078
201	71	18	50	6-01-74	S	87
203	33*	18	50-51	6-03-74	HR	1560
204	72	18	51	6-03-74	S	510
205	73	18	51-52	6-03-74	HR	1590
206	74	18	52	6-03-74	HR	2782
207	75	18	52	6-03-74	HR	3267
214	34*	18	53	6-05-74	HR	3169
215	76	18	53	6-05-74	HR	1394
216	35*	18	53-59	6-06-74	HR	1013
217	36*	18	59-61	6-06-74	HR	2545
218	37*	18	61	6-06-74	S	237
219	38*	18	61	6-06-74	HR	2452

PUBLIC ACTS OF THE FORTY-THIRD CONGRESS

Public Law/Resolution		Statutes at Large	Page	Date	Bill No.	
Chapter	Number					
220	39*	18	61	6-06-74	S	822
221	77	18	61	6-06-74	HR	3407
222	78	18	62	6-06-74	HR	2692
223	79	18	62	6-06-74	S	32
224	80	18	62-63	6-06-74	HR	2538
256	40*	18	63	6-08-74	S	229
259	41*	18	64	6-09-74	HR	2081
260	42*	18	64-65	6-09-74	HR	3160
261	81	18	65	6-09-74	HR	773
262	82	18	65	6-09-74	S	766
263	83	18	66	6-09-74	S	369
264	84	18	66	6-09-74	S	708
274	85	18	66	6-10-74	S	860
275	43*	18	66-71	6-11-74	HR	3095
283	86	18	72	6-15-74	HR	2019
285	44*	18	72-75	6-16-74	HR	1009
286	45*	18	75-76	6-16-74	S	693
287	46*	18	76	6-16-74	S	881
288	87	18	76	6-16-74	HR	1753
289	88	18	76	6-16-74	S	793
290	89	18	77	6-16-74	S	529
294	47*	18	77	6-17-74	HR	3073
295	90	18	77	6-17-74	HR	2697
298	48*	18	78	6-18-74	HR	735
299	49*	18	78	6-18-74	HR	2453
300	50*	18	78	6-18-74	HR	3359
301	51*	18	78-79	6-18-74	S	876
302	52*	18	79	6-18-74	HR	1828
303	53*	18	79	6-18-74	HR	3303
304	54*	18	80	6-18-74	HR	3574
305	91	18	80	6-18-74	S	624
306	92	18	80-81	6-18-74	HR	2208
307	93	18	81	6-18-74	HR	3335
308	94	18	81	6-18-74	HR	3575
309	95	18	81-82	6-18-74	HR	1051
310	96	18	82	6-18-74	HR	3601
311	97	18	82-83	6-18-74	HR	1706
312	98	18	83	6-18-74	HR	3672

PUBLIC ACTS OF THE FORTY-THIRD CONGRESS

Public Law/Resolution		Statutes at Large	Page	Date	Bill No.	
Chapter	Number					
313	99	18	83	6-18-74	HR	2416
314	100	18	83-84	6-18-74	HR	2359
315	101	18	84	6-18-74	HR	3237
322	102	18	84	6-19-74	S	571
323	103	18	85	6-19-74	HR	1931
328	55*	18	85-111	6-20-74	HR	2064
329	56*	18	111	6-20-74	HR	886
330	57*	18	111	6-20-74	HR	3090
331	58*	18	111-112	6-20-74	HR	3573
332	59*	18	112	6-20-74	HR	440
333	60*	18	113-114	6-20-74	HR	3652
334	61*	18	115	6-20-74	S	954
335	62*	18	115-116	6-20-74	HR	3421
336	63*	18	116	6-20-74	HR	3332
337	64*	18	116-121	6-20-74	HR	3680
338	65*	18	121	6-20-74	HR	2450
339	66*	18	121	6-20-74	S	176
340	67*	18	121-122	6-20-74	HR	203
341	68*	18	122	6-20-74	HR	1507
342	69*	18	123	6-20-74	HR	3740
343	70*	18	123-125	6-20-74	HR	1572
344	71*	18	125-128	6-20-74	HR	2655
345	104	18	128	6-20-74	HR	3166
346	105	18	129-130	6-20-74	HR	3351
347	106	18	130	6-20-74	HR	3748
348	107	18	130-131	6-20-74	HR	3309
349	108	18	131-132	6-20-74	HR	3265
388	72*	18	133-146	6-22-74	HR	3030
389	73*	18	146-178	6-22-74	HR	2343
390	74*	18	178-186	6-22-74	HR	792
391	75*	18	186-191	6-22-74	HR	3171
392	76*	18	191-192	6-22-74	S	716
393	77*	18	192	6-22-74	HR	3256
394	78*	18	192-193	6-22-74	HR	3354
395	79*	18	193	6-22-74	HR	3428
396	80*	18	193	6-22-74	HR	3508
397	81*	18	193	6-22-74	HR	225
398	82*	18	194	6-22-74	HR	3539

Public Law/Resolution		Statutes at Large	Page	Date	Bill No.	
Chapter	Number					
399	83*	18	194	6-22-74	HR	3678
400	84*	18	194	6-22-74	HR	3162
401	85*	18	195-196	6-22-74	HR	2246
402	86*	18	196	6-22-74	HR	899
403	109	18	196	6-22-74	S	758
404	110	18	196-197	6-22-74	S	482
405	111	18	197	6-22-74	HR	3586
406	112	18	197-198	6-22-74	S	732
407	113	18	198	6-22-74	HR	3591
408	114	18	198	6-22-74	HR	3741
409	115	18	198	6-22-74	HR	2539
410	116	18	199	6-22-74	HR	2787
411	117	18	199	6-22-74	HR	2988
412	118	18	200	6-22-74	HR	3163
413	119	18	200	6-22-74	HR	3257
414	120	18	200	6-22-74	HR	3282
415	121	18	201	6-22-74	HR	3431
416	122	18	201	6-22-74	HR	3522
417	123	18	201	6-22-74	HR	3757
418	124	18	201	6-22-74	S	688
419	125	18	202	6-22-74	S	784
420	126	18	202	6-22-74	HR	2384
421	127	18	202	6-22-74	HR	2801
422	128	18	202-203	6-22-74	HR	1764
423	129	18	203	6-22-74	HR	2347
424	130	18	203	6-22-74	S	486
453	87*	18	203-204	6-23-74	S	849
454	88*	18	204	6-23-74	HR	3098
455	89*	18	204-231	6-23-74	HR	3600
456	90*	18	231-237	6-23-74	HR	3094
457	91*	18	237-244	6-23-74	HR	3168
458	92*	18	244-245	6-23-74	S	321
459	93*	18	245-249	6-23-74	S	7
460	94*	18	250	6-23-74	HR	3327
461	95*	18	250	6-23-74	HR	3432
462	96*	18	250	6-23-74	HR	3413
463	97*	18	251	6-23-74	HR	3534
464	98*	18	251	6-23-74	HR	3581

PUBLIC ACTS OF THE FORTY-THIRD CONGRESS

Public Law/Resolution		Statutes at Large	Page	Date	Bill No.	
Chapter	Number					
465	99*	18	251-252	6-23-74	HR	3415
466	100*	18	252	6-23-74	S	806
467	101*	18	252	6-23-74	S	683
468	102*	18	252	6-23-74	HR	2770
469	103*	18	253-256	6-23-74	HR	3097
470	104*	18	256-272	6-23-74	HR	3604
471	131	18	272-273	6-23-74	HR	3528
472	132	18	273	6-23-74	HR	3352
473	133	18	274	6-23-74	HR	2884
474	134	18	274-275	6-23-74	HR	3025
475	135	18	275	6-23-74	HR	2909
476	136	18	275-276	6-23-74	HR	2653
477	137	18	276	6-23-74	HR	3211
478	138	18	276-277	6-23-74	S	313
479	139	18	277	6-23-74	S	930
480	140	18	277-280	6-23-74	S	733
481	141	18	280-281	6-23-74	S	854
482	142	18	281-282	6-23-74	S	775
483	143	18	282	6-23-74	S	406
484	144	18	282	6-23-74	HR	2187
485	145	18	282	6-23-74	HR	1767
486	146	18	282	6-23-74	HR	1410
487	147	18	283	6-23-74	HR	2897
488	148	18	283	6-23-74	HR	3088
489	149	18	283	6-23-74	HR	3761
490	150	18	283	6-23-74	HR	3773
491	151	18	283-284	6-23-74	HR	2771

RESOLUTIONS OF THE FORTY-THIRD CONGRESS

1	1	18	285	1-08-74	H Res.	16
3	1*	18	285	1-19-74	H Res.	35
4	2	18	285	2-13-74	H Res.	43
5	3	18	285-286	3-18-74	S Res.	6
6	2*	18	286	3-24-74	H Res.	52
7	4	18	286	3-25-74	H Res.	29
8	5	18	286-287	4-27-74	H Res.	45
9	6	18	287	5-28-74	H Res.	103
10	3*	18	287	6-17-74	H Res.	107

RESOLUTIONS OF THE FORTY-THIRD CONGRESS

Public Law/Resolution		Statutes at Large	Page	Date	Bill No.
Chapter	Number				
11	7	18	287	6-19-74	H Res. 53
12	8	18	288	6-20-74	H Res. 112
13	9	18	288	6-22-74	H Res. 113
14	10	18	288	6-22-74	H Res. 59
15	11	18	288-289	6-22-74	H Res. 95
16	12	18	289	6-23-74	H Res. 115
17	13	18	289	6-23-74	H Res. 114

PUBLIC ACTS OF THE FORTY-THIRD CONGRESS

Public Law/Resolution		Statutes at Large	Page	Date	Bill No.	
Chapter	Number					
1	1	18	291	12-15-74	HR	3822
2	2	18	291-292	12-15-74	HR	2104
4	3	18	292-293	12-19-74	HR	3743
5	4	18	293	12-21-74	HR	3339
7	5	18	293	12-24-74	S	1054
8	1*	18	293	12-28-74	S	974
9	2*	18	293-294	12-28-74	HR	4144
10	6	18	294	12-28-74	S	1023
12	3*	18	294	1-01-75	S	1043
13	4*	18	294-295	1-11-75	S	381
14	7	18	295	1-11-75	S	650
15	5*	18	296	1-14-75	S	1044
18	6*	18	296-302	1-18-75	HR	3819
19	7*	18	302	1-19-75	S	1068
20	8	18	302	1-19-75	S	924
22	8*	18	303	1-22-75	HR	4214
23	9	18	303	1-22-75	HR	4213
25	10	18	303	1-25-75	S	1009
26	11	18	303	1-28-75	HR	4119
27	12	18	304	1-28-75	HR	4163
29	9*	18	304	1-29-75	HR	3593
30	13	18	304	1-30-75	S	170
31	14	18	304	1-30-75	HR	3006
32	15	18	305	1-30-75	S	448
33	10*	18	305	2-01-75	S	1204
34	16	18	305-306	2-05-75	HR	3584
35	17	18	206-307	2-05-75	HR	4162
36	11*	18	307-313	2-08-75	HR	3572
37	18	18	313	2-09-75	HR	4443
39	12*	18	313-314	2-10-75	HR	3823
40	19	18	314-315	2-10-75	HR	4545
41	13*	18	315	2-11-75	HR	2032
76	20	18	315	2-15-75	HR	4531
77	14*	18	315-316	2-16-75	S	1076
78	21	18	316	2-17-75	HR	4563
80	15*	18	316-321	2-18-75	HR	4546
81	16*	18	321-328	2-18-75	HR	3911
82	22	18	328	2-18-75	HR	2103

PUBLIC ACTS OF THE FORTY-THIRD CONGRESS

Public Law/Resolution		Statutes at Large	Page	Date	Bill No.	
Chapter	Number					
83	23	18	329	2-18-75	S	1012
84	24	18	329	2-18-75	HR	4535
89	17*	18	329-330	2-19-75	HR	3825
90	25	18	330-331	2-19-75	HR	3080
91	26	18	331	2-19-75	HR	3915
92	27	18	332	2-19-75	HR	4126
93	28	18	332	2-19-75	HR	2109
94	18*	18	332	2-20-75	HR	4444
95	19*	18	333-334	2-22-75	HR	3623
99	29	18	334-335	2-23-75	HR	4676
108	30	18	335	2-27-75	HR	1938
114	20*	18	335-337	3-01-75	HR	796
115	21*	18	337	3-01-75	HR	844
116	22*	18	337	3-01-75	HR	4677
117	31	18	337-338	3-01-75	HR	4727
118	23*	18	338	3-02-75	S	320
119	24*	18	338	3-02-75	HR	4530
120	32	18	338	3-02-75	HR	4838
126	25*	18	338-339	3-03-75	HR	4835
127	26*	18	339-340	3-03-75	HR	4680
128	27*	18	340-343	3-03-75	HR	4529
129	28*	18	343-370	3-03-75	HR	3818
130	28*	18	371-402	3-03-75	HR	4729
131	30*	18	402-420	3-03-75	HR	4851
132	31*	18	420-451	3-03-75	HR	3821
133	32*	18	452-455	3-03-75	HR	3820
134	33	18	456-466	3-03-75	HR	4740
135	34	18	466-469	3-03-75	HR	4441
136	35	18	469-470	3-03-75	HR	2073
137	36	18	470-473	3-03-75	HR	3511
138	37	18	473	3-03-75	HR	1593
139	38	18	474-476	3-03-75	HR	435
140	39	18	476	3-03-75	S	679
141	40	18	477-478	3-03-75	HR	4747
142	41	18	478	3-03-75	HR	3912
143	42	18	478-479	3-03-75	S	468
144	43	18	479	3-03-75	HR	4744
145	44	18	479-480	3-03-75	HR	3504

Public Law/Resolution		Statutes at Large	Page	Date	Bill No.	
Chapter	Number					
146	45	18	480	3-03-75	HR	4856
147	46	18	480	3-03-75	HR	4850
148	47	18	480	3-03-75	HR	1995
149	48	18	481	3-03-75	HR	2080
150	49	18	481	3-03-75	HR	4141
151	50	18	481-482	3-03-75	S	524
152	51	18	482-483	3-03-75	S	378
153	52	18	483-484	3-03-75	S	1328
154	53	18	484	3-03-75	S	1237
155	54	18	484-485	3-03-75	S	706
156	55	18	485-486	3-03-75	S	976
157	56	18	486	3-03-75	S	1339
158	57	18	486-496	3-03-75	HR	4734
159	33*	18	497	3-03-75	S	588
160	34*	18	497	3-03-75	HR	4841
161	35*	18	498-501	3-03-75	HR	2102
162	36*	18	501-505	3-03-75	HR	4840
163	37*	18	505-506	3-03-75	S	1270
164	38*	18	506	3-03-75	HR	3923
165	39*	18	506	3-03-75	HR	4685
166	40*	18	506-507	3-03-75	HR	4573
167	41*	18	507	3-03-75	HR	4833
168	42*	18	507-508	3-03-75	HR	4445
169	43*	18	508	3-03-75	HR	4447
170	44*	18	509	3-03-75	S	1240
171	45*	18	509	3-03-75	S	608
172	46*	18	510	3-03-75	HR	3379
173	47*	18	510	3-03-75	HR	3641
174	48*	18	510-511	3-03-75	HR	3435
175	49*	18	511	3-03-75	HR	4449
176	50*	18	511	3-03-75	HR	4520
177	51*	18	511-512	3-03-75	HR	4528
178	52*	18	512	3-03-75	HR	2093
179	53*	18	512	3-03-75	HR	4857
180	54*	18	513	3-03-75	HR	4853
181	55*	18	513	3-03-75	S	1296
182	56*	18	513-514	3-03-75	HR	2179
183	57*	18	514	3-03-75	HR	2419

PUBLIC ACTS OF THE FORTY-THIRD CONGRESS

Public Law/Resolution		Statutes at Large	Page	Date	Bill No.	
Chapter	Number					
184	58	18	514-515	3-03-75	HR	4458
185	59	18	515	3-03-75	HR	4730
186	60	18	515	3-03-75	HR	1063
187	61	18	515	3-03-75	HR	4866
188	62	18	516	3-03-75	S	420
189	63	18	516-517	3-03-75	S	867
190	64	18	517	3-03-75	S	55
191	65	18	517-518	3-03-75	S	28
192	66	18	518	3-03-75	S	1097
193	67	18	518	3-03-75	S	1019
194	68	18	518	3-03-75	S	912
195	69	18	519	3-03-75	S	757
196	70	18	519	3-03-75	HR	2502
197	71	18	519	3-03-75	S	411
198	72	18	520	3-03-75	HR	4746
199	73	18	520	3-03-75	HR	4816
200	74	18	521	3-03-75	HR	4324
201	75	18	521	3-03-75	S	1222
202	76	18	521	3-03-75	S	1297
203	77	18	522	3-03-75	S	1230

RESOLUTIONS OF THE FORTY-THIRD CONGRESS

1	1	18	523	12-18-74	S Res.	11
2	2	18	523-524	12-21-74	H Res.	119
3	3	18	524	2-16-75	H Res.	148
5	4	18	524	2-26-75	H Res.	135
6	5	18	524	3-02-75	H Res.	161
7	1*	18	524-525	3-03-75	H Res.	162
8	6	18	525	3-03-75	H Res.	102

PUBLIC ACTS OF THE FORTY-FOURTH CONGRESS

Public Law/Resolution		Statutes at Large	Page	Date	Bill No.	
Chapter	Number					
1	1	19	1	12-24-75	S	78
2	2	19	1	1-18-76	HR	282
3	3	19	2	1-18-76	HR	283
4	4	19	2	1-25-76	S	236
5	5	19	2	2-01-76	HR	626
6	6	19	2	2-01-76	HR	1208
9	7	19	3	2-15-76	HR	1053
10	8	19	3-4	2-16-76	HR	514
11	9	19	4	2-18-76	S	53
12	10	19	4-5	2-18-76	S	305
13	11	19	5	2-25-76	HR	785
14	12	19	5	2-25-76	HR	217
15	3*	19	5	2-29-76	HR	1802
17	13	19	5-6	3-03-76	HR	1328
18	14	19	6	3-03-76	HR	1590
19	15	19	6	3-03-76	HR	1384
20	16	19	6-7	3-06-76	HR	1054
23	17	19	7	3-14-76	HR	2282
27	18	19	7	3-15-76	HR	2270
28	19	19	7	3-15-76	HR	2285
29	20	19	8	3-16-76	S	360
30	21	19	8	3-23-76	HR	811
31	22	19	8-9	3-23-76	HR	1962
40	23	19	9-12	3-30-76	S	359
42	24	19	12-25	4-03-76	HR	2262
43	25*	19	25-26	4-05-76	S	401
44	26	19	26-27	4-05-76	S	295
45	27*	19	27	4-05-76	S	644
46	28	19	27	4-06-76	HR	2821
47	29	19	28	4-06-76	HR	2589
50	30	19	28	4-10-76	S	682
51	31	19	28-30	4-10-76	HR	2678
52	21*	19	30-31	4-10-76	HR	1488
53	32	19	31-32	4-11-76	S	252
54	33	19	32	4-11-76	HR	2143
55	34	19	32	4-11-76	HR	2800
56	35	19	32-33	4-13-76	HR	2655
62	36	19	33	4-14-76	HR	356

PUBLIC ACTS OF THE FORTY-FOURTH CONGRESS

Public Law/Resolution		Statutes at Large	Page	Date	Bill No.	
Chapter	Number					
63	37	19	33-34	4-17-76	HR	2450
64	38	19	34	4-17-76	HR	2934
65	39	19	34	4-17-76	S	235
66	40	19	34	4-18-76	S	701
67	41	19	35	4-20-76	S	58
71	42	19	35	4-21-76	S	417
72	43	19	35-36	4-21-76	S	34
73	44	19	36	4-21-76	HR	1439
78	45	19	36-37	4-25-76	S	279
79	46	19	37	4-25-76	S	697
80	47	19	37	4-25-76	S	169
83	48	19	37	4-26-76	HR	726
84	49	19	38	4-27-76	HR	1052
85	50	19	38-40	4-27-76	HR	700
86	51	19	41	4-29-76	S	760
88	52	19	41-48	5-01-76	HR	3128
89	53	19	49	5-01-76	HR	2951
90	54	19	49-52	5-03-76	HR	1345
91	55	19	52	5-05-76	HR	1251
93	56	19	52-53	5-09-76	S	130
94	57	19	53	5-09-76	HR	3269
95	58	19	53	5-13-76	HR	522
96	59	19	53	5-13-76	HR	3356
101	60	19	54	5-19-76	HR	3368
102	61	19	54	5-20-76	HR	2427
103	62	19	54-55	5-23-76	S	679
104	63	19	55	5-23-76	HR	2452
105	64	19	55	5-23-76	HR	3136
106	65	19	55-56	5-23-76	HR	2286
108	67	19	56	5-23-76	S	258
112	68	19	56	5-24-76	S	153
114	69	19	56-57	5-25-76	S	293
118	70	19	57	6-02-76	HR	3479
119	71	19	57	6-02-76	HR	219
120	72	19	57-58	6-07-76	S	677
122	73	19	58	6-10-76	HR	2447
123	74	19	58	6-12-76	HR	1400
133	75	19	59	6-19-76	HR	2434

PUBLIC ACTS OF THE FORTY-FOURTH CONGRESS

Public Law/Resolution		Statutes at Large	Page	Date	Bill No.	
Chapter	Number					
134	76	19	59	6-19-76	HR	3573
135	77	19	59-60	6-20-76	HR	2134
136	78	19	60	6-20-76	HR	2135
137	79	19	60	6-20-76	HR	2140
144	80	19	60	6-26-76	HR	1846
145	81	19	61	6-26-76	S	863
146	82	19	61	6-26-76	S	320
147	83	19	61-62	6-26-76	S	546
154	84	19	62	6-29-76	HR	353
156	85	19	63-64	6-30-76	HR	2441
157	86	19	65	6-30-76	HR	3809
158	87	19	65	6-30-76	S	960
159	88	19	65-72	6-30-76	HR	3375
160	89	19	72	7-01-76	HR	2824
162	90	19	72	7-03-76	S	46
163	91	19	72-73	7-03-76	S	558
164	92	19	73	7-03-76	S	634
165	93	19	73-74	7-04-76	S	2
166	94	19	74	7-05-76	HR	525
167	95	19	74	7-05-76	S	166
168	96	19	74-76	7-05-76	HR	1797
169	97	19	76	7-06-76	S	336
172	98	19	76-77	7-08-76	HR	3670
177	99	19	78	7-10-76	HR	3858
179	100	19	78-82	7-12-76	HR	3263
180	101	19	83-88	7-12-76	HR	2676
181	102	19	88	7-12-76	HR	1100
182	103	19	88	7-12-76	HR	3839
183	104	19	88-89	7-12-76	S	435
184	105	19	89	7-12-76	S	176
185	106	19	90	7-12-76	S	369
186	107	19	90	7-12-76	HR	2575
187	108	19	91	7-12-76	S	962
191	109	19	91	7-18-76	HR	3884
192	110	19	91	7-18-76	HR	3200
212	112	19	91-92	7-19-76	HR	1970
213	113	19	92-94	7-19-76	HR	3411
214	114	19	94	7-19-76	HR	702

Public Law/Resolution		Statutes at Large	Page	Date	Bill No.	
Chapter	Number					
220	115	19	94-95	7-21-76	S	894
221	116	19	95	7-21-76	HR	3928
222	117	19	95	7-22-76	S	843
223	118	19	95-96	7-22-76	HR	2118
224	119	19	96	7-22-76	S	391
225	120	19	96	7-22-76	S	983
226	121	19	97-101	7-24-76	HR	3717
227	122	19	101	7-24-76	HR	1771
228	123	19	101	7-24-76	S	1000
234	124	19	102	7-26-76	S	332
239	125	19	102	7-29-76	HR	1692
246	126	19	102-122	7-31-76	HR	3749
248	127	19	122	8-01-76	HR	4054
249	128	19	122	8-02-76	HR	4055
250	129	19	123	8-02-76	S	982
251	130	19	123	8-02-76	HR	3927
253	131	19	123-124	8-03-76	HR	4053
254	132	19	124	8-05-76	HR	1972
255	133	19	124-126	8-07-76	HR	810
256	134	19	126-127	8-09-76	HR	1336
258	135	19	127	8-11-76	HR	2692
259	136	19	127-129	8-11-76	HR	3625
260	137	19	129-131	8-11-76	HR	3963
261	138	19	131	8-12-76	HR	2252
262	139	19	131	8-12-76	HR	1823
263	140	19	131	8-12-76	S	1007
264	141	19	131	8-12-76	HR	4087
265	142	19	132	8-14-76	HR	4060
266	143	19	132	8-14-76	HR	361
267	144	19	132-139	8-14-76	HR	3022
268	145	19	139	8-14-76	HR	3209
269	146	19	139	8-14-76	HR	3678
270	147	19	139-140	8-14-76	S	413
271	148	19	140	8-14-76	S	1021
272	149	19	140	8-14-76	S	1036
273	150	19	141	8-14-76	S	84
274	151	19	141-142	8-14-76	S	846
287	152	19	143-170	8-15-76	HR	2571

PUBLIC ACTS OF THE FORTY-FOURTH CONGRESS

Public Law/Resolution		Statutes at Large	Page	Date	Bill No.	
Chapter	Number					
288	153	19	170–175	8–15–76	HR	1594
289	154	19	176–200	8–15–76	HR	3478
290	155	19	200	8–15–76	HR	612
291	156	19	200	8–15–76	S	1014
292	157	19	201	8–15–76	S	1042
293	158	19	201	8–15–76	S	892
294	159	19	202	8–15–76	S	699
295	160	19	202	8–15–76	S	297
296	161	19	202	8–15–76	HR	3962
297	162	19	202–203	8–15–76	HR	3168
298	163	19	203	8–15–76	HR	4107
299	164	19	203	8–15–76	S	1006
300	165	19	203–204	8–15–76	HR	1516
301	166	19	204	8–15–76	HR	4106
302	167	19	204	8–15–76	HR	800
303	168	19	205–206	8–15–76	HR	2689
304	169	19	206	8–15–76	HR	1803
305	170	19	206–207	8–15–76	HR	2813
306	171	19	207	8–15–76	HR	4108
307	172	19	207–208	8–15–76	HR	351
308	173	19	208–209	8–15–76	S	779

RESOLUTIONS OF THE FORTY-FOURTH CONGRESS

3	1	19	211	3–13–76	H Res.	19
4	2	19	211–212	3–14–76	H Res.	52
6	3	19	212	4–06–76	H Res.	86
8	4	19	212	4–10–76	S Res.	12
9	5	19	212–213	4–27–76	H Res.	85
10	6	19	213	5–08–76	H Res.	99
11	7	19	213	5–13–76	H Res.	110
12	8	19	213	6–08–76	H Res.	115
13	9	19	214	7–03–76	H Res.	129
15	10	19	214	7–20–76	H Res.	146
16	11	19	214–215	7–22–76	H Res.	135
17	12	19	215	7–22–76	H Res.	109
18	13	19	215–216	7–25–76	H Res.	153
19	14	19	216	8–03–76	H Res.	77
20	15	19	216	8–05–76	H Res.	154

RESOLUTIONS OF THE FORTY-FOURTH CONGRESS

Public Law/Resolution		Statutes at Large	Page	Date	Bill No.
Chapter	Number				
21	16	19	216	8-15-76	S Res. 24
22	17	19	217	8-15-76	H Res. 166
23	18	19	217	8-15-76	H Res. 148
24	19	19	217	8-15-76	H Res. 165

PUBLIC ACTS OF THE FORTY-FOURTH CONGRESS

Public Law/Resolution		Statutes at Large	Page	Date	Bill No.	
Chapter	Number					
1	1	19	219	12-18-76	HR	4197
7	2	19	219	12-22-76	S	745
9	3	19	219-220	12-23-76	HR	4124
10	4	19	220	12-27-76	HR	3693
12	5	19	220-221	12-28-76	S	1057
18	6	19	221	1-12-77	HR	2260
19	7	19	221-222	1-12-77	HR	4272
21	8	19	222	1-13-77	HR	4116
22	9	19	222	1-16-77	S	526
23	10	19	222	1-16-77	S	752
24	11	19	223	1-16-77	S	739
25	12	19	223	1-16-77	HR	4281
27	13	19	223-224	1-19-77	HR	4120
31	14	19	224	1-20-77	S	842
34	15	19	225	1-24-77	HR	2653
36	16	19	225-227	1-26-77	HR	4307
37	17	19	227-229	1-29-77	S	1153
41	18	19	230	1-31-77	S	155
50	19	19	230-231	2-05-77	HR	4473
57	20	19	231	2-13-77	HR	4284
58	21	19	231	2-16-77	S	1222
59	22	19	231-232	2-16-77	HR	967
60	23	19	232	2-17-77	S	1139
63	24	19	232-233	2-20-77	S	1141
65	25	19	233-238	2-26-77	HR	4251
66	26	19	239	2-26-77	HR	7
67	27	19	239	2-27-77	HR	2690
68	28	19	239-240	2-27-77	HR	4576
69	29	19	240-254	2-27-77	HR	4668
72	30	19	254-264	2-28-77	S	1185
73	31	19	264	2-28-77	S	234
74	32	19	264-265	2-28-77	S	859
75	33	19	265	2-28-77	HR	1984
76	34	19	265	2-28-77	HR	3163
77	35	19	266-267	2-28-77	HR	3741
79	36	19	267	3-01-77	S	1270
80	37	19	267	3-01-77	S	1271
81	38	19	267-268	3-01-77	S	805

PUBLIC ACTS OF THE FORTY-FOURTH CONGRESS

Public Law/Resolution		Statutes at Large	Page	Date	Bill No.	
Chapter	Number					
82	39	19	268-269	3-02-77	S	1216
83	40	19	269	3-02-77	S	1231
84	41	19	269-270	3-02-77	HR	3566
85	42	19	270	3-02-77	HR	1947
99	43	19	270	3-03-77	HR	4657
100	44	19	270	3-03-77	S	1243
101	45	19	271-293	3-03-77	HR	4452
102	46	19	294-319	3-03-77	HR	4472
103	47	19	319-343	3-03-77	HR	3628
104	48	19	343-344	3-03-77	HR	186
105	49	19	344-362	3-03-77	HR	4680
106	50	19	363-376	3-03-77	HR	4559
107	51	19	377	3-03-77	HR	4261
108	52	19	377-380	3-03-77	HR	2382
109	53	19	380-383	3-03-77	HR	4306
110	54	19	383-385	3-03-77	HR	4187
111	55	19	385-391	3-03-77	HR	4616
112	56	19	391-392	3-03-77	HR	4188
113	57	19	392-393	3-03-77	HR	1765
114	58	19	393-395	3-03-77	HR	3925
115	59	19	395	3-03-77	HR	4276
116	60	19	395	3-03-77	HR	1253
117	61	19	396-402	3-03-77	HR	4554
118	62	19	402	3-03-77	S	1238
119	63	19	402-403	3-03-77	S	177
120	64	19	403	3-03-77	S	36
121	65	19	403	3-03-77	S	35
122	66	19	403-404	3-03-77	S	1225
123	67	19	404	3-03-77	S	1163
124	68	19	404	3-03-77	S	1128
125	69	19	404-405	3-03-77	S	1122
126	70	19	405	3-03-77	S	1083
127	71	19	405-406	3-03-77	S	1063
128	72	19	406	3-03-77	S	1019
129	73	19	406-407	3-03-77	S	1001
130	74	19	407	3-03-77	HR	4198
131	75	19	407	3-03-77	HR	1611
132	76	19	408	3-03-77	HR	1824

PUBLIC ACTS OF THE FORTY-FOURTH CONGRESS

Public Law/Resolution		Statutes at Large	Page	Date	Bill No.	
Chapter	Number					
133	77	19	408	3-03-77	S	189
134	76*	19	408	3-03-77	S	1111

RESOLUTIONS OF THE FORTY-FOURTH CONGRESS

1	1	19	409	12-09-76	S Res.	26
2	2	19	409	1-15-77	S Res.	29
3	3	19	409	1-26-77	H Res.	169
5	4	19	409	2-05-77	H Res.	181
6	5	19	410	3-03-77	H Res.	196
7	6	19	410	3-03-77	S Res.	30
8	7	19	410-411	3-03-77	H Res.	194
9	8	19	411	3-03-77	S Res.	32

PUBLIC ACTS OF THE FORTY-FIFTH CONGRESS

Public Law/Resolution		Statutes at Large	Page	Date	Bill No.	
Chapter	Number					
1	1	20	1-4	11-21-77	HR	902
2	2	20	4-5	11-21-77	HR	1220
3	3	20	5	11-21-77	HR	1265
5	4	20	5	11-24-77	S	289
6	5	20	5	12-10-77	HR	1279

RESOLUTIONS OF THE FORTY-FIFTH CONGRESS

2	1	20	6	11-23-77	S Res.	6

PUBLIC ACTS OF THE FORTY-FIFTH CONGRESS

Public Law/Resolution		Statutes at Large	Page	Date	Bill No.	
Chapter	Number					
1	1	20	7	12-14-77	HR	1532
3	2	20	7-13	12-15-77	HR	1526
4	3	20	13	12-15-77	S	192
5	4	20	13	12-15-77	S	315
6	5	20	14	12-15-77	HR	2115
7	6	20	14-21	1-14-78	HR	1637
8	7	20	22	1-18-78	HR	2142
9	8	20	22	1-31-78	HR	542
10	9	20	22	2-01-78	S	461
12	10	20	23	2-04-78	S	412
13	11	20	24	2-07-78	HR	2479
14	12	20	24	2-11-78	HR	1454
16	13	20	24	2-19-78	S	702
17	14	20	24	2-25-78	HR	789
18	15	20	25	2-25-78	HR	1201
20	16	20	25-26	2-28-78	HR	1093
22	17	20	26	3-04-78	HR	1928
25	18	20	26-27	3-08-78	HR	3551
26	19	20	27	3-09-78	S	541
27	20	20	27	3-09-78	HR	2860
28	21	20	27-29	2-09-78	S	17
32	22	20	29-30	3-13-78	HR	1074
34	23	20	30	3-15-78	HR	1474
37	24	20	30-31	3-16-78	HR	912
38	25	20	31	3-18-78	S	876
42	26	20	31	3-23-78	HR	2887
43	27	20	31-32	3-23-78	HR	2686
44	28	20	32	2-26-78	S	611
46	29	20	32-33	4-02-78	S	528
47	30	20	34	4-02-78	HR	3846
48	31	20	34-35	4-03-78	HR	2371
49	32	20	35	4-03-78	S	648
50	33	20	35	4-08-78	HR	1254
51	34	20	35-36	4-08-78	HR	596
58	35	20	36	4-10-78	HR	2287
59	36	20	36	4-17-78	S	691
60	37	20	36	4-17-78	HR	1412
61	38	20	36-37	4-19-78	S	1014

PUBLIC ACTS OF THE FORTY-FIFTH CONGRESS

Public Law/Resolution		Statutes at Large	Page	Date	Bill No.	
Chapter	Number					
62	39	20	37	4-20-78	S	484
64	40	20	37	4-23-78	HR	4242
66	41	20	37 38	4-29-78	HR	3739
67	42	20	39	4-29-78	HR	3712
68	43	20	39	4-29-78	HR	1411
69	44	20	39-40	4-29-78	HR	1432
72	45	20	40	4-30-78	HR	4658
73	46	20	40	4-30-78	HR	4222
74	47	20	40	4-30-78	S	1080
75	48	20	41-46	4-30-78	HR	3740
76	49	20	46-47	4-30-78	HR	3102
78	50	20	47	5-02-78	S	1045
79	51	20	47	5-02-78	HR	4394
80	52	20	47	5-02-78	S	120
87	53	20	48	5-03-78	S	706
88	54	20	48	5-03-78	HR	1887
91	55	20	48-56	5-04-78	HR	3822
95	56	20	56	5-06-78	HR	1639
96	57	20	56-61	5-07-78	S	15
106	58	20	61	5-16-78	HR	3679
107	59	20	61-63	5-17-78	HR	3987
109	60	20	63	5-25-78	HR	3123
140	61	20	63	5-27-78	HR	3373
141	62	20	63	5-27-78	HR	3546
142	63	20	63-87	5-27-78	HR	4549
145	64	20	87	5-28-78	S	933
146	65	20	87	5-31-78	HR	4663
147	66	20	88	5-31-78	HR	4713
148	67	20	88	6-01-78	S	1021
150	68	20	88-89	6-03-78	S	20
151	69	20	89-91	6-03-78	S	926
152	70	20	91	6-03-78	HR	3369
154	71	20	91	6-04-78	HR	4425
155	72	20	91-98	6-04-78	HR	3064
156	73	20	99	6-06-78	HR	4413
160	74	20	99	6-07-78	S	35
161	75	20	100	6-07-78	S	134
162	76	20	100-101	6-07-78	HR	3969

PUBLIC ACTS OF THE FORTY-FIFTH CONGRESS

Public Law/Resolution		Statutes at Large	Page	Date	Bill No.	
Chapter	Number					
168	77	20	101	6-08-78	S	330
169	78	20	101-102	6-08-78	S	380
170	79	20	102	6-08-78	HR	4988
180	80	20	102-108	6-11-78	HR	3259
181	81	20	108-111	6-11-78	HR	2507
182	82	20	111	6-11-78	HR	3892
183	83	20	111	6-11-78	HR	4519
184	84	20	112	6-11-78	HR	5124
188	85	20	112-113	6-14-78	HR	3974
189	86	20	113	6-14-78	S	138
190	87	20	113-115	6-14-78	S	396
191	88	20	115-130	6-14-78	HR	5117
192	89	20	130-131	6-14-78	HR	5066
193	90	20	131	6-14-78	S	1272
194	91	20	131	6-14-78	HR	4943
195	92	20	132	6-14-78	HR	2057
196	93	20	132	6-14-78	HR	2319
197	94	20	132	6-14-78	S	1208
198	95	20	133	6-14-78	HR	1271
199	96	20	133	6-14-78	HR	4525
211	97	20	133	6-15-78	HR	699
212	98	20	133-134	6-15-78	HR	4802
213	99	20	134-135	6-15-78	HR	4945
214	100	20	135-137	6-15-78	HR	4616
215	101	20	137-139	6-15-78	HR	3708
216	102	20	140	6-15-78	HR	3978
259	103	20	140-143	6-17-78	HR	4246
260	104	20	143-144	6-17-78	S	1047
261	105	20	144	6-17-78	HR	4976
262	106	20	144-145	6-18-78	S	1016
263	107	20	145-152	6-18-78	HR	4867
264	108	20	152-163	6-18-78	HR	4236
265	109	20	163-165	6-18-78	HR	3988
266	110	20	165	6-18-78	HR	775
267	111	20	165-166	6-18-78	HR	179
268	112	20	166	6-18-78	HR	4422
269	113	20	166	6-18-78	HR	431
309	114	20	166	6-19-78	S	1088

PUBLIC ACTS OF THE FORTY-FIFTH CONGRESS

Public Law/Resolution		Statutes at Large	Page	Date	Bill No.	
Chapter	Number					
310	115	20	167	6-19-78	S	1044
311	116	20	167	6-19-78	S	304
312	117	20	167-168	6-19-78	S	268
313	118	20	168-169	6-19-78	S	1262
314	119	20	169	6-19-78	HR	4572
315	120	20	169	6-19-78	S	1404
316	121	20	169-171	6-19-78	S	1200
317	122	20	171	6-19-78	HR	4
318	123	20	171	6-19-78	S	185
319	124	20	171-172	6-19-78	HR	923
320	125	20	172-173	6-19-78	HR	2401
321	126	20	173	6-19-78	HR	3968
322	127	20	173	6-19-78	HR	4024
323	128	20	173-174	6-19-78	HR	4055
324	129	20	175	6-19-78	HR	4674
325	130	20	175	6-19-78	HR	4931
326	131	20	175-177	6-19-78	HR	5070
327	132	20	177	6-19-78	HR	5137
328	133	20	177-178	6-19-78	HR	5053
329	135	20	178-206	6-19-78	HR	4104
330	211*	20	206	6-19-78	HR	2441
331	221*	20	206	6-19-78	HR	4420
359	134	20	206-240	6-20-78	HR	5130
360	136	20	241	6-20-78	S	566
361	137	20	241	6-20-78	S	493
362	138	20	241-242	6-20-78	S	1284
363	139	20	242	6-20-78	S	1411
364	140	20	242	6-20-78	HR	3343
365	141	20	242	6-20-78	HR	3435
366	142	20	243	6-20-78	HR	4989
367	143	20	243	6-20-78	HR	4981

RESOLUTIONS OF THE FORTY-FIFTH CONGRESS

1	1	20	245-246	12-15-77	H Res.	48
2	2	20	246	12-15-77	H Res.	56
3	3	20	246	12-15-77	H Res.	58
4	4	20	247	12-15-77	H Res.	59
6	5	20	247	1-26-78	S Res.	15

RESOLUTIONS OF THE FORTY-FIFTH CONGRESS

Public Law/Resolution		Statutes at Large	Page	Date	Bill No.	
Chapter	Number					
8	6	20	247	2-01-78	H Res.	83
9	7	20	247	2-07-78	H Res.	85
10	8	20	248	2-18-78	H Res.	54
11	9	20	248	2-18-78	H Res.	90
13	10	20	248	3-09-78	H Res.	82
14	11	20	248	3-09-78	H Res.	37
15	12	20	249	3-25-78	S Res.	21
16	13	20	249-250	3-28-78	H Res.	133
17	14	20	250	4-04-78	H Res.	142
18	15	20	250	4-11-78	S Res.	22
19	16	20	250	5-03-78	H Res.	158
20	17	20	251	5-04-78	H Res.	78
22	18	20	251-252	5-22-78	S Res.	23
24	19	20	252	5-31-78	H Res.	178
25	20	20	252	5-31-78	H Res.	173
26	21	20	252	6-07-78	H Res.	153
27	22	20	253	6-08-78	H Res.	177
28	23	20	253	6-14-78	S Res.	34
29	24	20	253	6-14-78	H Res.	182
30	25	20	253-254	6-14-78	H Res.	193
31	26	20	254	6-14-78	H Res.	152
32	27	20	254	6-15-78	H Res.	81
33	28	20	254	6-17-78	S Res.	36
34	29	20	254-255	6-17-78	S Res.	37
35	30	20	255	6-18-78	S Res.	39
36	31	20	255	6-18-78	H Res.	195
38	32	20	255	6-19-78	H Res.	199
39	33	20	255-256	6-19-78	H Res.	197
40	34	20	256	6-19-78	H Res.	196
41	35	20	256	6-20-78	S Res.	41
42	36	20	256	6-20-78	S Res.	42

Public Law/Resolution		Statutes at Large	Page	Date	Bill No.	
Chapter	Number					
2	1	20	257	12-12-78	S	824
3	2	20	257	12-12-78	S	1133
4	3	20	257-258	12-13-78	S	1367
5	4	20	258	12-16-78	HR	5307
8	5	20	259	12-21-78	HR	5532
9	6	20	259	12-21-78	HR	5535
10	7	20	259	12-21-78	HR	5682
11	8	20	259-260	12-23-78	HR	5683
12	9	20	260	1-13-79	S	882
19	10	20	260-262	1-20-79	HR	5230
20	11	20	263	1-21-79	HR	5067
21	12	20	264	1-24-79	S	1374
22	13	20	264	1-25-79	S	1297
23	14	20	265	1-25-79	HR	4234
24	15	20	265-266	1-25-79	HR	5808
25	16	20	266	1-27-79	S	893
26	17	20	266-267	1-27-79	HR	5501
27	18	20	267	1-27-79	HR	5655
28	19	20	267-274	1-27-79	HR	5312
30	20	20	274-275	1-28-79	S	109
33	21	20	275-276	1-29-79	HR	6141
34	22	20	276	1-29-79	S	1242
35	23	20	276	1-29-79	S	1435
36	24	20	276	1-30-79	HR	613
37	25	20	277	1-30-79	HR	4200
38	26	20	277	1-31-79	S	623
39	27	20	277-278	1-31-79	HR	5315
40	28	20	278-279	2-03-79	S	43
41	29	20	280	2-03-79	S	878
42	30	20	280	2-03-79	S	1151
43	31	20	280-281	2-03-79	S	1277
44	32	20	281	2-03-79	S	1060
45	33	20	281	2-04-79	HR	5052
46	34	20	281	2-04-79	S	1662
47	35	20	282	2-04-79	S	351
48	36	20	282	2-04-79	S	1135
49	37	20	282-283	2-06-79	S	1028
50	38	20	283	2-06-79	S	1344

PUBLIC ACTS OF THE FORTY-FIFTH CONGRESS

Public Law/Resolution		Statutes at Large	Page	Date	Bill No.	
Chapter	Number					
65	39	20	283-284	2-10-79	S	1560
68	40	20	284-292	2-14-79	HR	5313
81	41	20	292	2-15-79	HR	1077
82	42	20	292-294	2-15-79	S	763
83	43	20	294-295	2-15-79	HR	5180
87	44	20	295-316	2-17-79	HR	5534
90	45	20	316	2-19-79	HR	376
91	46	20	316	2-19-79	S	830
95	47	20	317	2-21-79	HR	5217
96	48	20	317-318	2-24-79	HR	4779
97	49	20	318-320	2-24-79	HR	1582
99	50	20	320-321	2-25-79	S	361
100	51	20	321	2-25-79	S	658
101	52	20	321	2-25-79	S	1307
102	53	20	321-322	2-26-79	HR	5477
103	54	20	322	2-26-79	HR	3828
104	55	20	322	2-26-79	HR	1008
105	56	20	322-323	2-26-79	HR	3055
106	57	20	323	2-26-79	HR	6225
109	58	20	323	2-27-79	HR	6150
110	59	20	323-324	2-27-79	S	1099
112	60	20	324	2-28-79	HR	5824
114	61	20	324	3-01-79	S	793
115	62	20	324	3-01-79	S	837
116	63	20	325	3-01-79	HR	1277
117	64	20	325	3-01-79	HR	1278
118	65	20	325	3-01-79	HR	4002
119	66	20	325	3-01-79	HR	6272
120	67	20	325-326	3-01-79	HR	3871
121	68	20	326	3-01-79	HR	3434
122	69	20	326	3-01-79	S	1365
123	70	20	326	3-01-79	S	1268
124	71	20	327	3-01-79	HR	3625
125	72	20	327-352	3-01-79	HR	4414
170	73	20	352	3-03-79	S	801
171	74	20	352	3-03-79	S	1073
172	75	20	353	3-03-79	S	1108
173	76	20	353	3-03-79	S	1285

PUBLIC ACTS OF THE FORTY-FIFTH CONGRESS

Public Law/Resolution		Statutes at Large	Page	Date	Bill No.	
Chapter	Number					
174	77	20	353-354	3-03-79	HR	1651
175	78	20	354	3-03-79	HR	1901
176	79	20	354	3-03-79	HR	5065
177	80	20	355	3-03-79	HR	5300
178	81	20	355	3-03-79	HR	6523
179	82	20	355	3-03-79	HR	6179
180	83	20	355-363	3-03-79	HR	6143
181	84	20	363-377	3-03-79	HR	6463
182	85	20	377-410	3-03-79	HR	6471
183	86	20	410-426	3-03-79	HR	6436
184	87	20	427-467	3-03-79	HR	6126
185	88	20	467	3-03-79	HR	5231
186	89	20	467-469	3-03-79	HR	4228
187	90	20	469-470	3-03-79	HR	6462
188	91	20	470	3-03-79	S	174
189	92	20	470-471	3-03-79	S	184
190	93	20	471-472	3-03-79	S	373
191	94	20	472	3-03-79	S	959
192	95	20	472	3-03-79	S	1087
193	96	20	473	3-03-79	HR	1475
194	97	20	473	3-03-79	S	1582
195	98	20	473-481	3-03-79	S	1685
196	99	20	481-483	3-03-79	S	1691
197	100	20	483	3-03-79	HR	2518
198	101	20	483	3-03-79	HR	3879
199	102	20	483-484	3-03-79	HR	4803
200	103	20	484	3-03-79	HR	6242
201	104	20	484	3-03-79	HR	6270
202	105	20	484-485	3-03-79	HR	6500

RESOLUTIONS OF THE FORTY-FIFTH CONGRESS

1	1	20	487	12-21-78	H Res.	206
2	2	20	487	12-21-78	H Res.	210
3	3	20	487	12-21-78	H Res.	211
5	4	20	487-488	2-05-79	H Res.	162
6	5	20	488	2-10-79	H Res.	229
9	6	20	488	2-27-79	S Res.	66
12	7	20	488-489	3-03-79	H Res.	127

RESOLUTIONS OF THE FORTY-FIFTH CONGRESS

Public Law/Resolution		Statutes at Large	Page	Date	Bill No.	
Chapter	Number					
13	8	20	489	3-03-79	S Res.	71
14	9	20	489-490	3-03-79	H Res.	63
15	10	20	490	3-03-79	H Res.	191
16	11	20	490	3-03-79	H Res.	207

This is a blank page.

PUBLIC ACTS OF THE FORTY SIXTH-CONGRESS

Public Law/Resolution		Statutes at Large	Page	Date	Bill No.	
Chapter	Number					
1	1	21	1	4-18-79	S	55
2	2	21	1	4-29-79	S	218
3	3	21	2-3	5-10-79	HR	1343
4	4	21	3	5-12-79	HR	67
5	5	21	3-4	5-12-79	HR	286
6	6	21	4	5-13-79	HR	1376
7	7	21	4	5-14-79	S	565
8	8	21	4	5-17-79	HR	1377
10	9	21	5	5-29-79	HR	178
11	10	21	5-7	6-02-79	S	108
12	11	21	7-8	6-09-79	HR	4
13	12	21	8	6-09-79	S	491
14	13	21	8	6-09-79	S	644
15	14	21	8-9	6-10-79	HR	1999
16	15	21	9	6-10-79	HR	2005
17	16	21	9-10	6-10-79	HR	1380
18	17	21	10-11	6-11-79	S	572
19	18	21	11	6-12-79	HR	1152
20	19	21	11	6-12-79	S	516
21	20	21	11-20	6-12-79	HR	2020
22	21	21	20	6-14-79	HR	435
23	22	21	20-21	6-14-79	S	678
26	23	21	21	6-18-79	HR	1478
27	24	21	21-22	6-18-79	HR	2263
32	25	21	23	6-19-79	HR	1734
33	26	21	23	6-21-79	HR	1369
34	27	21	23-30	6-21-79	HR	2251
35	28	21	30-35	6-23-79	HR	2175
38	29	21	35	6-27-79	HR	1856
39	30	21	35	6-27-79	HR	2267
40	31	21	35	6-27-79	HR	2274
41	32	21	36	6-27-79	HR	1379
42	33	21	36-37	6-27-79	HR	2329
43	34	21	37-38	6-28-79	HR	1847
44	35	21	38-40	6-28-79	S	697
45	36	21	40-41	6-28-79	HR	2002
47	37	21	41	6-30-79	S	719
48	38	21	41	6-30-79	S	506

PUBLIC ACTS OF THE FORTY-SIXTH CONGRESS

Public Law/Resolution		Statutes at Large	Page	Date	Bill No.	
Chapter	Number					
49	39	21	41-42	6-30-79	S	498
50	40	21	42	6-30-79	HR	1627
51	41	21	43	6-30-79	HR	2264
52	42	21	43-44	6-30-79	HR	2381
53	43	21	44	6-30-79	S	696
54	44	21	44	6-30-79	S	671
55	45	21	44-45	6-30-79	S	243
56	46	21	45	6-30-79	HR	2386
57	47	21	45	6-30-79	S	712
59	48	21	45-46	7-01-79	HR	609
60	49	21	46	7-01-79	S	641
61	50	21	46-47	7-01-79	S	675
62	51	21	47-48	7-01-79	S	716
63	52	21	48	7-01-79	HR	2275
64	53	21	48	7-01-79	HR	2406

RESOLUTIONS OF THE FORTY-SIXTH CONGRESS

1	1	21	48	4-18-79	S Res.	17
2	2	21	49	4-18-79	S Res.	20
3	3	21	49	6-09-79	S Res.	35
4	4	21	49-50	6-10-79	H Res.	82
5	5	21	50	6-14-79	H Res.	94
6	6	21	50	6-14-79	H Res.	72
9	7	21	50	6-19-79	S Res.	6
10	8	21	50-51	6-20-79	H Res.	34
11	9	21	51	6-20-79	H Res.	87
12	10	21	51-53	6-20-79	H Res.	1
13	11	21	53	6-24-79	H Res.	85
14	12	21	53	6-27-79	H Res.	71
15	13	21	53-54	6-27-79	H Res.	113
16	14	21	54	6-27-79	H Res.	32
17	15	21	54	6-28-79	S Res.	5
18	16	21	54	6-28-79	H Res.	114
19	17	21	54-55	6-28-79	H Res.	102
20	18	21	55-56	7-01-79	H Res.	118
21	19	21	56	7-01-79	H Res.	119
22	20	21	56-57	7-01-79	H Res.	79

PUBLIC ACTS OF THE FORTY-SIXTH CONGRESS

Public Law/Resolution		Statutes at Large	Page	Date	Bill No.	
Chapter	Number					
1	1	21	59	12-20-79	HR	1955
2	2	21	59	12-22-79	HR	1989
4	3	21	59-60	1-13-80	HR	2791
5	4	21	60	1-14-80	S	819
8	5	21	60	1-21-80	HR	1307
9	6	21	61	1-22-80	S	765
10	7	21	61	1-23-80	HR	3496
12	8	21	61	1-24-80	HR	55
13	9	21	62	1-24-80	HR	2790
14	10	21	62	1-24-80	HR	3518
16	11	21	62	1-28-80	HR	3108
17	12	21	62-63	1-29-80	HR	3034
18	13	21	63-64	2-04-80	HR	582
19	14	21	64-65	2-04-80	S	891
21	15	21	65	2-11-80	HR	325
22	16	21	65	2-11-80	HR	3497
25	17	21	66	2-14-80	S	857
30	18	21	66	2-24-80	HR	2785
33	19	21	66	3-05-80	HR	3288
34	20	21	66-67	3-05-80	HR	4903
36	21	21	67	3-10-80	HR	4432
37	22	21	67	3-10-80	HR	3462
38	23	21	67-68	3-16-80	HR	3258
39	24	21	68-69	3-16-80	HR	3968
40	25	21	69-70	4-01-80	HR	1153
41	26	21	70	4-01-80	S	605
42	27	21	70	4-01-80	S	1229
43	28	21	70-71	4-01-80	HR	5258
47	29	21	71	4-06-80	HR	4568
48	30	21	71-72	4-07-80	HR	4736
49	31	21	72	4-07-80	HR	2817
50	32	21	73	4-09-80	HR	5621
51	33	21	73	4-14-80	HR	5622
52	34	21	73-74	4-16-80	S	53
53	35	21	74	4-16-80	S	631
54	36	21	74	4-16-80	S	837
55	37	21	74	4-16-80	S	1475
56	38	21	74-75	4-16-80	HR	5048

PUBLIC ACTS OF THE FORTY-SIXTH CONGRESS

Public Law/Resolution		Statutes at Large	Page	Date	Bill No.	
Chapter	Number					
57	39	21	75-76	4-20-80	S	885
58	40	21	76	4-20-80	S	1027
60	41	21	77-81	4-23-80	S	1160
61	42	21	81	4-23-80	HR	5161
67	43	21	81	4-24-80	HR	5623
71	44	21	81	4-30-80	HR	1336
72	45	21	82	5-01-80	HR	3534
73	46	21	82-90	5-03-80	HR	5626
74	47	21	90-108	5-03-80	HR	5524
75	48	21	108	5-03-80	HR	4247
76	49	21	108-109	5-03-80	HR	3803
77	50	21	109	5-03-80	HR	2253
78	51	21	109	5-03-80	HR	2902
80	52	21	109-110	5-04-80	HR	2787
81	53	21	110-114	5-04-80	HR	5523
83	54	21	114	5-07-80	HR	6066
84	55	21	114	5-08-80	HR	5894
85	56	21	114-133	5-11-80	HR	4212
88	57	21	133-140	5-14-80	HR	3035
89	58	21	140-141	5-14-80	HR	4227
94	59	21	141	5-17-80	S	1670
95	60	21	141	5-18-80	HR	4507
100	61	21	141	5-24-80	HR	2481
101	62	21	142	5-24-80	HR	2850
102	63	21	142	5-26-80	S	464
103	64	21	142	5-26-80	S	1703
105	65	21	142-143	5-27-80	HR	580
106	66	21	143	5-27-80	HR	4214
107	67	21	143-145	5-28-80	HR	2326
108	68	21	145-150	5-28-80	HR	4812
113	69	21	150-151	5-31-80	HR	6239
115	70	21	151-153	6-01-80	HR	3015
116	71	21	154	6-01-80	S	1702
119	72	21	154	6-03-80	HR	5203
120	73	21	155	6-04-80	HR	5526
121	74	21	155-162	6-04-80	HR	5896
124	75	21	163	6-07-80	HR	3966
127	76	21	163-164	6-08-80	HR	165

PUBLIC ACTS OF THE FORTY-SIXTH CONGRESS

Public Law/Resolution		Statutes at Large	Page	Date	Bill No.	
Chapter	Number					
128	77	21	164	6-08-80	HR	2440
129	78	21	164	6-08-80	HR	2788
130	79	21	164	6-08-80	HR	3347
131	80	21	164-165	6-08-80	HR	5041
132	81	21	165	6-08-80	S	559
133	82	21	165	6-08-80	S	1117
134	83	21	165-166	6-08-80	S	1148
135	84	21	166	6-08-80	S	1256
136	85	21	166	6-08-80	S	1404
137	86	21	166-167	6-08-80	S	1408
161	87	21	167-168	6-09-80	S	640
162	88	21	168-169	6-09-80	S	849
163	89	21	169	6-09-80	S	1162
164	90	21	169	6-09-80	S	1247
165	91	21	170	6-09-80	S	1490
166	92	21	170	6-09-80	S	1501
167	93	21	170	6-09-80	S	1570
168	94	21	170-171	6-09-80	S	1723
169	95	21	171	6-09-80	HR	1064
170	96	21	171	6-09-80	HR	2046
171	97	21	171-172	6-09-80	HR	4849
186	98	21	172	6-10-80	S	1281
187	99	21	172	6-10-80	HR	1305
188	100	21	172	6-10-80	HR	2208
189	101	21	173	6-10-80	HR	2508
190	102	21	173-175	6-10-80	HR	4911
203	103	21	175-176	6-11-80	HR	698
204	104	21	176	6-11-80	HR	3794
205	105	21	176-177	6-11-80	HR	4606
206	106	21	177-179	6-11-80	HR	6036
207	107	21	179	7-14-80	HR	2528
208	108	21	179	6-14-80	HR	3274
209	109	21	180	7-14-80	HR	3275
210	110	21	180	7-14-80	HR	5304
211	111	21	180-197	7-14-80	HR	6237
212	112	21	197	7-14-80	HR	6467
213	113	21	198	7-14-80	HR	6471
214	114	21	198	7-14-80	HR	6472

PUBLIC ACTS OF THE FORTY-SIXTH CONGRESS

Public Law/Resolution		Statutes at Large	Page	Date	Bill No.	
Chapter	Number					
221	115	21	198	7-15-80	S	194
222	116	21	199	7-15-80	S	1315
223	117	21	199-205	7-15-80	S	1509
224	118	21	205-210	7-15-80	S	1771
225	119	21	210-237	7-15-80	HR	6185
226	120	21	237	7-15-80	HR	5153
227	121	21	237-238	7-15-80	HR	1846
234	122	21	238-258	7-16-80	HR	6325
235	123	21	259-281	7-16-80	HR	6266
236	124	21	281	7-16-80	S	815
237	125	21	282	7-16-80	S	1320
238	126	21	282	7-16-80	S	1371
239	127	21	283	7-16-80	HR	559
240	128	21	283	7-16-80	HR	952
241	129	21	283	7-16-80	HR	1023
242	130	21	283-284	7-16-80	HR	1291
243	131	21	284-287	7-16-80	HR	2328
244	132	21	287	7-16-80	HR	3171
245	133	21	287-288	7-16-80	HR	3708
246	134	21	288-290	7-16-80	HR	4244
247	135	21	290	7-16-80	HR	4268
248	136	21	290	7-16-80	HR	5502
249	137	21	290-291	7-16-80	HR	5628
250	138	21	291	7-16-80	HR	6109
251	139	21	291-292	7-16-80	HR	6112
252	140	21	292-296	7-16-80	HR	6207
253	141	21	296-297	7-16-80	HR	6492

RESOLUTIONS OF THE FORTY-SIXTH CONGRESS

1	1	21	299	12-19-79	S Res.	26
2	2	21	299	12-19-79	S Res.	50
3	3	21	299	12-19-79	S Res.	52
4	4	21	299-300	1-14-80	S Res.	58
6	5	21	300	1-23-80	H Res.	156
7	6	21	300	1-28-80	H Res.	145
8	7	21	300	2-04-80	H Res.	169
9	8	21	301	2-05-80	H Res.	163
10	9	21	301	2-11-80	H Res.	93

Public Law/Resolution		Statutes at Large	Page	Date	Bill No.
Chapter	Number				
11	10	21	301-302	2-16-80	H Res. 170
12	11	21	302	2-17-80	S Res. 75
13	12	21	302	2-25-80	H Res. 200
14	13	21	302-303	2-25-80	H Res. 203
15	14	21	303	2-25-80	H Res. 157
16	15	21	303	2-25-80	S Res. 80
17	16	21	303	4-01-80	H Res. 68
18	17	21	303-304	4-02-80	H Res. 237
22	18	21	304	4-16-80	S Res. 99
23	19	21	304	4-22-80	S Res. 56
25	20	21	304-305	4-24-80	H Res. 189
26	21	21	305	4-28-80	H Res. 290
28	22	21	305-306	4-29-80	S Res. 91
30	23	21	306	5-04-80	H Res. 297
31	24	21	306	5-08-80	H Res. 179
32	25	21	306	5-14-80	H Res. 296
33	26	21	306	5-14-80	S Res. 73
35	27	21	306-307	5-26-80	S Res. 84
38	28	21	307	5-31-80	H Res. 312
39	29	21	307	6-01-80	S Res. 100
44	30	21	308	6-07-80	S Res. 19
45	31	21	308	6-07-80	S Res. 64
48	32	21	308-309	6-09-80	H Res. 215
51	33	21	309	6-11-80	H Res. 293
52	34	21	309	6-14-80	H Res. 322
55	35	21	310	6-16-80	H Res. 328
56	36	21	310	6-16-80	S Res. 67
57	37	21	310	6-16-80	H Res. 123

PUBLIC ACTS OF THE FORTY-SIXTH CONGRESS

Public Law/Resolution		Statutes at Large	Page	Date	Bill No.	
Chapter	Number					
1	1	21	311	12-15-80	HR	3191
2	2	21	311	12-17-80	HR	3921
4	3	21	311-312	12-23-80	HR	6539
5	4	21	312	12-23-80	HR	6593
6	5	21	312	12-23-80	S	1583
7	6	21	312	12-23-80	HR	1760
8	7	21	312-313	12-23-80	HR	4429
9	8	21	313	12-23-80	HR	5384
10	9	21	313	12-23-80	S	1814
15	10	21	314	1-07-81	S	54
17	11	21	314	1-13-81	HR	460
18	12	21	314-315	1-13-81	HR	4006
19	13	21	315	1-13-81	HR	6256
23	14	21	315-317	1-18-81	S	323
24	15	21	317	1-20-81	HR	5047
25	16	21	317	1-21-81	HR	2658
27	17	21	318	1-25-81	HR	1894
28	18	21	318-321	1-27-81	HR	6614
29	19	21	321	1-28-81	S	1618
30	20	21	321	1-28-81	S	1922
31	21	21	322	1-31-81	HR	7029
33	22	21	322	2-01-81	HR	6025
34	23	21	322	2-08-81	S	939
35	24	21	322-323	2-08-81	S	1573
36	25	21	323	2-08-81	S	1805
39	26	21	323	2-09-81	HR	6527
40	27	21	323-324	2-09-81	HR	4596
41	28	21	324	2-09-81	HR	6229
42	29	21	324	2-09-81	HR	7098
45	30	21	324	2-14-81	HR	6599
46	31	21	325	2-15-81	S	201
47	32	21	325	2-15-81	S	1487
60	33	21	325-326	2-17-81	HR	6451
61	44	21	326	2-18-81	HR	1327
62	35	21	326	2-18-81	HR	6942
64	36	21	326-328	2-21-81	S	711
68	37	21	328	2-23-81	HR	6062
69	38	21	328-330	2-23-81	HR	1381

Public Law/Resolution		Statutes at Large	Page	Date	Bill No.	
Chapter	Number					
70	39	21	330	2-23-81	HR	3047
71	40	21	330	2-23-81	S	1292
72	41	21	331	2-23-81	S	1349
73	42	21	331-339	2-23-81	HR	6969
78	43	21	339-345	2-24-81	HR	6613
79	44	21	346-350	2-24-81	HR	6719
80	45	21	350-351	2-26-81	HR	6532
81	46	21	351-352	2-26-81	HR	6514
82	47	21	352	2-26-81	HR	4572
90	48	21	352-373	2-28-81	HR	7036
91	49	21	373	2-28-81	HR	7033
92	50	21	373	2-28-81	HR	7103
93	51	21	373	3-01-81	S	1905
94	52	21	374	3-01-81	S	2184
95	53	21	374	3-01-81	HR	6545
96	54	21	374-377	3-01-81	HR	6972
97	55	21	377	3-01-81	HR	1197
107	56	21	377	3-02-81	HR	6023
108	57	21	378	3-02-81	HR	3785
109	58	21	378	3-02-81	HR	4590
110	59	21	378-379	3-02-81	HR	5097
111	60	21	379	3-02-81	HR	5532
112	61	21	379-380	3-02-81	HR	6493
128	62	21	380-381	3-03-81	S	753
129	63	21	381-385	3-03-81	HR	7099
130	64	21	385-413	3-03-81	HR	7101
131	65	21	414	3-03-81	HR	7032
132	66	21	414-434	3-03-81	HR	7251
133	67	21	435-458	3-03-81	HR	7203
134	68	21	458-468	3-03-81	HR	7035
135	69	21	468	3-03-81	HR	6529
136	70	21	468-485	3-03-81	HR	7104
137	71	21	485-502	3-03-81	HR	6730
138	72	21	502-504	3-03-81	HR	5088
139	73	21	504-505	3-03-81	HR	440
140	74	21	505	3-03-81	HR	1280
141	75	21	505	3-03-81	HR	2769
142	76	21	505-506	3-03-81	HR	3742

PUBLIC ACTS OF THE FORTY-SIXTH CONGRESS

Public Law/Resolution		Statutes at Large	Page	Date	Bill No.	
Chapter	Number					
143	77	21	506	3-03-81	HR	3751
144	78	21	507-508	3-03-81	HR	4050
145	79	21	508	3-03-81	HR	4206
146	80	21	508-509	3-03-81	HR	4411
147	81	21	509	3-03-81	HR	4477
148	82	21	509	3-03-81	HR	5066
149	83	21	509-510	3-03-81	HR	5629
150	84	21	510	3-03-81	HR	5627
151	85	21	510	3-03-81	HR	2058
152	86	21	510-511	3-03-81	HR	1729
153	87	21	511	3-03-81	HR	2165
154	88	21	511	3-03-81	HR	2384
155	89	21	511-512	3-03-81	HR	3132
156	90	21	512	3-03-81	HR	3520
157	91	21	512	3-03-81	HR	4451
158	92	21	513	3-03-81	HR	4905
159	93	21	513	3-03-81	HR	5715
160	94	21	513	3-03-81	HR	6324

RESOLUTIONS OF THE FORTY-SIXTH CONGRESS

1	1	21	515	12-18-80	H Res.	338
2	2	21	515	1-21-81	H Res.	358
3	3	21	515	1-27-81	H Res.	340
4	4	21	515-516	1-27-81	H Res.	369
6	5	21	516	2-01-81	H Res.	224
7	6	21	516	2-01-81	H Res.	266
8	7	21	516	2-08-81	S Res.	143
9	8	21	516-517	2-08-81	S Res.	146
10	9	21	517	2-09-81	H Res.	388
11	10	21	517	2-14-81	H Res.	362
12	11	21	517-518	2-14-81	H Res.	372
13	12	21	518	2-14-81	H Res.	83
14	13	21	518	2-18-81	H Res.	337
17	14	21	518	2-23-81	H Res.	378
18	15	21	518-519	2-23-81	H Res.	386
19	16	21	519	2-23-81	H Res.	178
20	17	21	519	2-26-81	H Res.	315
21	18	21	519-520	2-26-81	H Res.	387

RESOLUTIONS OF THE FORTY-SIXTH CONGRESS

Public Law/Resolution		Statutes at Large	Page	Date	Bill No.	
Chapter	Number					
22	19	21	520	3-01-81	S Res.	156
23	20	21	520	3-01-81	H Res.	401
24	21	21	520	3-02-81	H Res.	373
25	22	21	520-521	3-03-81	S Res.	79
26	23	21	521	3-03-81	H Res.	186
27	24	21	521	3-03-81	H Res.	402
28	25	21	521	3-03-81	H Res.	419
29	26	21	522	3-03-81	S Res.	137
30	27	21	522	3-03-81	S Res.	164

PUBLIC ACTS OF THE FORTY-SEVENTH CONGRESS

Public Law/Resolution		Statutes at Large	Page	Date		Bill No.
Chapter	Number					
1	1	22	1	12-20-81	S	127
2	2	22	1	12-20-81	S	209
3	3	22	1-2	12-21-81	S	485
4	4	22	2	1-27-82	S	873
5	5	22	2	1-28-82	HR	2775
7	6	22	2-3	2-08-82	HR	3181
12	7	22	3	2-13-82	HR	2796
13	8	22	3	2-15-82	HR	2341
14	9	22	3-4	2-17-82	HR	3870
15	10	22	4	2-20-82	HR	4240
16	11	22	4	2-25-82	S	937
17	12	22	4	2-25-82	S	977
18	13	22	5	2-25-82	HR	3210
19	14	22	5	2-25-82	HR	2944
20	15	22	5-6	2-25-82	HR	3550
21	16	22	7	3-04-82	S	1046
22	17	22	7	3-04-82	S	1211
23	18	22	7	3-04-82	S	58
24	19	22	7-13	3-06-82	HR	4221
25	20	22	13	3-06-82	HR	2192
26	21	22	13	3-06-82	HR	4679
27	22	22	13-28	3-06-82	HR	3844
28	23	22	28	3-09-82	S	1233
30	24	22	28	3-10-82	S	578
31	25	22	28-29	3-11-82	S	387
32	26	22	29	3-11-82	S	1092
41	27	22	29-30	3-17-82	HR	3251
44	28	22	30	3-21-82	HR	1514
46	29	22	30	3-22-82	HR	2736
47	30	22	30-32	3-22-82	S	353
48	31	22	32-33	3-23-82	HR	4439
49	32	22	33-34	3-23-82	HR	4698
51	33	22	34-35	3-28-82	HR	4440
52	34	22	35-36	3-28-82	S	17
53	35	22	36	3-28-82	S	650
55	36	22	36-37	3-31-82	S	864
58	37	22	37	4-01-82	HR	697
59	38	22	37-38	4-01-82	S	827

PUBLIC ACTS OF THE FORTY-SEVENTH CONGRESS

Public Law/Resolution		Statutes at Large	Page	Date	Bill No.	
Chapter	Number					
60	39	22	38-39	4-01-82	HR	879
61	40	22	40	4-01-82	S	1415
67	41	22	40	4-05-82	S	383
68	42	22	40	4-05-82	S	1594
71	43	22	41	4-07-82	S	667
72	44	22	41	4-07-82	HR	1776
73	45	22	41	4-07-82	HR	5588
74	46	22	42-43	4-11-82	S	768
75	47	22	43-44	4-11-82	S	731
76	48	22	44	4-11-82	S	1501
77	49	22	44	4-11-82	HR	5665
79	50	22	44-46	4-14-82	S	308
80	51	22	46	4-15-82	S	1361
82	52	22	46-47	4-17-82	HR	5573
83	53	22	47	4-18-82	S	1558
85	54	22	47	4-21-82	HR	5801
87	55	22	47	4-25-82	HR	124
88	56	22	48	4-25-82	S	1290
89	57	22	49	4-25-82	HR	5221
106	58	22	49	4-26-82	S	26
107	59	22	49-50	4-26-82	S	361
108	60	22	50	4-26-82	S	1677
109	61	22	50	4-26-82	HR	3246
110	62	22	50-52	4-26-82	HR	4454
111	63	22	52	5-01-82	HR	721
112	64	22	52	5-01-82	HR	813
113	65	22	52	5-01-82	S	1598
116	66	22	52-55	5-04-82	HR	3548
117	67	22	55-58	5-04-82	HR	1049
118	68	22	58	5-04-82	HR	5352
119	69	22	58	5-04-82	HR	5908
120	70	22	58	5-04-82	HR	4680
126	71	22	58-61	5-06-82	HR	5804
127	72	22	61	5-08-82	S	24
128	73	22	62	5-09-82	HR	4133
129	74	22	62	5-09-82	HR	4176
130	75	22	62	5-09-82	S	238
144	76	22	63	5-15-82	S	328

Public Law/Resolution		Statutes at Large	Page	Date	Bill No.	
Chapter	Number					
145	77	22	64	5-15-82	HR	2315
146	78	22	64	5-15-82	HR	3196
147	79	22	64-65	5-17-82	HR	459
148	80	22	65	5-17-82	HR	605
149	81	22	65	5-17-82	HR	679
150	82	22	66	5-17-82	HR	1287
151	83	22	66	5-17-82	HR	2195
152	84	22	66	5-17-82	HR	2552
153	85	22	66	5-17-82	HR	3001
154	86	22	66	5-17-82	HR	3333
155	87	22	67	5-17-82	HR	3738
156	88	22	67	5-17-82	HR	3877
157	89	22	67	5-17-82	HR	4299
158	90	22	67	5-17-82	HR	4545
159	91	22	67-68	5-17-82	HR	4585
160	92	22	68	5-17-82	HR	4745
161	93	22	68	5-17-82	HR	5211
162	94	22	68	5-17-82	HR	5240
163	95	22	68-88	5-17-82	HR	4185
170	96	22	88-89	5-19-82	HR	5575
171	97	22	89-92	5-19-82	HR	4466
172	98	22	93	5-19-82	HR	3208
173	99	22	93	5-19-82	HR	6179
181	100	22	93-94	5-25-82	HR	880
182	101	22	94	5-25-82	HR	3846
183	102	22	94-95	5-25-82	HR	3847
184	103	22	94	5-25-82	HR	3858
185	104	22	95	5-25-82	HR	4172
186	105	22	95-96	5-25-82	HR	4177
187	106	22	96-97	5-25-82	HR	4701
188	107	22	97	5-25-82	HR	5346
189	108	22	97	5-26-82	HR	909
190	109	22	97	5-26-82	HR	5540
195	110	22	98-99	6-05-82	HR	4197
197	111	22	99	6-10-82	S	6
198	112	22	100	6-10-82	S	726
199	113	22	100-101	6-10-82	S	1034
200	114	22	101	6-10-82	HR	4199

PUBLIC ACTS OF THE FORTY-SEVENTH CONGRESS

Public Law/Resolution		Statutes at Large	Page	Date	Bill No.	
Chapter	Number					
218	115	22	101-103	6-15-82	S	1168
219	116	22	103-104	6-15-82	HR	1765
220	117	22	104	6-15-82	HR	5127
222	118	22	104-105	6-16-82	S	1420
223	119	22	105-106	6-16-82	HR	1993
230	120	22	106	6-19-82	S	1531
231	121	22	107-108	6-19-82	HR	797
236	122	22	108	6-22-82	S	841
239	123	22	108-109	6-27-82	S	102
240	124	22	109-111	6-27-82	S	1608
241	125	22	111-112	6-27-82	S	1673
242	126	22	112-114	6-27-82	HR	2313
243	127	22	114	6-27-82	HR	4710
244	128	22	114-115	6-27-82	HR	4842
245	129	22	115-116	6-27-82	HR	6335
246	130	22	116	6-27-82	HR	6410
253	131	22	116-117	6-28-82	HR	6014
254	132	22	117-123	6-30-82	HR	5559
255	133	22	123-126	6-30-82	HR	4222
257	134	22	126	7-01-82	HR	713
258	135	22	126-127	7-01-82	S	789
259	136	22	127	7-01-82	S	1158
260	137	22	128	7-01-82	HR	2202
261	138	22	128	7-01-82	HR	3082
262	139	22	128-135	7-01-82	HR	3830
263	140	22	135-144	7-01-82	HR	5664
266	141	22	144-146	7-03-82	S	1020
267	142	22	146-148	7-03-82	S	1810
268	143	22	148-150	7-03-82	HR	5004
269	144	22	150	7-03-82	HR	6004
270	145	22	150	7-05-82	S	2034
271	146	22	150-151	7-05-82	S	2068
272	147	22	151	7-06-82	HR	6225
273	148	22	151-152	7-06-82	S	188
274	149	22	152	7-07-82	S	62
275	150	22	152-153	7-07-82	S	750
276	151	22	153	7-07-82	S	1875
277	152	22	153	7-07-82	HR	3831

PUBLIC ACTS OF THE FORTY-SEVENTH CONGRESS

Public Law/Resolution		Statutes at Large	Page	Date	Bill No.	
Chapter	Number					
278	153	22	154	7-07-82	HR	6394
279	154	22	154	7-07-82	HR	6413
281	155	22	154-155	7-08-82	S	121
282	156	22	155-156	7-08-82	S	2033
283	157	22	156-157	7-08-82	HR	6519
284	158	22	157-160	7-10-82	S	1045
285	159	22	160-161	7-11-82	S	1825
286	160	22	161	7-12-82	HR	4173
287	161	22	161	7-12-82	HR	4179
288	162	22	161-162	7-12-82	HR	5535
289	163	22	162	7-12-82	HR	6676
290	164	22	162-166	7-12-82	HR	4167
291	165	22	166-167	7-12-82	S	1960
293	166	22	168	7-15-82	S	1432
294	167	22	168-170	7-15-82	S	1723
295	168	22	170-171	7-15-82	S	1095
308	169	22	171	7-19-82	S	1886
309	170	22	171	7-19-82	S	1942
310	171	22	171	7-19-82	S	2050
311	172	22	171	7-19-82	S	2057
312	173	22	172-173	7-20-82	HR	4166
313	174	22	173	7-21-82	S	1774
348	175	22	173-174	7-25-82	S	2084
349	176	22	174-176	7-25-82	HR	6514
350	177	22	176	7-27-82	S	329
351	178	22	176	7-27-83	HR	5388
352	179	22	177	7-27-82	HR	4174
353	180	22	177	7-27-82	HR	4178
356	181	22	177-178	7-28-82	S	469
357	182	22	178	7-28-82	S	698
358	183	22	179	7-28-82	S	1620
360	184	22	179-180	7-31-82	S	114
361	185	22	180	7-31-82	S	314
362	186	22	180	7-31-82	S	838
363	187	22	181	7-31-82	HR	1858
364	188	22	181	7-31-82	HR	2374
366	189	22	181	8-01-82	S	1582
371	190	22	181-185	8-02-82	S	60

Public Law/Resolution		Statutes at Large	Page	Date	Bill No.	
Chapter	Number					
372	191	22	185	8-02-82	S	972
373	192	22	185-186	8-02-82	HR	4443
374	193	22	186-191	8-02-82	HR	6722
375	194	22	191-213	8-02-82	HR	6242
376	195	22	214-215	8-03-82	HR	6677
377	196	22	215	8-03-82	S	740
378	197	22	215-216	8-03-82	S	979
379	198	22	216	8-03-82	S	1845
380	199	22	217	8-03-82	HR	209
381	200	22	217	8-03-82	HR	4460
384	201	22	217-218	8-04-82	S	346
385	202	22	218	8-04-82	HR	2402
386	203	22	218	8-04-82	HR	5222
389	204	22	219-256	8-05-82	HR	6244
390	205	22	257-284	9-05-82	HR	6243
391	206	22	284-297	8-05-82	HR	6616
392	207	22	297-298	9-05-82	S	50
393	208	22	298-299	8-05-82	S	1440
394	209	22	299	8-05-82	S	1959
395	210	22	299	8-05-82	HR	720
396	211	22	299	8-05-82	HR	6111
397	212	22	299-300	8-05-82	HR	929
398	213	22	300-301	8-05-82	HR	5841
399	214	22	301	8-05-82	HR	6743
431	215	22	301	8-07-82	HR	6715
432	216	22	301-302	8-07-82	S	126
433	217	22	302-340	8-07-82	HR	6716
434	218	22	341-343	8-07-82	S	1255
435	219	22	343	8-07-82	S	1612
436	220	22	344	8-07-82	S	2002
437	221	22	344-345	8-07-82	S	2151
438	222	22	345	8-07-82	S	2172
439	223	22	345-346	8-07-82	HR	1364
440	224	22	346	8-07-82	HR	2299
441	225	22	346-347	8-07-82	HR	4684
442	226	22	347-348	8-07-82	HR	5224
443	227	22	348	8-07-82	HR	6265
444	228	22	348	8-07-82	HR	6520

PUBLIC ACTS OF THE FORTY-SEVENTH CONGRESS

Public Law/Resolution		Statutes at Large	Page	Date	Bill No.	
Chapter	Number					
445	229	22	348–349	8–07–82	HR	6593
446	230	22	349	8–07–82	HR	6687
447	231	22	349–350	8–07–82	HR	6845
448	232	22	350–369	8–07–82	HR	5812
464	233	22	369–370	8–08–82	S	670
465	234	22	370–371	8–08–82	S	1787
466	232	22	371–372	8–08–82	S	2164
467	236	22	372	8–08–82	HR	3825
468	237	22	372–373	8–08–82	HR	3854
469	238	22	373–374	8–08–82	HR	3920
470	239	22	374	8–08–82	HR	5978
471	240	22	374	8–08–82	HR	6103
472	241	22	374–375	8–08–82	HR	6149
473	242	22	375	8–08–82	HR	6525
474	243	22	375	8–08–82	HR	6679
475	244	22	375–376	8–08–82	HR	6692
476	245	22	376	8–08–82	HR	6695
477	246	22	376	8–08–82	HR	6702
478	247	22	376	8–08–82	HR	6718
479	248	22	376	8–08–82	HR	6721

RESOLUTIONS OF THE FORTY-SEVENTH CONGRESS

1	1	22	377	12–21–81	H Res.	57
3	2	22	377	1–12–82	H Res.	66
4	3	22	377	2–15–82	H Res.	89
5	4	22	378	2–17–82	H Res.	127
6	5	22	378	2–25–82	S Res.	41
7	6	22	378	3–06–82	H Res.	104
8	7	22	378	3–10–82	S Res.	45
9	8	22	378–379	3–11–82	S Res.	47
11	9	22	379	3–15–82	H Res.	140
12	10	22	379	3–21–82	S Res.	49
15	11	22	379	4–01–82	S Res.	30
16	12	22	379–380	4–01–82	H Res.	183
19	13	22	380	4–18–82	S Res.	56
20	14	22	380	4–21–82	H Res.	197
21	15	22	380	5–01–82	H Res.	161
23	16	22	380	5–05–82	H Res.	96

Public Law/Resolution		Statutes at Large	Page	Date	Bill No.
Chapter	Number				
24	17	22	381	5-05-82	H Res. 204
25	18	22	381	5-17-82	H Res. 8
27	19	22	381	5-19-82	H Res. 111
28	20	22	382-383	5-19-82	H Res. 211
29	21	22	383	5-25-82	H Res. 212
30	22	22	383	6-05-82	S Res. 71
32	23	22	383	6-07-82	S Res. 53
33	24	22	383-384	6-07-82	H Res. 213
34	25	22	384	6-10-82	H Res. 227
36	26	22	384	6-27-82	H Res. 239
38	27	22	384-385	6-30-82	H Res. 248
39	28	22	385-386	7-01-82	H Res. 176
40	29	22	386	7-01-82	S Res. 58
41	30	22	386	7-06-82	H Res. 224
42	31	22	386-387	7-07-82	H Res. 243
43	32	22	387	7-07-82	H Res. 247
47	33	22	387	7-12-82	H Res. 69
48	34	22	387	7-12-82	S Res. 91
49	35	22	387-389	7-12-82	H Res. 237
50	36	22	389	7-19-82	H Res. 174
51	37	22	389	7-20-82	H Res. 261
52	38	22	389	7-21-82	H Res. 240
57	39	22	389	7-31-82	S Res. 83
58	40	22	390	8-01-82	S Res. 81
59	41	22	390	8-01-82	H Res. 274
61	42	22	390-391	8-02-82	H Res. 220
62	43	22	391	8-02-82	H Res. 266
63	44	22	391	8-03-82	H Res. 122
64	45	22	391	8-03-82	S Res. 73
65	46	22	391-392	8-03-82	S Res. 90
66	47	22	392	8-03-82	H Res. 178
68	48	22	392	8-04-82	S Res. 102
70	49	22	392	8-05-82	H Res. 288
71	50	22	392-393	8-05-82	H Res. 131
72	51	22	393	8-05-82	H Res. 92
73	52	22	393	8-07-82	H Res. 203
74	53	22	393	8-07-82	H Res. 254
77	54	22	394	8-08-82	S Res. 107

RESOLUTIONS OF THE FORTY-SEVENTH CONGRESS

Public Law/Resolution		Statutes at Large	Page	Date	Bill No.
Chapter	Number				
78	55	22	394	8-08-82	S Res. 108
79	56	22	394	8-08-82	H Res. 266
80	57	22	394-395	8-08-82	H Res. 278
81	58	22	395	8-08-82	H Res. 279
82	59	22	395	8-08-82	H Res. 282
83	60	22	395	8-08-82	H Res. 290

PUBLIC ACTS OF THE FORTY-SEVENTH CONGRESS

Public Law/Resolution		Statutes at Large	Page	Date	Bill No.	
Chapter	Number					
1	1	22	397	12-13-82	S	2198
5	2	22	397	12-21-82	S	2155
6	3	22	398	12-23-82	HR	6187
7	4	22	398	12-23-82	S	506
8	5	22	399	12-23-82	S	1703
12	6	22	399-400	1-06-83	S	145
13	7	22	400	1-06-83	HR	429
14	8	22	401	1-09-83	S	265
15	9	22	401	1-09-83	S	335
16	10	22	401	1-09-83	S	390
17	11	22	402	1-09-83	S	1026
23	12	22	402	1-13-83	S	2150
24	13	22	402	1-13-83	HR	5014
25	14	22	402-403	1-15-83	S	1860
26	15	22	403	1-15-83	S	2290
27	16	22	403-407	1-16-83	S	133
32	17	22	407	1-18-83	S	173
33	18	22	407	1-19-83	HR	3506
34	19	22	408	1-19-83	HR	6627
36	20	22	408-411	1-20-83	HR	7052
40	21	22	411-412	1-31-83	HR	1294
41	22	22	412-413	1-31-83	HR	3575
42	23	22	413-414	2-10-83	S	2412
43	24	22	414	2-12-83	S	2370
44	25	22	414-416	2-14-83	HR	5380
46	26	22	416-419	2-15-83	HR	7050
47	27	22	419-420	2-17-83	S	2239
48	28	22	420	2-17-83	S	2305
49	29	22	420-421	2-17-83	S	2356
50	30	22	421	2-19-83	S	325
51	31	22	421-422	2-22-83	HR	1052
52	32	22	422-423	2-22-83	S	2264
55	33	22	423-424	2-26-83	S	2490
56	34	22	424-431	2-26-83	HR	6957
57	35	22	431	2-28-83	HR	2997
58	36	22	431-432	2-28-83	HR	7193
59	37	22	432	3-01-83	HR	1078
60	38	22	432-433	3-01-83	HR	2871

PUBLIC ACTS OF THE FORTY-SEVENTH CONGRESS

Public Law/Resolution		Statutes at Large	Page	Date	Bill No.	
Chapter	Number					
61	39	22	433-451	3-01-83	HR	6900
64	40	22	451-452	3-02-83	HR	7486
90	41	22	453	3-03-83	S	889
91	42	22	453	3-03-83	HR	1410
92	43	22	453-455	3-03-83	HR	7049
93	44	22	456-460	3-03-83	HR	7077
94	45	22	460-462	3-03-83	HR	7115
95	46	22	462-471	3-03-83	HR	7181
96	47	22	471	3-03-83	HR	7191
97	48	22	472-481	3-03-83	HR	7314
98	49	22	481	3-03-83	HR	7597
99	50	22	481-482	3-03-83	HR	7623
100	51	22	482-484	3-03-83	HR	7682
101	52	22	484	3-03-83	S	171
102	53	22	484-485	3-03-83	S	1829
115	54	22	485	3-03-83	HR	110
116	55	22	385-586	3-03-83	HR	684
117	56	22	486	3-03-83	HR	3220
118	57	22	487	3-03=83	HR	4757
119	58	22	487	3-03-83	HR	5200
120	59	22	487-488	3-03-83	HR	5300
121	60	22	488-526	3-03-83	HR	5538
122	61	22	526	3-03-83	HR	5543
123	62	22	526-529	3-03-83	HR	5661
124	63	22	529-530	3-03-83	HR	6236
125	64	22	530	3-03-83	HR	7226
126	65	22	530	3-03-83	HR	7289
127	66	22	530-531	3-03-83	HR	5674
128	67	22	531-564	3-03-83	HR	7482
129	68*	22	564	3-03-83	S Res.	143
130	69	22	564-565	3-03-83	S	1821
131	70	22	565-566	3-03-83	S	2433
132	71	22	566	3-03-83	HR	814
133	72	22	566	3-03-83	HR	1226
134	73	22	567	3-03-83	HR	1926
135	74	22	567	3-03-83	HR	6682
136	75	22	567-568	3-03-83	HR	6683
137	76	22	568-571	3-03-83	HR	6930

PUBLIC ACTS OF THE FORTY-SEVENTH CONGRESS

Public Law/Resolution		Statutes at Large	Page	Date	Bill No.	
Chapter	Number					
138	77	22	571-572	3-03-83	HR	7148
139	78	22	572-581	3-03-83	HR	7327
140	79	22	582	3-03-83	HR	7462
141	80	22	582-600	3-03-83	HR	7637
142	81	22	600-602	3-03-83	HR	7611
143	82	22	603-633	3-03-83	HR	7595

RESOLUTIONS OF THE FORTY-SEVENTH CONGRESS

1	1	22	635	12-12-82	H Res.	292
3	2	22	635	12-22-82	S Res.	116
4	3	22	635	1-18-83	H Res.	308
5	4	22	635-636	1-24-83	H Res.	190
6	5	22	636	2-01-83	H Res.	323
7	6	22	636	2-05-83	S Res.	109
8	7	22	637	2-06-83	S Res.	132
9	8	22	637	2-17-83	H Res.	109
10	9	22	637	2-17-83	H Res.	335
11	10	22	637-638	2-23-83	S Res.	137
12	11	22	638	2-23-83	H Res.	346
13	12	22	638	2-23-83	H Res.	348
14	13	22	638	2-24-83	H Res.	347
15	14	22	639	2-24-83	H Res.	349
16	15	22	639	2-24-83	H Res.	356
17	16	22	639-640	2-26-83	H Res.	337
19	17	22	640	3-02-83	H Res.	358
20	18	22	640	3-03-83	H Res.	324
21	19	22	640-641	3-03-83	H Res.	359
22	20	22	641	3-03-83	S Res.	123
23	21	22	641-642	3-03-83	H Res.	331
24	22	22	642	3-03-83	S Res.	64
25	23	22	642	3-03-83	S Res.	95
26	24	22	642-643	3-03-83	S Res.	138
27	25	22	643	3-03-83	S Res.	139
28	26	22	643-644	3-03-83	H Res.	277
29	27	22	644	3-03-83	H Res.	281
30	28	22	644	3-03-83	H Res.	333
31	29	22	644	3-03-83	H Res.	367

Public Law/Resolution		Statutes at Large	Page	Date	Bill No.	
Chapter	Number					
1	1	23	1	1-18-84	HR	686
2	2	23	1	1-19-84	S	1038
3	3	23	1-2	1-29-84	S	844
4	4	23	2	1-31-84	S	1256
6	5	23	2-3	2-14-84	HR	3948
7	6	23	3	2-21-84	HR	2555
8	7	23	3	2-23-84	HR	448
9	8	23	3	3-01-84	HR	1482
10	9	23	4	3-03-84	S	1490
11	10	23	4	3-12-84	HR	5462
12	11	23	4	3-13-84	S	616
14	12	23	5	3-22-84	S	1314
16	13	23	5	3-24-84	HR	4779
17	14	23	5-6	3-28-84	S	1847
18	15	23	6	3-31-84	S	1692
19	16	23	6-9	3-31-84	HR	4971
20	17	23	10	4-02-84	S	74
21	18	23	10	4-10-84	S	1819
23	19	23	11	4-17-84	S	1871
24	20	23	11	4-18-84	S	874
25	21	23	11	4-18-84	HR	3956
26	22	23	11-12	4-18-84	HR	4993
27	23	23	12	4-23-84	S	503
28	24	23	13-14	4-23-84	S	1063
31	25	23	14-15	4-28-84	HR	6538
36	26	23	15	5-01-84	S	652
37	27	23	15-18	5-01-84	HR	6073
38	28	23	18-19	5-02-84	HR	3931
39	29	23	19	5-03-84	HR	5966
43	30	23	19-20	5-13-84	S	258
44	31	23	21	5-13-84	S	2093
45	32	23	21	5-13-84	HR	2334
46	33	23	21-22	5-13-84	HR	3926
50	34	23	22	5-14-84	S	241
52	35	23	22-24	5-16-84	S	1369
53	36	23	24-28	5-17-84	S	153
55	37	23	28-29	5-21-84	HR	6856
57	38	23	29-30	5-29-84	S	51

PUBLIC ACTS OF THE FORTY-EIGHTH CONGRESS

Public Law/Resolution		Statutes at Large	Page	Date	Bill No.	
Chapter	Number					
58	39	23	30-31	5-29-84	S	664
59	40	23	31	5-29-84	HR	450
60	41	23	31-33	5-29-84	HR	3967
62	42	23	33-34	6-03-84	S	247
63	43	23	34-35	6-03-84	HR	355
64	44	23	35-36	6-03-84	HR	2824
65	45	23	36	6-03-84	HR	4994
71	46	23	36-39	6-05-84	HR	5261
72	47	23	39-40	6-07-84	HR	7076
73	48	23	40	6-09-84	HR	1323
74	49	23	40	6-11-84	HR	578
75	50	23	40	6-11-84	HR	1761
79	51	23	41	6-12-84	HR	1483
80	52	23	41	6-12-84	HR	4359
81	53	23	41-43	6-12-84	HR	6539
82	54	23	43-45	6-12-84	HR	6762
98	55	23	45	6-18-84	HR	2240
99	56	23	45-47	6-18-84	HR	6406
101	57	23	47-48	6-20-84	S	304
102	58	23	48	6-20-84	S	802
103	59	23	48	6-20-84	S	1149
104	60	23	49	6-20-84	S	1232
105	61	23	49-50	6-20-84	S	1950
106	62	23	50	6-20-84	HR	4701
107	63	23	50	6-20-84	HR	6933
117	64	23	50	6-21-84	S	2145
118	65	23	50-52	6-23-84	S	312
119	66	23	52-53	6-24-84	S	820
121	67	23	53-60	6-26-84	HR	2228
122	68	23	60	6-26-84	HR	2265
123	69	23	60	6-26-84	HR	4411
126	70	23	60	6-27-84	S	1727
127	71	23	60-61	6-27-84	HR	1340
131	72	23	61-62	6-28-84	S	353
132	73	23	62	6-28-84	HR	6021
134	74	23	62-63	6-30-84	HR	6526
142	75	23	63-64	7-02-84	HR	6215
143	76	23	64-66	7-02-84	HR	7164

PUBLIC ACTS OF THE FORTY-EIGHTH CONGRESS

Public Law/Resolution		Statutes at Large	Page	Date	Bill No.	
Chapter	Number					
147	77	23	66-67	7-03-84	S	675
148	78	23	67	7-03-84	HR	4977
149	79	23	67-69	7-03-84	HR	2031
176	80	23	69	7-04-84	HR	1628
177	81	23	69-72	7-04-84	HR	3961
178	82	23	72-73	7-04-84	HR	4651
179	83	23	73-76	7-04-84	HR	4680
180	84	23	76-98	7-04-84	HR	6092
181	85	23	98-101	7-04-84	HR	6094
182	86	23	101-102	7-04-84	HR	1682
214	87	23	103-104	7-05-84	S	1581
215	88	23	104-106	7-05-84	S	2243
216	89	23	106	7-05-84	HR	6761
217	90	23	107-113	7-05-84	HR	6861
218	91	23	113	7-05-84	S	838
219	92	23	113-115	7-05-84	S	1721
220	93	23	115-118	7-05-84	HR	1798
221	94	23	118-119	7-05-84	HR	3056
222	95	23	119-120	7-05-84	HR	4383
223	96	23	120-121	7-05-84	HR	4696
224	97	23	121	7-05-84	HR	5709
225	98	23	122	7-05-84	HR	6370
226	99	23	122-123	7-05-84	HR	6409
227	100	23	123-132	7-05-84	HR	6656
228	101	23	132-133	7-05-84	HR	6925
229	102	23	133-154	7-05-84	HR	7012
230	103	23	154	7-05-84	HR	3337
231	104	23	154-155	7-05-84	HR	6657
232	105	23	155	7-05-84	HR	6750
233	106	23	155	7-05-84	HR	4985
234	107	23	156-158	7-05-84	HR	5459
235	108	23	158-159	7-05-84	HR	7440
331	109	23	159-194	7-07-84	HR	7069
332	110	23	194-227	7-07-84	HR	7380
333	111	23	227-236	7-07-84	HR	6770
334	112	23	236-262	7-07-84	HR	7235
335	113	23	262-263	7-07-84	HR	7509

RESOLUTIONS OF THE FORTY-EIGHTH CONGRESS

Public Law/Resolution		Statutes at Large	Page	Date	Bill No.
Chapter	Number				
1	1	23	265	12-12-83	H Res. 1
2	2	23	265	12-21-83	S Res. 31
3	3	23	265-266	12-26-83	H Res. 65
4	4	23	266	2-01-84	H Res. 127
5	5	23	266	2-02-84	H Res. 113
6	6	23	266	2-02-84	H Res. 117
7	7	23	266-267	2-07-84	H Res. 116
8	8	23	267	2-08-84	H Res. 121
9	9	23	267	2-12-84	H Res. 154
10	10	23	267-268	2-13-84	H Res. 119
11	11	23	268	2-15-84	H Res. 24
12	12	23	268	2-15-84	H Res. 160
14	13	23	268-269	2-25-84	S Res. 51
15	14	23	269	3-03-84	S Res. 58
17	15	23	269	3-13-84	H Res. 191
18	16	23	269	3-27-84	H Res. 215
19	17	23	269-270	3-31-84	S Res. 64
20	18	23	270	4-23-84	H Res. 193
21	19	23	270	4-28-84	H Res. 224
22	20	23	270-271	4-29-84	S Res. 80
23	21	23	271	5-03-84	H Res. 223
24	22	23	271	5-03-84	H Res. 236
25	23	23	271	5-03-84	H Res. 240
26	24	23	272	5-13-84	S Res. 81
27	25	23	272	5-13-84	S Res. 82
28	26	23	272-273	5-16-84	H Res. 231
29	27	23	273	5-16-84	H Res. 239
30	28	23	273	5-29-84	H Res. 245
32	29	23	273	6-07-84	H Res. 255
33	30	23	274	6-11-84	S Res. 88
34	31	23	274	6-11-84	H Res. 179
36	32	23	274	6-20-84	H Res. 235
37	33	23	274-275	6-20-84	H Res. 257
38	34	23	275	6-23-85	H Res. 167
39	35	23	275	6-26-84	H Res. 135
40	36	23	275	6-26-84	H Res. 137
41	37	23	276	6-27-84	H Res. 138
42	38	23	276	6-27-84	H Res. 264

RESOLUTIONS OF THE FORTY-EIGHTH CONGRESS

Public Law/Resolution		Statutes at Large	Page	Date	Bill No.
Chapter	Number				
43	39	23	276-277	6-30-84	H Res. 283
44	40	23	277	7-01-84	H Res. 251
45	41	23	277	7-05-84	H Res. 260
46	42	23	277	7-05-84	H Res. 276
47	43	23	277-278	7-07-84	H Res. 286
48	44	23	278	7-07-84	H Res. 287

Public Law/Resolution		Statutes at Large	Page	Date	Bill No.	
Chapter	Number					
1	1	23	279	12-18-84	S	1309
2	2	23	279	12-18-84	S	2402
3	3	23	280	12-18-84	HR	7428
4	4	23	280	12-20-84	S	2041
7	5	23	280	12-27-84	HR	2728
8	6	23	281	1-08-85	S	2393
9	7	23	281	1-10-85	S	2348
18	8	23	281	1-13-85	HR	4539
19	9	23	281-282	1-13-85	S	55
20	10	23	282	1-13-85	S	52
22	11	23	282	1-17-85	S	1432
23	12	23	283	1-17-85	HR	7964
25	13	23	283-284	1-20-85	S	1820
26	14	23	284	1-20-85	HR	7329
29	15	23	284-285	1-21-85	S	478
30	16	23	285-286	1-21-85	S	2061
38	17	23	287	1-27-85	HR	7768
41	18	23	287	1-28-85	HR	5639
43	19	23	287-295	1-30-85	HR	7874
45	20	23	295-296	1-31-85	HR	7619
46	21	23	296	1-31-85	HR	181
47	22	23	296-297	1-31-85	HR	1565
50	23	23	297	2-05-85	HR	1017
52	24	23	298	2-10-85	S	674
55	25	23	298	2-11-85	S	1793
56	26	23	298-302	2-12-85	HR	7577
58	27	23	302-303	2-13-85	S	729
59	28	23	303-304	2-13-85	HR	8121
64	29	23	304	2-14-85	S	235
65	30	23	304-305	2-14-85	HR	1013
66	31	23	305	2-14-85	HR	1339
67	32	23	305	2-14-85	HR	5670
68	33	23	305-306	2-14-85	HR	5674
123	34	23	306	2-16-85	S	1705
124	35	23	306	2-17-85	S	1751
125	36	23	307	2-17-85	S	2278
126	37	23	307	2-17-85	HR	7131
137	38	23	307-308	2-20-85	S	1251

Public Law/Resolution		Statutes at Large	Page	Date	Bill No.	
Chapter	Number					
138	39	23	308	2-20-85	S	2246
139	40	23	308	2-20-85	S	2594
144	41	23	309-310	2-25-85	HR	3258
145	42	23	310-319	2-25-85	HR	8039
146	43	23	320	2-25-85	S	1412
147	44	23	320	2-25-85	S	1839
148	45	23	320-321	2-25-85	HR	483
149	46	23	321-322	2-25-85	HR	5479
150	47	23	322-331	2-25-85	HR	7857
160	48	23	331	2-26-85	S	194
161	49	23	331-332	2-26-85	S	1117
162	50	23	332	2-26-85	S	1473
163	51	23	332	2-26-85	S	2551
164	52	23	332-333	2-26-85	HR	2550
165	53	23	333-335	2-26-85	HR	2799
166	54	23	335	2-26-85	HR	8273
260	55	23	335-336	2-28-85	S	78
261	56	23	336	2-28-85	S	229
262	57	23	336-337	2-28-85	S	1810
263	58	23	337	2-28-85	S	2084
264	59	23	337	2-28-85	S	2375
265	60	23	337-338	2-28-85	HR	3933
314	61	23	338-339	3-02-85	S	1609
315	62	23	339	3-02-85	HR	48
316	63	23	340	3-02-85	HR	3108
318	64	23	340	3-03-85	HR	6824
319	65	23	340-343	3-03-85	S	66
320	66	23	344	3-03-85	S	84
321	67	23	344	3-03-85	S	2577
322	68	23	344-345	3-03-85	S	2666
323	69	23	345	3-03-85	HR	441
324	70	23	345	3-03-85	HR	577
325	71	23	345-346	3-03-85	HR	870
326	72	23	346	3-03-85	HR	1321
327	73	23	346-347	3-03-85	HR	1618
328	74	23	347	3-03-85	HR	2123
329	75	23	347-348	3-03-85	HR	2949
330	76	23	348	3-03-85	HR	3058

PUBLIC ACTS OF THE FORTY-EIGHTH CONGRESS

Public Law/Resolution		Statutes at Large	Page	Date	Bill No.	
Chapter	Number					
331	77	23	348	3-03-85	HR	3343
332	78	23	349	3-03-85	HR	3593
333	79	23	349	3-03-85	HR	4067
334	80	23	349-350	3-03-85	HR	4088
335	81	23	350	3-03-85	HR	5713
336	82	23	350-351	3-03-85	HR	5747
337	83	23	351-353	3-03-85	HR	6658
338	84	23	353-356	3-03-85	HR	8038
339	85	23	356-361	3-03-85	HR	8120
340	86	23	361-362	3-03-85	HR	7785
341	87	23	362-285	3-03-85	HR	7970
342	88	23	385-388	3-03-85	HR	8138
343	89	23	388-425	3-03-85	HR	8179
344	90	23	426-433	3-03-85	HR	8239
345	91	23	434	3-03-85	HR	8279
346	92	23	434-435	3-03-85	S	2530
347	93	23	435	3-03-85	HR	445
348	94	23	436	3-03-85	HR	449
349	95	23	436	3-03-85	HR	1004
350	96	23	436-437	3-03-85	HR	1401
351	97	23	437	3-03-85	HR	4089
352	98	23	437	3-03-85	HR	5509
353	99	23	437	3-03-85	HR	5691
354	100	23	438-442	3-03-85	HR	5692
355	101	23	443	3-03-85	HR	6220
356	102	23	443-444	3-03-85	HR	6760
357	103	23	444	3-03-85	HR	7034
358	104	23	445-546	3-03-85	HR	8102
359	105	23	446-478	3-03-85	HR	8255
360	106	23	478-514	3-03-85	HR	8256

RESOLUTIONS OF THE FORTY-EIGHTH CONGRESS

1	1	23	515	12-18-84	S Res.	98
2	2	23	515	12-18-84	S Res.	101
3	3	23	515	12-18-84	H Res.	300
4	4	23	516	12-18-84	H Res.	289
5	5	23	516	1-06-85	S Res.	32
6	6	23	516	1-12-85	H Res.	308

RESOLUTIONS OF THE FORTY-EIGHTH CONGRESS

Public Law/Resolution		Statutes at Large	Page	Date	Bill No.
Chapter	Number				
7	7	23	516-517	2-09-85	S Res. 104
8	8	23	517	2-12-85	H Res. 323
9	9	23	518	2-12-85	H Res. 327
10	10	23	518	2-13-85	H Res. 309
11	11	23	518	2-19-85	S Res. 92
12	12	23	518	2-26-85	H Res. 335
14	13	23	519	3-02-85	H Res. 320
15	14	23	519	3-02-85	H Res. 338
16	15	23	519	3-02-85	H Res. 339
17	16	23	519	3-02-85	H Res. 340
18	17	23	520	3-03-85	S Res. 100
19	18	23	520	3-03-85	S Res. 114
20	19	23	520	3-03-85	H Res. 341
21	20	23	520-521	3-03-85	H Res. 342
22	21	23	521	3-03-85	H Res. 347

PUBLIC ACTS OF THE FORTY-NINTH CONGRESS

Public Law/Resolution		Statutes at Large	Page	Date	Bill No.	
Chapter	Number					
3	1	24	1	1-19-86	S	128
4	2	24	1-2	1-19-86	S	471
5	3	24	2	1-19-86	S	602
6	4	24	2-3	2-02-86	S	671
7	5	24	3	2-09-86	HR	5186
8	6	24	3	2-15-86	S	126
9	7	24	3-4	2-15-86	S	382
19	8	24	4	3-13-86	S	491
20	9	24	4-5	3-16-86	S	610
21	10	24	5	3-18-86	HR	5219
22	11	24	5-6	3-19-86	HR	545
27	12	24	6-8	3-26-86	HR	5893
28	13	24	8	3-29-86	S	1136
29	14	24	8	3-29-86	HR	1245
30	15	24	9	3-29-86	HR	4982
40	16	24	9	3-30-86	HR	4420
41	17	24	9	3-31-86	HR	5544
47	18	24	10	4-15-86	S	44
48	19	24	12-12	4-15-86	S	60
49	20	24	12	4-15-86	HR	1270
50	21	24	12-14	4-15-86	HR	1297
57	22	24	14	4-17-86	HR	1151
58	23	24	14	4-22-86	S	633
59	24	24	15	4-22-86	S	1476
60	25	24	15	4-22-86	HR	2239
61	26	24	15	4-22-86	HR	7632
64	27	24	15-16	4-29-86	HR	444
67	28	24	16	4-30-86	S	2239
69	29	24	16	5-01-86	S	82
70	30	24	17	5-01-86	S	481
71	31	24	17-18	5-01-86	S	880
72	32	24	18	5-01-86	S	2224
73	33	24	18-19	5-01-86	HR	327
74	34	24	19	5-01-86	HR	6980
75	35	24	19	5-01-86	HR	7467
76	36	24	19	5-01-86	HR	7647
81	37	24	20	5-03-86	S	1487
82	38	24	20-21	5-03-86	HR	4493

Public Law/Resolution		Statutes at Large	Page	Date	Bill No.	
Chapter	Number					
83	39	24	21	5-03-86	HR	5549
87	40	24	21-22	5-06-86	S	1377
88	41	24	22	5-06-86	HR	129
326	42	24	23	5-11-86	S	214
327	43	24	23	5-15-86	S	216
328	44	24	23	5-15-86	S	102
329	45	24	23-25	5-15-86	HR	2993
330	46	24	25-27	5-15-86	HR	3370
331	24	24	27-28	5-15-86	HR	3371
332	48	24	28-29	5-15-86	HR	4765
333	49	24	29-47	5-15-86	HR	5543
334	50	24	47-48	5-15-86	HR	5673
335	51	24	48-49	5-15-86	HR	6558
338	52	24	50	5-17-86	S	223
339	53	24	50	5-17-86	S	1013
340	54	24	50	5-17-86	S	1105
341	55	24	51	5-17-86	S	1471
342	56	24	51	5-17-86	HR	606
343	57	24	51	5-17-86	HR	1027
344	28	24	52-53	5-17-86	HR	1360
345	59	24	53-54	5-17-86	HR	2309
346	60	24	54-55	5-17-86	HR	2410
347	61	24	55-56	5-17-86	HR	3369
348	62	24	57	5-17-86	HR	3519
349	63	24	57	5-17-86	HR	3775
350	64	24	58-59	5-17-86	HR	4569
351	65	24	59-60	5-17-86	HR	5677
352	66	24	60-61	5-17-86	HR	5684
353	67	24	62-63	5-17-86	HR	5685
354	68	24	63-64	5-17-86	HR	5786
355	69	24	64-65	5-17-86	HR	6013
356	70	24	65-67	5-17-86	HR	7646
357	71	24	67-68	5-17-86	HR	7651
361	72	24	68	5-18-86	HR	661
362	73	24	69	5-20-86	S	1405
363	74	24	69	5-20-86	HR	7938
376	75	24	69-70	5-24-86	S	1387
377	76	24	70	5-26-86	HR	7207

PUBLIC ACTS OF THE FORTY-NINTH CONGRESS

Public Law/Resolution		Statutes at Large	Page	Date	Bill No.	
Chapter	Number					
381	77	24	70-71	5-27-86	S	1394
391	78	24	71-72	5-28-86	HR	4968
392	79	24	72	5-28-86	HR	8762
395	80	24	73-76	6-01-86	S	1484
396	81	24	76	6-01-86	HR	5789
397	82	24	76	6-01-86	S	91
416	83	24	77-78	6-02-86	HR	6661
417	84	24	78-79	6-16-86	S	121
421	85	24	79-83	6-19-86	HR	4838
422	86	24	83-84	6-19-86	HR	5910
423	87	24	84	6-19-86	HR	6965
424	88	24	84	6-19-86	HR	6975
463	89	24	84-86	6-21-86	S	200
567	90	24	86	6-29-86	S	1657
568	91	24	86	6-29-86	HR	4177
569	92	24	87	6-29-86	HR	4415
570	93	24	87-90	6-29-86	HR	5886
572	94	24	91	6-30-86	HR	544
573	95	24	91-92	6-30-86	HR	5887
574	96	24	93-99	6-30-86	HR	6395
575	97	24	100-104	6-30-86	HR	7481
576	98	24	104	6-30-86	S	2222
577	99	24	104-105	6-30-86	HR	5547
578	100	24	105	6-30-86	HR	7735
579	101	24	105	6-30-86	HR	368
580	102	24	106	6-30-86	HR	868
581	103	24	106	6-30-86	HR	5221
582	104	24	106	6-30-85	HR	5251
583	105	24	106	6-30-86	HR	5401
584	106	24	107	6-30-86	HR	5888
585	107	24	107	6-30-86	HR	6665
599	108	24	107-108	7-01-86	HR	67
600	109	24	108-117	7-01-86	HR	6392
601	110	24	117-120	7-02-86	S	1486
608	111	24	121	7-02-86	HR	138
609	112	24	121	7-02-86	HR	1341
610	113	24	121-122	7-02-86	HR	3440
611	114	24	122	7-02-86	HR	5201

PUBLIC ACTS OF THE FORTY-NINTH CONGRESS

Public Law/Resolution		Statutes at Large	Page	Date	Bill No.	
Chapter	Number					
622	115	24	122-123	7-03-86	S	1352
623	116	24	123	7-03-86	HR	4063
636	117	24	123	7-06-86	S	2732
637	118	24	123-124	7-06-86	HR	453
744	119	24	124-127	7-06-86	HR	6391
745	120	24	127	7-08-86	S	2152
746	121	24	128	7-08-86	HR	1357
747	122	24	128-129	7-08-86	HR	7183
755	123	24	129	7-09-86	HR	3037
756	124	24	129	7-09-86	HR	4232
757	125	24	130-138	7-09-86	HR	6397
758	126	24	138	7-10-86	S	503
759	127	24	138-140	7-10-86	HR	41
760	128	24	140-141	7-10-86	HR	392
761	129	24	141	7-10-86	HR	2148
762	130	24	141-142	7-10-86	HR	4498
763	131	24	142-143	7-10-86	HR	5862
764	132	24	143	7-10-86	HR	5874
765	133	24	144	7-12-86	HR	985
775	134	24	144-146	7-19-86	HR	8973
776	135	24	146	7-19-86	HR	4139
778	136	24	147-148	7-20-86	HR	1205
779	137	24	148	7-26-86	HR	6979
780	138	24	149	7-26-86	HR	7471
781	139	24	149-157	7-26-86	HR	8975
782	140	24	158	7-26-86	HR	9438
797	141	24	158	7-28-86	S	57
798	142	24	158	7-28-86	S	582
799	143	24	159	7-28-86	S	2332
800	144	24	159	7-28-86	HR	5866
801	145	24	159	7-28-86	HR	7627
802	146	24	160-161	7-29-86	S	236
803	147	24	161	7-29-86	S	453
804	148	24	161-162	7-29-86	S	901
805	149	24	163-164	7-29-86	S	1937
806	150	24	164-165	7-29-86	S	2115
807	151	24	165-166	7-29-86	S	2880
808	152	24	166	7-29-86	HR	1983

PUBLIC ACTS OF THE FORTY-NINTH CONGRESS

Public Law/Resolution		Statutes at Large	Page	Date	Bill No.	
Chapter	Number					
809	153	24	166-167	7-29-86	HR	4670
810	154	24	167-168	7-29-86	HR	7191
811	155	24	168-169	7-29-86	HR	8023
812	156	24	169	7-29-86	HR	9208
816	157	24	169	7-30-86	HR	2475
817	158	24	170	7-30-86	HR	4335
818	159	24	170-171	7-30-86	HR	5179
827	160	24	172-209	7-31-86	HR	8974
840	161	24	209-213	8-02-86	HR	8328
841	162	24	213	8-02-86	S	2794
842	163	24	213	8-02-86	HR	28
843	164	24	214	8-02-86	HR	4503
844	165	24	214	8-02-86	HR	7087
848	166	24	214-215	8-03-86	HR	3014
849	167	24	215-217	8-03-86	HR	6664
893	168	24	217	8-04-86	S	71
894	169	24	218	8-04-86	S	1008
895	170	24	218	8-04-86	S	2796
896	171	24	218	8-04-86	HR	8585
897	172	24	219	8-04-86	S	632
898	173	24	219	8-04-86	S	885
899	174	24	220	8-04-86	S	2056
900	175	24	220	8-04-86	S	2438
901	176	24	220-221	8-04-86	HR	4865
902	177	24	222-256	8-04-86	HR	9478
903	178	24	256-308	8-04-86	HR	9726
928	179	24	308-310	8-05-86	HR	5196
929	180	24	310-335	8-05-86	HR	7480
930	181	24	335-336	8-05-86	S	335
931	182	24	336	8-05-86	HR	2124
932	183	24	337	8-05-86	HR	9857

RESOLUTIONS OF THE FORTY-NINTH CONGRESS

1	1	24	339	12-21-85	H Res.	2
2	2	24	339	12-26-85	S Res.	1
3	3	24	339	12-26-85	H Res.	1
4	4	24	340	3-13-86	H Res.	105
5	5	24	340	3-13-86	H Res.	124

RESOLUTIONS OF THE FORTY-NINTH CONGRESS

Public Law/Resolution		Statutes at Large	Page	Date	Bill No.
Chapter	Number				
6	6	24	340	3-29-86	S Res. 39
7	7	24	340-341	3-29-86	H Res. 71
8	8	24	341	4-07-86	H Res. 58
9	9	24	341	4-07-86	H Res. 115
10	10	24	341	4-15-86	H Res. 18
11	11	24	341	4-15-86	H Res. 73
12	12	24	342	5-01-86	S Res. 10
15	13	24	342	6-28-86	H Res. 76
17	14	24	342	6-30-86	S Res. 18
18	15	24	343	7-01-86	H Res. 196
19	16	24	343	7-03-86	H Res. 57
20	17	24	343	7-03-86	H Res. 177
21	18	24	344	7-03-86	H Res. 183
22	19	24	344	7-08-86	H Res. 185
23	20	24	344	7-15-86	H Res. 199
24	21	24	345	7-15-86	H Res. 202
25	22	24	345	7-28-86	S Res. 62
26	23	24	345	7-28-86	H Res. 129
27	24	24	345-346	7-29-86	H Res. 22
28	25	24	346	7-29-86	H Res. 54
29	26	24	346	8-02-86	H Res. 142
30	27	24	346-347	8-04-86	H Res. 87
31	28	24	347	8-04-86	H Res. 138
32	29	24	347	8-04-86	H Res. 201
33	30	24	347	8-04-86	H Res. 160
34	31	24	348	8-04-86	H Res. 209
35	32	24	348	8-05-86	S Res. 46
36	33	24	348	8-05-86	S Res. 82
37	34	24	349	8-05-86	H Res. 120
38	35	24	349	8-05-86	H Res. 213

PUBLIC ACTS OF THE FORTY-NINTH CONGRESS

Public Law/Resolution		Statutes at Large	Page	Date	Bill No.	
Chapter	Number					
2	1	24	351	12-20-86	S	1424
3	2	24	351	12-20-86	S	830
4	3	24	351-352	12-20-86	S	1110
5	4	24	352	12-20-86	HR	6983
7	5	24	352-353	12-21-86	HR	68
8	6	24	353	12-22-86	HR	10239
9	7	24	353	12-23-86	S	1526
11	8	24	354	1-03-87	S	263
12	9	24	354	1-03-87	HR	3504
13	10	24	354-355	1-03-87	HR	5878
14	11	24	355-356	1-03-87	HR	7536
15	12	24	356-357	1-03-87	HR	9987
16	13	24	358	1-03-87	HR	2013
21	14	24	358-359	1-17-87	S	1353
22	15	24	359	1-17-87	S	1829
23	16	24	360	1-17-87	S	2901
24	17	24	360	1-17-87	HR	1085
25	18	24	361	1-17-87	HR	7879
26	19	24	361-363	1-17-87	HR	9763
40	20	24	363	1-26-87	S	228
41	21	24	364	1-26-87	S	634
42	22	24	364	1-26-87	S	766
43	23	24	364	1-26-87	S	1130
44	24	24	364-365	1-26-87	S	1188
45	25	24	365-366	1-26-87	S	1212
46	26	24	366-367	1-26-87	S	1213
47	27	24	367-368	1-26-87	S	1577
48	28	24	368	1-26-87	S	1882
49	29	24	368-369	1-26-87	S	2600
50	30	24	369	1-26-87	S	2791
67	31	24	370	1-29-87	HR	191
68	32	24	370	1-29-87	S	230
69	33	24	370-371	1-29-87	S	1386
70	34	24	371-372	1-29-87	HR	807
71	35	24	372	1-29-87	HR	6313
72	36	24	372	1-29-87	HR	7192
90	37	24	373-375	2-03-87	S	9
91	38	24	375-377	2-03-87	S	2589

Public Law/Resolution		Statutes at Large	Page	Date	Bill No.	
Chapter	Number					
92	39	24	377-378	2-03-87	HR	1171
93	40	24	378	2-03-87	HR	5894
103	41	24	378-379	2-04-87	S	129
104	42	24	379-387	2-04-87	S	1532
105	43	24	387-388	2-04-87	S	1813
119	44	24	388-391	2-08-87	S	54
120	45	24	391-392	2-08-87	HR	3186
123	46	24	392	2-09-87	HR	8923
124	47	24	393	2-09-87	HR	9371
125	48	24	393	2-09-87	HR	9644
126	49	24	393-394	2-09-87	HR	10051
127	50	24	394-401	2-09-87	HR	10242
128	51	24	401	2-11-87	HR	1280
129	52	24	401-402	2-12-87	S	222
130	53	24	402-403	2-15-87	HR	10056
131	54	24	403-404	2-16-87	S	1536
132	55	24	404	2-17-87	S	129
133	56	24	404	2-17-87	S	388
134	57	24	404-405	2-17-87	S	574
135	58	24	405	2-17-87	S	2477
136	59	24	405	2-17-87	S	2652
137	60	24	406	2-17-87	HR	1684
138	61	24	406	2-17-87	HR	3110
139	62	24	406	2-17-87	HR	3160
156	63	24	407	2-21-87	HR	7218
157	64	24	407	2-21-87	HR	9895
158	65	24	408	2-21-87	HR	10412
208	66	24	408	2-23-87	S	1154
209	67	24	408-409	2-23-87	S	2428
210	68	24	409-410	2-23-87	S	3044
211	69	24	410	2-23-87	HR	1143
212	70	24	410	2-23-87	HR	1336
213	71	24	411	2-23-87	HR	1622
214	72	24	411	2-23-87	HR	1993
215	73	24	411-412	2-23-87	HR	3289
216	74	24	412-413	2-23-87	HR	4806
217	75	24	413	2-23-87	HR	7083
218	76	24	414	2-23-87	HR	7860

PUBLIC ACTS OF THE FORTY-NINTH CONGRESS

Public Law/Resolution		Statutes at Large	Page	Date	Bill No.	
Chapter	Number					
219	77	24	414	2-23-87	HR	8893
220	78	24	414-415	2-23-87	HR	9232
221	79	24	415-416	2-23-87	HR	9653
222	80	24	416	2-23-87	HR	9918
249	81	24	416-417	2-24-87	S	93
250	82	24	417	2-24-87	S	305
251	83	24	417-418	2-24-87	S	712
252	84	24	418	2-24-87	S	1592
253	85	24	418	2-24-87	S	2225
254	86	24	419-422	2-24-87	HR	6393
257	87	24	422	2-25-87	HR	7508
258	88	24	422-423	2-25-87	HR	7775
259	89	24	423	2-25-87	HR	10305
269	90	24	423	2-28-87	S	1458
270	91	24	424	2-28-87	S	2982
271	92	24	424-427	2-28-87	HR	2929
272	93	24	427	2-28-87	HR	4308
273	94	24	428	2-28-87	HR	9116
274	95	24	428	2-28-87	HR	9642
275	96	24	429	2-28-87	S	2992
276	97	24	429	2-28-87	HR	1173
277	98	24	429-430	2-28-87	HR	2646
278	99	24	430	2-28-87	HR	6538
279	100	24	430-431	2-28-87	HR	6764
280	101	24	431	2-28-87	HR	7209
281	102	24	431	2-28-87	HR	7596
282	103	24	432	2-28-87	HR	8030
283	104	24	432-433	2-28-87	HR	8880
284	105	24	433	2-28-87	HR	9339
285	106	24	434	2-28-87	HR	10048
286	107	24	434	2-28-87	HR	10091
287	108	24	434	2-28-87	HR	10804
288	109	24	434-435	2-28-87	HR	5538
311	110	24	435-436	3-01-87	S	1119
312	111	24	436-439	3-01-87	HR	10395
313	112	24	439-440	3-01-87	HR	10397
314	113	24	440-442	3-02-87	S	372
315	114	24	442-443	3-02-87	HR	367

Public Law/Resolution		Statutes at Large	Page	Date	Bill No.	
Chapter	Number					
316	115	24	444	3-02-87	HR	2075
317	116	24	444	3-02-87	HR	2539
318	117	24	445	3-02-87	HR	6637
319	118	24	446-449	3-02-87	HR	8594
320	119	24	449-467	3-02-87	HR	10394
333	120	24	468	3-03-87	S	1131
334	121	24	468-469	3-03-87	S	2898
335	122	24	470-471	3-03-87	S	2930
336	123	24	471-472	3-03-87	S	2958
337	124	24	472-474	3-03-87	S	3039
338	125	24	474-475	3-03-87	S	3165
339	126	24	475-576	3-03-87	S	3173
340	127	24	476-477	3-03-87	HR	3280
341	128	24	477-478	3-03-87	HR	5959
342	129	24	478-487	3-03-87	HR	10396
343	130	24	487	3-03-87	HR	10731
344	131	24	487-488	3-03-87	S	3296
345	132*	24	488-492	3-03-87	H Res.	170
346	133	24	492	3-03-87	HR	8346
347	134	24	492	3-03-87	HR	8599
348	135	24	492-493	3-03-87	HR	9859
349	136	24	493-494	3-03-87	HR	10717
350	137	24	494	3-03-87	HR	10799
351	138	24	495-499	3-03-87	HR	10912
352	139	24	499	3-03-87	HR	10991
353	140	24	500	3-03-87	S	512
354	141	24	500	3-03-87	S	1255
355	142	24	501	3-03-87	S	1854
356	143	24	501-502	3-03-87	S	2896
357	144	24	502-503	3-03-87	HR	34
358	145	24	504-505	3-03-87	HR	3853
359	146	24	505-508	3-03-87	HR	6974
360	147	24	508	3-03-87	HR	8593
361	148	24	508-509	3-03-87	HR	9858
362	149	24	509-543	3-03-87	HR	10072
363	150	24	543-544	3-03-87	HR	10233
364	151	24	544	3-03-87	HR	11202
365	152	24	544-545	3-03-87	S	856

PUBLIC ACTS OF THE FORTY-NINTH CONGRESS

Public Law/Resolution		Statutes at Large	Page	Date	Bill No.	
Chapter	Number					
366	153	24	545–546	3–03–87	S	3095
367	154	24	546–548	3–03–87	S	3104
368	155	24	548–549	3–03–87	S	3184
369	156	24	549	3–03–87	S	3358
370	157	24	550	3–03–87	HR	1413
371	158	24	551	3–03–87	HR	1686
372	159	24	551–552	3–03–87	HR	2252
373	160	24	552–555	3–03–87	HR	2441
374	161	24	555	3–03–87	HR	4981
375	162	24	555–556	3–03–87	HR	6066
376	163	24	556–558	3–03–87	HR	7021
377	164	24	558–559	3–03–87	HR	8978
378	165	24	559–560	3–03–87	HR	9110
379	166	24	560	3–03–87	HR	9469
380	167	24	560	3–03–87	HR	9818
381	168	24	561–562	3–03–87	HR	10023
382	169	24	562–563	3–03–87	HR	10055
383	170	24	564–565	3–03–87	HR	10098
384	171	24	565–566	3–03–87	HR	10146
385	172	24	566–567	3–03–87	HR	10425
386	173	24	567–568	3–03–87	HR	10644
387	174	24	568–569	3–03–87	HR	10790
388	175	24	569–570	3–03–87	HR	10793
389	176	24	571–580	3–03–87	HR	10802
390	177	24	580	3–03–87	HR	10900
391	178	24	481–594	3–03–87	HR	11020
392	179	24	595–632	3–03–87	HR	11028
393	180	24	632–633	3–03–87	HR	11061
394	181	24	633	3–03–87	HR	11063
395	182	24	633–634	3–03–87	HR	11103
396	183	24	634–635	3–03–87	S	199
397	184	24	635–641	3–03–87	S	10

RESOLUTIONS OF THE FORTY-NINTH CONGRESS

1	1	24	643	12–17–86	H Res.	220
2	2	24	643	12–20–86	S Res.	19
3	3	24	643	12–21–86	H Res.	118
4	4	24	644	1–03–87	H Res.	67

RESOLUTIONS OF THE FORTY-NINTH CONGRESS

Public Law/Resolution		Statutes at Large	Page	Date	Bill No.
Chapter	Number				
5	5	24	644	1-19-87	S Res. 90
6	6	24	644	2-23-87	S Res. 40
7	7	24	644-645	2-23-87	H Res. 72
8	8	24	645	2-28-87	S Res. 51
9	9	24	645	2-28-87	H Res. 215
10	10	24	646	3-03-87	S Res. 88
11	11	24	646	3-03-87	H Res. 263
12	12	24	646	3-03-87	S Res. 78
13	13	24	647	3-03-87	S Res. 108
14	14	24	647	3-03-87	S Res. 117
15	15	24	647	3-03-87	S Res. 118
16	16	24	647	3-03-87	H Res. 130
17	17	24	648	3-03-87	H Res. 264
18	18	24	648	3-03-87	S Res. 73
19	19	24	648	3-03-87	H Res. 182
20	20	24	649	3-03-87	H Res. 229
21	21	24	649	3-03-87	H Res. 238
22	22	24	649	3-03-87	H Res. 253

PUBLIC ACTS OF THE FIFTIETH CONGRESS

Public Law/Resolution		Statutes at Large	Page	Date	Bill No.	
Chapter	Number					
1	1	25	1	1-20-88	S	261
2	2	25	1-2	1-20-88	HR	3318
3	3	25	2-4	1-31-88	S	290
4	4	25	4-32	2-01-88	HR	4271
5	5	25	32	2-01-88	HR	4881
7	6	25	33	2-06-88	S	191
9	7	25	33	2-15-88	HR	5352
10	8	25	33	2-15-88	HR	1213
12	9	25	34-35	2-17-88	S	274
13	10	25	35-39	2-18-88	S	1346
14	11	25	39-40	2-18-88	HR	2578
15	12	25	40-41	2-18-88	HR	5514
16	13	25	41	2-20-88	S	1022
17	14	25	41-43	2-29-88	S	1900
18	15	25	43	2-29-88	HR	6439
19	16	25	43	3-01-88	S	601
20	17	25	43-44	3-05-88	S	642
21	18	25	44	3-05-88	HR	1495
22	19	25	44	3-05-88	HR	2993
23	20	25	44-45	3-05-88	HR	4359
29	21	25	45	3-08-88	S	158
30	22	25	45	3-09-88	HR	4756
34	23	25	45	3-23-88	S	1027
42	24	25	46	3-26-88	S	2494
43	25	25	46	3-26-88	HR	5617
45	26	25	46	3-29-88	HR	1611
47	27	25	47-71	3-30-88	HR	6437
48	28	25	72	4-02-88	S	2220
49	29	25	73	4-02-88	S	2550
50	30	25	73	4-02-88	HR	1528
51	31	25	73	4-02-88	HR	5373
52	32	25	73	4-02-88	S	643
53	33	25	74-75	4-02-88	HR	4327
54	34	25	76	4-02-88	HR	5723
56	35	25	76	4-04-88	S	1564
57	36	25	76-78	4-04-88	S	1663
58	37	25	78-79	4-04-88	HR	1589
59	38	25	79	4-04-88	HR	4487

Public Law/Resolution		Statutes at Large	Page	Date	Bill No.	
Chapter	Number					
60	39	25	79	4-04-88	HR	4556
61	40	25	79	4-04-88	HR	5728
63	41	25	80-81	4-05-88	HR	1481
64	42	25	81	4-05-88	HR	1678
65	43	25	81	4-05-88	HR	3508
69	44	25	82-83	4-09-88	HR	3470
70	45	25	83	4-09-88	HR	7217
80	46	25	84	4-11-88	HR	4472
81	47	25	84	4-11-88	HR	8808
107	48	25	84-85	4-16-88	S	1387
108	49	25	85	4-16-88	HR	1262
109	50	25	85	4-16-88	S	1371
121	51	25	85	4-17-88	HR	5639
123	52	25	86	4-19-88	HR	1818
124	53	25	86	4-19-88	HR	3796
125	54	25	86-87	4-19-88	HR	5062
126	55	25	87	4-19-88	HR	5673
127	56	25	87	4-19-88	HR	6051
128	57	25	87-88	4-19-88	HR	7262
129	58	25	88	4-19-88	HR	8044
137	59	25	88-90	4-20-88	HR	1076
155	60	25	90	4-23-88	HR	7220
191	61	25	90	4-24-88	S	2565
192	62	25	90-92	4-24-88	HR	1584
193	63	25	92-94	4-24-88	HR	2927
194	64	25	94	4-24-88	HR	9381
204	65	25	94	4-26-88	HR	4964
206	66	25	94-104	4-30-88	HR	7315
207	67	25	105	5-01-88	S	1431
208	68	25	105	5-01-88	S	2085
209	69	25	105-107	5-01-88	S	2179
210	70	25	107	5-01-88	HR	1805
211	71	25	107-108	5-01-88	HR	4365
212	72	25	108-112	5-01-88	HR	6894
213	73	25	113-133	5-01-88	HR	1956
214	74	25	134	5-01-88	HR	3253
227	75	25	134	5-02-88	HR	7546
230	76	25	134	5-09-88	S	1483

PUBLIC ACTS OF THE FIFTIETH CONGRESS

Public Law/Resolution		Statutes at Large	Page	Date	Bill No.	
Chapter	Number					
231	77	25	135	5-09-88	HR	1158
232	78	25	135-136	5-09-88	HR	1438
233	79	25	136	5-09-88	HR	1788
234	80	25	136-137	5-09-88	HR	3333
241	81	25	137	5-11-88	HR	1712
242	82	25	137	5-14-88	S	1828
243	83	25	138	5-14-88	S	2458
244	84	25	138	5-14-88	S	2506
245	85	25	138-139	5-14-88	S	2614
246	86	25	139-140	5-14-88	HR	3215
247	87	25	140	5-14-88	HR	9430
248	88	25	140-144	5-14-88	S	1148
249	89	25	144-145	5-14-88	S	1889
250	90	25	145-147	5-14-88	S	2198
251	91	25	147-149	5-14-88	S	2671
252	92	25	149	5-14-88	HR	1325
253	93	25	149-150	5-14-88	HR	7218
255	94	25	150-151	5-15-88	S	2267
257	95	25	151	5-16-88	S	2605
261	96	25	151	5-17-88	S	1204
295	97	25	152	5-19-88	HR	1697
297	98	25	152-153	5-21-88	S	555
298	99	25	153	5-21-88	HR	6831
299	100	25	153-154	5-21-88	HR	7348
306	101	25	155	5-24-88	S	354
307	102	25	155-156	5-24-88	HR	1473
308	103	25	157	5-24-88	HR	1645
309	104	25	157	5-24-88	HR	4358
310	105	25	157-158	5-24-88	HR	7936
319	106	25	158	5-28-88	S	850
320	107	25	159	5-28-88	HR	1640
321	108	25	159-160	5-28-88	HR	9711
336	109	25	160-161	5-30-88	S	38
337	110	25	162-165	5-30-88	S	269
338	111	25	165	6-01-88	S	2210
339	112	25	165-166	6-04-88	HR	2068
340	113	25	166	6-04-88	HR	8006
341	114	25	166-167	6-04-88	HR	1540

PUBLIC ACTS OF THE FIFTIETH CONGRESS

Public Law/Resolution		Statutes at Large	Page	Date	Bill No.	
Chapter	Number					
342	115	25	167	6-04-88	HR	6098
343	116	25	167	6-04-88	HR	8394
344	117	25	167-168	6-04-88	S	325
345	118	25	169	6-04-88	S	2901
361	119	25	169-170	6-06-88	S	786
362	120	25	170-171	6-06-88	S	1747
363	121	25	171-172	6-06-88	S	2345
364	122	25	172-173	6-06-88	S	2481
365	123	25	173	6-06-88	HR	7938
369	124	25	173-174	6-07-88	HR	5445
370	125	25	174-175	6-07-88	S	1083
371	126	25	175	6-07-88	S	1554
372	127	25	175	6-07-88	S	1978
373	128	25	176	6-07-88	HR	7222
374	129	25	176	6-08-88	HR	9788
375	130	25	177-178	6-08-88	S	2123
382	131	25	178	6-09-88	HR	4920
383	132	25	178-179	6-09-88	HR	5929
384	133	25	179-180	6-09-88	HR	7564
385	134	25	180-181	6-09-88	HR	8623
389	135	25	182-184	6-13-88	HR	8560
390	136	25	184-185	6-18-88	S	1948
391	137	25	185	6-18-88	S	2551
392	138	25	186	6-18-88	HR	1483
393	139	25	186-187	6-18-88	HR	1844
394	140	25	187-188	6-18-88	HR	7052
395	141	25	188	6-18-88	HR	7509
396	142	25	188-189	6-18-88	HR	8279
397	143	25	189	6-18-88	HR	8965
398	144	25	189-190	6-18-88	HR	7265
419	145	25	190-194	6-19-88	HR	6899
420	146	25	194	6-19-88	HR	7263
421	147	25	195	6-19-88	HR	7264
422	148	25	195-197	6-19-88	HR	7340
423	149	25	197-198	6-19-88	HR	1184
472	150	25	198-199	6-22-88	HR	6440
478	151	25	199-203	6-23-88	HR	2017
486	152	25	203-204	6-25-88	S	1507

Public Law/Resolution		Statutes at Large	Page	Date	Bill No.	
Chapter	Number					
487	153	25	204–205	6–25–88	HR	7783
494	154	25	205–209	6–26–88	S	2929
496	155	25	209–210	6–29–88	S	1241
497	156	25	210–211	6–29–88	S	2930
498	157	25	211–212	6–29–88	HR	2097
499	158	25	212–214	6–29–88	HR	2527
500	159	25	214–215	6–29–88	HR	2528
501	160	25	215–216	6–29–88	HR	4320
502	161	25	216–217	6–29–88	HR	8343
503	162	25	217–239	6–29–88	HR	8565
519	163	25	240	7–04–88	HR	8372
590	164	25	240–241	7–09–88	S	23
591	165	25	241–242	7–09–88	S	1484
592	166	25	242–243	7–09–88	S	1525
593	167	25	243–244	7–09–88	S	1851
594	168	25	244–245	7–09–88	S	2601
595	169	25	245–246	7–09–88	HR	1361
596	170	25	246	7–09–88	HR	1451
597	171	25	246–247	7–09–88	HR	1514
598	172	25	247	7–09–88	HR	3290
614	173	25	247–255	7–11–88	HR	6833
615	174	25	256–295	7–11–88	HR	9377
621	175	25	295–296	7–16–88	S	322
622	176	25	296–297	7–16–88	S	560
623	177	25	298–299	7–16–88	S	667
624	178	25	299–301	7–16–88	S	1405
625	179	25	301–302	7–16–88	S	1524
626	180	25	302–303	7–16–88	S	1526
627	181	25	303–305	7–16–88	S	1882
628	182	25	305–307	7–16–88	S	1883
629	183	25	307–309	7–16–88	S	2199
630	184	25	309–311	7–16–88	S	2674
631	185	25	311–312	7–16–88	HR	9610
666	186	25	312–314	7–17–88	S	1404
676	187	25	314–328	7–18–88	HR	8989
677	188	25	328–334	7–18–88	HR	10233
678	189	25	334–336	7–19–88	S	1669
679	190	25	336	7–19–88	HR	1983

Public Law/Resolution		Statutes at Large	Page	Date	Bill No.	
Chapter	Number					
680	191	25	336-337	7-19-88	HR	5096
685	192	25	337-338	7-19-88	HR	9816
690	193	25	338-339	7-20-88	HR	1387
691	194	25	339	7-23-88	S	671
692	195	25	339-340	7-23-88	HR	3376
693	196	25	340	7-23-88	HR	4423
694	197	25	340	7-23-88	HR	8039
695	198	25	341	7-23-88	HR	8391
696	199	25	341-343	7-23-88	HR	10628
700	200	25	343-344	7-24-88	S	3215
701	201	25	344-345	7-24-88	HR	7749
702	202	25	345-347	7-24-88	HR	9345
715	203	25	347	7-25-88	HR	5064
716	204	25	347-348	7-26-88	S	1129
717	205	25	349-350	7-26-88	S	2536
718	206	25	350-352	7-26-88	S	2807
720	207	25	352	7-31-88	S	735
722	208	25	352	8-01-88	HR	1338
723	209	25	353	8-01-88	HR	10053
724	210	25	353-354	8-01-88	S	1051
725	211	25	355	8-01-88	S	1612
726	212	25	355	8-01-88	S	2307
727	213	25	355-357	8-01-88	S	2493
728	214	25	357	8-01-88	HR	6153
729	215	25	357-358	8-01-88	HR	8180
730	216	25	358	8-01-88	HR	8183
738	217	25	358-359	8-06-88	S	558
739	218	25	359	8-06-88	S	1709
740	219	25	359-360	8-06-88	S	3365
741	220	25	360-362	8-06-88	HR	2170
742	221	25	362-363	8-06-88	HR	2625
743	222	25	363-364	8-06-88	HR	3070
744	223	25	365	8-06-88	HR	5095
745	224	25	365-367	8-06-88	HR	6699
746	225	25	367-369	8-06-88	HR	7438
747	226	25	369-370	8-06-88	HR	7899
748	227	25	370-372	8-06-88	HR	8353
749	228	25	372-373	8-06-88	HR	8354

PUBLIC ACTS OF THE FIFTIETH CONGRESS

Public Law/Resolution		Statutes at Large	Page	Date	Bill No.	
Chapter	Number					
750	229	25	373-374	8-06-88	HR	8355
751	230	25	374-375	8-06-88	HR	9086
752	231	25	375-377	8-06-88	HR	9420
753	232	25	377-378	8-06-88	HR	9611
754	233	25	378	8-06-88	HR	10524
755	234	25	378-380	8-06-88	HR	10527
756	235	25	380-382	8-06-88	HR	10538
757	236	25	382	8-06-88	S	2845
772	237	25	382-385	8-07-88	HR	1426
773	238	25	385-386	8-07-88	HR	3523
785	239	25	386	8-08-88	S	64
786	240	25	387	8-08-88	S	143
787	241	25	387	8-08-88	S	183
788	242	25	387-388	8-08-88	HR	1312
789	243	25	388	8-08-88	HR	1477
790	244	25	388-389	8-08-88	HR	1648
791	245	25	389	8-08-88	HR	1705
792	246	25	389-390	8-08-88	HR	3361
793	247	25	390-391	8-08-88	HR	9512
794	248	25	391	8-08-88	HR	9771
816	249	25	391-392	8-08-88	S	196
817	250	25	392	8-09-88	S	856
818	251	25	392	8-09-88	S	928
819	252	25	393	8-09-88	S	1782
820	253	25	394-395	8-09-88	HR	9079
821	254	25	395-396	8-09-88	HR	10128
822	255	25	396-397	8-09-88	HR	10347
823	256	25	398-399	8-09-88	HR	10573
824	257	25	399	8-09-88	HR	10758
859	258	25	399-400	8-10-88	S	2624
860	259	25	400-433	8-11-88	HR	9859
866	260	25	433-437	8-13-88	S	783
867	261	25	437	8-13-88	S	907
868	262	25	437	8-13-88	HR	1560
869	263	25	438	8-13-88	HR	7398
870	264	25	438	8-13-88	HR	8783
871	265	25	439	8-13-88	HR	9056
872	266	25	439	8-13-88	HR	9977

PUBLIC ACTS OF THE FIFTIETH CONGRESS

Public Law/Resolution		Statutes at Large	Page	Date	Bill No.	
Chapter	Number					
873	267	25	440-442	8-13-88	HR	10604
890	268	25	442-443	8-14-88	HR	1508
891	269	25	443	8-14-88	HR	1612
892	270	25	443-444	8-14-88	HR	5067
899	271	25	444	8-21-88	HR	8592
900	272	25	444-446	8-21-88	HR	10165
912	273	25	446-449	8-22-88	HR	7647
913	274	25	449-450	8-27-88	S	509
914	275	25	450	8-27-88	S	2116
915	276	25	450-451	8-27-88	HR	1321
916	277	25	451	8-27-88	HR	3329
917	278	25	451-452	8-27-88	HR	5863
936	279	25	452-457	9-01-88	HR	8662
948	280	25	457-458	9-06-88	HR	11118
991	281	25	458-473	9-07-88	HR	10556
999	282	25	473-474	9-10-88	S	1880
1000	283	25	474	9-10-88	S	3226
1001	284	25	474-475	9-10-88	S	3474
1006	285	25	475	9-11-88	S	2197
1007	286	25	475-476	9-11-88	S	3364
1015	287	25	476-479	9-13-88	S	3304
1018	288	25	479-480	9-14-88	HR	1661
1026	289	25	480-481	9-22-88	HR	5670
1027	290	25	481-488	9-22-88	HR	10234
1028	291	25	489-491	9-22-88	HR	10998
1037	292	25	491-492	9-26-88	S	186
1038	293	25	492-496	9-26-88	S	2252
1039	294	25	496-497	9-26-88	S	3447
1040	295	25	497	9-26-88	HR	1604
1041	296	26	497-498	9-26-88	HR	11446
1056	297	25	498	10-01-88	S	3539
1057	298	25	498	10-01-88	HR	1216
1058	299	25	499	10-01-88	HR	5059
1059	300	25	499-500	10-01-88	HR	8751
1060	301	25	500	10-01-88	HR	8752
1061	302	25	500	10-01-88	HR	10679
1062	303	25	501	10-01-88	HR	10931
1063	304	25	501-504	10-01-88	HR	8665

Public Law/Resolution		Statutes at Large	Page	Date	Bill No.	
Chapter	Number					
1064	305	25	504	10-01-88	HR	11336
1065	306	25	504-505	10-01-88	HR	11391
1069	307	25	505-548	10-02-88	HR	10540
1070	308	25	548-549	10-09-88	S	3471
1090	309	25	549-551	10-12-88	S	249
1091	310	25	552	10-12-88	S	554
1092	311	25	552	10-12-88	S	2519
1093	312	25	552-553	10-12-88	S	2613
1094	313	25	553	10-12-88	S	3098
1095	314	25	554	10-12-88	S	3168
1096	315	25	555-556	10-12-88	HR	9619
1097	316	25	556-557	10-12-88	HR	10060
1098	317	25	557	10-12-88	HR	10934
1099	318	25	557	10-12-88	HR	11101
1113	319	25	557-558	10-13-88	HR	1923
1186	320	25	558-560	10-17-88	HR	10112
1194	321	25	560	10-18-88	S	70
1195	322	25	560	10-18-88	S	1856
1196	323	25	560-564	10-18-88	S	2742
1197	324	25	564	10-18-88	S	3427
1208	325	25	564	10-19-88	HR	2972
1209	326	25	565	10-19-88	HR	10606
1210	327	25	565-607	10-19-88	HR	10896
1211	328	25	608-609	10-19-88	S	1494
1212	329	25	609-610	10-19-88	S	2110
1213	330	25	610-611	10-19-88	S	2802
1214	331	25	611-612	10-19-88	S	3433
1215	332	25	612-613	10-19-88	S	3597
1216	334	25	613-614	10-19-88	S	3620
1217	335	25	614	10-19-88	HR	1249
1218	335	25	614	10-19-88	HR	1641
1219	336	25	614	10-19-88	HR	5700
1220	337	25	614	10-19-88	HR	7421
1221	338	25	614	10-19-88	HR	7604
1222	339	25	615	10-19-88	HR	11581
1223	340	25	615	10-19-88	HR	11599

Public Law/Resolution		Statutes at Large	Page	Date	Bill No.	
Chapter	Number					
1	1	25	617	12-22-87	H Res.	2
2	2	25	617	2-01-88	H Res.	72
4	3	25	617	2-15-88	S Res.	50
5	4	25	618	3-05-88	H Res.	113
6	5	25	618	3-10-88	S Res.	4
7	6	25	618-619	3-20-88	S Res.	60
8	7	25	619	3-26-88	H Res.	117
9	8	25	620	4-02-88	S Res.	65
10	9	25	620	4-05-88	H Res.	77
12	10	25	620	4-11-88	H Res.	140
14	11	25	620-621	5-10-88	H Res.	83
15	12	25	622	5-11-88	S Res.	70
16	13	25	622	5-14-88	S Res.	68
17	14	25	622	5-14-88	S Res.	73
18	15	25	623	5-21-88	H Res.	148
19	16	25	623	5-24-88	H Res.	95
20	17	25	623	5-29-88	S Res.	87
21	18	25	623-624	6-20-88	H Res.	183
22	19	25	624	6-25-88	S Res.	42
23	20	25	624	6-30-88	H Res.	187
24	21	25	625	6-30-88	H Res.	188
25	22	25	625	7-02-88	H Res.	178
26	23	25	625	7-10-88	H Res.	191
27	24	25	625-626	7-10-88	H Res.	193
29	25	25	626	7-16-88	H Res.	184
30	26	25	626-627	7-16-88	H Res.	196
31	27	25	627	7-19-88	S Res.	96
32	28	25	627	7-23-88	H Res.	161
33	29	25	627	7-25-88	H Res.	195
34	30	25	628	7-31-88	H Res.	206
35	31	25	628	8-01-88	H Res.	103
36	32	25	628	8-08-88	S Res.	77
37	33	25	629	8-13-88	S Res.	27
38	34	25	629	8-14-88	S Res.	99
39	35	25	629	8-14-88	S Res.	100
41	36	25	630	9-01-88	H Res.	219
42	37	25	630	9-06-88	H Res.	201
43	38	25	630	9-15-88	H Res.	221

RESOLUTIONS OF THE FIFTIETH CONGRESS

Public Law/Resolution		Statutes at Large	Page	Date	Bill No.
Chapter	Number				
44	39	25	630	9-26-88	S Res. 102
45	40	25	631	9-26-88	H Res. 225
46	41	25	631	10-01-88	H Res. 223
47	42	25	631	10-12-88	S Res. 10
48	43	25	631	10-12-88	S Res. 110
49	44	25	631-632	10-12-88	H Res. 210
50	45	25	632	10-18-88	H Res. 101
51	46	25	632	10-19-88	S Res. 112
52	47	25	632-633	10-19-88	S Res. 116
54	48	25	633	10-20-88	H Res. 229
55	49	25	633	10-20-88	H Res. 231
56	50	25	633-634	10-20-88	H Res. 232
57	51	25	634	10-20-88	H Res. 233

Public Law/Resolution		Statutes at Large	Page	Date	Bill No.	
Chapter	Number					
1	1	25	635-636	12-10-88	HR	11139
2	2	25	636-637	12-10-88	HR	11262
3	3	25	637	12-17-88	S	3475
4	4	25	637	12-17-88	HR	11764
6	5	26	637-638	12-18-88	S	2040
7	6	25	638	12-22-88	HR	11878
8	7	25	638	12-24-88	HR	2579
18	8	25	639	1-01-89	HR	7843
19	9	25	639-640	1-04-89	S	1786
20	10	25	640	1-04-89	HR	10323
21	11	25	640-641	1-08-89	HR	10023
22	12	25	641-642	1-08-89	HR	10869
24	13	25	642-646	1-14-89	HR	7935
47	14	25	646	1-16-89	HR	1959
48	15	25	646-647	1-16-89	HR	5009
49	16	25	647-650	1-16-89	HR	7261
50	17	25	650	1-16-89	HR	11794
66	18	25	651	1-17-89	S	3732
91	19	25	652	1-21-89	S	154
92	20	25	652-653	1-21-89	S	182
93	21	25	653-654	1-21-89	S	1931
99	22	25	654	1-30-89	S	3782
100	23	25	654	1-30-89	HR	12107
111	24	25	654-655	2-01-89	HR	11785
113	25	25	655-656	2-06-89	S	3733
115	26	25	657	2-08-89	HR	4353
116	27	25	657	2-08-89	HR	6105
117	28	25	657	2-08-89	HR	11683
119	29	25	657-658	2-09-89	HR	4351
120	30	25	658	2-09-89	HR	5870
121	31	25	658	2-09-89	HR	12060
122	32	25	659	2-09-89	HR	8191
132	33	25	659	2-12-89	S	379
133	34	25	659	2-12-89	S	1092
134	35	25	660-661	2-12-89	S	3794
135	36	25	661-662	2-12-89	HR	1860
136	37	25	662	2-12-89	HR	12009
137	38	25	662-667	2-12-89	HR	11854

Public Law/Resolution		Statutes at Large	Page	Date	Bill No.	
Chapter	Number					
149	39	25	667	2-13-89	S	2318
150	40	25	668	2-13-89	S	3804
151	41	25	668	2-13-89	S	3824
152	42	25	668-669	2-13-89	S	3830
153	43	25	669	2-13-89	S	3869
154	44	25	669-670	2-13-89	HR	1599
165	45	25	670	2-14-89	HR	4496
166	46	25	670	2-14-89	HR	9396
168	47	25	671-672	2-15-89	HR	3312
169	48	25	672	2-15-89	HR	11693
171	49	25	672	2-16-89	S	2305
172	50	25	673	2-16-89	S	3858
176	51	25	673-675	2-20-89	S	1305
180	52	25	676-684	2-22-89	S	185
201	53	25	684	2-23-89	S	259
202	54	25	684-687	2-23-89	S	2315
203	55	25	687-689	2-23-89	S	2992
204	56	25	689-690	2-23-89	S	3734
205	57	25	690	2-23-89	S	3786
206	58	25	690	2-23-89	S	3795
207	59	25	690-691	2-23-89	S	3800
208	60	25	691	2-23-89	S	3897
234	61	25	691	2-25-89	S	1804
235	62	25	691-693	2-25-89	S	3663
236	63	25	693	2-25-89	S	3865
237	64	25	693-694	2-25-89	HR	3060
238	65	25	694	2-25-89	HR	1407
239	66	25	695	2-25-89	S	3949
240	67	25	695	2-25-89	HR	11604
241	68	25	696	2-25-89	HR	12443
278	68	25	696-705	2-26-89	HR	11879
279	70	25	705-745	2-26-89	HR	11795
280	71	25	745-748	2-26-89	HR	11777
302	72	25	748-749	2-27-89	S	3560
308	73	25	749-750	3-01-89	S	3640
309	74	25	750	3-01-89	S	24
310	75	25	750-751	3-01-89	S	1128
311	76	25	751	3-01-89	S	1721

PUBLIC ACTS OF THE FIFTIETH CONGRESS

Public Law/Resolution		Statutes at Large	Page	Date	Bill No.	
Chapter	Number					
312	77	25	751-752	3-01-89	S	3146
313	78	25	752-753	3-01-89	S	3284
314	79	25	754-755	3-01-89	S	3285
315	80	25	755	3-01-89	S	3645
316	81	25	756	3-01-89	S	3666
317	82	25	757-759	3-01-89	S	3920
318	83	25	760	3-01-89	S	3921
319	84	25	760-767	3-01-89	HR	1659
320	85	25	767	3-01-89	HR	3721
321	86	25	768-769	3-01-89	HR	6364
322	87	25	769-770	3-01-89	HR	11338
323	88	25	770	3-01-89	HR	11643
324	89	25	770	3-01-89	S	1283
325	90	25	770-771	3-01-89	S	3431
326	91	25	771	3-01-89	S	3751
327	92	25	772	3-01-89	S	3778
328	93	25	772-781	3-01-89	HR	4961
329	94	25	781	3-01-89	HR	5690
330	95	25	781	3-01-89	HR	7864
331	96	25	781	3-01-89	HR	10652
332	97	25	782-783	3-01-89	HR	11658
333	98	25	783-788	3-01-89	HR	1874
356	99	25	788	3-02-89	S	1974
357	100	25	788-790	3-02-89	S	2816
358	101	25	790	3-02-89	HR	5032
359	102	25	791	3-02-89	HR	7028
360	103	25	791	3-02-89	HR	7066
361	104	25	791	3-02-89	HR	8053
362	105	25	791	3-02-89	HR	11216
363	106	25	792	3-02-89	HR	11342
364	107	25	792	3-02-89	HR	11527
365	108	25	792	3-02-89	HR	11901
366	109	25	792	3-02-89	HR	12113
367	110	25	792	3-02-89	HR	12310
368	111	25	793	3-02-89	HR	12414
369	112	25	793	3-02-89	HR	12431
370	113	25	793-809	3-02-89	HR	11651
371	114	25	809-825	3-02-89	HR	12329

PUBLIC ACTS OF THE FIFTIETH CONGRESS

Public Law/Resolution		Statutes at Large	Page	Date	Bill No.	
Chapter	Number					
372	115	25	825-834	3-02-89	HR	12383
373	116	25	835-841	3-02-89	HR	12485
374	117	25	841-845	3-02-89	HR	12490
375	118	25	846-849	3-02-89	S	1631
376	119	25	849-850	3-02-89	S	1701
377	120	25	850-852	3-02-89	S	1939
378	121	25	852-853	3-02-89	S	2029
379	122	25	853	3-02-89	S	2442
380	123	25	853	3-02-89	S	2475
381	124	25	854-855	3-02-89	S	2511
382	125	25	855-863	3-02-89	S	2851
383	126	25	863	3-02-89	S	3653
384	127	25	863	3-02-89	S	3696
385	128	25	864	3-02-89	S	3818
386	129	25	864	3-02-89	S	3929
387	130	25	864-866	3-02-89	S	3951
388	131	25	866-867	3-02-89	S	3995
389	132	25	867-869	3-02-89	HR	5509
390	133	25	869-871	3-02-89	HR	6106
391	134	25	871-872	3-02-89	HR	7777
392	135	25	872	3-02-89	HR	8309
393	136	25	873-874	3-02-89	HR	9268
394	137	25	874-877	3-02-89	HR	9418
395	138	25	877-878	3-02-89	HR	9423
396	139	25	878-879	3-02-89	HR	9674
397	140	25	879-880	3-02-89	HR	10319
398	141	25	880-881	3-02-89	HR	10588
399	142	25	882	3-02-89	HR	10832
400	143	25	882-883	3-02-89	HR	11573
401	144	25	883-884	3-02-89	HR	11649
402	145	25	884-885	3-02-89	HR	11735
403	146	25	885-886	3-02-89	HR	11782
404	147	25	886-888	3-02-89	HR	11917
405	148	25	888-889	3-02-89	HR	11970
406	149	25	899-901	3-01-89	HR	12389
407	150	25	901-903	3-02-89	HR	12489
408	151	25	903-904	3-02-89	HR	12515
409	152	25	904-905	3-02-89	HR	12524

Public Law/Resolution		Statutes at Large	Page	Date	Bill No.	
Chapter	Number					
410	153	25	905-939	3-02-89	HR	12571
411	154	25	939-980	3-02-89	HR	12008
412	155	25	980-1006	3-02-89	HR	12578
413	156	25	1006-1008	3-02-89	HR	12154
414	157	25	1008-1009	3-02-89	S	858
415	158	25	1009-1010	3-02-89	S	3993
416	159	25	1010-1011	3-02-89	S	3918
417	160	25	1011	3-02-89	S	2828
418	161	25	1012	3-02-89	S	2182
419	162	25	1012	3-02-89	HR	5716
420	163	25	1012	3-02-89	HR	8740
421	164	25	1012-1013	3-02-89	HR	11128
422	165	25	1013-1016	3-02-89	HR	11634
423	166	25	1016	3-02-89	HR	11678
424	167	25	1017	3-02-89	HR	12324
425	168	25	1017	3-02-89	HR	12430

RESOLUTIONS OF THE FIFTIETH CONGRESS

1	1	25	1019	12-20-88	H Res.	236
2	2	25	1019	1-23-89	S Res.	104
3	3	25	1019	2-05-89	H Res.	181
5	4	25	1020	2-14-89	H Res.	25
7	5	25	1020	2-28-89	S Res.	137
8	6	25	1020	3-01-89	H Res.	258
9	7	25	1020-1021	3-01-89	H Res.	262
10	8	25	1021	3-01-89	S Res.	140
11	9	25	1021	3-01-89	H Res.	266
12	10	25	1021-1022	3-02-89	H Res.	268
13	11	25	1022	3-02-89	H Res.	252

PUBLIC ACTS OF THE FIFTY-FIRST CONGRESS

Public Law/Resolution		Statutes at Large	Page	Date	Bill No.	
Chapter	Number					
1	1	26	1	12-19-89	HR	5
2	2	26	2	1-23-90	S	1417
3	3	26	2	1-25-90	HR	153
4	4	26	3	2-04-90	HR	11
5	5	26	3	2-04-90	HR	845
6	6	26	3-5	2-06-90	S	600
7	7	26	5-6	2-06-90	S	1098
8	8	26	6	2-07-90	HR	495
9	9	26	6-7	2-11-90	HR	583
10	10	26	7	2-13-90	S	881
11	11	26	7	2-13-90	S	1023
12	12	26	8	2-13-90	S	1093
13	13	26	8	2-18-90	HR	584
14	14	26	8-9	2-19-90	HR	24
15	15	26	9-10	2-19-90	HR	3298
16	16	26	10-11	2-19-90	HR	3834
17	17	26	11-12	2-21-90	S	940
18	18	26	12-13	2-21-90	S	2015
19	19	26	13	2-22-90	S	1181
20	20	26	13-14	2-27-90	S	226
21	21	26	14-15	2-27-90	S	620
22	22	26	15	2-27-90	HR	7159
23	23	26	15	3-01-90	S	896
24	24	26	16	3-01-90	HR	3923
25	25	26	16	3-04-90	S	835
26	26	26	17	3-05-90	S	1359
27	27	26	17	3-06-90	HR	7215
28	28	26	17	3-07-90	HR	5235
29	29	26	17-18	3-08-90	S	993
31	30	26	18	3-13-90	HR	5682
32	31	26	18-20	3-15-90	S	1297
33	32	26	20	3-15-90	S	1858
34	33	26	20-21	3-15-90	S	1905
35	34	26	21-22	3-15-90	S	2994
36	35	26	22	3-17-90	S	1701
37	36	26	22	3-19-90	S	296
38	37	26	22-23	3-19-90	S	306
39	38	26	24	3-19-90	S	308

Public Law/Resolution		Statutes at Large	Page	Date	Bill No.	
Chapter	Number					
40	39	26	24-25	3-19-90	HR	5825
46	40	26	25-28	3-24-90	HR	7617
47	41	26	28	2-24-90	S	1083
48	42	26	29	3-24-90	S	280
49	43	26	29	3-24-90	S	1272
50	44	26	29-31	3-24-90	HR	4130
51	45	26	31-32	3-27-90	S	140
52	46	26	32	3-27-90	HR	417
55	47	26	32	3-28-90	HR	346
56	48	26	33	3-29-90	S	3279
58	49	26	33	3-31-90	HR	8458
60	50	26	33-34	4-01-90	HR	525
61	51	26	34	4-03-90	HR	7025
62	52	26	34	4-03-90	S	2447
63	53	26	34-44	4-04-90	HR	7496
64	54	26	44	4-05-90	S	2501
65	55	26	45-46	4-05-90	S	2653
66	56	26	46	4-05-90	S	3025
70	57	26	46	4-09-90	S	1612
71	58	26	47-48	4-09-90	S	1738
72	59	26	48-49	4-09-90	S	2324
73	60	26	50	4-09-90	S	567
74	61	26	50	4-09-90	S	2026
75	62	26	51-53	4-09-90	S	2323
76	63	26	53	4-10-90	S	1332
77	64	26	53	4-10-90	S	1984
78	65	26	54	4-11-90	S	428
79	66	26	54	4-11-90	HR	4539
80	67	26	55	4-14-90	S	381
82	68	26	55	4-15-90	HR	5874
83	69	26	55-56	4-16-90	S	368
84	70	26	56	4-16-90	S	2860
85	71	26	56	4-16-90	HR	4975
89	72	26	57	4-17-90	S	430
98	73	26	57	4-18-90	HR	7164
100	74	26	58	4-19-90	HR	2849
101	75	26	58	4-19-90	HR	3352
148	76	26	58-59	4-22-90	HR	400

PUBLIC ACTS OF THE FIFTY-FIRST CONGRESS

Public Law/Resolution		Statutes at Large	Page	Date	Bill No.	
Chapter	Number					
149	77	26	59	4-22-90	HR	5667
150	78	26	60	4-22-90	HR	8906
152	79	26	60-61	4-23-90	S	2402
153	80	26	61-62	4-23-90	HR	7498
156	81	26	62-66	4-25-90	HR	8393
159	82	26	66	4-26-90	HR	105
160	83	26	66-67	4-26-90	HR	386
161	84	26	67-68	4-26-90	HR	6942
162	85	26	69	4-26-90	HR	200
163	86	26	69-71	4-26-90	HR	505
164	87	26	71	4-26-90	HR	605
165	88	26	71-72	4-26-90	HR	778
166	89	26	72	4-26-90	HR	3331
167	90	26	72-73	4-26-90	HR	4587
168	91	26	73-74	4-28-90	HR	139
169	92	26	74-75	4-28-90	HR	507
170	93	26	75-77	4-28-90	HR	3876
171	94	26	77	4-29-90	S	3026
172	95	26	77-78	4-30-90	S	157
173	96	26	78	4-30-90	S	2284
174	97	26	79-80	4-30-90	HR	8250
180	98	26	80	5-01-90	S	3063
181	99	26	80-81	5-01-90	S	1873
182	100	26	81-100	5-02-90	S	895
183	101	26	100	5-02-90	HR	7156
195	102	26	100	5-05-90	HR	164
196	103	26	101	5-05-90	HR	533
197	104	26	102	5-06-90	HR	5179
198	105	26	102-104	5-08-90	HR	5964
199	106	26	104-105	5-08-90	HR	7509
200	107	26	105	5-09-90	HR	9548
201	108	26	105-106	5-12-90	S	3472
202	109	26	106-107	5-14-90	HR	7166
203	110	26	107	5-14-90	HR	10102
204	111	26	107	5-14-90	S	361
205	112	26	107-108	5-14-90	S	954
206	113	26	108	5-14-90	HR	389
207	114	26	109-110	5-14-90	HR	1015

Public Law/Resolution		Statutes at Large	Page	Date	Bill No.	
Chapter	Number					
208	115	26	110	5-14-90	HR	4553
209	116	26	110-111	5-14-90	HR	7904
211	117	26	111	5-15-90	HR	6474
213	118	26	111-112	5-16-90	S	606
214	119	26	112-113	5-16-90	S	859
215	120	26	113-114	5-16-90	S	2304
216	121	26	114-115	5-16-90	S	2406
217	122	26	115	5-16-90	HR	1590
233	123	26	115-116	5-20-90	HR	3872
234	124	26	116	5-21-90	S	3821
235	125	26	116	5-21-90	HR	753
236	122	26	116-118	5-21-90	HR	5729
270	127	26	118	5-22-90	S	1477
271	128	26	118-119	5-22-90	HR	4652
288	129	26	119	5-23-90	HR	7993
291	130	26	119-120	5-24-90	HR	749
292	131	26	120-121	5-24-90	HR	7985
355	132	26	121	5-26-90	HR	6419
382	133	26	121-123	5-28-90	S	2601
388	134	26	123-124	6-02-90	S	1900
389	135	26	124-125	6-02-90	S	2630
390	136	26	125	6-02-90	HR	448
391	137	26	126	6-02-90	HR	7898
399	138	26	126-127	6-06-90	S	2714
400	139	26	127	6-09-90	S	55
401	140	26	127-128	6-09-90	S	278
402	141	26	128-129	6-09-90	S	903
403	142	26	129-130	6-09-90	S	3622
405	143	26	130	6-10-90	S	84
406	144	26	130	6-10-90	S	2415
407	145	26	131-142	6-10-90	HR	4970
408	146	26	142	6-10-90	S	2296
409	147	26	143-144	6-10-90	S	2960
410	148	26	144	6-10-90	S	3337
412	149	26	145	6-11-90	S	3131
413	150	26	145	6-11-90	S	3401
414	151	26	145-146	6-11-90	S	3599
415	152	26	146	6-11-90	S	826

PUBLIC ACTS OF THE FIFTY-FIRST CONGRESS

Public Law/Resolution		Statutes at Large	Page	Date	Bill No.	
Chapter	Number					
418	153	26	146-147	6-12-90	S	3639
419	154	26	147-148	6-12-90	HR	856
422	155	26	148	6-13-90	HR	6845
423	156	26	148-157	6-13-90	HR	7619
424	157	26	157	6-16-90	S	2548
425	158	26	157	6-16-90	HR	445
426	159	26	157-158	6-16-90	HR	8235
427	160	26	158-159	6-17-90	HR	8295
428	161	26	159	6-17-90	S	2784
429	162	26	159-160	6-17-90	HR	10390
430	163	26	160-161	6-18-90	HR	10906
431	164	26	161	6-18-90	S	2311
432	165	26	162	6-18-90	S	2317
433	166	26	162	6-18-90	HR	1306
435	167	26	162-163	6-20-90	S	977
436	168	26	163	6-20-90	HR	10813
437	169	26	163-169	6-20-90	HR	8152
438	170	26	169	6-20-90	HR	8555
479	171	26	170-173	6-21-90	HR	347
480	172	26	173	6-21-90	HR	8544
540	173	26	173	6-24-90	S	3052
612	174	26	174	6-25-90	S	3571
613	175	26	174-175	6-25-90	HR	407
614	176	26	175-179	6-25-90	HR	3365
615	177	26	179-180	6-25-90	HR	7856
616	178	26	180	6-25-90	HR	10065
631	179	26	180	6-26-90	HR	75
632	180	26	180-181	6-26-90	S	595
633	181	26	181-182	6-27-90	S	3982
634	182	26	182-183	6-27-90	S	389
635	183	26	183	6-28-90	HR	7217
636	184	26	183-184	6-28-90	HR	8831
638	185	26	184-187	6-30-90	HR	344
639	186	26	187-189	6-30-90	HR	7160
640	187	26	189-206	6-30-90	HR	8909
641	188	26	206-208	6-30-90	HR	9856
646	189	26	209	7-01-90	HR	578
647	190	26	209-210	7-02-90	S	1

Public Law/Resolution		Statutes at Large	Page	Date	Bill No.	
Chapter	Number					
648	191	26	210-211	7-02-90	S	2403
649	192	26	211-212	7-02-90	HR	401
650	193	26	212	7-02-90	HR	3940
651	194	26	212	7-02-90	HR	9289
652	195	26	213	7-02-90	HR	887
653	196	26	213	7-02-90	HR	4635
654	197	26	213-214	7-02-90	HR	6946
655	198	26	214	7-03-90	HR	516
656	199	26	215-219	7-03-90	HR	4562
657	200	26	219-220	7-03-90	HR	9677
658	201	26	220	7-03-90	HR	11223
660	202	26	220	7-08-90	HR	9048
661	203	26	221	7-09-90	HR	8342
662	204	26	221	7-09-90	HR	833
663	205	26	221-222	7-09-90	HR	8149
664	206	26	222-226	7-10-90	HR	982
665	207	26	226-227	7-10-90	HR	5966
666	208	26	227	7-10-90	HR	8245
667	209	26	228-268	7-11-90	HR	9066
668	210	26	268	7-11-90	HR	9104
669	211	26	268-271	7-11-90	HR	3886
706	212	26	272-282	7-14-90	HR	9603
707	213	26	282-288	7-14-90	HR	10716
708	214	26	289-290	7-14-90	HR	5381
714	215	26	290-291	7-22-90	HR	7754
717	216	26	291-292	7-25-90	HR	4570
721	217	26	292	7-26-90	HR	278
722	218	26	292	7-30-90	HR	529
723	219	26	292-293	7-30-90	HR	8296
724	220	26	293-311	8-06-90	HR	3711
726	221	26	311-312	8-07-90	HR	9521
727	222	26	312	8-08-90	S	4000
728	223	26	313	8-08-90	S	398
729	224	26	313	8-08-90	S	3555
735	225	26	313	8-14-90	HR	11690
736	226	26	313-315	8-15-90	HR	9523
796	227	26	315	8-18-90	S	4225
797	228	26	315-320	8-18-90	HR	8391

PUBLIC ACTS OF THE FIFTY-FIRST CONGRESS

Public Law/Resolution		Statutes at Large	Page	Date	Bill No.	
Chapter	Number					
801	229	26	320	8-19-90	S	3787
802	230	26	320-328	8-19-90	S	3917
803	231	26	329	8-19-90	S	4207
804	232	26	329-333	8-19-90	HR	7058
805	233	26	333	8-19-90	S	3329
806	234	26	333-336	8-19-90	HR	6454
807	235	26	336-362	8-19-90	HR	10726
812	236	26	362	8-28-90	S	276
813	237	26	362	8-28-90	S	3127
814	238	26	363	8-28-90	S	3163
815	239	26	363-364	8-29-90	S	2661
816	240	26	364-366	8-29-90	S	2979
817	241	26	366-369	8-29-90	S	3795
818	242	26	369	8-29-90	S	4335
819	243	26	369-370	8-29-90	HR	8951
820	244	26	370-371	8-29-90	HR	11380
837	245	26	371-414	8-30-90	HR	10884
838	246	26	414	8-30-90	S	4312
839	247	26	414-417	8-30-90	S	2594
840	248	26	417	8-30-90	S	3064
841	249	26	417-419	8-30-90	S	3714
854	250	26	419-420	9-01-90	S	3172
856	251	26	420-421	9-02-90	HR	8523
857	252	26	421-422	9-02-90	HR	10060
871	253	26	422-423	9-04-90	S	1442
872	254	26	424	9-04-90	S	3031
873	255	26	424	9-04-90	S	3174
874	256	26	424	9-04-90	S	3202
875	257	26	425	9-04-90	S	3918
876	258	26	425	9-04-90	S	4213
906	259	26	426	9-13-90	S	885
907	260	26	426-465	9-19-90	HR	9486
908	261	26	465-466	9-19-90	HR	11569
909	262	26	466-467	9-25-90	S	897
910	263	26	467	9-25-90	S	3089
911	264	26	467	9-25-90	S	3843
912	265	26	467-468	9-25-90	S	2835
913	266	26	468	9-25-90	HR	526

Public Law/Resolution		Statutes at Large	Page	Date	Bill No.	
Chapter	Number					
914	267	26	468	9-25-90	HR	785
915	268	26	468	9-25-90	HR	3715
916	269	26	469-470	9-25-90	HR	8047
917	270	26	470	9-25-90	HR	8631
918	271	26	470-472	9-25-90	HR	8792
919	272	26	472	9-25-90	HR	8950
920	273	26	472-473	9-25-90	HR	10835
921	274	26	474	9-25-90	HR	10907
922	275	26	474	9-25-90	HR	11206
923	276	26	474-476	9-25-90	HR	11240
924	277	26	476-477	9-25-90	HR	11241
925	278	26	477-478	9-25-90	HR	11272
926	279	26	478	9-25-90	HR	11570
938	280	26	478-479	9-26-90	S	20
939	281	26	479	9-26-90	S	1872
940	282	26	479-480	9-26-90	S	3751
941	283	26	481-482	9-26-90	S	4278
942	284	26	482-483	9-26-90	S	4280
943	285	26	483-484	9-26-90	S	4281
944	286	26	484-485	9-26-90	HR	3895
945	287	26	485	9-26-90	HR	5596
946	288	26	485	9-26-90	S	2392
947	289	26	485-489	9-26-90	S	3556
948	290	26	489	9-26-90	S	3596
949	291	26	490	9-26-90	HR	7056
950	292	26	490	9-26-90	HR	7795
951	293	26	490-491	9-26-90	HR	8155
998	294	26	491	9-27-90	HR	8201
999	295	26	491	9-27-90	HR	11654
1000	296	26	491	9-27-90	S	1689
1001	297	26	492-495	9-27-90	S	4
1002	298	26	495	9-27-90	S	3851
1003	299	26	495-596	9-27-90	S	4375
1040	300	26	496-499	9-29-90	S	2781
1041	301	26	500	9-29-90	S	1037
1042	302	26	500	9-29-90	S	1636
1043	303	26	500	9-29-90	HR	5323
1044	304	26	500-501	9-29-90	HR	5711

Public Law/Resolution		Statutes at Large	Page	Date	Bill No.	
Chapter	Number					
1045	305	26	501	9-29-90	HR	573
1046	306	26	501	9-29-90	HR	7983
1047	307	26	501	9-29-90	HR	8943
1048	208	26	502	9-29-90	HR	11154
1120	309	26	502	9-30-90	S	4074
1121	310	26	502	9-30-90	HR	8247
1122	311	26	502-503	9-30-90	S	3852
1123	312	26	503	9-30-90	S	3996
1124	313	26	503	9-30-90	HR	3857
1125	314	26	504	9-30-90	HR	8394
1126	315	26	504-551	9-30-90	HR	11459
1127	316	26	552	9-30-90	S	497
1128	317	26	552-553	9-30-90	S	728
1129	318	26	553-554	9-30-90	S	3798
1130	319	26	554-555	9-30-90	S	3801
1131	320	26	555-558	9-30-90	S	4011
1132	321	26	558	9-30-90	S	4297
1133	322	26	558-559	9-30-90	S	4322
1134	323	26	559-560	9-30-90	S	4334
1135	324	26	561	9-30-90	S	4403
1239	325	26	561	10-01-90	S	160
1240	326	26	561-562	10-01-90	S	2805
1241	327	26	562	10-01-90	S	3716
1242	328	26	563-564	10-01-90	S	3895
1243	329	26	564-566	10-01-90	S	3952
1244	330	26	567-625	10-01-90	HR	9416
1245	331	26	625	10-01-90	S	4021
1246	332	26	625-632	10-01-90	S	4081
1247	333	26	632	10-01-90	S	4221
1248	334	26	632-636	10-01-90	S	4309
1249	335	26	636-637	10-01-90	S	4354
1250	336	26	637-638	10-01-90	S	4395
1251	337	26	639-640	10-01-90	S	4396
1252	338	26	640-643	10-01-90	S	4398
1253	339	26	643-644	10-01-90	S	4405
1254	340	26	644-645	10-01-90	S	2212
1255	341	26	645	10-01-90	HR	12163
1256	342	26	645-646	10-01-90	HR	11928

PUBLIC ACTS OF THE FIFTY-FIRST CONGRESS

Public Law/Resolution		Statutes at Large	Page	Date	Bill No.	
Chapter	Number					
1257	343	26	646-647	10-01-90	HR	789
1258	344	26	647-648	10-01-90	HR	5939
1259	345	26	648	10-01-90	HR	7989
1260	346	26	648-649	10-01-90	HR	10486
1261	347	26	649-650	10-01-90	HR	10265
1262	348	26	650	10-01-90	HR	10639
1263	349	26	650-652	10-01-90	HR	12187
1264	350	26	652	10-01-90	S	161
1265	351	26	652-653	10-01-90	S	597
1266	352	26	653-655	10-01-90	S	1454
1267	353	26	655	10-01-90	S	1658
1268	354	26	655-657	10-01-90	S	1904
1269	355	26	657	10-01-90	S	2014
1270	356	26	657-658	10-01-90	S	2562
1271	357	26	658-659	10-01-90	S	2782
1272	358	26	659-660	10-01-90	S	3280
1273	359	26	660-661	10-01-90	S	3314
1274	260	26	661	10-01-90	S	3545
1275	261	26	661-662	10-01-90	S	3745
1276	362	26	662-663	10-01-90	S	3817
1277	363	26	663-664	10-01-90	S	3863
1278	364	26	664-665	10-01-90	S	3938

RESOLUTIONS OF THE FIFTY-FIRST CONGRESS

1	1	26	667	12-19-89	H Res.	1
2	2	26	667	12-19-89	H Res.	2
3	3	26.	667	12-19-89	H Res.	3
4	4	26	668	12-21-89	H Res.	16
5	5	26	668	1-06-90	S Res.	32
6	6	26	668	1-10-90	H Res.	19
8	7	26	668	2-06-90	S Res.	48
9	8	28	669	2-06-90	H Res.	79
10	9	26	669	2-19-90	S Res.	54
11	10	26	669-670	2-22-90	S Res.	37
12	11	26	670	3-19-90	S Res.	63
13	12	26	670	4-03-90	H Res.	136
14	13	26	670	4-11-90	S Res.	46
15	14	26	671	4-19-90	H Res.	119

Public Law/Resolution		Statutes at Large	Page	Date	Bill No.
Chapter	Number				
16	15	26	671	4-25-90	H Res. 155
17	16	26	671-672	5-01-90	H Res. 14
18	17	26	672	5-01-90	H Res. 128
20	18	26	672	5-14-90	H Res. 105
21	19	26	673	5-19-90	H Res. 12
22	20	26	673	5-22-90	H Res. 149
23	21	26	673	5-22-90	H Res. 153
25	22	26	673	5-27-90	H Res. 167
26	23	26	674	6-05-90	H Res. 127
27	24	26	674	6-05-90	H Res. 134
28	25	26	674-675	6-19-90	S Res. 28
29	22	26	675	6-21-90	H Res. 37
30	27	26	675-676	6-30-90	H Res. 185
31	28	26	676	7-02-90	H Res. 183
33	29	26	676-677	7-16-90	H Res. 150
34	30	26	677	7-30-90	H Res. 203
35	31	26	677	8-08-90	S Res. 111
36	32	26	677	8-08-90	H Res. 209
38	33	26	677-678	8-14-90	H Res. 211
39	34	26	678	8-14-90	S Res. 75
40	35	26	678	8-28-90	S Res. 71
41	36	26	678	8-28-90	S Res. 116
42	37	26	679	8-30-90	S Res. 115
43	38	26	679	9-01-90	H Res. 213
44	39	26	679	9-01-90	S Res. 120
45	40	26	679-680	9-19-90	H Res. 170
46	41	26	680	9-19-90	H Res. 184
47	42	26	680	9-19-90	H Res. 215
48	43	26	681	9-25-90	S Res. 102
49	44	26	681	9-25-90	S Res. 109
50	45	26	681	9-25-90	S Res. 6
51	46	26	682	9-26-90	S Res. 51
52	47	26	682	9-26-90	H Res. 224
53	48	26	682	9-27-90	S Res. 128
54	49	26	683	9-29-90	H Res. 152
55	50	26	683	9-29-90	H Res. 228
56	51	26	683	9-29-90	H Res. 231
57	52	26	684	9-30-90	S Res. 123

RESOLUTIONS OF THE FIFTY-FIRST CONGRESS

Public Law/Resolution		Statutes at Large	Page	Date	Bill No.
Chapter	Number				
58	53	26	684	9-30-90	S Res. 95
59	54	26	684-685	9-30-90	S Res. 125
60	55	26	685	10-01-90	H Res. 104
61	56	26	685	10-01-90	H Res. 169
62	57	26	686	10-01-90	H Res. 214
63	58	26	686	10-01-90	H Res. 218

PUBLIC ACTS OF THE FIFTY-FIRST CONGRESS

Public Law/Resolution		Statutes at Large	Page	Date	Bill No.	
Chapter	Number					
1	1	26	687	12-11-90	HR	7666
2	2	26	687-688	12-11-90	HR	9707
3	3	26	688-689	12-11-90	HR	9852
4	4	26	689	12-15-90	S	169
5	5	26	689	12-15-90	HR	11527
6	6	26	689	12-15-90	HR	12447
7	7	26	690	12-15-90	S	3841
8	8	26	690	12-15-90	S	4072
22	9	26	690	12-18-90	S	2237
23	10	26	690-691	12-18-90	S	4468
25	11	26	691-692	12-20-90	S	2884
26	12	26	692	12-22-90	S	3122
27	13	26	693	12-24-90	S	1044
28	14	26	694	12-24-90	S	1512
29	15	26	695	12-24-90	S	1977
30	16	26	696	12-24-90	S	3282
31	17	26	696-697	12-24-90	S	3796
32	18	26	697-298	12-24-90	S	4158
33	19	26	698-700	12-26-90	S	3929
34	20	26	700-701	12-26-90	S	4561
38	21	26	701-702	12-27-90	S	2404
39	22	26	702	12-27-90	HR	93
40	23	26	703	12-27-90	HR	4608
42	24	26	703-704	1-02-91	S	875
43	25	26	704-705	1-02-91	S	1548
44	26	26	705-706	1-02-91	S	2349
45	27	26	706	1-02-91	HR	256
46	28	26	706-707	1-02-91	HR	630
47	29	26	707	1-02-91	HR	3279
50	30	26	707-708	1-05-91	HR	196
60	31	26	708-709	1-07-91	S	884
61	32	26	709-710	1-08-91	HR	12498
63	33	26	710-711	1-12-91	S	1230
64	34	26	711-712	1-12-91	S	1590
65	35	26	712-714	1-12-91	S	2783
66	36	26	714-715	1-12-91	S	2816
67	37	26	715-716	1-12-91	S	4493
70	38	26	716	1-13-91	S	4112

343

PUBLIC ACTS OF THE FIFTY-FIRST CONGRESS

Public Law/Resolution		Statutes at Large	Page	Date	Bill No.	
Chapter	Number					
72	39	26	717	1-15-91	S	902
73	40	26	718	1-15-91	S	4547
74	41	26	718	1-16-91	HR	9919
76	42	26	718-719	1-19-91	HR	8243
77	43	26	720-721	1-19-91	S	3271
78	44	26	721	1-19-91	HR	7630
79	45	26	721	1-19-91	HR	9490
80	46	26	722	1-19-91	HR	11237
83	47	26	722-723	1-21-91	S	507
84	48	26	723-724	1-21-91	S	953
85	49	26	724-725	1-21-91	S	2405
86	50	26	725-726	1-21-91	S	3417
87	51	26	726-727	1-21-91	HR	178
91	52	26	727-728	1-24-91	S	77
92	53	26	728	1-24-91	HR	11814
98	54	26	728	1-26-91	HR	7119
99	55	26	729	1-26-91	S	1354
100	56	26	730	1-26-91	S	2082
101	57	26	730-731	1-26-91	S	2427
102	58	26	731	1-26-91	HR	4403
103	59	26	731-732	1-26-91	HR	5380
109	60	26	732-733	1-27-91	S	1384
113	61	26	733	2-06-91	HR	13453
114	62	26	733-734	2-07-91	HR	154
115	63	26	734	2-07-91	HR	608
116	64	26	735-736	2-07-91	HR	12500
117	65	26	736	2-07-91	S	4560
121	66	26	736-737	2-09-91	S	4886
122	67	26	737	2-09-91	HR	7976
123	68	26	737-738	2-09-91	S	4592
124	69	26	738-739	2-09-91	HR	188
125	70	26	739-740	2-09-91	HR	4559
126	71	26	740-741	2-09-91	HR	8341
127	72	26	742-743	2-10-91	HR	10862
128	73	26	743-744	2-10-91	S	3173
129	74	26	745-746	2-10-91	S	4937
130	75	26	746-747	2-10-91	HR	8589
131	76	26	747	2-11-91	HR	6975

PUBLIC ACTS OF THE FIFTY-FIRST CONGRESS

Public Law/Resolution		Statutes at Large	Page	Date	Bill No.	
Chapter	Number					
163	77	26	747-748	2-13-91	HR	8049
164	78	26	748-749	2-13-91	HR	12042
165	79	26	749-759	2-13-91	HR	11915
166	80	26	759	2-13-91	HR	6460
167	81	26	760-762	2-13-91	HR	13071
168	82	26	762	2-13-91	HR	9193
237	83	26	763	2-16-91	S	654
238	84	26	763	2-16-91	S	2105
239	85	26	764	2-16-91	S	3062
240	86	26	764	2-16-91	HR	11391
244	87	26	764-765	2-18-91	S	4814
248	88	26	765	2-21-91	S	4397
249	89	26	765	2-21-91	S	4754
250	90	26	765-766	2-21-91	HR	8588
251	91	26	766	2-21-91	HR	9602
252	92	26	766	2-21-91	HR	12536
282	93	26	767	2-24-91	HR	6586
283	94	26	767-770	2-24-91	HR	12499
284	95	26	770-779	2-24-91	HR	12573
285	96	26	780	2-24-91	S	874
286	97	26	781-783	2-24-91	S	5000
287	98	26	783	2-24-91	S	174
288	99	26	783-787	2-24-91	S	2675
289	100	26	787	2-24-91	S	4746
290	101	26	787	2-24-91	HR	8628
291	102	26	788	2-24-91	HR	13055
342	103	26	788-789	2-27-91	S	2648
382	104	26	789-794	2-28-91	S	3770
383	105	26	794-796	2-28-91	S	3043
384	106	26	796-797	2-28-91	S	1395
385	107	26	797	2-28-91	HR	10787
492	108	26	797-799	3-02-91	S	5037
493	109	26	799	3-02-91	HR	11003
494	110	26	799-815	3-02-91	HR	12782
495	111	26	816-822	3-02-91	HR	12922
496	112	26	822-823	3-02-91	S	172
497	113	26	824	3-02-91	S	5100
498	114	26	824	3-02-91	HR	3902

PUBLIC ACTS OF THE FIFTY-FIRST CONGRESS

Public Law/Resolution		Statutes at Large	Page	Date	Bill No.	
Chapter	Number					
499	115	26	824	3-02-91	HR	9955
500	116	26	824-825	3-02-91	HR	10500
501	117	26	825-826	3-02-91	HR	12839
517	118	26	826-230	3-03-91	HR	9014
518	119	26	830	3-03-91	S	4520
519	120	26	830-832	3-03-91	S	3738
520	121	26	833	3-03-91	S	4119
521	122	26	833	3-03-91	S	4897
522	123	26	833-834	3-03-91	S	4939
523	124	26	835	3-03-91	S	4951
524	125	26	835-836	3-03-91	S	5013
525	126	26	836	3-03-91	S	5044
526	127	26	836-838	3-03-91	S	5072
527	218	26	838-839	3-03-91	S	5110
528	129	26	839	3-03-91	S	5125
529	130	26	839-840	3-03-91	HR	182
530	131	26	840-841	3-03-91	HR	6498
531	132	26	841-842	3-03-91	HR	7342
532	133	26	842	3-03-91	HR	7938
533	134	26	842-844	3-03-91	HR	11736
534	135	26	844	3-03-91	HR	12333
535	136	26	844-848	3-03-91	HR	12993
536	137	26	848-850	3-03-91	HR	13218
537	138	26	850-851	3-03-91	S	4224
538	139	26	851-854	3-03-91	HR	8150
539	140	26	854-862	3-03-91	HR	9798
540	141	26	862-908	3-03-91	HR	13658
541	142	26	908-948	3-03-91	HR	13049
542	143	26	948-989	3-03-91	HR	13462
543	144	26	989-1044	3-03-91	HR	13388
544	145	26	1044-1052	3-03-91	HR	13552
545	146	26	1053-1062	3-03-91	HR	13069
546	147	26	1062-1079	3-03-91	HR	12729
547	148	26	1079-1081	3-03-91	HR	13511
548	149	26	1081-1083	3-03-91	HR	12227
549	150	26	1083	3-03-91	HR	8239
550	151	26	1084	3-03-91	HR	8046
551	152	26	1084-1086	3-03-91	HR	13586

PUBLIC ACTS OF THE FIFTY-FIRST CONGRESS

Public Law/Resolution		Statutes at Large	Page	Date	Bill No.	
Chapter	Number					
552	153	26	1087	3-03-91	S	2692
553	154	26	1087-1089	3-03-91	S	5089
554	155	26	1089	3-03-91	S	5105
555	156	26	1089-1091	3-03-91	S	4155
556	157	26	1091-1092	3-03-91	S	4733
557	158	26	1092-1093	3-03-91	S	3238
558	159	26	1093	3-03-91	S	4557
559	160	26	1093-1094	3-03-91	S	5129
560	161	26	1094-1095	3-03-91	S	1453
561	162	26	1095-1103	3-03-91	HR	7254
562	163	26	1103	3-03-91	HR	949
563	164	26	1103-1104	3-03-91	HR	13266
564	165	26	1104-1106	3-03-91	HR	3839
565	166	26	1106-1110	3-03-91	HR	10881
566	167	26	1110	3-03-91	HR	187

RESOLUTIONS OF THE FIFTY-FIRST CONGRESS

1	1	26	1111	12-05-90	S Res.	53
2	2	26	1111	12-09-90	S Res.	122
3	3	26	1111-1112	12-09-90	S Res.	132
4	4	26	1112	12-18-90	S Res.	90
5	5	26	1112	12-20-90	S Res.	253
6	6	26	1112-1113	12-24-90	S Res.	82
7	7	26	1113	12-24-90	S Res.	131
8	8	26	1113	1-28-91	H Res.	210
9	9	26	1113	2-05-91	H Res.	240
10	10	26	1114	2-07-91	H Res.	234
11	11	26	1114	2-18-91	H Res.	251
12	12	26	1114	3-02-91	S Res.	158
13	13	26	1114-1115	3-02-91	S Res.	166
14	14	26	1115	3-02-91	H Res.	156
15	15	26	1115	3-02-91	H Res.	158
17	16	26	1115-1116	3-03-91	S Res.	169
18	17	26	1116	3-03-91	S Res.	168
19	18	26	1116	3-03-91	H Res.	154
20	19	26	1117	3-03-91	H Res.	287
21	20	26	1117	3-03-91	H Res.	138
22	21	26	1117	3-03-91	H Res.	98

RESOLUTIONS OF THE FIFTY-FIRST CONGRESS

Public Law/Resolution		Statutes at Large	Page	Date	Bill No.
Chapter	Number				
23	22	26	1118	3-03-91	H Res. 278

PUBLIC ACTS OF THE FIFTY-SECOND CONGRESS

Public Law/Resolution		Statutes at Large	Page	Date	Bill No.	
Chapter	Number					
1	1	27	1	1-22-92	HR	123
2	2	27	1-2	1-28-92	HR	517
3	3	27	2	2-03-92	HR	28
5	4	27	2-3	2-09-92	HR	2785
6	5	27	3	2-09-92	HR	3931
7	6	27	3	2-11-92	S	1604
8	7	27	3-4	2-15-92	HR	217
9	8	27	4	2-18-92	HR	4107
10	9	27	4-5	2-26-92	S	1183
11	10	27	5	3-08-92	HR	532
12	11	27	5-6	3-08-92	HR	5399
14	12	27	7	3-09-92	HR	435
15	13	27	7	3-10-92	S	821
16	14	27	7	3-18-92	HR	3980
17	15	27	7-8	3-18-92	HR	6836
18	16	27	8-10	3-18-92	HR	6876
19	17	27	10	3-21-92	S	1058
20	18	27	11	3-21-92	HR	5755
21	19	27	11	3-24-92	HR	2568
22	20	27	11	3-25-92	HR	3933
23	21	27	12	3-26-92	HR	128
25	22	27	12	3-29-92	HR	6071
28	23	27	12	3-31-92	HR	497
29	24	27	12	3-31-92	HR	2384
30	25	27	13	3-31-92	HR	5118
31	26	27	13	4-01-92	HR	5891
32	27	27	13	4-01-92	S	494
34	28	27	14	4-05-92	S	1884
35	29	27	14	4-06-92	S	2315
36	30	27	14	4-06-92	S	2643
37	31	27	14	4-07-92	S	808
38	32	27	15	4-07-92	HR	4631
39	33	27	15	4-07-92	HR	5176
40	34	27	15	4-11-92	HR	3867
41	35	27	16	4-11-92	S	2056
43	36	27	16	4-13-92	HR	610
44	37	27	16	4-13-92	HR	4534
45	38	27	16-18	4-15-92	S	440

PUBLIC ACTS OF THE FIFTY-SECOND CONGRESS

Public Law/Resolution		Statutes at Large	Page	Date	Bill No.	
Chapter	Number					
46	39	27	18–19	4–15–92	S	1643
47	40	27	19	4–15–92	S	1645
49	41	27	19–20	4–18–92	S	2388
50	42	27	20	4–19–92	S	418
52	43	27	20–21	4–23–92	S	113
53	44	27	21	4–23–92	S	1492
54	45	27	22	4–28–92	HR	5978
55	46	27	22	4–28–92	HR	4429
56	47	27	22–23	4–30–92	HR	2786
57	48	27	23–24	4–30–92	HR	6286
59	49	27	24–25	5–03–92	HR	7020
60	50	27	25–26	5–05–92	HR	6185
61	51	27	26–27	5–09–92	S	3022
62	52	27	27	5–09–92	S	2305
63	53	27	27–28	5–10–92	HR	7023
64	54	27	28	5–11–92	HR	8503
65	55	27	28–29	5–11–92	HR	6295
66	56	27	29	5–11–92	HR	6788
67	57	27	29–30	5–11–92	HR	5444
68	58	27	30–31	5–12–92	HR	250
69	59	27	31–32	5–12–92	HR	5354
70	60	27	33	5–12–92	HR	5108
71	61	27	33	5–12–92	HR	8001
72	62	27	33–37	5–13–92	HR	7818
73	63	27	37	5–13–92	HR	7727
74	64	27	37–38	5–13–92	HR	4845
76	65	27	38–39	5–23–92	HR	7360
77	66	27	39	5–23–92	HR	507
78	67	27	39–40	5–25–92	HR	6658
79	68	27	40	5–25–92	HR	4533
83	69	27	40	5–31–92	S	1975
85	70	27	40–41	6–03–92	S	1646
86	71	27	41	6–03–92	S	2613
87	72	27	41	6–03–92	S	2460
88	73	27	41–42	6–04–92	HR	4004
89	74	27	42–43	6–06–92	S	661
90	75	27	43–45	6–06–92	S	1935
91	76	27	45	6–06–92	S	2107

Public Law/Resolution		Statutes at Large	Page	Date	Bill No.	
Chapter	Number					
92	77	27	46	6-06-92	S	2437
93	78	27	46-47	6-06-92	HR	7092
108	79	27	47-49	6-08-92	HR	7365
116	80	27	50	6-10-92	S	1950
117	81	27	50	6-14-92	HR	9118
118	82	27	50-51	6-15-92	HR	8420
119	83	27	51-52	6-15-92	HR	8295
120	84	27	52-53	6-17-92	HR	38
123	85	27	53-54	6-21-92	S	2021
124	86	27	54-56	6-22-92	S	442
125	87	27	56-57	6-22-92	S	1644
126	88	27	57-58	6-22-92	S	2254
127	89	27	58	6-22-92	S	2597
130	90	27	59	6-24-92	S	3036
132	91	27	59	6-25-92	S	153
133	92	27	59	6-25-92	S	1380
134	93	27	60	6-25-92	S	81
135	94	27	60-61	6-25-92	S	1714
137	95	27	61	6-30-92	S	1952
138	96	27	61	6-30-92	HR	8861
139	97	27	61-62	7-01-92	S	2049
140	98	27	62-64	7-01-92	HR	7557
143	99	27	65-66	7-05-92	HR	410
144	100	27	66-72	7-05-92	HR	429
145	101	27	72-73	7-05-92	HR	626
146	102	27	74	7-05-92	HR	8888
147	103	27	74-82	7-05-92	HR	9089
148	104	27	82	7-06-92	HR	1080
149	105	27	83	7-06-92	HR	4620
150	106	27	83-85	7-06-92	HR	5133
151	107	27	86	7-06-92	HR	6591
152	108	27	86	7-06-92	HR	7081
153	109	27	86-87	7-06-92	HR	7696
154	110	27	87	7-06-92	S	1768
156	111	27	87	7-13-92	HR	5499
157	112	27	87	7-13-92	HR	6663
158	113	27	88-116	7-13-92	HR	7820
159	114	27	116-117	7-13-92	HR	8294

Public Law/Resolution		Statutes at Large	Page	Date	Bill No.	
Chapter	Number					
160	115	27	118-119	7-13-92	HR	8580
161	116	27	119-120	7-13-92	HR	6875
162	117	27	120	7-13-92	S	552
163	118	27	120	7-13-92	HR	5431
164	119	27	120-145	7-13-92	HR	5974
165	120	27	145-148	7-13-92	HR	8224
168	121	27	148-149	7-14-92	S	1393
169	122	27	149	7-14-92	S	1910
170	123	27	149-150	7-14-92	HR	5726
171	124	27	150-168	7-14-92	HR	6746
172	125	27	168-174	7-14-92	HR	4636
173	126	27	174	7-14-92	HR	7688
195	127	27	174-183	7-16-92	HR	6923
196	128	27	183-223	7-16-92	HR	9040
197	129	27	223-234	7-16-92	HR	7624
198	130	27	234	7-16-92	S	3299
199	131	27	234	7-16-92	S	3273
201	132	27	235	7-18-92	S	1741
205	133	27	235-236	7-19-92	HR	6792
206	134	27	236-251	7-19-92	HR	7093
208	135	27	252	7-20-92	S	3201
209	136	27	252	7-20-92	HR	8153
214	137	27	253	7-21-92	S	2022
215	138	27	254	7-21-92	S	3447
216	139	27	254	7-21-92	HR	9283
227	140	27	254	7-22-92	S	3454
228	141	27	254-255	7-22-92	HR	5119
229	142	27	255	7-22-92	HR	3947
230	143	27	255-257	7-22-92	HR	3971
231	144	27	257	7-22-92	S	1775
233	145	27	257-260	7-23-92	HR	8533
234	146	27	260-261	7-23-92	S	1988
235	147	27	261	7-23-92	S	2968
236	148	27	261-262	7-23-92	S	3011
237	149	27	262-263	7-23-92	S	3406
238	150	27	263	7-23-92	S	2519
239	151	27	264	7-23-92	HR	7454
240	152	27	264-265	7-23-92	HR	402

Public Law/Resolution		Statutes at Large	Page	Date	Bill No.	
Chapter	Number					
241	153	27	265-267	7-23-92	HR	9144
248	154	27	267-268	7-26-92	HR	9324
249	155	27	268	7-26-92	HR	6073
250	156	27	268-270	7-26-92	HR	5446
251	157	27	270	7-26-92	HR	5997
252	158	27	270-271	7-26-92	HR	8579
253	159	27	271	7-26-92	HR	6091
254	160	27	271-272	7-26-92	HR	7322
255	161	27	272	7-26-92	HR	2713
256	162	27	272-273	7-26-92	S	1793
257	163	27	273	7-26-92	HR	6891
264	164	27	273	7-27-92	HR	8124
265	165	27	274-275	7-27-92	HR	7720
266	166	27	275	7-27-92	S	1498
267	167	27	275	7-27-92	S	621
268	168	27	276	7-27-92	S	898
269	169	27	276	7-27-92	S	1230
270	170	27	276-277	7-27-92	S	1039
271	171	27	277	7-27-92	S	1295
272	172	27	277-278	7-27-92	S	2470
273	173	27	278	7-27-92	S	3154
274	174	27	279-280	7-27-92	HR	5941
275	175	27	280-281	7-27-92	HR	9581
276	176	27	281	7-27-92	S	620
277	177	27	281-282	7-27-92	HR	7296
311	178	27	282-319	7-28-92	HR	9284
312	179	27	319-320	7-28-92	S	3211
313	180	27	320	7-28-92	HR	4827
314	181	27	320-321	7-28-92	HR	9023
315	182	27	321	7-28-92	HR	9022
316	183	27	321-322	7-28-92	S	1040
317	184	27	322	7-28-92	HR	6183
320	185	27	322-325	7-29-92	S	267
321	186	27	325-326	7-29-92	HR	6793
322	187	27	326-334	7-29-92	HR	9172
323	188	27	334	7-29-92	HR	8122
327	189	27	334-336	7-30-92	HR	7974
328	190	27	336	7-30-92	S	1722

PUBLIC ACTS OF THE FIFTY-SECOND CONGRESS

Public Law/Resolution		Statutes at Large	Page	Date	Bill No.	
Chapter	Number					
329	191	27	336-339	7-30-92	HR	5684
351	192	27	340	8-01-92	S	2137
352	193	27	340	8-01-92	HR	8537
353	194	27	341-345	8-01-92	HR	4667
360	195	27	345-346	8-03-92	HR	7213
361	196	27	347	8-03-92	HR	6262
362	197	27	347	8-03-92	HR	222
374	198	27	347	8-04-92	S	3394
375	199	27	348	8-04-92	S	1273
376	200	27	348	8-04-92	HR	9482
379	201	27	348-349	8-05-92	HR	7294
380	202	27	349-388	8-05-92	HR	7520
381	203	27	389-390	8-05-92	HR	9710
382	204	27	390-392	8-05-92	S	3134
383	205	27	392	8-05-92	S	3126

RESOLUTIONS OF THE FIFTY-SECOND CONGRESS

1	1	27	393	12-23-91	H Res.	1
2	2	27	393	1-26-92	S Res.	18
3	3	27	393	2-25-92	H Res.	81
4	4	27	394	2-26-92	S Res.	45
5	5	27	394	3-24-92	S Res.	44
6	6	27	394	4-06-92	S Res.	49
7	7	27	394-395	4-06-92	H Res.	115
8	8	27	395	4-12-92	H Res.	92
9	9	27	396	4-14-92	H Res.	69
11	10	27	396	5-10-92	H Res.	97
12	11	27	396	5-12-92	H Res.	118
13	12	27	396	5-27-92	H Res.	132
15	13	27	396-397	6-14-92	H Res.	121
16	14	27	397	6-22-92	S Res.	84
17	15	27	397	6-24-92	S Res.	47
18	16	27	397	6-29-92	S Res.	83
19	17	27	397-398	6-30-92	H Res.	145
20	18	27	398	7-15-92	H Res.	151
21	19	27	398	7-18-92	S Res.	76
22	20	27	399	7-20-92	S Res.	46
23	21	27	399	7-22-92	H Res.	108

RESOLUTIONS OF THE FIFTY-SECOND CONGRESS

Public Law/Resolution		Statutes at Large	Page	Date	Bill No.
Chapter	Number				
24	22	27	399	7-23-92	H Res. 155
25	23	27	399-400	7-23-92	H Res. 102
26	24	27	400	7-26-92	H Res. 105
27	25	27	400	7-26-92	S Res. 104
29	26	27	401	7-28-92	H Res. 142
30	27	27	401	8-01-92	H Res. 159
31	28	27	401	8-04-92	H Res. 160
32	29	27	401	8-05-92	S Res. 42
33	30	27	402	8-05-92	S Res. 106
34	31	27	402	8-05-92	S Res. 100
35	32	27	403	8-05-92	H Res. 161

PUBLIC ACTS OF THE FIFTY-SECOND CONGRESS

Public Law/Resolution		Statutes at Large	Page	Date	Bill No.	
Chapter	Number					
1	1	27	405	12-16-92	S	139
6	2	27	405-406	12-22-92	S	3418
7	3	27	406-407	12-22-92	S	2451
8	4	27	407	12-22-92	S	1956
9	5	27	407-408	12-22-92	HR	8760
10	6	27	408	12-22-92	S	869
11	7	27	408	12-22-92	S	3188
12	8	27	408-409	12-22-92	S	2093
14	9	27	409-410	12-28-92	S	539
15	10	27	410-412	12-28-92	S	606
16	11	27	412-413	12-28-92	S	1647
17	12	27	413	1-05-93	S	570
18	13	27	413	1-05-93	S	1675
20	14	27	414	1-06-93	HR	9417
21	15	27	414-415	1-06-93	S	3298
22	16	27	415	1-06-93	S	2981
23	17	27	415	1-07-93	HR	6644
24	18	27	415	1-09-93	HR	9487
25	19	27	416	1-09-93	HR	9488
28	20	27	416-417	1-10-93	S	3029
29	21	27	417	1-10-93	S	1831
32	22	27	417-419	1-12-93	S	3048
38	23	27	420	1-14-93	S	3623
39	24	27	420	1-20-93	S	3195
41	25	27	421	1-23-93	S	3580
42	26	27	421	1-23-93	S	1292
43	27	27	421-422	1-23-93	HR	4844
44	28	27	422	1-23-93	HR	9824
46	29	27	422	1-25-93	S	3537
47	30	27	422-424	1-26-93	HR	10015
48	31	27	424-426	1-26-93	S	2345
50	32	27	426	1-27-93	S	1631
51	33	27	426	1-28-93	S	3117
52	34	27	426-427	1-28-93	S	3407
53	35	27	427	1-28-93	S	3727
54	36	27	427	1-31-93	S	3581
56	37	27	427-428	2-02-93	HR	5597
57	38	27	428-429	2-03-93	HR	10062

Public Law/Resolution		Statutes at Large	Page	Date	Bill No.	
Chapter	Number					
58	39	27	429	2-03-93	HR	10189
61	40	27	430	2-04-93	HR	10007
62	41	27	430	2-04-93	S	985
63	42	27	430	2-06-93	HR	8956
64	43	27	431	2-06-93	S	3753
65	44	27	431	2-07-93	HR	5752
66	45	27	431-434	2-07-93	HR	8602
67	46	27	434	2-07-93	HR	10063
69	47	27	434	2-08-93	HR	9531
74	48	27	434-436	2-09-93	HR	10010
75	49	27	437-439	2-09-93	HR	6748
76	50	27	439-440	2-09-93	HR	9930
77	51	27	440	2-09-93	HR	6649
81	52	27	441	2-11-93	S	3798
82	53	27	441-443	2-11-93	HR	6797
83	54	27	443-444	2-11-93	S	1933
103	55	27	444	2-13-93	HR	8268
104	56	27	444-445	2-13-93	HR	9758
105	57	27	445-446	2-13-93	HR	9176
106	58	27	446-447	2-14-93	S	3826
107	59	27	447-448	2-14-93	S	3787
108	60	27	448-449	2-14-93	S	3825
114	61	27	449-452	2-15-93	HR	9757
115	62	27	453-455	2-15-93	HR	9955
116	63	27	455	2-15-93	S	3859
117	64	27	455	2-15-93	S	3510
118	65	27	456	2-15-93	S	3843
119	66	27	456	2-15-93	HR	7625
120	67	27	456-457	2-15-93	S	3788
121	68	27	457-458	2-15-93	HR	9786
136	69	27	458-461	2-18-93	HR	9923
137	70	27	461-462	2-18-93	S	741
138	71	27	462	2-18-93	HR	8123
139	72	27	462	2-18-93	S	2852
140	73	27	462-463	2-18-93	S	3836
143	74	27	464	2-20-93	S	2946
144	75	27	465-467	2-20-93	HR	3627
145	76	27	468	2-20-93	HR	7762

Public Law/Resolution		Statutes at Large	Page	Date	Bill No.	
Chapter	Number					
146	77	27	468-469	2-20-93	HR	9592
147	78	27	469-470	2-20-93	HR	9527
148	79	27	470	2-20-93	HR	10206
149	80	27	470-471	2-21-93	HR	8340
150	81	27	472	2-21-93	S	3629
151	82	27	472	2-21-93	HR	10391
153	83	27	472-473	2-23-93	HR	9826
154	84	27	473	2-23-93	HR	8582
156	85	27	474	2-24-93	HR	10241
157	86	27	474	2-24-93	HR	10236
158	87	27	475	2-24-93	HR	10039
159	88	27	475-476	2-24-93	S	3857
160	89	27	476	2-24-93	HR	10304
164	90	27	477	2-25-93	HR	10489
165	91	27	477	2-25-93	HR	1036
167	92	27	477-478	2-27-93	HR	9069
168	93	27	478-487	2-27-93	HR	9825
169	94	27	487-490	2-27-93	S	3873
170	95	27	490-491	2-27-93	HR	9730
171	96	27	492-494	2-27-93	S	3602
174	97	27	494-495	2-28-93	S	3725
175	98	27	495-496	2-28-93	S	3702
176	99	27	496	2-28-93	S	3811
182	100	27	496-506	3-01-93	HR	10267
183	101	27	507-511	3-01-93	HR	9286
184	102	27	511-513	3-01-93	S	3876
185	103	27	513-515	3-01-93	S	3871
186	104	27	515-523	3-01-93	HR	10290
187	105	27	523-524	3-01-93	HR	10345
188	106	27	524-527	3-01-93	HR	3626
189	107	27	527	3-01-93	HR	4275
190	108	27	528	3-01-93	S	3886
191	109	27	529	3-01-93	HR	10484
192	110	27	529-530	3-01-93	S	3317
193	111	27	530	3-01-93	S	2722
195	112	27	530-531	3-02-93	HR	8677
196	113	27	531-532	3-02-93	HR	9350
197	114	27	532-537	3-02-93	S	1307

PUBLIC ACTS OF THE FIFTY-SECOND CONGRESS

Public Law/Resolution		Statutes at Large	Page	Date	Bill No.	
Chapter	Number					
199	115	27	537-554	3-03-93	HR	10038
200	116	27	555	3-03-93	S	2931
201	117	27	555-557	3-03-93	HR	10280
202	118	27	557	3-03-93	S	2966
203	119	27	557-563	3-03-93	HR	7633
204	120	27	563-568	3-03-93	HR	10266
205	121	27	568-569	3-03-93	S	782
206	122	27	569-571	3-03-93	S	3240
207	123	27	571-572	3-03-93	S	203
208	124	27	572-612	3-03-93	HR	10238
209	125	27	612-646	3-03-93	HR	10415
210	122	27	646-674	3-03-93	HR	10258
211	127	27	675-715	3-03-93	HR	10331
212	128	27	715-732	3-03-93	HR	10488
213	129	27	732-734	3-03-93	HR	10349
214	130	27	734-743	3-03-93	HR	10421
215	131	27	743	3-03-93	S	3881
216	132	27	743	3-03-93	HR	10351
217	133	27	744	3-03-93	S	2566
218	134	27	744	3-03-93	S	3890
219	135	27	744-745	3-03-93	HR	3594
220	136	27	745-746	3-03-93	HR	9612
221	137	27	746	3-03-93	HR	10375
222	138	27	747	3-03-93	S	204
223	139	27	747	3-03-93	S	3711
224	140	27	747-751	3-03-93	S	3473
225	141	27	751	3-03-93	HR	5816
226	142	27	751	3-03-93	S	2171

RESOLUTIONS OF THE FIFTY-SECOND CONGRESS

1	1	27	752	12-13-92	H Res.	167
2	2	27	752	12-20-92	H Res.	170
4	3	27	752	1-07-93	S Res.	112
5	4	27	752	1-09-93	S Res.	123
6	5	27	753	1-16-93	S Res.	113
7	6	27	753	1-18-93	H Res.	166
8	7	27	753	1-25-93	S Res.	135
9	8	27	754	1-26-93	S Res.	128

RESOLUTIONS OF THE FIFTY-SECOND CONGRESS

Public Law/Resolution		Statutes at Large	Page	Date	Bill No.
Chapter	Number				
10	9	27	754	2-03-93	S Res. 124
11	10	27	754	2-09-93	S Res. 144
12	11	27	754-755	2-12-93	S Res. 134
13	12	27	755	2-14-93	S Res. 140
14	13	27	755	2-15-93	H Res. 204
15	14	27	755-756	2-18-93	S Res. 130
16	15	27	756	2-25-93	S Res. 102
17	16	27	756	2-25-93	S Res. 121
19	17	27	757	3-03-93	S Res. 148
20	18	27	757	3-03-93	S Res. 159
21	19	27	757	3-03-93	H Res. 196

PUBLIC ACTS OF THE FIFTY-THIRD CONGRESS

Public Law/Resolution		Statutes at Large	Page	Date	Bill No.	
Chapter	Number					
1	1	28	1	9-01-93	S	50
2	2	28	2	9-07-93	HR	4
3	3	28	2	10-02-93	S	721
4	4	28	3	10-03-93	HR	3607
5	5	28	3	10-20-93	S	824
6	6	28	4	10-31-93	HR	3421
7	7	28	4	11-01-93	HR	1986
8	8	28	4	11-01-93	HR	1
9	9	28	5	11-03-93	HR	2002
10	10	28	5-6	11-03-93	HR	2799
11	11	28	6	11-03-93	HR	3297
12	12	28	6	11-03-93	HR	3545
13	13	28	7	11-03-93	HR	3571
14	14	28	7-8	11-03-93	HR	3684
15	15	28	8-9	11-03-93	HR	4015
16	16	28	9	11-03-93	HR	4186

RESOLUTIONS OF THE FIFTY-THIRD CONGRESS

1	1	28	10	8-17-93	H Res.	1
2	2	28	10	8-17-93	H Res.	2
3	3	28	11	8-21-93	H Res.	3
4	4	28	11	9-01-93	H Res.	4
5	5	28	11	9-09-93	H Res.	6
6	6	28	11	9-09-93	H Res.	7
7	7	28	12	9-13-93	S Res.	17
8	8	28	12	10-02-93	H Res.	57
9	9	28	12	10-14-93	H Res.	14
10	10	28	13	10-17-93	H Res.	65
12	11	28	13	10-28-93	H Res.	66
13	12	28	13	10-31-93	H Res.	55
14	13	28	13	11-03-93	H Res.	22
15	14	28	14	11-03-93	H Res.	83
16	15	28	14	11-03-93	S Res.	36

Public Law/Resolution		Statutes at Large	Page	Date	Bill No.	
Chapter	Number					
1	1	28	15	12-12-93	HR	3544
2	2	28	15-16	12-21-93	HR	4177
3	3	28	16-20	12-21-93	HR	4763
4	4	28	20	12-21-93	HR	146
5	5	28	20-21	12-21-93	HR	288
6	6	28	21	12-21-93	HR	2668
7	7	28	21	12-21-93	HR	3629
8	8	28	21-22	12-21-93	HR	4243
9	9	28	22-26	12-21-93	S	1021
10	10	28	26	1-11-94	HR	2796
12	11	28	26-27	1-22-94	S	1378
13	12	28	27	1-22-94	HR	156
14	13	28	27	1-22-94	HR	299
15	14	28	27-28	1-22-94	HR	340
16	15	28	28	1-22-94	HR	1920
17	16	28	28-29	1-22-94	HR	4340
18	17	28	29	1-22-94	HR	4414
19	18	28	29-30	1-27-94	S	339
20	19	28	30	1-27-94	HR	3627
21	20	28	30-33	1-27-94	HR	4610
22	21	28	33-34	1-27-94	HR	4292
23	22	28	34	2-01-94	HR	356
24	23	28	35-36	2-02-94	HR	3689
25	24	28	36-37	2-08-94	HR	2331
26	25	28	37	2-08-94	S	758
27	26	28	37	2-10-94	S	824
29	27	28	38	2-21-94	HR	4449
30	28	28	38	2-24-94	S	1126
31	29	28	38	3-06-94	HR	5414
32	30	28	39	3-09-94	HR	5833
33	31	28	39-40	3-09-94	HR	4770
34	32	28	40	3-10-94	S	1306
35	33	28	40-41	3-12-94	S	1217
36	34	28	41	3-12-94	S	1460
37	35	28	41-43	3-12-94	HR	5646
38	36	28	43	3-14-94	HR	9
39	37	28	43-44	3-14-94	S	432
40	38	28	44	3-14-94	HR	4571

PUBLIC ACTS OF THE FIFTY-THIRD CONGRESS

Public Law/Resolution		Statutes at Large	Page	Date	Bill No.	
Chapter	Number					
41	39	28	44	3-14-94	HR	5485
45	40	28	44-45	3-24-94	HR	4831
46	41	28	45	3-29-94	S	260
47	42	28	45-46	3-29-94	HR	5425
48	43	28	47	3-29-94	HR	5529
49	44	28	47	3-29-94	HR	5530
51	45	28	47-48	4-02-94	S	1749
52	46	28	48-50	4-02-94	HR	1918
56	47	28	50-51	4-05-94	HR	1919
57	48	28	52-55	4-06-94	S	1836
58	49	28	55-57	4-21-94	HR	1917
59	50	28	57	4-21-94	HR	5041
60	51	28	57-58	4-21-94	HR	5356
61	52	28	58-62	4-21-94	HR	6556
62	53	28	62-64	4-21-94	HR	1916
63	54	28	64	4-24-94	S	1928
64	55	28	64-67	4-24-94	HR	5978
66	56	28	67-68	4-30-94	HR	3713
67	57	28	68-71	5-01-94	HR	4765
68	58	28	71	5-04-94	HR	5065
69	59	28	72	5-07-94	S	1403
70	60	28	72-73	5-07-94	HR	6055
71	61	28	73	5-07-94	HR	6073
72	62	28	73-75	5-07-94	HR	6442
73	63	28	75-76	5-11-94	HR	3740
75	64	28	76	5-12-94	HR	4419
76	65	28	76-77	5-12-94	HR	6110
77	66	28	78	5-25-94	S	443
79	67	28	78	5-28-94	S	1808
80	68	28	78-80	5-28-94	HR	5771
81	69	28	80-82	5-28-94	HR	6610
82	70	28	82	5-28-94	HR	6770
83	71	28	82-83	5-28-94	HR	6970
84	72	28	83-84	5-28-94	HR	6838
85	73	28	84	5-29-94	HR	7072
86	74	28	84	5-30-94	S	1467
87	75	28	84-85	5-30-94	HR	73
91	76	28	85	6-05-94	S	2020

Public Law/Resolution		Statutes at Large	Page	Date	Bill No.	
Chapter	Number					
92	77	28	85–86	6-05-94	S	1886
93	78	28	86	6-06-94	S	123
94	79	28	86	6-06-94	S	1226
95	80	28	87	6-06-94	S	755
99	81	28	88	6-07-94	HR	5779
100	82	28	88–89	6-07-94	HR	6123
101	83	28	89–90	6-07-94	HR	6448
102	84	28	90–91	6-08-94	S	1424
103	85	28	91	6-08-94	HR	82
104	86	28	91	6-14-94	S	591
105	87	28	92–93	6-14-94	S	1950
106	88	28	93	6-14-94	HR	3715
107	89	28	93	6-19-94	HR	6126
108	90	28	93–94	6-19-94	HR	7458
109	91	28	94	6-19-94	HR	6576
110	92	28	94–95	6-20-94	HR	5778
113	93	28	95	6-21-94	S	513
117	94	28	95–96	6-27-94	S	1995
118	95	28	96	6-28-94	S	730
119	96	28	96–97	6-29-94	HR	4701
120	97	28	97–98	6-29-94	HR	5806
121	98	28	98–99	7-02-94	HR	4961
122	99	28	99	7-03-94	S	1954
123	100	28	99	7-03-94	S	2135
125	101	28	99–100	7-06-94	S	2000
126	102	28	100–101	7-06-94	S	171
127	103	28	101	7-06-94	HR	7449
129	104	28	101	7-11-94	S	1759
131	105	28	101–102	7-12-94	HR	6500
132	106	28	102	7-12-94	HR	7293
133	107	28	103	7-13-94	S	1045
134	108	28	103	7-13-94	S	2070
135	109	28	103	7-16-94	S	1573
136	110	28	103–104	7-16-94	HR	5601
137	111	28	104–107	7-16-94	HR	6016
138	112	28	107–112	7-16-94	HR	352
140	113	28	112–113	7-18-94	S	1694
141	114	28	113–114	7-18-94	HR	5482

PUBLIC ACTS OF THE FIFTY-THIRD CONGRESS

Public Law/Resolution		Statutes at Large	Page	Date	Bill No.	
Chapter	Number					
142	115	28	114	7-18-94	HR	6558
143	116	28	114	7-18-94	HR	7506
144	117	28	114-115	7-18-94	HR	6447
147	118	28	115	7-23-94	S	1390
148	119	28	116	7-23-94	S	2208
149	120	28	117	7-23-94	HR	51
150	121	28	117	7-23-94	HR	4734
151	122	28	117-118	7-23-94	HR	3135
152	123	28	118-119	7-23-94	HR	2015
153	124	28	119-120	7-23-94	HR	7498
162	125	28	120-121	7-26-94	S	1930
163	126	28	122-123	7-26-94	HR	69
164	127	28	123	7-26-94	HR	3458
165	128	28	123-141	7-26-94	HR	6748
166	129	28	141-151	7-26-94	HR	6108
167	130	28	151-159	7-26-94	HR	5894
168	131	28	159	7-26-94	HR	236
170	132	28	159-160	7-30-94	HR	4322
171	133	28	160	7-30-94	S	1076
172	134	28	160-162	7-30-94	HR	5860
174	135	28	162-211	7-31-94	HR	7097
175	136	28	211	7-31-94	HR	2586
176	137	28	212	8-01-94	HR	38
177	138	28	212	8-01-94	HR	3202
178	139	28	212-215	8-01-94	HR	4858
179	140	28	215-216	8-01-94	S	1209
180	141	28	216	8-01-94	S	1426
181	142	28	217	8-01-94	HR	7197
189	143	28	217-218	8-02-94	HR	6171
190	144	28	219	8-03-94	S	2150
191	145	28	219	8-03-94	S	207
192	145	28	219-220	8-03-94	S	1399
193	147	28	220-221	8-03-94	S	2245
194	148	28	221	8-03-94	HR	108
195	149	28	221	8-03-94	HR	7734
196	150	28	222	8-03-94	HR	83
197	151	28	222	8-03-94	HR	4452
198	152	28	222-223	8-03-94	HR	5293

Public Law/Resolution		Statutes at Large	Page	Date	Bill No.	
Chapter	Number					
199	153	28	223	8-03-94	HR	6111
200	154	28	224	8-03-94	HR	6754
201	155	28	224-225	8-03-94	HR	7753
202	156	28	225	8-03-94	HR	2795
206	157	28	225-226	8-04-94	S	320
207	158	28	226	8-04-94	HR	366
208	159	28	226-227	8-04-94	HR	4448
209	160	28	227	8-04-94	HR	4567
210	161	28	227	8-04-94	HR	5312
211	162	28	227-228	8-04-94	HR	6719
212	163	28	228	8-04-94	HR	7518
213	164	28	229	8-04-94	HR	4346
214	165	28	229	8-04-94	HR	4903
215	166	28	229-232	8-04-94	HR	7335
226	167	28	232-233	8-06-94	HR	213
227	168	28	233	8-06-94	HR	4600
228	169	28	233-243	8-06-94	HR	6373
231	170	28	243	8-07-94	HR	4611
232	171	28	243-262	8-07-94	HR	5481
233	172	28	262	8-07-94	HR	5371
234	173	28	263	8-07-94	HR	7488
235	174	28	263	8-07-94	HR	7494
236	175	28	263	8-08-94	HR	3606
237	176	28	264	8-08-94	HR	6080
238	177	28	264-274	8-08-94	HR	6937
243	178	28	274	8-09-94	HR	6042
244	179	28	274-275	8-09-94	HR	6542
245	180	28	275	8-09-94	HR	6720
246	181	28	275	8-09-94	HR	7419
253	182	28	275-276	8-11-94	HR	6893
254	183	28	276	8-11-94	S	2217
255	184	28	276-277	8-11-94	HR	6814
256	185	28	277	8-11-94	HR	7187
278	186	28	277	8-13-94	S	1852
279	187	28	277-278	8-13-94	S	1896
280	188	28	278	8-13-94	HR	86
281	189	28	278	8-13-94	HR	4326
282	190	28	279-280	8-13-94	HR	4954

Public Law/Resolution		Statutes at Large	Page	Date	Bill No.	
Chapter	Number					
283	191	28	280-281	9-13-94	HR	6577
284	192	28	281	8-13-94	HR	7383
285	193	28	282	8-13-94	HR	7827
287	194	28	282-285	8-14-94	HR	6415
288	195	28	285	8-15-94	S	2234
289	196	28	286	8-15-94	HR	2669
290	197	28	286-338	8-15-94	HR	6913
299	198	28	338-372	8-18-94	HR	6518
300	199	28	372	8-18-94	S	2280
301	200	28	372-423	8-18-94	HR	5575
302	201	28	423	8-20-94	HR	7803
307	202	28	424-488	8-23-94	HR	7477
308	203	28	488	8-23-94	S	1007
309	204	28	488	8-23-94	S	1772
310	205	28	488	8-23-94	S	1885
311	206	28	489	8-23-94	S	2107
312	207	28	489-490	8-23-94	S	2303
313	208	28	491	8-23-94	HR	387
314	209	28	491	8-23-94	HR	4667
315	210	28	491-492	8-23-94	HR	6038
316	211	28	492	8-23-94	HR	6060
317	212	28	492-494	8-23-94	HR	6777
318	213	28	494-499	8-23-94	HR	7006
319	214	28	499	8-23-94	HR	7294
320	215	28	499-501	8-23-94	HR	7667
328	216	28	501	8-24-94	S	971
329	217	28	501	8-24-94	S	1005
330	218	28	502-504	8-24-94	HR	7680
341	219	28	504	8-27-94	HR	7461
342	220	28	504-505	8-27-94	S	1458
343	221	28	505	8-27-94	S	2290
344	222	28	506	8-27-94	S	2293
345	223	28	506-507	8-27-94	HR	6529
346	224	28	507-508	8-27-94	S	870
347	225	28	508	8-27-94	HR	6888
348	226	28	508	8-27-94	HR	8007
349	227	28	509-570	8-27-94	HR	4864
350	228	28	571	8-27-94	HR	5478

PUBLIC ACTS OF THE FIFTY-THIRD CONGRESS

Public Law/Resolution		Statutes at Large	Page	Date	Bill No.	
Chapter	Number					
351	229	28	571-572	8-27-94	HR	7571
352	230	28	573-574	8-27-94	HR	7572

RESOLUTIONS OF THE FIFTY-THIRD CONGRESS

1	1	28	575	12-07-93	H Res.	88
3	2	28	575-576	12-15-93	H Res.	77
4	3	28	576	12-19-93	H Res.	98
5	4	28	576	12-19-93	H Res.	31
6	5	28	576-577	12-19-93	H Res.	96
7	6	28	577	12-25-93	S Res.	43
8	7	28	577	1-15-94	H Res.	93
9	8	28	577	1-27-94	H Res.	112
10	9	28	578	2-02-94	S Res.	55
12	10	28	578	3-12-94	S Res.	53
13	11	28	578-579	3-14-94	S Res.	51
14	12	28	579	3-19-94	S Res.	62
15	13	28	579	3-30-94	H Res.	147
16	14	28	579-580	3-31-94	H Res.	144
17	15	28	580	4-02-94	S Res.	8
18	16	28	580-581	4-02-94	S Res.	37
19	17	28	581	4-04-94	H Res.	146
20	18	28	581	4-10-94	H Res.	139
21	19	28	581-582	4-27-94	S Res.	77
22	20	28	582	5-04-94	S Res.	66
23	21	28	582	5-04-94	S Res.	81
24	22	28	582-583	5-05-94	H Res.	150
26	23	28	583	5-11-94	H Res.	123
27	24	28	583	5-11-94	H Res.	168
28	25	28	583	5-28-94	H Res.	178
29	26	28	583	6-05-94	S Res.	89
30	27	28	584	6-05-94	H Res.	185
31	28	28	584-585	6-22-94	H Res.	172
32	29	28	585-586	6-29-94	H Res.	196
33	30	28	586	6-29-94	S Res.	57
34	31	28	586	7-03-94	H Res.	193
35	32	28	586-587	7-09-94	H Res.	201
37	33	28	587	7-23-94	H Res.	126
38	34	28	587	7-31-94	H Res.	208

RESOLUTIONS OF THE FIFTY-THIRD CONGRESS

Public Law/Resolution		Statutes at Large	Page	Date	Bill No.
Chapter	Number				
39	35	28	587	8-01-94	H Res. 94
40	36	28	588-589	8-01-94	H Res. 32
42	37	28	589-590	8-06-94	H Res. 121
43	38	28	590	8-15-94	H Res. 95
44	39	28	590	8-15-94	H Res. 217
45	40	28	590	8-23-94	S Res. 96
46	41	28	591	8-23-94	S Res. 101
49	42	28	591	8-27-94	S Res. 102
50	43	28	591	8-27-94	H Res. 5
51	44	28	591-592	8-27-94	H Res. 220
52	45	28	592	8-27-94	H Res. 221
53	46	28	592	8-28-94	S Res. 105

Public Law/Resolution		Statutes at Large	Page	Date	Bill No.	
Chapter	Number					
1	1	28	593-594	12-08-94	HR	7515
3	2	28	594	12-13-94	S	679
6	3	28	595	12-15-94	HR	4453
7	4	28	595	12-15-94	HR	7796
8	5	28	595-596	12-24-94	S	2327
9	6	28	596	12-24-94	HR	8249
10	7	28	596	12-24-94	HR	8288
11	8	28	596-597	12-26-94	S	2416
12	9	28	597-599	12-27-94	HR	6499
14	10	28	599	12-29-94	HR	7489
15	11	28	599	12-29-94	HR	7953
19	12	28	599-600	1-07-95	S	2325
20	13	28	600	1-08-95	S	2353
21	14	28	601	1-08-95	S	2384
23	15	28	601-624	1-12-95	HR	2650
24	16	28	624-625	1-16-95	S	588
25	17	28	625-626	1-16-95	S	1706
26	18	28	626	1-16-95	S	2337
27	19	28	626	1-16-95	HR	7109
28	20	28	626	1-16-95	HR	8067
29	21	28	627-634	1-16-95	HR	8125
33	22	28	634	1-19-95	S	2363
34	23	28	634-635	1-19-95	HR	8094
36	24	28	635	1-21-95	S	756
37	25	28	635-636	1-21-95	HR	7828
38	26	28	636	1-21-95	HR	8172
39	27	28	636	1-22-95	HR	8077
43	28	28	636-639	1-25-95	HR	8148
44	29	28	639	1-25-95	S	1683
45	30	28	639-640	1-25-95	HR	6321
46	31	28	640-641	1-25-95	HR	8251
50	32	28	641	1-26-95	S	2295
54	33	28	641-642	2-01-95	HR	8164
55	34	28	642	2-04-95	S	686
56	35	28	643	2-04-95	HR	8336
59	36	28	643	2-08-95	S	1478
60	37	28	643	2-08-95	S	2562
61	38	28	643-644	2-08-95	HR	3291

Public Law/Resolution		Statutes at Large	Page	Date	Bill No.	
Chapter	Number					
62	39	28	644	2-08-95	HR	7811
63	40	28	645	2-08-95	HR	8277
64	41	28	645-650	2-08-95	HR	8635
78	42	28	650	2-09-95	S	2736
79	43	28	650	2-11-95	S	445
80	44	28	651-653	2-11-95	HR	8253
81	45	28	653-654	2-12-95	S	2352
82	46	28	654	2-12-95	HR	7334
83	47	28	654-663	2-12-95	HR	8226
84	48	28	633	2-12-95	HR	8552
87	49	28	664	2-13-94	S	2165
88	50	28	664	2-13-95	HR	397
92	51	28	664-665	2-15-95	S	2433
94	52	28	665	2-18-95	S	1813
95	53	28	665-666	2-18-95	S	2697
96	54	28	666-667	2-18-95	HR	5216
97	55	28	667	2-18-95	HR	5603
98	56	28	668	2-18-95	HR	7839
100	57	28	668-671	2-19-95	S	655
101	58	28	671-672	2-19-95	HR	7020
102	59	28	672	2-19-95	HR	8563
103	60	28	672	2-19-95	S	2595
105	61	28	673	2-20-95	S	1667
106	62	28	673	2-20-95	S	2699
107	63	28	673	2-20-95	HR	27
108	64	28	674	2-20-95	HR	109
109	65	28	675	2-20-95	HR	116
110	66	28	675	2-20-95	HR	155
111	67	28	676	2-20-95	HR	2337
112	68	28	676-677	2-20-95	HR	4283
113	69	28	677-679	2-20-95	HR	6792
114	70	28	679	2-20-95	HR	7731
115	71	28	679	2-21-95	S	2589
127	72	28	680	2-23-95	S	2783
128	73	28	680	2-25-95	HR	5219
129	74	28	681-682	2-25-95	HR	8499
130	75	28	682-683	2-26-95	S	2521
131	76	28	683-686	2-26-95	HR	3476

Public Law/Resolution		Statutes at Large	Page	Date	Bill No.	
Chapter	Number					
132	77	28	686-687	2-26-95	HR	4693
133	78	28	687	2-26-95	HR	4952
134	79	28	687-688	2-26-95	HR	5711
135	80	28	688-689	2-26-95	HR	6750
137	81	28	689	2-27-95	HR	6323
138	82	28	689-690	2-28-95	S	444
139	83	28	690-691	2-28-95	HR	4475
140	84	28	691-693	2-28-95	HR	8272
144	85	28	693	3-01-95	S	1717
145	86	28	693-698	3-01-95	S	2173
146	87	28	699-700	3-01-95	HR	2377
147	88	28	700	3-01-95	HR	7834
148	89	28	700-701	3-01-95	HR	8337
149	90	28	701	3-01-95	HR	8459
150	91	28	701	3-01-95	HR	8680
159	92	28	701	3-02-95	S	2798
160	93	28	702-703	3-02-95	HR	6078
161	94	28	703-704	3-02-95	HR	8092
162	95	28	704-707	3-02-95	HR	8093
163	96	28	708-709	3-02-95	HR	8189
164	97	28	709-711	3-02-95	HR	8231
165	98	28	711-713	3-02-95	HR	8327
166	99	28	713-717	3-02-95	HR	8638
168	100	28	717-721	3-02-95	HR	8698
168	101	28	721-727	3-02-95	HR	8714
169	102	28	727-738	3-02-95	HR	8727
170	103	28	738-739	3-02-95	HR	8880
171	104	28	739-740	3-02-95	HR	8882
172	105	28	740-741	3-02-95	S	1503
173	106	28	741-743	3-02-95	S	2790
174	107	28	744	3-02-95	HR	4605
175	108	28	744	3-02-95	HR	8900
176	109	28	744-764	3-02-95	HR	8388
177	110	28	764-809	3-02-95	HR	8767
178	111	28	809-811	3-02-95	S	1921
179	112	28	811-813	3-02-95	HR	3246
180	113	28	813-814	3-02-95	HR	6979
181	114	28	814	3-02-95	HR	8122

PUBLIC ACTS OF THE FIFTY-THIRD CONGRESS

Public Law/Resolution		Statutes at Large	Page	Date	Bill No.	
Chapter	Number					
182	115	28	814	3-02-95	HR	8614
183	116	28	814-815	3-02-95	HR	8696
184	117	28	815	3-02-95	S	2463
185	118	28	815-825	3-02-95	HR	8234
186	119	28	825-843	3-02-95	HR	8665
187	120	29	843-876	3-02-95	HR	8892
188	121	28	876-910	3-02-95	HR	8479
189	122	28	910-962	3-02-95	HR	8518
190	123	28	962-963	3-02-95	S	1201
191	124	28	963-964	3-02-95	S	1620
192	125	28	964	3-02-95	S	1841
193	126	28	964-965	3-02-95	S	1876
194	127	28	965	3-02-95	HR	8407
195	128	28	966	3-02-95	HR	8979

RESOLUTIONS OF THE FIFTY-THIRD CONGRESS

1	1	28	967	12-15-94	H Res. 237
2	2	28	967	12-24-94	H Res. 231
3	3	28	967	1-12-95	H Res. 97
5	4	28	967-968	1-21-95	H Res. 246
8	5	28	968	2-01-95	H Res. 254
9	6	28	968-969	2-05-95	S Res. 115
10	7	28	969	2-08-95	H Res. 92
11	8	28	969	2-13-95	H Res. 269
12	9	28	969	2-15-95	S Res. 128
13	10	28	970	2-15-95	S Res. 125
14	11	28	970	2-18-95	S Res. 113
15	12	28	970	2-18-95	H Res. 261
16	13	28	970-971	2-20-95	H Res. 140
17	14	28	971	2-20-95	H Res. 252
18	15	28	971	2-21-95	H Res. 273
19	16	28	9710972	2-26-95	H Res. 209
20	17	28	972	2-26-95	H Res. 227
21	18	28	972	2-27-95	S Res. 109
22	19	28	972	2-27-95	S Res. 138
23	20	28	973	3-01-95	H Res. 277
24	21	28	973	3-02-95	S Res. 117
25	22	28	973	3-02-95	S Res. 139

RESOLUTIONS OF THE FIFTY-THIRD CONGRESS

Public Law/Resolution		Statutes at Large	Page	Date	Bill No.
Chapter	Number				
26	23	28	973-974	3-02-95	S Res. 141
27	24	28	974	3-02-95	S Res. 142
28	25	28	974	3-02-95	H Res. 119
29	26	28	975	3-02-95	S Res. 91
30	27	28	975	3-02-95	S Res. 134
31	28	28	975	3-02-95	H Res. 286

Public Law/Resolution		Statutes at Large	Page	Date	Bill No.	
Chapter	Number					
1	1	29	1	12-21-95	HR	2173
2	2	29	1	12-27-95	HR	803
3	3	29	2	1-04-96	HR	2264
4	4	29	2	1-06-96	HR	2720
5	5	29	2-3	1-21-96	S	30
6	6	29	3	1-21-96	HR	4241
7	7	29	3	1-22-96	S	628
8	8	29	4	1-23-96	S	43
9	9	29	4	2-05-96	S	1450
10	10	29	4-5	2-07-96	S	650
11	11	29	5	2-07-96	HR	173
12	12	29	5	2-07-96	HR	5566
14	13	29	6	2-08-96	S	1547
18	14	29	6	2-12-96	S	708
19	15	29	6-7	2-13-96	S	1046
20	16	29	7	2-15-96	HR	1464
21	17	29	7	2-15-96	HR	2175
22	18	29	8	2-18-96	HR	4145
23	19	29	8-9	2-20-96	HR	3553
24	20	29	9	2-20-96	S	1591
25	21	29	10	2-20-96	HR	2654
26	22	29	10-11	2-20-96	HR	3728
27	23	29	11	2-20-96	HR	4810
28	24	29	11	2-20-96	HR	4991
29	25	29	12-13	2-24-96	HR	3009
30	26	29	13-16	2-24-96	HR	3812
31	27	29	16-17	2-26-96	HR	2642
32	28	29	17	2-26-96	HR	1442
33	29	29	17-28	2-26-96	HR	4321
34	30	29	28-38	2-26-96	HR	4960
35	31	29	39	2-27-96	HR	1676
36	32	29	39	2-27-96	HR	1785
37	33	29	39	3-02-96	S	1740
38	34	29	40-42	3-02-96	HR	4153
39	35	29	42-43	3-02-96	HR	5474
40	36	29	43-44	3-04-96	S	103
41	37	29	44	3-04-96	S	879
42	38	29	44-45	3-06-96	S	259

PUBLIC ACTS OF THE FIFTY-FOURTH CONGRESS

Public Law/Resolution		Statutes at Large	Page	Date	Bill No.	
Chapter	Number					
46	39	29	45–46	3–06–96	HR	3537
47	40	29	46	3–06–96	HR	3962
48	41	29	46–54	3–06–96	HR	4043
49	42	29	54–55	3–06–96	HR	4779
51	43	29	55	3–07–96	HR	3982
52	44	29	55	3–13–96	S	477
53	45	29	55–57	3–13–96	S	636
54	46	29	57	3–13–96	HR	162
55	47	29	57	3–13–96	HR	1712
56	48	29	58	3–13–96	HR	2300
57	49	29	58–60	3–16–96	S	1825
58	50	29	60	3–16–96	HR	3964
59	51	29	60–69	3–16–96	HR	5359
60	52	29	69–72	3–18–96	HR	1691
62	53	29	72	3–20–96	S	1230
63	54	29	73	3–20–96	S	1804
64	55	29	73	3–20–96	HR	3265
65	56	29	73–74	3–20–96	HR	7137
66	57	29	74	3–23–96	HR	2921
67	58	29	74–75	3–23–96	HR	6250
73	59	29	75	3–28–96	S	732
74	60	29	75–76	3–28–96	S	990
75	61	29	76–77	3–28–96	S	2251
76	62	29	77–78	3–28–96	HR	5382
77	63	29	78–79	3–28–96	HR	5979
78	64	29	79–80	3–28–96	HR	6304
79	65	29	80	3–28–96	HR	6936
82	66	29	80–84	3–30–96	HR	67
83	67	29	84	3–31–96	HR	4463
84	68	29	84	3–31–96	S	1179
85	69	29	84	3–31–96	HR	5286
87	70	29	85	4–01–96	HR	5828
88	71	29	85	4–04–96	HR	4698
90	72	29	85	4–06–96	S	494
91	73	29	86	4–06–96	HR	55
92	74	29	86–87	4–06–96	HR	6408
93	75	29	87–90	4–06–96	HR	5564
94	76	29	90	4–07–96	HR	1244

Public Law/Resolution		Statutes at Large	Page	Date	Bill No.	
Chapter	Number					
95	77	29	90-91	4-07-96	S	2419
96	78	29	91	4-13-96	HR	5736
98	79	29	91	4-14-96	S	2132
99	80	29	91-92	4-14-96	HR	4053
100	81	29	92-93	4-14-96	HR	4254
101	82	29	93	4-14-96	HR	5914
103	83	29	94	4-15-96	HR	5363
104	84	29	94-95	4-16-96	HR	6996
107	85	29	95	4-18-96	S	628
108	86	29	95-96	4-18-96	HR	2912
119	87	29	96	4-24-96	HR	8313
120	88	29	96-97	4-24-96	S	744
121	89	29	97	4-24-96	S	1317
122	90	29	98	4-24-96	S	2141
123	91	29	98-99	4-24-96	HR	3281
140	92	29	99-108	4-25-96	HR	5161
141	93	29	109-110	4-25-96	HR	5672
147	94	29	110	5-01-96	HR	2265
150	95	29	110	5-04-96	S	1176
151	96	29	111	5-04-96	S	1353
152	97	29	111-112	5-04-96	HR	3549
153	98	29	112	5-04-96	HR	4781
154	99	29	112-113	5-04-96	HR	5488
155	100	29	113-114	5-04-96	HR	7905
161	101	29	115	5-07-96	S	2997
162	102	29	115	5-08-96	HR	3544
163	103	29	115	5-09-96	S	1846
164	104	29	115-116	5-09-96	S	661
167	105	29	116	5-11-96	S	1872
168	106	29	116-117	5-11-96	HR	1191
169	107	29	117	5-11-96	HR	4456
175	108	29	117	5-13-96	HR	8820
176	109	29	118	5-13-96	HR	6505
177	110	29	118-120	5-13-96	S	1904
179	111	29	120	5-14-96	HR	3018
181	112	29	120	5-15-96	S	2870
182	113	29	120-121	5-15-96	HR	175
191	114	29	121	5-18-96	HR	6

Public Law/Resolution		Statutes at Large	Page	Date	Bill No.	
Chapter	Number					
192	115	29	121	5-18-96	HR	1980
193	116	29	121	5-18-96	HR	3448
194	117	29	122	5-18-96	HR	3462
195	118	29	122	5-13-96	HR	7865
199	119	29	122-123	5-19-96	S	2642
200	120	29	123	5-19-96	HR	4787
201	121	29	123	5-19-96	HR	5105
202	122	29	123	5-19-96	HR	5481
203	123	29	124	5-19-96	HR	5790
204	124	29	124	5-19-96	HR	6195
205	125	29	124-125	5-19-96	HR	6663
206	126	29	125-126	5-19-96	HR	7264
207	127	29	126	5-19-96	HR	7395
208	128	29	126-127	5-19-96	HR	8532
212	129	29	127	5-21-96	S	2032
213	130	29	128	5-21-96	S	2488
214	131	29	128	5-21-96	HR	227
215	132	29	128-129	5-21-96	HR	6172
216	133	29	129	5-21-96	HR	6666
217	134	29	129	5-21-96	HR	6836
218	135	29	129-130	5-21-96	HR	7100
219	136	29	130	5-21-96	HR	7140
220	137	29	130	5-21-96	HR	7143
221	138	29	130	5-21-96	HR	7172
222	139	29	130-131	5-21-96	HR	7216
223	140	29	131	5-21-96	HR	7671
224	141	29	131-132	5-21-96	HR	7973
225	142	29	132-133	5-21-96	HR	8012
226	143	29	133	5-21-96	HR	8013
227	144	29	133	5-21-96	HR	8077
230	145	29	133	5-22-96	HR	8266
231	146	29	133-134	5-22-96	S	1865
232	147	29	134	5-22-96	S	2508
233	148	29	134-135	5-22-96	S	2936
238	149	29	135-136	5-25-96	HR	270
239	150	29	136	5-25-96	HR	4179
240	151	29	136	5-25-96	HR	4324
241	152	29	136	5-25-96	HR	5217

Public Law/Resolution		Statutes at Large	Page	Date	Bill No.	
Chapter	Number					
242	153	29	136-137	5-25-96	HR	5379
243	154	29	137	5-25-96	HR	4255
244	155	29	138	5-25-96	HR	8260
245	156	29	138	5-25-96	S	981
246	157	29	138-140	5-25-96	S	2843
252	158	29	140-186	5-28-96	HR	6248
253	159	29	186-187	5-28-96	HR	8167
254	160	29	187-188	5-28-96	S	888
255	161	29	188-189	5-28-96	HR	3013
256	162	29	189	5-28-96	HR	7324
257	163	29	190	5-28-96	HR	8590
258	164	29	190-191	5-28-96	HR	9030
270	165	29	191-192	5-29-96	HR	4452
274	166	29	192-193	5-30-96	HR	6833
275	167	29	193	5-30-96	HR	248
303	168	29	193-194	6-01-96	S	1659
304	169	29	194	6-01-96	HR	4785
309	170	29	195	6-03-96	HR	886
310	171	29	195	6-03-96	HR	3282
311	172	29	195-197	6-03-96	HR	5675
312	173	29	197	6-03-96	HR	1436
313	174	29	198-202	6-03-96	HR	5731
314	175	29	202-244	6-03-96	HR	7977
315	176	29	244-245	6-03-96	S	1247
316	177	29	245-246	6-03-96	S	2221
317	178	29	246-250	6-03-96	S	2499
331	179	29	251	6-05-96	HR	3337
335	180	29	251-253	6-06-96	HR	6994
336	181	29	253	6-06-96	HR	7578
337	182	29	253-256	6-06-96	HR	8008
338	183	29	256-261	6-06-96	HR	8109
339	184	29	262	6-06-96	S	3161
370	185	29	262	6-08-96	S	2169
371	186	29	263	6-08-96	HR	6259
372	187	29	264-266	6-08-96	HR	8469
373	188	29	267-313	6-08-96	HR	9404
386	189	29	313-316	6-09-96	HR	6614
387	190	29	316-317	6-09-96	S	2022

PUBLIC ACTS OF THE FIFTY-FOURTH CONGRESS

Public Law/Resolution		Statutes at Large	Page	Date	Bill No.	
Chapter	Number					
394	191	29	317	6-10-96	S	2859
395	192	29	318-320	6-10-96	S	2928
396	193	29	321	6-10-96	S	2978
397	194	29	321	6-10-96	HR	2
398	195	29	321-360	6-10-96	HR	6249
399	196	29	361-380	6-10-96	HR	7542
400	197	29	380-381	6-10-96	HR	8383
401	198	29	381-382	6-10-96	HR	9253
402	199	29	382-384	6-10-96	S	1306
403	200	29	384	6-10-96	S	1767
404	201	29	384	6-10-96	S	2412
405	202	29	384-385	6-10-96	S	2490
406	203	29	385	6-10-96	S	2783
407	204	29	385	6-10-96	HR	2777
408	205	29	385	6-10-96	HR	6256
409	206	29	386	6-10-96	S	3206
414	207	29	386-388	6-11-96	S	2943
415	208	29	388-391	6-11-96	S	2944
416	209	29	391	6-11-96	S	2945
417	210	29	391-393	6-11-96	S	3170
418	211	29	393	6-11-96	HR	180
419	212	29	393-413	6-11-96	HR	5210
420	213	29	413-455	6-11-96	HR	7664
421	214	29	455-456	6-11-96	HR	8321
422	215	29	456-457	6-11-96	HR	9226
423	216	29	457	6-11-96	HR	9406
424	217	29	458	6-11-96	HR	9447

RESOLUTIONS OF THE FIFTY-FOURTH CONGRESS

1	1	29	459	12-18-95	H Res.	7
2	2	29	459	12-20-95	H Res.	26
3	3	29	459-460	12-23-95	S Res.	13
4	4	29	460	12-27-95	H Res.	27
5	5	29	460	1-04-96	S Res.	32
6	6	29	461	1-04-96	H Res.	56
7	7	29	461	1-14-96	H Res.	19
8	8	29	461	1-17-96	H Res.	60
9	9	29	461-462	1-21-96	H Res.	25

RESOLUTIONS OF THE FIFTY-FOURTH CONGRESS

Public Law/Resolution		Statutes at Large	Page	Date	Bill No.	
Chapter	Number					
10	10	29	462	1-08-96	S Res.	50
11	11	29	462-463	1-30-96	H Res.	88
12	12	29	463	2-05-96	H Res.	89
13	13	29	463	2-07-96	S Res.	23
14	14	29	463	2-07-96	H Res.	66
16	15	29	464	2-13-96	H Res.	79
17	16	29	464	2-20-96	S Res.	39
18	17	29	464	2-26-96	S Res.	17
19	18	29	465	2-26-96	S Res.	59
20	19	29	465	3-02-96	H Res.	121
22	20	29	465	3-11-96	H Res.	108
23	21	29	466	3-11-96	S Res.	65
24	22	29	466	3-13-96	S Res.	78
25	23	29	466-467	3-13-96	S Res.	85
26	24	29	467	3-13-96	H Res.	98
27	25	29	467	3-14-96	S Res.	43
28	26	29	467	3-16-96	S Res.	24
29	27	29	467-468	3-16-96	S Res.	54
30	28	29	468	3-19-96	S Res.	47
31	29	29	468	3-19-96	S Res.	72
32	30	29	468-469	3-20-96	H Res.	105
33	31	29	469	3-20-96	H Res.	140
34	32	29	469	3-23-96	H Res.	133
35	33	29	469	3-24-96	S Res.	79
36	34	29	469	3-24-96	H Res.	141
38	35	29	470	4-02-96	S Res.	114
40	36	29	470	4-06-96	S Res.	99
41	37	29	470	4-06-96	S Res.	103
42	38	29	470-471	4-06-96	H Res.	24
43	39	29	471	4-10-96	H Res.	159
44	40	29	471	4-18-96	S Res.	104
45	41	29	471	4-18-96	S Res.	123
46	42	29	471	4-20-96	S Res.	116
47	43	29	472	4-21-96	H Res.	160
48	44	29	472	4-24-96	S Res.	131
49	45	29	472	4-24-96	H Res.	163
50	46	29	472-473	4-30-96	H Res.	170
51	47	29	473	5-02-96	H Res.	85

RESOLUTIONS OF THE FIFTY-FOURTH CONGRESS

Public Law/Resolution		Statutes at Large	Page	Date	Bill No.
Chapter	Number				
52	48	29	473	5-18-96	S Res. 15
53	49	29	473-474	5-18-96	H Res. 167
55	50	29	474-475	5-21-96	H Res. 122
56	51	29	475	5-28-96	H Res. 174
57	52	29	475	5-28-96	H Res. 193
58	53	29	475-476	6-08-96	S Res. 155
59	54	29	476	6-09-96	H Res. 195
60	55	29	476	6-10-96	S Res. 161
62	56	29	476	6-11-96	S Res. 149

PUBLIC ACTS OF THE FIFTY-FOURTH CONGRESS

Public Law/Resolution		Statutes at Large	Page	Date	Bill No.	
Chapter	Number					
1	1	29	477–479	12–22–96	S	2889
2	2	29	479	12–22–96	HR	9473
3	3	29	479–481	12–22–96	HR	9753
4	4	29	481–482	1–06–97	S	2306
5	5	29	482–483	1–06–97	HR	9700
7	6	29	483	1–08–97	S	2047
8	7	29	483	1–09–97	S	337
9	8	29	483	1–09–97	HR	9472
11	9	29	484	1–13–97	S	264
12	10	29	484–485	1–13–97	S	1723
13	11	29	485–486	1–13–97	S	1724
29	12	29	487	1–15–97	HR	878
30	13	29	487–489	1–16–97	HR	4052
61	14	29	489	1–18–97	S	1646
62	15	29	490–491	1–18–97	HR	7945
66	16	29	491	1–20–97	S	206
67	17	29	491–492	1–20–97	S	1424
68	18	29	492	1–20–97	S	1448
69	19	29	492–493	1–20–97	S	1726
70	20	29	493–494	1–20–97	S	3050
83	21	29	494	1–21–97	S	2334
86	22	29	494	1–22–97	HR	7777
90	23	29	495–496	1–26–97	S	3071
91	24	29	496–497	1–26–97	HR	9733
92	25	29	497	1–26–97	S	319
93	26	29	497–499	1–26–97	S	1725
94	27	29	499	1–26–97	HR	6883
95	28	29	499–500	1–26–97	HR	8676
96	29	29	500–501	1–26–97	HR	8726
99	30	29	501–502	1–27–97	S	3375
106	31	29	502	1–28–97	HR	9901
108	32	29	502–506	1–29–97	S	1741
109	33	29	506–507	1–30–97	HR	280
110	34	29	507	1–30–97	HR	7255
111	35	29	507	1–30–97	HR	8413
112	36	29	507–509	1–30–97	HR	8551
113	37	29	509	1–30–97	HR	9865
121	38	29	509	2–01–97	S	3525

PUBLIC ACTS OF THE FIFTY-FOURTH CONGRESS

Public Law/Resolution		Statutes at Large	Page	Date	Bill No.	
Chapter	Number					
122	39	29	509-510	2-01-97	HR	9935
136	40	29	510-511	2-03-97	HR	8298
145	41	29	511	2-04-97	HR	7781
146	42	29	511	2-04-97	HR	9710
167	43	29	511-512	2-05-97	HR	8038
169	44	29	512	2-06-97	S	738
170	45	29	512	2-06-97	S	3555
172	46	29	512	2-08-97	S	1675
173	47	29	513	2-08-97	S	1722
174	48	29	513-514	2-08-97	S	3303
175	49	29	514-515	2-08-97	S	3401
176	50	29	515-516	2-08-97	HR	6750
177	51	29	516	2-08-97	HR	8190
178	52	29	516-517	2-08-97	HR	9469
179	53	29	517	2-08-97	HR	3772
205	54	29	517	2-09-97	S	666
213	55	29	517-518	2-10-97	S	1624
214	56	29	518-526	2-10-97	HR	9707
216	57	29	526	2-11-97	S	3551
221	58	29	526	2-13-97	S	1296
222	59	29	527	2-13-97	HR	6776
223	60	29	527	2-13-97	HR	8356
224	61	29	527	2-13-97	HR	9734
228	62	29	527-528	2-15-97	HR	9029
229	63	29	528-529	2-15-97	HR	9775
230	64	29	529-530	2-15-97	HR	9863
231	65	29	530	2-15-97	HR	10067
234	66	29	530	2-16-97	HR	3719
236	67	29	531	2-17-97	S	3333
237	68	29	531	2-17-97	HR	4985
238	69	29	531-532	2-17-97	HR	5482
239	70	29	532	2-17-97	HR	8010
240	71	29	533-534	2-17-97	HR	8814
241	72	29	534	2-17-97	HR	9345
242	73	29	534-535	2-17-97	HR	9799
243	74	29	535	2-17-97	HR	9841
244	75	29	535	2-17-97	HR	10012
250	76	29	535	2-18-97	HR	9493

Public Law/Resolution		Statutes at Large	Page	Date	Bill No.	
Chapter	Number					
251	77	29	536	2-18-97	S	3320
263	78	29	536	2-19-97	S	1862
264	79	29	536-538	2-19-97	HR	8672
265	80	29	538-578	2-19-97	HR	9643
267	81	29	578-579	2-20-97	HR	6713
268	82	29	579-590	2-20-97	HR	10134
269	83	29	590-592	2-20-97	HR	10278
308	84	29	592	2-23-97	S	3603
310	85	29	592	2-24-97	S	1169
311	86	29	593	2-24-97	S	2101
312	87	29	593-594	2-24-97	HR	853
313	88	29	594	2-24-97	HR	9123
315	89	29	594-595	2-25-97	HR	5490
316	90	29	595	2-25-97	HR	6834
317	91	29	595-596	2-25-97	HR	9168
332	92	29	596-597	2-26-97	S	2923
333	93	29	597-598	2-26-97	S	3614
334	94	29	598-599	2-26-97	S	3718
335	95	29	599	2-26-97	HR	1984
336	96	29	599	2-26-97	HR	9494
340	97	29	599	2-27-97	HR	4156
341	98	29	600	2-27-97	S	3666
342	99	29	600	2-27-97	HR	9647
353	100	29	600	3-02-97	S	3561
354	101	29	600-602	3-02-97	HR	1708
355	102	29	602-603	3-02-97	S	1743
356	103	29	603	3-02-97	S	2232
357	104	29	603-604	3-02-97	S	3721
358	105	29	604-607	3-02-97	S	3725
359	106	29	607	3-02-97	S	3680
360	107	29	607-608	3-02-97	HR	3623
361	108	29	608-609	3-02-97	HR	7469
362	109	29	609-618	3-02-97	HR	9638
363	110	29	618-619	3-02-97	HR	9709
364	111	29	619-620	3-02-97	HR	9976
365	112	29	620	3-02-97	HR	10122
366	113	29	620-621	3-02-97	S	2037
372	114	29	621-622	3-03-97	HR	7320

PUBLIC ACTS OF THE FIFTY-FOURTH CONGRESS

Public Law/Resolution		Statutes at Large	Page	Date	Bill No.	
Chapter	Number					
373	115	29	622	3-03-97	HR	9101
374	116	29	622-624	3-03-97	S	1832
375	117	29	624	3-03-97	S	3307
376	118	29	624-625	3-03-97	S	3547
377	119	29	625	3-03-97	HR	5732
378	120	29	625-626	3-03-97	HR	8443
379	121	29	626-628	3-03-97	HR	8582
380	122	29	628	3-03-97	HR	9703
381	123	29	628-629	3-03-97	HR	10272
382	124	29	630-635	3-03-97	HR	10108
383	125	29	635-641	3-03-97	HR	9023
384	126	29	641-644	3-03-97	HR	10288
385	127	29	644-648	3-03-97	HR	10289
386	128	29	648-665	3-03-97	HR	10336
387	129	29	665-685	3-03-97	HR	10167
388	130	29	685-687	3-03-97	HR	2698
389	131	29	687-691	3-03-97	HR	2663
390	132	29	692	3-03-97	S	3538
391	133	29	692-694	3-03-97	HR	3014
392	134	29	694-695	3-03-97	HR	10223
393	135	29	695	3-03-97	HR	9821
394	136	29	695	3-03-97	HR	10203
395	137	29	695-696	3-03-97	HR	10202
396	138	29	696	3-03-97	HR	10304
397	139	29	696	3-03-97	HR	10367

RESOLUTIONS OF THE FIFTY-FOURTH CONGRESS

1	1	29	697	12-21-96	H Res.	209
2	2	29	697	1-08-97	S Res.	162
3	3	29	697	1-11-97	H Res.	205
4	4	29	697-698	1-16-97	H Res.	213
5	5	29	698	1-21-97	S Res.	189
7	6	29	698	1-30-97	H Res.	152
8	7	29	698-699	2-03-97	H Res.	215
9	8	29	699-700	2-06-97	H Res.	214
10	9	29	700	2-13-97	H Res.	243
11	10	29	700	2-15-97	H Res.	249
12	11	29	700-701	2-17-97	H Res.	237

RESOLUTIONS OF THE FIFTY-FOURTH CONGRESS

Public Law/Resolution		Statutes at Large	Page	Date	Bill No.
Chapter	Number				
13	12	29	701	2-18-97	H Res. 234
14	13	29	701	2-19-97	S Res. 201
15	14	29	701-702	2-19-97	S Res. 204
16	15	29	702	2-20-97	S Res. 148
17	16	29	702-703	2-23-97	S Res. 121
18	17	29	703	2-24-97	H Res. 239
19	18	29	703	2-24-97	H Res. 252
20	19	29	703-704	2-26-97	H Res. 229
21	20	29	704	2-26-97	H Res. 257
23	21	29	704	3-03-97	S Res. 205
24	22	29	704	3-03-97	H Res. 211

PUBLIC ACTS OF THE FIFTY-FIFTH CONGRESS

Public Law/Resolution		Statutes at Large	Page	Date	Bill No.	
Chapter	Number					
1	1	30	1-10	4-23-97	HR	14
2	2	30	11-62	6-04-97	HR	16
3	3	30	62-96	6-07-97	HR	15
4	4	30	96-103	6-07-97	S	1886
5	5	30	103-104	6-09-97	S	1944
6	6	30	104	6-18-97	S	956
7	7	30	104-105	6-18-97	S	1979
8	8	30	105	6-23-97	S	2150
9	9	30	105-150	7-19-97	HR	13
10	10	30	151	7-19-97	HR	3486
11	11	30	151-213	7-24-97	HR	379
12	12	30	214	7-24-97	S	2138
13	13	30	214-215	7-24-97	HR	3941
14	14	30	215	7-24-97	HR	3950

RESOLUTIONS OF THE FIFTY-FIFTH CONGRESS

1	1	30	216	3-24-97	H Res.	32
2	2	30	216	3-24-97	H Res.	33
3	3	30	216	3-24-97	S Res.	18
4	4	30	217	3-25-97	S Res.	7
5	5	30	217	3-26-97	H Res.	25
6	6	30	217-218	3-31-97	S Res.	21
7	7	30	219	4-07-97	S Res.	20
8	8	30	219	4-07-97	S Res.	24
9	9	30	219	4-07-97	H Res.	47
10	10	30	220	5-07-97	S Res.	39
11	11	30	220	5-24-97	S Res.	42
12	12	30	220	6-01-97	S Res.	43
13	13	30	220-221	6-01-97	S Res.	44
14	14	30	221	6-09-97	S Res.	45
15	15	30	221	6-15-97	H Res.	64
17	16	30	222	6-26-97	H Res.	61
18	17	30	222-223	6-30-97	S Res.	50
19	18	30	223	7-15-97	H Res.	76
20	19	30	224	7-19-97	S Res.	52
21	20	30	224	7-24-97	H Res.	79
22	21	30	224	7-24-97	H Res.	82

PUBLIC ACTS OF THE FIFTY-FIFTH CONGRESS

Public Law/Resolution		Statutes at Large	Page	Date	Bill No.	
Chapter	Number					
1	1	30	225	12-16-97	HR	4752
2	2	30	226	12-18-97	HR	5173
3	3	30	226-227	12-29-97	S	2612
4	4	30	227	1-13-98	HR	4769
5	5	30	227-228	1-18-98	HR	4221
6	6	30	228-231	1-25-98	S	467
7	7	30	231	1-25-98	S	468
8	8	30	231-234	1-25-98	S	1258
10	9	30	234	1-27-98	HR	5493
11	10	30	234-239	1-28-98	HR	6251
12	11	30	240	1-31-98	S	3053
13	12	30	240	2-03-98	HR	5516
14	13	30	240	2-09-98	S	1788
15	14	30	240	2-09-98	HR	6554
16	15	30	241	2-11-98	HR	5029
17	16	30	241	2-14-98	HR	4760
18	17	30	241-244	2-14-98	S	2858
23	18	30	245	2-15-98	HR	5982
24	19	30	245-246	2-15-98	S	2553
25	20	30	246-248	2-17-98	S	471
26	21	30	248-249	2-17-98	S	3580
27	22	30	249	2-17-98	HR	4581
28	23	30	249	2-17-98	HR	7559
30	24	30	249	2-19-98	S	3192
31	25	30	249-250	2-19-98	HR	7933
32	26	30	250-252	2-28-98	HR	2283
35	27	30	252-253	3-04-98	S	3578
37	28	30	253	3-05-98	HR	4934
38	29	30	253-261	3-05-98	HR	7555
53	30	30	261	3-08-98	S	2640
54	31	30	262	3-08-98	HR	2484
55	32	30	262-273	3-09-98	HR	6449
56	33	30	273-274	3-09-98	HR	8927
57	34	30	274	3-11-98	HR	5434
59	35	30	275-276	3-12-98	S	3839
60	36	30	276-277	3-14-98	HR	4303
68	37	30	277-318	3-15-98	HR	4751
69	38	30	318-327	3-15-98	HR	6546

Public Law/Resolution		Statutes at Large	Page	Date	Bill No.	
Chapter	Number					
70	39	30	327	3-17-98	S	1865
71	40	30	327-328	3-17-98	HR	8386
72	41	30	328-329	3-18-98	S	2323
74	42	30	329	3-19-98	HR	4066
75	43	30	329	3-19-98	HR	4385
76	44	30	330	3-19-98	HR	7203
82	45	30	330	3-21-98	S	4078
85	46	30	330-340	3-22-98	HR	6351
86	47	30	340	3-23-98	S	2781
87	48	30	341-344	3-23-98	S	3077
88	49	30	344	3-23-98	HR	7344
89	50	30	344	3-23-98	HR	7541
100	51	30	344-345	3-26-98	S	2508
102	52	30	345	3-29-98	HR	6079
103	53	30	346-347	3-30-98	HR	8618
104	54	30	347-350	3-30-98	HR	6358
105	55	30	350-351	3-30-98	S	3873
113	56	30	351	4-04-98	HR	5865
116	57	30	352	4-09-98	S	771
118	58	30	352-353	4-11-98	S	3056
119	59	30	354	4-11-98	HR	5030
120	60	30	354-355	4-11-98	HR	5489
121	61	30	355-357	4-11-98	HR	6906
166	62	30	357-358	4-15-98	S	3472
183	63	30	359-360	4-21-98	S	3457
184	64	30	360	4-21-98	S	3627
185	65	30	360-361	4-21-98	HR	7445
186	66	30	361	4-21-98	HR	7943
187	67	30	361-363	4-22-98	HR	9944
188	68	30	363-364	4-25-98	S	3154
189	69	30	364	4-25-98	HR	10086
191	70	30	364-366	4-26-98	HR	9878
226	71	30	366	4-29-98	HR	4929
227	72	30	366-367	4-29-98	HR	8569
228	73	30	367	4-29-98	HR	8875
229	74	30	367-368	4-29-98	S	3
231	75	30	369	5-02-98	HR	3963
234	76	30	369-390	5-04-98	HR	9378

PUBLIC ACTS OF THE FIFTY-FIFTH CONGRESS

Public Law/Resolution		Statutes at Large	Page	Date	Bill No.	
Chapter	Number					
235	77	30	390-397	5-04-98	HR	10197
236	78	30	397	5-04-98	HR	7337
237	79	30	397-398	5-04-98	HR	7748
238	80	30	398	5-04-98	HR	9552
241	81	30	398	5-05-98	HR	409
245	82	30	399	5-07-98	S	924
246	83	30	399	5-07-98	HR	2691
247	84	30	399-400	5-07-98	HR	5511
248	85	30	400-403	5-07-98	HR	7441
249	86	30	403	5-07-98	HR	8738
290	87	30	403	5-09-98	HR	6468
292	88	30	404	5-11-98	HR	1595
293	89	30	404	5-11-98	S	1316
294	90	30	405	5-11-98	HR	4468
295	91	30	405-406	5-11-98	HR	5885
296	92	30	406	5-12-98	HR	9638
297	93	30	406	5-14-98	S	4142
298	94	30	407-408	5-14-98	S	4452
299	95	30	409-415	5-14-98	HR	5975
338	96	30	415-416	5-17-98	HR	6161
339	97	30	416-417	5-17-98	HR	4099
340	98	30	417	5-17-98	HR	5521
341	99	30	417	5-17-98	S	3132
342	100	30	417-418	5-18-98	S	4567
343	101	30	418	5-18-98	HR	9956
344	102	30	418-419	5-18-98	S	1586
345	103	30	419	5-18-98	S	4518
346	104	30	419	5-18-98	S	4566
347	105	30	419	5-19-98	HR	1596
348	106	30	420	5-21-98	S	3145
349	107	30	420	5-21-98	S	3953
350	108	30	420	5-21-98	S	4582
363	109	30	420	5-26-98	S	4607
364	110	30	421	5-27-98	S	4645
366	111	30	421	5-28-98	S	4206
367	112	30	421	5-28-98	S	4621
368	113	30	422-423	5-31-98	HR	10378
369	114	30	423-424	6-01-98	S	3088

Public Law/Resolution		Statutes at Large	Page	Date	Bill No.	
Chapter	Number					
370	115	30	424-428	6-01-98	HR	4372
371	116	30	428	6-01-98	S	4556
372	117	30	429	6-02-98	HR	9604
376	118	30	429-430	6-04-98	S	1883
377	119	30	430-431	6-04-98	S	4108
378	120	30	431	6-04-98	HR	8349
379	121	30	431	6-04-98	HR	9815
388	122	30	432	6-06-98	S	4554
389	123	30	432	6-06-98	S	4578
390	124	30	432	6-07-98	S	4699
391	125	30	433	6-07-98	HR	9477
392	126	30	433-434	6-07-98	HR	10121
393	127	30	434	6-07-98	HR	10525
394	128	30	434-437	6-08-98	S	1910
395	129	30	437-440	6-08-98	HR	10565
423	130	30	440	6-10-98	S	4168
446	131	30	440-445	6-13-98	HR	9008
447	132	30	445-448	6-13-98	HR	9205
448	133	30	448-470	6-13-98	HR	10100
449	134	30	470	6-15-98	HR	10682
450	135	30	470-471	6-15-98	HR	5149
451	136	30	471	6-15-98	HR	5522
452	137	30	471-472	6-15-98	HR	9075
456	138	30	473	6-16-98	S	4749
457	139	30	473	6-16-98	S	4740
458	140	30	473	6-16-98	S	4676
459	141	30	473-474	6-16-98	HR	8871
460	142	30	474	6-16-98	HR	10087
463	143	30	474-475	6-17-98	HR	10220
464	144	30	475	6-18-98	S	4763
465	145	30	475-476	6-18-98	S	4048
466	146	30	476-477	6-18-98	HR	4073
467	147	30	477	6-18-98	HR	6954
468	148	30	478-483	6-18-98	HR	10293
469	149	30	483-484	6-18-98	HR	10423
489	150	30	484-486	6-21-98	HR	8226
490	151	30	487	6-21-98	HR	9554
494	152	30	487	6-23-98	S	3209

Public Law/Resolution		Statutes at Large	Page	Date	Bill No.	
Chapter	Number					
495	153	30	487-488	6-24-98	S	1726
496	154	30	488-489	6-24-98	HR	8541
497	155	30	489-490	6-25-98	S	914
499	156	30	490-492	6-27-98	HR	6148
500	157	30	492	6-27-98	S	4738
501	158	30	493	6-27-98	S	4750
502	159	30	493-494	6-27-98	S	4759
503	160	30	494-495	6-27-98	HR	5879
504	161	30	495	6-27-95	HR	10290
517	162	30	495-519	6-28-98	HR	8581
518	163	30	519	6-28-98	HR	9338
519	164	30	519-520	6-28-98	HR	10209
534	165	30	520-521	6-29-98	S	2916
535	166	30	521-522	6-29-98	S	3871
536	167	30	522	6-29-98	S	4456
537	168	30	522-524	6-29-98	HR	1073
538	169	30	525	6-29-98	HR	10606
540	170	30	525-544	6-30-98	HR	6897
541	171	30	544-566	7-01-98	S	1035
542	172	30	567-569	7-01-98	S	3596
543	173	30	570-571	7-01-98	HR	5880
544	174	30	571	7-01-98	S	3277
545	175	30	571-597	7-01-98	HR	6896
546	176	30	597-650	7-01-98	HR	8428
547	177	30	650-651	7-01-98	S	2063
548	178	30	651	7-01-98	S	3368
563	179	30	651	7-02-98	S	4439
564	180	30	652	7-02-98	HR	10585
568	181	30	652	7-05-98	S	4713
571	182	30	652-714	7-07-98	HR	10691
572	183	30	714-715	7-07-98	S	4809
573	184	30	715	7-07-98	S	4810
574	185	30	715-716	7-07-98	S	3707
575	186	30	716-717	7-07-98	S	4710
576	187	30	717	7-07-98	S	4714
577	188	30	718	7-07-98	S	4741
578	189	30	718-719	7-07-98	HR	6160
579	190	30	719-720	7-07-98	HR	10280

PUBLIC ACTS OF THE FIFTY-FIFTH CONGRESS

Public Law/Resolution		Statutes at Large	Page	Date	Bill No.	
Chapter	Number					
580	191	30	720	7-07-98	HR	10424
581	192	30	720	7-07-98	HR	10477
582	193	30	720	7-07-98	HR	10561
583	194	30	721	7-07-98	HR	10693
584	195	30	721	7-07-98	HR	10805
635	196	30	721-722	7-08-98	HR	5883
636	197	30	722	7-08-98	HR	6149
637	198	30	722	7-08-98	HR	7018
638	199	30	723-724	7-08-98	HR	8063
639	200	30	724	7-08-98	HR	8064
640	201	30	724-725	7-08-98	HR	9204
641	202	30	725-728	7-08-98	HR	9206
642	203	30	728	7-08-98	HR	10051
643	204	30	728-729	7-08-98	HR	10510
644	205	30	729	7-08-98	HR	10685
645	206	30	729	7-08-98	HR	10766
646	207	30	730	7-08-98	HR	10885
647	208	30	730-731	7-08-98	S	4853

RESOLUTIONS OF THE FIFTY-FIFTH CONGRESS

1	1	30	732	12-16-97	H Res.	103
2	2	30	732	12-18-97	H Res.	102
3	3	30	732-733	1-20-98	S Res.	81
4	4	30	733	1-24-98	H Res.	121
5	5	30	733-734	1-25-98	S Res.	75
6	6	30	734	2-01-98	S Res.	82
8	7	30	734	2-17-98	S Res.	98
9	8	30	735	2-17-98	H Res.	99
10	9	30	735	2-19-98	S Res.	53
11	10	30	735	2-23-98	H Res.	148
12	11	30	735-736	3-05-98	S Res.	94
13	12	30	736	3-05-98	S Res.	108
14	13	30	736	3-05-98	H Res.	120
16	14	30	736	3-18-98	S Res.	91
18	15	30	737	3-19-98	H Res.	166
19	16	30	737	4-01-98	H Res.	182
20	17	30	737	4-09-98	H Res.	178

RESOLUTIONS OF THE FIFTY-FIFTH CONGRESS

Public Law/Resolution		Statutes at Large	Page	Date	Bill No.
Chapter	Number				
21	18	30	737-738	4-11-98	S Res. 129
22	19	30	738	4-11-98	S Res. 105
23	20	30	738	4-11-98	S Res. 28
24	21	30	738-739	4-20-98	H Res. 233
25	22	30	739	4-22-98	S Res. 157
26	23	30	739	4-25-98	S Res. 110
27	24	30	739-740	4-25-98	S Res. 150
28	25	30	740	4-25-98	H Res. 227
29	26	30	740-741	4-29-98	H Res. 116
30	27	30	741	5-04-98	H Res. 24
31	28	30	741	5-07-98	H Res. 119
32	29	30	741	5-07-98	H Res. 149
33	30	30	742	5-10-98	H Res. 260
34	31	30	742-743	5-12-98	S Res. 6
35	32	30	743-744	5-18-98	H Res. 214
37	33	30	744	5-24-98	H Res. 237
38	34	30	744-745	5-26-98	H Res. 257
39	35	30	745	5-26-98	S Res. 167
40	36	30	745	5-27-98	H Res. 245
41	37	30	745-746	5-28-98	H Res. 195
42	38	30	746	6-03-98	S Res. 163
43	39	30	746	6-04-98	S Res. 148
44	40	30	746	6-04-98	H Res. 150
45	41	30	747	6-06-98	H Res. 271
46	42	30	747	6-07-98	H Res. 189
47	43	30	747	6-08-98	H Res. 175
48	44	30	747	6-14-98	S Res. 172
49	45	30	748	6-15-98	S Res. 95
50	46	30	748	6-16-98	H Res. 7
51	47	30	748-749	6-25-98	S Res. 168
52	48	30	749	6-28-98	S Res. 175
53	49	30	749-750	6-29-98	H Res. 251
54	50	30	750	7-01-98	H Res. 221
55	51	30	750-751	7-07-98	H Res. 259
56	52	30	751-752	7-07-98	S Res. 139
57	53	30	752	7-08-98	H Res. 270
58	54	30	752-753	7-08-98	S Res. 141
59	55	30	753	7-08-98	S Res. 182

PUBLIC ACTS OF THE FIFTY-FIFTH CONGRESS

Public Law/Resolution		Statutes at Large	Page	Date	Bill No.	
Chapter	Number					
28	1	30	755–764	12–21–98	S	95
29	2	30	764–765	12–21–98	S	622
30	3	30	765–767	12–21–98	S	3941
31	4	30	768–769	12–21–98	S	4080
32	5	30	769	12–21–98	S	4326
33	6	30	769–770	12–21–98	S	4717
34	7	30	770	12–21–98	HR	9068
35	8	30	770	12–21–98	HR	10915
36	9	30	770–771	12–21–98	HR	8925
41	10	30	772–782	1–05–98	HR	10989
42	11	30	782–783	1–10–98	S	4891
43	12	30	783	1–10–98	HR	5527
44	13	30	783–784	1–10–98	HR	11061
46	14	30	784	1–12–98	HR	11248
47	15	30	785–802	1–12–99	HR	5370
48	16	30	802–803	1–12–99	HR	10106
56	17	30	803–804	1–25–99	HR	421
57	18	30	804	1–25–99	HR	10709
61	19	30	804	1–28–99	S	626
62	20	30	804	1–28–99	S	1601
63	21	30	804–805	1–28–99	S	4316
64	22	30	805–806	1–28–99	S	5004
65	23	30	806–810	1–28–99	S	5045
66	24	30	810	1–28–99	HR	11716
78	25	30	811	1–31–99	S	4626
79	26	30	812	2–02–99	HR	5887
80	27	30	812	2–02–99	HR	8882
81	28	30	812–813	2–02–99	HR	9955
82	29	30	813–814	2–02–99	HR	11019
83	30	30	814	2–02–99	HR	11029
84	31	30	814–815	2–02–99	HR	10459
86	32	30	815	2–04–99	S	2944
87	33	30	815–816	2–04–99	S	5191
88	34	30	816–820	2–04–99	HR	11116
89	35	30	820	2–04–99	HR	11157
120	36	30	821–822	2–08–99	S	5047
121	37	30	822	2–08–99	HR	6901
122	38	30	822	2–08–99	HR	10666

Public Law/Resolution		Statutes at Large	Page	Date	Bill No.	
Chapter	Number					
123	39	30	822-823	2-08-99	HR	10912
127	40	30	823	2-09-99	S	5224
128	41	30	823-833	2-09-99	HR	11487
129	42	30	834	2-09-99	HR	10509
150	43	30	834-835	2-10-99	S	4571
151	44	30	835	2-10-99	S	4700
152	45	30	835-836	2-11-99	HR	12009
153	46	30	836	2-13-99	S	4070
154	47	30	836	2-14-99	S	5088
155	48	30	836	2-14-99	HR	10563
157	49	30	837	2-15-99	HR	10398
160	50	30	837	2-18-99	S	2768
161	51	30	837	2-18-99	HR	26
162	52	30	837	2-18-99	HR	5019
163	53	30	838	2-18-99	HR	11142
164	54	30	838	2-18-99	HR	12094
167	55	30	838	2-20-99	HR	10281
168	56	30	838	2-20-99	HR	11440
171	57	30	839	2-21-99	S	1273
172	58	30	839	2-21-99	S	5186
173	59	30	839-840	2-21-99	S	1964
174	60	30	840	2-21-99	S	5355
175	61	30	840	2-21-99	HR	2683
176	62	30	841-843	2-21-99	HR	4382
177	63	30	843-844	2-21-99	HR	10997
178	64	30	844-845	2-21-99	HR	11098
179	65	30	845-846	2-21-99	HR	11358
186	66	30	846	2-23-99	HR	7094
187	67	30	846-890	2-24-99	HR	11414
189	68	30	890	2-25-99	S	4690
190	69	30	890	2-25-99	S	4808
191	70	30	890	2-25-99	S	5533
192	71	30	891	2-25-99	HR	6670
193	72	30	891	2-25-99	HR	11084
194	73	30	891-892	2-25-99	HR	11605
205	74	30	892	2-27-99	HR	11971
206	75	30	893	2-27-99	S	5126
207	76	30	893-894	2-27-99	HR	6551

PUBLIC ACTS OF THE FIFTY-FIFTH CONGRESS

Public Law/Resolution		Statutes at Large	Page	Date	Bill No.	
Chapter	Number					
208	77	30	894-895	2-27-99	HR	9219
209	78	30	895	2-27-99	HR	9513
210	79	30	895-904	2-27-99	HR	11717
211	80	30	904-905	2-27-99	HR	11732
212	81	30	905-906	2-27-99	HR	11736
218	82	30	906	2-28-99	S	4159
219	83	30	906-908	2-28-99	S	5265
220	84	30	908	2-28-99	S	5391
221	85	30	908	2-28-99	HR	8162
222	86	30	909-910	2-28-99	HR	8480
223	87	30	910-911	2-28-99	HR	11618
224	88	30	911-912	2-28-99	HR	11737
225	89	30	912-914	2-28-99	S	5076
226	90	30	914	2-28-99	S	5514
227	91	30	915	2-28-99	HR	7346
228	92	30	915-916	2-28-99	HR	11455
313	93	30	916-918	3-01-99	S	146
314	94	30	918	3-01-99	S	1040
315	95	30	918	3-01-99	S	5169
316	96	30	918-919	3-01-99	S	5427
317	97	30	919-920	3-01-99	HR	521
318	98	30	920	3-01-99	HR	2314
319	99	30	920	3-01-99	HR	4076
320	100	30	921	3-01-99	HR	6248
321	101	30	921-922	3-01-99	HR	8739
322	102	30	922	3-01-99	HR	11023
323	103	30	923-924	3-01-99	HR	11024
324	104	30	924-947	3-01-99	HR	11217
325	105	30	947-958	3-01-99	HR	11266
326	106	30	959	3-01-99	HR	11570
327	107	30	959-966	3-01-99	HR	11683
328	108	30	966-967	3-01-99	HR	11771
329	109	30	967	3-01-99	HR	11867
330	110	30	968	3-01-99	HR	11883
335	111	30	968	3-02-99	S	1271
336	112	30	968-969	3-02-99	HR	4306
337	113	30	969-970	3-02-99	HR	9077
338	114	30	970	3-02-99	HR	10969

PUBLIC ACTS OF THE FIFTY-FIFTH CONGRESS

Public Law/Resolution		Statutes at Large	Page	Date	Bill No.	
Chapter	Number					
339	115	30	970-971	3-02-99	S	88
340	116	30	971	3-02-99	S	109
341	117	30	972	3-02-99	S	164
342	118	30	972-973	3-02-99	S	244
343	119	30	973-974	3-02-99	S	346
344	120	30	974	3-02-99	S	706
345	121	30	975	3-02-99	S	926
346	122	30	975	3-02-99	S	927
347	123	30	975-976	3-02-99	S	1896
348	124	30	976	3-02-99	S	2048
349	125	30	976	3-02-99	S	2904
350	126	30	976	3-02-99	S	5319
351	127	30	977	3-02-99	S	5376
352	128	30	977-981	3-02-99	S	5578
353	129	30	981-982	3-02-99	HR	6
354	130	30	982	3-02-99	HR	75
355	131	30	982	3-02-99	HR	447
356	132	30	982	3-02-99	HR	484
357	133	30	982-983	3-02-99	HR	524
358	134	30	983	3-02-99	HR	1088
359	135	30	983-984	3-02-99	HR	1139
360	136	30	984	3-02-99	HR	2056
361	137	30	984	3-02-99	HR	2129
362	138	30	984	3-02-99	HR	4304
363	139	30	985	3-02-99	HR	4313
364	140	30	985	3-02-99	HR	5536
365	141	30	985-986	3-02-99	HR	8587
366	142	30	986	3-02-99	HR	9281
367	143	30	986-987	3-02-99	HR	10962
368	144	30	987	3-02-99	HR	11056
369	145	30	988	3-02-99	HR	11495
370	146	30	988	3-02-99	HR	11530
371	147	30	988-989	3-02-99	HR	11677
372	148	30	989	3-02-99	HR	11686
373	149	30	989-990	3-02-99	HR	11861
374	150	30	990-992	3-02-99	HR	11868
375	151	30	992-993	3-02-99	HR	11965
376	152	30	993	3-02-99	HR	12125

Public Law/Resolution		Statutes at Large	Page	Date	Bill No.	
Chapter	Number					
377	153	30	993-995	3-02-99	S	2552
378	154	30	995	3-02-99	S	5352
379	155	30	995	3-02-99	S	5450
380	156	30	995	3-02-99	S	5513
381	157	30	996	3-02-99	HR	84
382	158	30	996-997	3-02-99	HR	431
383	159	30	997	2-02-99	HR	477
384	160	30	997	3-02-99	HR	1079
385	161	30	997-998	3-02-99	HR	1631
386	162	30	998-999	3-02-99	HR	1663
387	163	30	999	3-02-99	HR	1859
388	164	30	999	3-02-99	HR	2598
389	165	30	999-1000	3-02-99	HR	2879
390	166	30	1000	3-02-99	HR	4113
391	167	30	1000-1001	3-02-99	HR	5528
392	168	30	1001-1002	3-02-99	HR	4595
393	169	30	1002	3-02-99	HR	5497
394	170	30	1002	3-02-99	HR	10753
395	171	30	1003	3-02-99	HR	10804
396	172	30	1003	3-02-99	HR	11314
397	173	30	1003	3-02-99	HR	11141
398	174	30	1004	3-02-99	HR	11162
399	175	30	1004	3-02-99	HR	11360
400	176	30	1004	3-02-99	HR	11919
413	177	30	1004-1009	3-03-99	HR	10403
414	178	30	1010	3-03-99	S	5144
415	179	30	1010	3-03-99	HR	1136
416	180	30	1010-1011	3-03-99	HR	1959
417	181	30	1012-1013	3-03-99	HR	2524
418	182	30	1013-1014	3-03-99	HR	11733
419	183	30	1014-1021	3-03-99	HR	11815
420	184	30	1022-1024	3-03-99	HR	12064
421	185	30	1024-1045	3-03-99	HR	12122
422	186	30	1045-1064	3-04-99	HR	11083
423	187	30	1064-1074	3-03-99	HR	12106
424	188	30	1074-1120	3-03-99	HR	12008
425	189	30	1121-1161	3-03-99	HR	11795
426	190	30	1161-1214	3-03-99	HR	4936

Public Law/Resolution		Statutes at Large	Page	Date	Bill No.	
Chapter	Number					
427	191	30	1214-1250	3-03-99	HR	12203
428	192	30	1250-1252	3-03-99	HR	12198
429	193	30	1253-1343	3-03-99	HR	8571
430	194	30	1343-1344	3-03-99	HR	11799
431	195	30	1344-1345	3-03-99	HR	11597
432	196	30	1346	3-03-99	HR	8626
433	197	30	1346	3-03-99	HR	631
434	198	30	1346-1349	3-03-99	HR	12102
435	199	30	1349-1350	3-03-99	HR	10253
436	200	30	1350-1351	3-03-99	HR	11879
437	201	30	1351-1352	3-03-99	HR	9335
438	202	30	1352	3-03-99	HR	8694
439	203	30	1352-1353	3-03-99	HR	500
440	204	30	1353	3-03-99	HR	7343
441	205	30	1354	3-03-99	HR	11178
442	206	30	1354-1355	3-03-99	HR	11882
443	207	30	1355-1356	3-03-99	S	710
444	208	30	1356	3-03-99	S	1056
445	209	30	1356-1358	3-03-99	S	5260
446	210	30	1358-1359	3-03-99	S	5130
447	211	30	1359-1360	3-03-99	S	2675
448	212	30	1360-1361	3-03-99	S	5258
449	213	30	1361-1362	3-03-99	HR	414
450	214	30	1362-1366	3-03-99	S	4852
451	215	30	1366-1368	3-03-99	HR	5428
452	216	30	1368	3-03-99	HR	11160
453	217	30	1368-1372	3-03-99	HR	11916
454	218	30	1372	3-03-99	HR	7271
455	219	30	1372-1373	3-03-99	HR	11712
456	220	30	1373-1376	3-03-99	HR	9428
457	221	30	1376-1377	3-03-99	HR	12184
458	222	30	1377-1378	3-03-99	HR	10294
459	223	30	1379	3-03-99	HR	6359
460	224	30	1379-1380	3-03-99	HR	1055
461	225	30	1380-1383	3-03-99	HR	11629
462	226	30	1383-1384	3-03-99	HR	9760
463	227	30	1384	3-03-99	S	1114

Public Law/Resolution		Statutes at Large	Page	Date	Bill No.
Chapter	Number				
1	1	30	1385	12-20-98	H Res. 311
2	2	30	1385	1-10-99	H Res. 274
3	3	30	1385	1-10-99	H Res. 275
4	4	30	1385-1386	1-10-99	H Res. 299
5	5	30	1386	1-12-99	S Res. 16
6	6	30	1386	1-12-99	S Res. 197
7	7	30	1386	1-12-99	H Res. 313
8	8	30	1387	1-16-99	S Res. 151
9	9	30	1387	1-21-99	H Res. 90
10	10	30	1387	1-24-99	H Res. 338
11	11	30	1387	1-28-99	S Res. 210
12	12	30	1388	1-28-99	S Res. 222
13	13	30	1388	2-09-99	H Res. 344
14	14	30	1388	2-15-99	S Res. 218
15	15	30	1388	2-15-99	S Res. 219
16	16	30	1388-1389	2-20-99	S Res. 245
17	17	30	1389	2-25-99	H Res. 307
18	18	30	1389	2-27-99	S Res. 231
20	19	30	1389	2-28-99	H Res. 339
21	20	30	1390	2-28-99	S Res. 34
22	21	30	1390	2-28-99	S Res. 252
23	22	30	1390	2-28-99	H Res. 358
24	23	30	1390-1391	3-01-99	S Res. 242
25	24	30	1391	3-01-99	S Res. 202
26	25	30	1391	3-01-99	S Res. 239
27	26	30	1391-1392	3-03-99	S Res. 189

PUBLIC ACTS OF THE FIFTY-SIXTH CONGRESS

Public Law/Resolution		Statutes at Large	Page	Date	Bill No.	
Chapter	Number					
1	1	31	1	12-20-99	HR	4152
2	2	31	1-2	1-25-00	S	1484
3	3	31	2	1-27-00	S	2884
4	4	31	2-3	1-30-00	HR	6777
5	5	31	3	1-31-00	S	1933
6	6	31	3	1-31-00	HR	4602
7	7	31	3-4	2-01-00	S	2179
8	8	31	5	2-03-00	S	2431
9	9	31	5	2-07-00	S	2727
10	10	31	5-6	2-07-00	HR	947
11	11	31	6	2-07-00	HR	6272
12	12	31	6-7	2-08-00	HR	5042
13	13	31	7	2-09-00	HR	549
14	14	31	7-27	2-09-00	HR	6237
15	15	31	27	2-10-00	S	734
16	16	31	27	2-10-00	HR	5076
17	17	31	28	2-10-00	HR	6073
18	18	31	28-29	2-13-00	HR	284
19	19	31	29	2-14-00	HR	5066
20	20	31	29	2-14-00	HR	3718
21	21	31	29-30	2-15-00	HR	4000
22	22	31	30-31	2-19-00	HR	5288
23	23	31	31-32	2-20-00	HR	7739
24	24	31	32-33	2-24-00	HR	6267
25	25	31	33	2-26-00	HR	5493
26	26	31	33-34	2-27-00	S	3003
27	27	31	34-35	2-28-00	S	160
28	28	31	35-36	2-28-00	HR	7660
29	29	31	36-37	3-01-00	S	2925
30	30	31	37-38	3-01-00	HR	4473
31	31	31	38-39	3-01-00	HR	5487
33	32	31	39-41	3-02-00	HR	4006
34	33	31	41-42	3-06-00	HR	2477
35	34	31	42	3-08-00	S	3266
36	35	31	42	3-09-00	S	282
37	36	31	43-44	3-09-00	S	1931
38	37	31	44	3-09-00	S	3360
39	38	31	45	3-10-00	HR	7731

PUBLIC ACTS OF THE FIFTY-SIXTH CONGRESS

Public Law/Resolution		Statutes at Large	Page	Date	Bill No.	
Chapter	Number					
41	39	31	45-50	3-14-00	HR	1
45	40	31	50	3-16-00	HR	6767
88	41	31	50	3-23-00	S	2279
89	42	31	50	3-23-00	S	2114
90	43	31	50-51	3-23-00	HR	1040
91	44	31	51	3-24-00	HR	9080
92	45	31	51	3-24-00	S	3138
108	46	31	51-52	3-26-00	HR	2956
110	47	31	52	3-28-00	S	68
111	48	31	52-53	3-28-00	S	2354
112	49	31	53	3-28-00	HR	4008
116	50	31	53-54	3-29-00	S	2882
118	51	31	54-58	3-30-00	HR	9249
120	52	31	58	3-31-00	HR	5067
121	53	21	58	3-31-00	HR	9497
156	54	31	59	4-04-00	S	3207
157	55	31	59	4-04-00	HR	99
158	56	31	59-60	4-04-00	HR	6627
159	57	31	60-71	4-04-00	HR	7941
178	58	31	72	4-05-00	HR	8128
180	59	31	72	4-07-00	S	1475
182	60	31	72-73	4-09-00	HR	5049
183	61	31	73	4-09-00	HR	7649
184	62	31	73	4-09-00	HR	8463
185	63	31	73-74	4-12-00	HR	60
186	64	31	74	4-12-00	HR	9284
187	65	31	74-75	4-12-00	S	2679
188	66	31	75	4-12-00	HR	7939
189	67	31	75	4-12-00	HR	9713
190	68	31	76-77	4-12-00	HR	10311
191	69	31	77-86	4-12-00	HR	8245
192	70	31	86-134	4-17-00	HR	8347
193	71	31	134-135	4-17-00	HR	8876
243	72	31	135-136	4-18-00	HR	1092
244	73	31	136	4-18-00	S	2336
245	74	31	136	4-18-00	HR	65
246	75	31	137	4-18-00	HR	963
250	76	31	137	4-21-00	HR	8063

PUBLIC ACTS OF THE FIFTY-SIXTH CONGRESS

Public Law/Resolution		Statutes at Large	Page	Date	Bill No.	
Chapter	Number					
251	77	31	137-138	4-23-00	HR	6959
252	78	31	138	4-23-00	HR	8466
253	79	31	138-139	4-23-00	HR	10449
254	80	31	139-140	4-23-00	HR	5485
338	81	31	141	4-27-00	S	3465
339	82	31	141-162	4-30-00	S	222
340	83	31	162-163	4-30-00	S	3924
341	84	31	163-165	4-30-00	S	4051
342	85	31	165	4-30-00	HR	4604
343	86	31	165	4-30-00	HR	9566
344	87	31	165-166	5-03-00	HR	6868
345	88	31	166-167	5-04-00	S	2869
346	89	31	167	5-04-00	HR	7945
347	90	31	167-168	5-04-00	HR	8962
348	91	31	168-169	5-04-00	HR	10097
349	92	31	169-170	5-05-00	HR	8585
384	93	31	170	5-07-00	S	3018
385	94	31	170-171	5-09-00	S	1477
386	95	31	171	5-09-00	HR	8188
387	96	31	172	5-09-00	HR	9824
388	97	31	172-174	5-10-00	HR	10310
389	98	31	174	5-10-00	HR	10696
390	99	31	174-175	5-10-00	HR	10279
391	100	31	175-177	5-12-00	S	268
392	101	31	177	5-12-00	S	2366
393	102	31	177-178	5-12-00	S	2559
394	103	31	178	5-12-00	S	3537
469	104	31	178-179	5-14-00	S	2499
479	105	31	179	5-17-00	HR	996
481	106	31	179	5-18-00	HR	8963
482	107	31	180	5-18-00	HR	10780
484	108	31	180	5-19-00	HR	9496
485	109	31	180	5-19-00	HR	9635
486	110	31	180-181	5-21-00	HR	2757
487	111	31	181	5-21-00	HR	3334
489	112	31	181	5-22-00	S	4291
541	113	31	182	5-23-00	HR	92
542	114	31	182	5-23-00	S	906

PUBLIC ACTS OF THE FIFTY-SIXTH CONGRESS

Public Law/Resolution		Statutes at Large	Page	Date	Bill No.	
Chapter	Number					
546	115	31	182-183	5-24-00	HR	7740
549	116	31	183	5-24-00	S	4129
550	117	31	183	5-24-00	HR	969
552	118	31	183-187	5-25-00	HR	9711
553	119	31	187-189	5-25-00	HR	6634
554	120	31	189-190	5-25-00	HR	9559
555	121	31	191-204	5-25-00	HR	10538
556	122	31	204	5-25-00	HR	6876
586	123	31	205-217	5-26-00	HR	8582
587	124	31	217-218	5-26-00	S	124
588	125	31	218	5-26-00	S	4048
589	126	31	218	5-26-00	S	4560
590	127	31	218-219	5-26-00	HR	8369
591	128	31	219	5-26-00	HR	11081
594	129	31	219-221	5-29-00	HR	9879
595	130	31	221	5-29-00	S	2883
598	131	31	221-248	5-31-00	HR	7433
599	132	31	248-249	5-31-00	HR	10740
600	133	31	249	5-31-00	S	4615
601	134	31	249-250	6-01-00	HR	2537
610	135	31	250-251	6-02-00	S	3055
611	136	31	251	6-02-00	HR	6243
612	137	31	251-252	6-02-00	HR	8498
613	138	31	252-261	6-02-00	HR	10301
614	139	31	262	6-04-00	HR	10997
615	140	31	262	6-04-00	HR	11816
619	141	31	262-263	6-04-00	HR	9884
620	142	31	264	6-04-00	HR	11281
621	143	31	264-265	6-04-00	HR	2826
622	144	31	265-266	6-04-00	HR	10812
623	145	31	266	6-04-00	HR	11283
714	146	31	266	6-05-00	S	359
715	147	31	266-267	6-05-00	S	3490
716	148	31	267-270	6-05-00	HR	6250
717	149	31	270	6-05-00	HR	8366
718	150	31	270-274	6-05-00	HR	11650
779	151	31	274	6-06-00	S	3598
780	152	31	274	6-06-00	HR	2864

Public Law/Resolution		Statutes at Large	Page	Date	Bill No.	
Chapter	Number					
1	1	31	725-726	12-07-00	HR	12283
3	2	31	726	12-19-00	S	5076
6	3	31	726	12-21-00	S	5053
8	4	31	727-728	1-04-01	HR	12838
9	5	31	728	1-11-01	HR	13394
10	6	31	729	1-14-01	HR	2955
11	7	31	729	1-14-01	HR	11588
12	8	31	729-730	1-14-01	HR	11213
13	9	31	730-731	1-14-01	HR	12447
75	10	31	731-733	1-15-01	S	2582
92	11	31	733	1-16-01	HR	12395
93	12	31	733-734	1-16-01	HR	12740
101	13	31	734	1-19-01	S	5231
102	14	31	735	1-19-01	HR	12546
103	15	31	735-736	1-19-01	S	2884
105	16	31	736-738	1-22-01	HR	953
106	17	31	738	1-22-01	HR	13274
107	18	31	738	1-22-01	HR	13599
164	19	31	739	1-24-01	HR	10498
166	20	31	740	1-25-01	S	1996
167	21	31	740	1-25-01	S	4816
180	22	31	740	1-26-01	S	5258
181	23	31	741-744	1-26-01	HR	12548
183	24	31	744	1-28-01	S	122
184	25	31	745	1-28-01	S	3252
186	26	31	745	1-31-01	S	3313
189	27	31	745	2-01-01	HR	428
190	28	31	746	2-01-01	HR	4728
191	29	31	746-748	2-01-01	HR	11785
192	30	31	748-758	2-02-01	S	4300
193	31	31	758	2-04-01	S	5337
194	32	31	759	2-04-01	HR	4910
195	33	31	759	2-04-01	HR	12281
199	34	31	759	2-05-01	S	5585
200	35	31	760	2-05-01	S	5583
217	36	31	760-761	2-06-01	HR	8856
218	37	31	761	2-06-01	HR	12899
219	38	31	762	2-06-01	HR	13279

Public Law/Resolution		Statutes at Large	Page	Date	Bill No.	
Chapter	Number					
781	153	31	274	6-06-00	HR	5296
782	154	31	275-276	6-06-00	HR	9679
783	155	31	276-277	6-06-00	HR	10650
784	156	31	277-280	6-06-00	S	2931
785	157	31	280-321	6-06-00	HR	11537
786	158	31	321-552	6-06-00	S	3419
787	159	31	553-554	6-06-00	HR	4468
788	160	31	554	6-06-00	S	41
789	161	31	554-578	6-06-00	HR	9139
790	162	31	578-588	6-06-00	HR	11646
791	163	31	588-645	6-06-00	HR	11212
792	164	31	645-656	6-06-00	HR	11538
793	165	31	656-657	6-06-00	HR	11719
794	166	31	657	6-06-00	HR	2916
795	167	31	657-658	6-06-00	HR	2936
796	168	31	658	6-06-00	HR	5763
797	169	31	658	6-06-00	HR	9388
798	170	31	658	6-06-00	HR	9389
799	171	31	659	6-06-00	HR	10152
800	172	31	659	6-06-00	HR	11214
801	173	31	660	6-06-00	HR	10308
802	174	31	660	6-06-00	HR	10665
803	175	31	660-661	6-06-00	HR	4915
804	176	31	661	6-06-00	HR	6063
805	177	31	662	6-06-00	HR	9510
806	178	31	662-663	6-06-00	HR	3597
807	179	31	664-665	6-06-00	HR	7663
808	180	31	665	6-06-00	HR	11326
809	181	31	665-668	6-06-00	HR	7950
810	182	31	668-671	6-06-00	HR	8665
811	183	31	671	6-06-00	HR	8925
812	184	31	671-672	6-06-00	HR	9827
813	185	31	672-681	6-06-00	S	255
814	186	31	681	6-06-00	S	1746
815	187	31	681	6-06-00	S	2438
816	188	31	682	6-06-00	S	4448
817	189	31	682	6-06-00	S	4532
818	190	31	682	6-06-00	S	3296

PUBLIC ACTS OF THE FIFTY-SIXTH CONGRESS

Public Law/Resolution		Statutes at Large	Page	Date	Bill No.	
Chapter	Number					
819	191	31	682	6-06-00	S	4658
820	192	31	683	6-06-00	S	4075
821	193	31	683	6-06-00	S	4020
822	194	31	684	6-06-00	S	3301
859	195	31	684-707	6-07-00	HR	10450
860	196	31	708	6-07-00	S	3616
861	197	31	708	6-07-00	HR	11599

RESOLUTIONS OF THE FIFTY-SIXTH CONGRESS

Chapter	Number	Statutes at Large	Page	Date	Bill No.	
1	1	31	709	12-16-99	HJR	80
2	2	31	709	1-24-00	S Res.	52
3	3	31	709	1-31-00	S Res.	3
4	4	31	710	1-31-00	HJR	129
5	5	31	710	2-09-00	HJR	6
6	6	31	710	2-10-00	HJR	136
7	7	31	710-711	2-17-00	S Res.	83
8	8	31	711	2-17-99	HJR	77
9	9	31	711	2-23-00	S Res.	55
10	10	31	711-712	3-08-00	HJR	170
11	11	31	712	3-12-00	HJR	119
12	12	31	712	3-16-00	S Res.	75
13	13	31	712	3-19-00	HJR	204
14	14	31	713	3-21-00	S Res.	91
15	15	31	713	3-26-00	HJR	159
16	16	31	713	4-09-00	HJR	216
17	17	31	713-714	4-17-00	S Res.	77
18	18	31	714	4-18-00	S Res.	34
19	19	31	714	4-23-00	S Res.	108
20	20	31	714	4-23-00	S Res.	114
21	21	31	714-715	4-23-00	HJR	235
22	22	31	715	4-30-00	S Res.	10
23	23	31	715-716	5-01-00	S Res.	116
24	24	31	716-717	5-03-00	S Res.	51
25	25	31	717	5-03-00	HJR	168
26	26	31	717	5-14-00	HJR	198
27	27	31	717	5-25-00	HJR	225
28	28	31	718	5-31-00	S Res.	76
29	29	31	718	6-02-00	S Res.	127

RESOLUTIONS OF THE FIFTY-SIXTH CONGRESS

Public Law/Resolution		Statutes at Large	Page	Date	Bi
Chapter	Number				
30	30	31	718	6-02-00	HJR
31	31	31	719	6-04-00	S Re
32	32	31	719	6-06-00	HJR
33	33	31	719	6-06-00	S R
34	34	31	720	6-06-00	S R
35	35	31	720	6-06-00	S R
36	36	31	720	6-06-00	S R
37	37	31	721	6-06-00	S
38	38	31	721-722	6-06-00	S
39	39	31	722	6-06-00	HJ
40	40	31	722	6-06-00	HJ
41	41	31	722	6-07-00	S
42	42	31	723	6-07-00	HJ

PUBLIC ACTS OF THE FIFTY-SIXTH CONGRESS

Public Law/Resolution		Statutes at Large	Page	Date	Bill No.	
Chapter	Number					
342	39	31	762	2-08-01	S	5910
343	40	31	762	2-08-01	S	2871
344	41	31	763	2-08-01	S	5351
345	42	31	763-764	2-08-01	S	5717
346	43	31	764	2-08-01	HR	10921
347	44	31	764-765	2-08-01	HR	11548
348	45	31	765	2-08-01	HR	13399
350	46	31	766	2-11-01	S	3901
351	47	31	766	2-11-01	HR	12513
352	48	31	766	2-11-01	HR	13371
353	49	31	767-774	2-12-01	S	1929
354	50	31	774-781	2-12-01	S	2329
355	51	31	781-783	2-12-01	HR	971
356	52	31	783-784	2-12-01	HR	9595
357	53	31	784-785	2-12-01	HR	11970
358	54	31	785	2-12-01	HR	13491
359	55	31	785	2-12-01	HR	13606
360	56	31	785	2-12-01	HR	10664
361	57	31	786	2-12-01	HR	10967
362	58	31	786-787	2-12-01	HR	12284
363	59	31	787-788	2-12-01	HR	12737
364	60	31	788-789	2-12-01	HR	13255
365	61	31	789-790	2-12-01	HR	13437
370	62	31	790	2-13-01	HR	8814
371	63	31	790	2-15-01	S	5776
372	64	31	790-791	2-15-01	HR	11973
373	65	31	791	2-15-01	HR	12897
374	66	31	791-792	2-15-01	HR	13438
377	67	31	792-793	2-18-01	S	419
378	68	31	793-794	2-18-01	S	5775
379	69	31	794-796	2-18-01	HR	3369
380	70	31	796	2-18-01	HR	5048
381	71	31	796-797	2-18-01	HR	13374
382	72	31	798	2-19-01	HR	13531
383	73	31	798	2-20-01	S	5023
384	74	31	798	2-20-01	S	5364
385	75	31	799	2-20-01	S	5404
386	76	31	799	2-20-01	HR	13633

PUBLIC ACTS OF THE FIFTY-SIXTH CONGRESS

Public Law/Resolution		Statutes at Large	Page	Date	Bill No.	
Chapter	Number					
461	77	31	799–800	2–21–01	HR	13706
463	78	31	800	2–23–01	HR	7840
464	79	31	800	2–23–01	HR	13731
465	80	31	800–801	2–23–01	HR	13782
466	81	31	801	2–23–01	HR	13193
467	82	31	801–802	2–23–01	S	2991
468	83	31	802–803	2–23–01	S	5814
469	84	31	803	2–23–01	HR	6240
470	85	31	804	2–23–01	HR	11716
472	86	31	804	2–25–01	HR	8067
473	87	31	804–805	2–25–01	HR	9154
474	88	31	805–806	2–25–01	HR	10869
475	89	31	806–807	2–25–01	HR	11110
476	90	31	807–808	2–25–01	HR	11111
477	91	31	808–809	2–25–01	HR	13635
478	92	31	809–810	2–25–01	HR	13802
607	93	31	810–811	2–26–01	HR	4742
608	94	31	811–812	2–26–01	HR	5056
613	96	31	812–815	2–27–01	HR	11789
614	96	31	815	2–27–01	HR	12327
615	97	31	816	2–27–01	S	5350
616	98	31	816	2–27–01	HR	10700
619	99	31	816–817	2–28–01	HR	5137
620	100	31	817–818	2–28–01	S	95
621	101	31	818–819	2–28–01	S	6050
622	101	31	819	2–28–01	HR	4718
623	102	31	819–820	2–28–01	HR	12456
668	104	31	821	3–01–01	S	3481
669	105	31	821–822	3–01–01	S	5014
670	106	31	822–846	3–01–01	HR	13575
671	107	31	846	3–01–01	S	3205
672	108	31	846	3–01–01	S	5857
673	109	31	846	3–01–01	S	5925
674	110	31	847–848	3–01–01	HR	9140
675	111	31	848–861	3–01–01	HR	11820
676	112	31	861–873	3–01–01	HR	11821
677	113	31	873–876	3–01–01	HR	13822
678	114	31	876–877	3–01–01	HR	13951

Public Law/Resolution		Statutes at Large	Page	Date	Bill No.	
Chapter	Number					
800	115	31	877-880	3-02-01	S	2799
801	116	31	880-882	3-02-01	HR	4345
802	117	31	882-895	3-02-01	HR	13850
803	118	31	895-910	3-02-01	HR	14017
804	119	31	910-922	3-02-01	HR	12846
805	120	31	922-938	3-02-01	HR	13801
806	121	31	938-950	3-02-01	HR	12394
807	122	31	950	3-02-01	S	4306
808	123	31	950	3-02-01	S	5978
809	124	31	950-951	3-02-01	HR	7571
810	125	31	952	3-02-01	HR	10899
811	126	31	952-953	3-02-01	HR	11161
812	127	31	953-954	3-02-01	HR	12396
813	128	31	954-956	3-02-01	HR	13707
814	129	31	956	3-02-01	HR	13803
815	130	31	956-957	3-02-01	HR	13865
816	131	31	957	3-02-01	HR	13907
817	132	31	957-958	3-02-01	HR	13992
818	133	31	958-959	3-02-01	HR	14144
819	134	31	960	3-02-01	S	3270
830	135	31	960-1009	3-03-01	HR	12291
831	136	31	1010-1058	3-03-01	HR	14236
832	137	31	1058-1085	3-03-01	HR	12904
833	139	31	1085	3-03-01	S	323
834	139	31	1086	3-03-01	S	1632
835	140	31	1086	3-03-01	S	3489
836	141	31	1086-1087	3-03-01	S	4171
837	142	31	1087	3-03-01	S	5022
838	143	31	1087	3-03-01	S	5331
839	144	31	1088	3-03-01	S	5698
840	145	31	1088-1089	3-03-01	S	5935
841	146	31	1089	3-03-01	S	6012
842	147	31	1089-1090	3-03-01	S	6054
843	148	31	1090-1091	3-03-01	HR	8068
844	149	31	1091-1093	3-03-01	HR	11881
845	150	31	1093	3-03-01	HR	12665
846	151	31	1093-1094	3-03-01	HR	12901
847	152	31	1095-1096	3-03-01	HR	13067

PUBLIC ACTS OF THE FIFTY-SIXTH CONGRESS

Public Law/Resolution		Statutes at Large	Page	Date	Bill No.	
Chapter	Number					
848	153	31	1096	3-03-01	HR	13776
849	154	31	1097-1098	3-03-01	HR	13947
850	155	31	1099	3-03-01	HR	14309
851	156	31	1099-1107	3-03-01	HR	13729
852	157	31	1107-1133	3-03-01	HR	13705
853	158	31	1133-1189	3-03-01	HR	14018
854	159	31	1189-1436	3-03-01	HR	9835
855	160	31	1436	3-03-01	S	2866
856	161	31	1436-1437	3-03-01	S	3670
857	162	31	1437	3-03-01	S	4509
858	163	31	1437	3-03-01	S	5484
859	164	31	1438	3-03-01	S	5573
860	165	31	1438-1439	3-03-01	S	5715
861	166	31	1439	3-03-01	S	5943
862	167	31	1439-1440	3-03-01	S	6048
863	168	31	1440	3-03-01	HR	3003
864	169	31	1440-1445	3-03-01	HR	9829
865	170	31	1445-1446	3-03-01	HR	9886
866	171	31	1446	3-03-01	HR	10302
867	172	31	1446-1447	3-03-01	HR	10698
868	173	31	1447	3-03-01	HR	10701
869	174	31	1447	3-03-01	HR	11900
870	175	31	1448	3-03-01	HR	12331
871	176	31	1448-1449	3-03-01	HR	13195
872	177	31	1449-1450	3-03-01	HR	11350
873	178	31	1450-1451	3-03-01	HR	13396
874	179	31	1451-1453	3-03-01	HR	13436
875	180	31	1453	3-03-01	HR	13530
876	181	31	1453-1454	3-03-01	HR	13609
877	182	31	1454-1455	3-03-01	HR	14093
878	183	31	1455-1456	3-03-01	HR	14138
879	184	31	1456-1457	3-03-01	HR	14165
880	185	31	1457	3-03-01	HR	14228
881	186	31	1458	3-03-01	HR	14260

RESOLUTIONS OF THE FIFTY-SIXTH CONGRESS

1	1	31	1459	12-18-00	HJR	281
2	2	31	1459	1-14-01	S Res.	144

RESOLUTIONS OF THE FIFTY-SIXTH CONGRESS

Public Law/Resolution		Statutes at Large	Page	Date	Bill No.	
Chapter	Number					
3	3	31	1459	1-14-01	HJR	101
4	4	31	1460	1-14-01	HJR	277
5	5	31	1460-1461	1-22-01	S Res.	145
7	6	31	1461	2-08-01	S Res.	142
8	7	31	1462	2-23-01	HJR	285
9	8	31	1462	2-23-01	HJR	292
10	9	31	1462	2-28-01	S Res.	157
11	10	31	1462-1463	2-28-01	HJR	74
12	11	31	1463	3-01-01	S Res.	159
13	12	31	1463	3-01-01	S Res.	163
14	13	31	1464	3-02-01	S Res.	164
15	14	31	1464	3-02-01	HJR	249
16	15	31	1464-1465	3-02-01	HJR	259
17	16	31	1465	3-02-01	HJR	306
18	17	31	1465	3-03-01	S Res.	115
19	18	31	1465-1466	3-03-01	S Res.	158

PUBLIC ACTS OF THE FIFTY-SEVENTH CONGRESS

Public Law/Resolution		Statutes at Large	Page	Date	Bill No.	
Chapter	Number					
1	1	32	1	12-14-01	S	632
2	2	32	1	1-13-02	HR	7471
3	3	32	2	1-22-02	S	2044
5	4	32	2	1-31-02	HR	9342
6	5	32	2	1-31-02	HR	10368
7	6	32	3	2-04-02	HR	8759
15	7	32	3-4	2-07-02	HR	2008
16	8	32	4-5	2-11-02	S	74
17	9	32	5-33	2-14-02	HR	9315
18	10	32	33	2-14-02	S	1747
19	11	32	33-34	2-14-02	HR	4372
20	12	32	34	2-14-02	HR	8761
22	13	32	34	2-15-02	HR	10076
23	14	32	34-35	2-15-02	S	946
24	15	32	35	2-19-02	S	1970
25	16	32	35	2-21-02	S	910
26	17	32	36-37	2-21-02	S	1165
27	18	32	37	2-21-02	HR	11470
28	19	32	37-38	2-24-02	S	73
29	20	32	38-39	2-24-02	S	1838
30	21	32	40-41	2-24-02	S	1839
31	22	32	41	2-24-02	S	651
32	23	32	41-42	2-26-02	S	650
33	24	32	42	2-26-02	HR	10780
34	25	32	43	2-28-02	S	88
134	26	32	43-51	2-28-02	HR	3104
139	27	32	51-53	3-06-02	HR	10308
140	28	32	54-55	3-08-02	HR	5833
141	29	32	55-56	3-10-02	S	2977
142	30	32	56-57	3-10-02	S	3107
143	31	32	58	3-10-02	HR	61
144	32	32	58	3-10-02	HR	10070
145	33	32	58-60	3-10-02	HR	5801
146	34	32	60-61	3-10-02	HR	2678
147	35	32	62	3-10-02	HR	8581
179	36	32	63	3-11-02	HR	4748
180	37	32	63	3-11-02	HR	7933
181	38	32	63	3-11-02	HR	8336

PUBLIC ACTS OF THE FIFTY-SEVENTH CONGRESS

Public Law/Resolution		Statutes at Large	Page	Date	Bill No.	
Chapter	Number					
182	39	32	63-64	3-11-02	HR	202
183	40	32	64-70	3-11-02	HR	11611
216	41	32	70	3-14-02	S	646
217	42	32	70	3-14-02	S	3090
218	43	32	70	3-14-02	HR	199
221	44	32	71-72	3-18-02	HR	4381
222	45	32	72	3-18-02	HR	7458
223	46	32	72-73	3-18-02	HR	9332
224	47	32	73-74	3-18-02	HR	10305
227	48	32	74	3-20-02	HR	11306
228	49	32	74	3-20-02	HR	6300
229	50	32	74-75	3-20-02	HR	11241
235	51	32	75	3-21-02	S	3312
236	52	32	75	3-21-02	HR	1980
237	53	32	75	3-21-02	HR	11719
272	54	32	76-88	3-22-02	HR	11471
273	55	32	88	3-22-02	HR	11474
275	56	32	89-90	3-24-02	S	3261
276	57	32	90	3-24-02	S	3267
277	58	32	90-91	3-24-02	HR	3148
278	59	32	91-92	3-26-02	HR	4607
385	60	32	93	3-29-02	S	3865
387	61	32	93	3-31-02	HR	3136
414	62	32	93-94	4-07-02	HR	13360
415	63	32	94-95	4-11-02	S	3231
416	64	32	95	4-11-02	HR	6196
417	65	32	95	4-11-02	HR	12095
418	66	32	95-96	4-11-02	HR	11053
500	67	32	96-99	4-12-02	HR	10530
501	68	32	100-101	4-12-02	S	1025
502	69	32	101	4-12-02	HR	10363
503	70	32	102	4-12-02	S	176
504	71	32	102-104	4-15-02	S	3513
505	72	32	104-105	4-15-02	HR	11409
506	73	32	105	4-15-02	S	2442
507	74	32	106	4-15-02	HR	3084
508	75	32	106	4-15-02	HR	184
530	76	32	106	4-17-02	S	1178

PUBLIC ACTS OF THE FIFTY-SEVENTH CONGRESS

Public Law/Resolution		Statutes at Large	Page	Date	Bill No.	
Chapter	Number					
562	77	32	107	4-18-02	HR	7675
563	78	32	107-118	4-21-02	HR	11354
585	79	32	118	4-22-02	HR	13627
586	80	32	119-120	4-23-02	HR	12452
588	81	32	120	4-24-02	S	4798
592	82	32	120	4-26-02	HR	12536
594	83	32	120-171	4-28-02	HR	10847
595	84	32	171-172	4-28-02	S	3449
596	85	32	172	4-28-02	HR	11636
637	86	32	172-173	4-29-02	S	2479
638	87	32	173-175	4-29-02	S	5046
639	88	32	175	4-29-02	S	305
640	89	32	176	4-29-02	HR	11096
641	90	32	176-177	4-29-02	HR	13031
642	91	32	177-178	4-29-02	HR	13819
669	92	32	178-179	4-30-02	HR	2062
670	93	32	180	4-30-02	HR	12093
671	94	32	181	4-30-02	HR	12498
672	95	32	181-183	4-30-02	HR	12867
673	96	32	183	4-30-02	S	3663
675	97	32	184	5-01-02	S	4148
679	98	32	184-185	5-02-02	S	715
680	99	32	185-186	5-03-02	S	4339
681	100	32	187	5-03-02	HR	11839
682	101	32	187-188	5-03-02	HR	12938
683	102	32	188-189	5-03-02	HR	13025
684	103	32	189-190	5-03-02	HR	13575
778	104	32	190	5-07-02	S	3361
779	105	32	190-191	5-07-02	S	4768
780	106	32	191	5-07-02	HR	1964
781	107	32	192-193	5-07-02	HR	13246
782	108	32	193	5-07-02	S	4932
783	109	32	193	5-09-02	S	4647
784	110	32	193-197	5-09-02	HR	9206
785	111	32	197-198	5-09-02	S	5105
787	112	32	198	5-13-02	S	5736
788	113	32	198	5-14-02	S	2632
789	114	32	198-199	5-14-02	S	4992

PUBLIC ACTS OF THE FIFTY-SEVENTH CONGRESS

Public Law/Resolution		Statutes at Large	Page	Date	Bill No.	
Chapter	Number					
790	115	32	199	5-14-02	S	5387
792	116	32	199	5-16-02	HR	13996
816	117	32	200	5-19-02	HR	53
817	118	32	200-201	5-19-02	HR	13076
818	119	32	201-202	5-20-02	HR	13288
819	120	32	202	5-22-02	S	3439
820	121	32	202-203	5-22-02	HR	4393
821	122	32	203-204	5-22-02	HR	9037
823	123	32	204-207	5-23-02	S	1295
887	124	32	207-245	5-27-02	HR	8587
888	125	32	245-277	5-27-02	HR	11353
889	126	32	277	5-28-02	S	89
890	127	32	277-280	5-28-02	S	2782
891	128	32	280-281	5-28-02	S	5406
941	129	32	282	5-29-02	S	593
942	130	32	282	5-31-02	S	1464
943	131	32	282-283	5-31-02	S	3129
944	132	32	283	5-31-02	S	3666
945	133	32	283	5-31-02	S	3908
946	134	32	284	5-31-02	S	4264
980	135	32	284	6-02-02	S	3208
981	136	32	284-285	6-02-02	HR	14589
983	137	32	285	6-03-02	HR	10995
984	138	32	285	6-03-02	HR	13168
985	139	32	286-303	6-03-02	HR	13895
986	140	32	303-304	6-03-02	HR	14189
987	141	32	304	6-03-02	HR	10144
989	142	32	304	6-04-02	S	2276
1030	143	32	304-305	6-05-02	HR	8752
1032	144	32	305	6-06-02	S	2510
1033	145	32	305-310	6-06-02	HR	13359
1036	146	32	310-327	6-06-02	HR	14018
1037	147	32	327-328	6-07-02	HR	11535
1071	148	32	329	6-09-02	S	312
1073	149	32	329	6-10-02	S	259
1074	150	32	329-330	6-10-02	HR	12085
1076	151	32	330	6-13-02	S	3800
1077	152	32	330	6-13-02	HR	7034

Public Law/Resolution		Statutes at Large	Page	Date	Bill No.	
Chapter	Number					
1078	153	32	330	6-13-02	HR	8736
1079	154	32	331-384	6-13-02	HR	12346
1080	155	32	384	6-13-02	HR	12796
1081	156	32	384-385	6-13-02	HR	1992
1082	157	32	385-386	6-13-02	HR	11599
1088	158	32	386	6-14-02	HR	8129
1089	159	32	386-387	6-14-02	HR	12797
1090	160	32	387	6-14-02	HR	14380
1093	161	32	388-390	6-17-02	S	3057
1121	162	32	390-391	6-18-02	S	4777
1122	163	32	391-392	6-18-02	S	5062
1123	164	32	392	6-18-02	HR	11657
1135	165	32	392-393	6-19-02	HR	9334
1136	166	32	393-395	6-20-02	HR	12865
1137	167	32	395	6-21-02	S	2769
1138	168	32	396	6-21-02	S	4769
1139	169	32	396-397	6-21-02	S	6030
1140	170	32	397-398	6-21-02	HR	14411
1151	171	32	398	6-23-02	S	282
1154	172	32	398	6-24-02	S	5906
1155	173	32	398-399	6-24-02	HR	11725
1156	174	32	399-400	6-27-02	S	640
1157	175	32	400-404	6-27-02	S	4284
1158	176	32	405	6-27-02	HR	4636
1159	177	32	405-406	6-27-02	HR	10299
1160	178	32	406-407	6-27-02	HR	13204
1161	179	32	407-408	6-27-02	HR	15004
1299	180	32	408-409	6-28-02	S	6270
1300	181	32	409-419	6-28-02	HR	13676
1301	182	32	419-481	6-28-02	HR	13123
1302	183	32	481-484	6-28-02	HR	3110
1303	184	32	484	6-28-02	S	1026
1304	185	32	484	6-28-02	S	2848
1305	186	32	485	6-28-02	S	3375
1306	187	32	485	6-28-02	S	3651
1307	188	32	485-486	6-28-02	S	3746
1308	189	32	486	6-28-02	S	5269
1309	190	32	486-491	6-28-02	HR	3641

PUBLIC ACTS OF THE FIFTY-SEVENTH CONGRESS

Public Law/Resolution		Statutes at Large	Page	Date	Bill No.	
Chapter	Number					
1310	191	32	491	6-28-02	HR	10933
1311	192	32	492	6-28-02	HR	11019
1312	193	32	492	6-28-02	HR	12097
1313	194	32	492-493	6-28-02	HR	14111
1314	195	32	493-495	6-28-02	HR	14247
1315	196	32	496-497	6-28-02	HR	14691
1316	197	32	497	6-28-02	HR	14802
1321	198	32	497-499	6-30-02	S	4611
1322	199	32	499-500	6-30-02	S	4776
1323	200	32	500-505	6-30-02	S	4923
1324	201	32	505	6-30-02	S	5434
1325	202	32	506	6-30-02	S	6178
1326	203	32	506	6-30-02	HR	4556
1327	204	32	506-507	6-30-02	HR	6570
1328	205	32	507-520	6-30-02	HR	12804
1329	206	32	520-546	6-30-02	S	493
1330	207	32	546	6-30-02	S	4450
1331	208	32	546-547	6-30-02	S	4762
1332	209	32	547-548	6-30-02	S	4792
1333	210	32	548	6-30-02	S	5383
1334	211	32	548	6-30-02	S	6091
1335	212	32	549	6-30-02	HR	2063
1336	213	32	549	6-30-02	HR	2066
1337	214	32	549-550	6-30-02	HR	8586
1338	215	32	550-551	6-30-02	HR	12205
1339	216	32	551-552	6-30-02	HR	12648
1351	217	32	552-590	7-01-02	HR	15108
1352	218	32	590-629	7-01-02	HR	14019
1353	219	32	629	7-01-02	HR	97
1354	220	32	629-630	7-01-02	HR	2494
1355	221	32	630-631	7-01-02	HR	5809
1356	222	32	631-632	7-01-02	HR	8327
1357	223	32	632	7-01-02	HR	9960
1358	224	32	632-635	7-01-02	HR	11400
1359	225	32	636	7-01-02	HR	11987
1360	226	32	636	7-01-02	HR	12086
1361	227	32	636-641	7-01-02	HR	12597
1362	228	32	641-657	7-01-02	HR	13172

PUBLIC ACTS OF THE FIFTY-SEVENTH CONGRESS

Public Law/Resolution		Statutes at Large	Page	Date	Bill No.	
Chapter	Number					
1363	229	32	657	7-01-02	HR	13875
1364	230	32	658-659	7-01-02	HR	14082
1365	231	32	660-661	7-01-02	HR	15003
1366	232	32	661	7-01-02	HR	15270
1367	233	32	661-662	7-01-02	HR	11656
1368	234	32	662-691	7-01-02	HR	14046
1369	235	32	691-712	7-01-02	S	2295
1370	236	32	712-714	7-01-02	S	2162
1371	237	32	714-715	7-01-02	S	3896
1372	238	32	715	7-01-02	S	4139
1373	239	32	715	7-01-02	S	4546
1374	240	32	716	7-01-02	S	4815
1375	241	32	716-727	7-01-02	S	5956
1376	242	32	727-728	7-01-02	S	6016
1377	243	32	728	7-01-02	S	6148
1378	244	32	728-729	7-01-02	S	6196
1379	245	32	730	7-01-02	HR	4346
1380	246	32	730	7-01-02	HR	9501
1381	247	32	730	7-01-02	HR	12702
1382	248	32	731	7-01-02	HR	12805
1383	249	32	731-732	7-01-02	HR	14244
1384	250	32	732	7-01-02	HR	15257
1385	251	32	732-733	7-01-02	HR	15258
1386	252	32	733	7-01-02	HR	11573

RESOLUTIONS OF THE FIFTY-SEVENTH CONGRESS

1	1	32	734	12-06-01	HJR	36
2	2	32	734-735	12-17-01	HJR	76
3	3	32	735	1-08-02	SJR	22
4	4	32	735	1-21-02	SJR	15
5	5	32	735	2-07-02	SJR	49
6	6	32	736	2-21-02	HJR	131
7	7	32	736	2-26-02	HJR	88
8	8	32	737	3-12-02	HJR	106
9	9	32	737	3-17-02	SJR	65
10	10	32	737	3-21-02	HJR	161
11	11	32	737-738	3-21-02	HJR	162
12	12	32	738	3-28-02	SJR	21

RESOLUTIONS OF THE FIFTY-SEVENTH CONGRESS

Public Law/Resolution		Statutes at Large	Page	Date	Bill No.	
Chapter	Number					
13	13	32	738	3-29-02	HJR	171
14	14	32	738	4-15-02	HJR	173
15	15	32	739	4-21-02	HJR	155
16	16	32	739	4-23-02	SJR	56
17	17	32	739	4-29-02	SJR	80
18	18	32	740	4-29-02	HJR	180
19	19	32	740	5-03-02	HJR	61
20	20	32	740	5-13-02	HJR	177
21	21	32	741	5-15-02	HJR	189
22	22	32	741	5-16-02	SJR	74
23	23	32	741-742	5-19-02	SJR	82
24	24	32	742	5-27-02	SJR	99
25	25	32	742	5-27-02	HJR	192
26	26	32	742	5-28-02	SJR	46
27	27	32	743	6-02-02	SJR	87
28	28	32	743	6-05-02	SJR	91
29	29	32	743	6-05-02	HJR	113
30	30	32	743-744	6-06-02	HJR	172
31	31	32	744-745	6-19-02	SJR	105
32	32	32	745	6-23-02	SJR	100
33	33	32	745	6-24-02	SJR	92
34	34	32	745	6-24-02	HJR	200
35	35	32	746	6-28-02	HJR	103
36	36	32	746	6-30-02	SJR	103
37	37	32	746-747	6-30-02	SJR	111
38	38	32	747	6-30-02	SJR	118
39	39	32	747	6-30-02	HJR	6
40	40	32	747-748	6-30-02	HJR	182
41	41	32	748-749	6-30-02	HJR	198
42	42	32	750	7-01-02	SJR	8
43	43	32	750	7-01-02	SJR	23
44	44	32	751	7-01-02	SJR	113
45	45	32	751	7-01-02	SJR	120
46	46	32	751	7-01-02	SJR	130
47	47	32	751	7-01-02	HJR	210

PUBLIC ACTS OF THE FIFTY-SEVENTH CONGRESS

Public Law/Resolution		Statutes at Large	Page	Date	Bill No.	
Chapter	Number					
1	1	32	753	12-15-02	HR	15794
2	2	32	753	12-16-02	S	215
3	3	32	754-755	12-17-02	S	6070
4	4	32	756	12-18-02	HR	15140
5	5	32	756-757	12-18-02	S	4204
7	6	32	757	12-19-02	HR	619
9	7	32	758	12-22-02	HR	15372
10	8	32	758-759	12-22-02	HR	16057
11	9	32	760	12-23-02	HR	14801
12	10	32	760-761	12-23-02	HR	15445
13	11	32	761-762	12-23-02	HR	15593
58	12	32	762-763	1-08-03	S	911
59	13	32	764	1-08-03	S	6399
61	14	32	764-765	1-09-03	S	3083
62	15	32	765	1-09-03	S	257
63	16	32	765-766	1-09-03	S	6138
87	17	32	766	1-10-03	HR	15605
88	18	32	766-767	1-10-03	HR	15606
89	19	32	767	1-10-03	S	4617
90	20	32	767-768	1-12-03	S	1833
91	21	32	768-769	1-12-03	S	4419
92	22	32	770	1-12-03	S	4355
133	23	32	770	1-13-03	S	1099
134	24	32	770	1-13-03	HR	179
186	25	32	770-771	1-14-03	S	2210
187	26	32	771	1-14-03	S	6439
188	27	32	772-773	1-15-03	S	6119
189	28	32	773	1-15-03	HR	16649
190	29	32	773	1-15-03	S	1359
192	30	32	773	1-16-03	S	4616
194	31	32	774	1-20-03	HR	16642
195	32	32	774-775	1-21-03	HR	16066
196	33	32	775-780	1-21-03	HR	15345
197	34	32	780	1-22-03	HR	15006
332	35	32	780-781	1-26-03	S	6216
333	36	32	781-783	1-29-03	HR	10522
334	37	32	783	1-30-03	HR	15510
335	38	32	784	1-30-03	HR	14839

PUBLIC ACTS OF THE FIFTY-SEVENTH CONGRESS

Public Law/Resolution		Statutes at Large	Page	Date	Bill No.	
Chapter	Number					
336	39	32	784-785	1-30-03	HR	15066
337	40	32	785	1-30-03	HR	15506
338	41	32	786	1-30-03	S	2296
339	42	32	786-788	1-30-03	S	6333
340	43	32	788	1-30-03	HR	15708
342	44	32	788-789	1-31-03	S	3243
343	45	32	789-790	1-31-03	S	4221
344	46	32	790-791	1-31-03	HR	7664
345	47	32	791	1-31-03	S	5316
346	48	32	791	1-31-03	S	5914
349	49	32	791-792	2-02-03	HR	15922
350	50	32	792-793	2-02-03	S	3512
351	51	32	793	2-02-03	HR	10300
397	52	32	793-794	2-03-03	HR	15711
398	53	32	794	2-03-03	S	6595
399	54	32	795	2-03-03	HR	10698
400	55	32	795	2-03-03	HR	16333
402	56	32	795	2-04-03	S	6461
482	57	32	796	2-05-03	S	3317
483	58	32	796	2-05-03	S	5329
484	59	32	796	2-05-03	S	5891
485	60	32	796	2-05-03	S	6034
486	61	32	797	2-05-03	S	6104
487	62	32	797-801	2-05-03	HR	13679
512	63	32	801-802	2-07-03	S	6446
513	64	32	802-803	2-07-03	S	7063
514	65	32	803	2-07-03	HR	159
515	66	32	804	2-07-03	HR	5756
516	67	32	804-805	2-07-03	HR	9360
517	68	32	805	2-07-03	HR	16099
518	69	32	805	2-07-03	S	5381
527	70	32	805	2-09-03	HR	16724
528	71	32	806	2-09-03	S	4722
529	72	32	806-807	2-09-03	S	7124
530	73	32	807-820	2-09-03	HR	16604
531	74	32	820	2-09-03	S	6278
532	75	32	820	2-09-03	HR	16330
533	76	32	820-821	2-09-03	HR	16651

PUBLIC ACTS OF THE FIFTY-SEVENTH CONGRESS

Public Law/Resolution		Statutes at Large	Page	Date	Bill No.	
Chapter	Number					
537	77	32	821	2-10-03	S	4222
538	78	32	821-822	2-10-03	HR	9503
539	79	32	822	2-10-03	S	2450
542	80	32	822	2-11-03	S	5212
543	81	32	822-823	2-11-03	S	5505
544	82	32	823	2-11-03	S	6773
545	83	32	824	2-11-03	HR	14899
546	84	32	824-825	2-12-03	S	661
547	85	32	825	2-12-03	S	3287
548	86	32	825	2-12-03	HR	15198
552	87	32	825-830	2-14-03	S	569
553	88	32	830-831	2-14-03	HR	15449
554	89	32	832-833	2-16-03	HR	14512
555	90	32	833	2-16-03	HR	16334
560	91	32	833-834	2-18-03	S	6961
561	92	32	834-836	2-18-03	S	7159
562	93	32	836-837	2-18-03	S	7185
563	94	32	837-838	2-18-03	S	7226
564	95	32	838	2-18-03	HR	7
565	96	32	839	2-18-03	HR	16602
566	97	32	839	2-18-03	HR	16646
567	98	32	839-840	2-18-03	HR	16975
568	99	32	840-841	2-18-03	HR	12952
569	100	32	841	2-18-03	HR	16731
706	101	32	841	2-19-03	S	149
707	102	32	841-847	2-19-03	S	5678
708	103	32	847-849	2-19-03	S	7053
709	104	32	849	2-19-03	HR	7642
710	105	32	849	2-19-03	HR	14047
745	106	32	850	2-21-03	S	4577
746	107	32	850	2-21-03	S	7245
747	108	32	850-851	2-21-03	HR	15767
748	109	32	852	2-21-03	HR	16915
749	110	32	852-853	2-23-03	HR	14764
750	111	32	853	2-24-03	S	265
751	112	32	853	2-24-03	S	1905
752	113	32	853	2-24-03	S	7043
753	114	32	854	2-24-03	S	7363

Public Law/Resolution		Statutes at Large	Page	Date	Bill No.	
Chapter	Number					
755	115	32	854-906	2-25-03	HR	16021
756	116	32	907	2-25-03	S	7288
757	117	32	907	2-25-03	S	6968
852	118	32	907	2-27-03	S	6515
853	119	32	908	2-27-03	S	7223
854	120	32	908	2-27-03	HR	16
855	121	32	908-909	2-27-03	HR	17192
856	122	32	909-918	2-28-03	S	4825
857	123	32	918-920	2-28-03	HR	7648
858	124	32	920-921	2-28-03	HR	12141
859	125	32	921	2-28-03	HR	15595
860	126	32	921-923	2-28-03	HR	17052
970	127	32	923-924	3-02-03	S	6525
971	128	32	924-925	3-02-03	HR	16509
972	129	32	925	3-02-03	HR	16909
973	130	32	926	3-02-03	HR	17204
974	131	32	926-927	3-02-03	HR	17088
975	132	32	927-943	3-02-03	HR	16567
976	133	32	943-944	3-02-03	S	3560
977	134	32	944	3-02-03	S	4850
978	135	32	944-952	3-02-03	S	6139
979	136	32	952	3-02-03	HR	3100
980	137	32	952-955	3-02-03	HR	15520
981	138	32	955	3-02-03	HR	15985
982	139	32	955	3-02-03	HR	16885
990	140	32	955-956	3-02-03	S	5437
991	141	32	956	3-03-03	HR	13605
992	142	32	956-981	3-03-03	HR	16842
993	143	32	982	3-03-03	HR	14384
994	144	32	982-1011	3-03-03	HR	15804
995	145	32	1011-1022	3-03-03	HR	16970
996	146	32	1022	3-03-03	S	6895
997	147	32	1022-1023	3-03-03	HR	14050
998	148	32	1023-1024	3-03-03	HR	16656
999	149	32	1024	3-03-03	HR	16069
1000	150	32	1024-1028	3-03-03	HR	17046
1001	151	32	1028	3-03-03	S	7425
1002	152	32	1028-1030	3-03-03	HR	12098

PUBLIC ACTS OF THE FIFTY-SEVENTH CONGRESS

Public Law/Resolution		Statutes at Large	Page	Date	Bill No.	
Chapter	Number					
1003	153	32	1030	3-03-03	HR	15243
1004	154	32	1030	3-03-03	HR	16138
1005	155	32	1031	3-03-03	HR	16573
1006	156	32	1031-1082	3-03-03	HR	17493
1007	157	32	1083-1147	3-03-03	HR	17202
1008	158	32	1147-1165	3-03-03	HR	16910
1009	159	32	1165-1176	3-03-03	HR	16990
1010	160	32	1177-1203	3-03-03	HR	17288
1011	161	32	1203-1213	3-03-03	S	7414
1012	162	32	1213-1222	3-03-03	HR	12199
1013	163	32	1222-1223	3-03-03	HR	15802
1014	164	32	1223	3-03-03	HR	7659
1015	165	32	1223-1224	3-03-03	HR	13075
1016	166	32	1224	3-03-03	HR	15155
1017	167	32	1224	3-03-03	HR	15799
1018	168	32	1225	3-03-03	HR	16881
1019	169	32	1225-1227	3-03-03	HR	17085
1020	170	32	1227-1228	3-03-03	S	7307
1021	171	32	1228	3-03-03	S	3522

RESOLUTIONS OF THE FIFTY-SEVENTH CONGRESS

1	1	32	1229	12-17-02	HJR	227
2	2	32	1229	1-12-03	SJR	57
3	3	32	1229	1-30-03	HJR	16
4	4	32	1230	2-02-03	HJR	216
5	5	32	1230	2-07-03	SJR	146
6	6	32	1230	2-10-03	SJR	156
7	7	32	1231	2-11-03	HJR	184
8	8	32	1231	2-21-03	SJR	108
9	9	32	1231-1232	2-24-03	SJR	148
10	10	32	1232	2-27-03	SJR	159

Volume I

Ch. 42.	1 Stat	372

Ch. 47.	1 Stat	376

Note: S 16 This bill number appears twice in the House Journal, but the subject matter is different for each one.

Volume 2

Ch. 8.	2 Stat	453

Note: HR 26 This bill number appears twice in the House Journal, the subject matter in this case is related.

Ch. 66.	2 Stat	499

Note: S 1a and S 1b appears in the House Journal but the subject matter differs.

Volume 3

Ch. 1.	3 Stat	88

Note: This bill number HR 197b appears in the House Journal.

Ch. 65.	3 Stat	427

Note: In the House Journal S 14 2d is the number.

Ch. 134.	3 Stat	607

Note: The bill number HR 145b as it appears in the House Journal.

Volume 4

Ch. 62.	4 Stat	239

Note: S 53 a appears like this in the House Journal.

Ch. 93.	4 Stat	242

Note: S 52 b appears like this in the House Journal.

Ch. 2.	4 Stat	668

Note: HJR 15b appears like this in the House Journal.

<u>Volume 5</u>

All asterisks are for private laws, where the distinction was
unclear, therefore several private (sic) are printed with public
laws. This pattern will occur throughout the remaining of this
text.

In the text of the House and Senate Journals H. Res. and S.
Res. are referred to as Joint Resolutions, hence they are joint
resolutions which requires favorable action by both chambers of
Congress to become a law.

<u>Volume 9</u>

All asterisks are for private laws and resolutions.

<u>Volume 10</u>

All asterisks are for private laws and resolutions.

<u>Volume 11</u>

All asterisks are for private laws and resolutions.

<u>Volume 12</u>

All asterisks are for private laws and resolutions.

<u>Volume 13</u>

Asterisks indicate the numbering of a law or bill (1/2) and
H. Res. 170 which passed both chambers.

<u>Volume 14</u>

" None "

<u>Volume 15</u>

" None "

<u>Volume 16</u>

Asterisks are for private laws.

<u>Volume 17</u>

Asterisks are for private laws that are printed with
the public laws.

<u>Volume 18</u>

Asterisks are for private laws.

<u>Volume 19</u>

Asterisks are for private laws.

Volume 20

    Asterisks are for private laws.

Volume 21

    " None "

Volume 22

    Asterisks indicate a resolution that passed.

Volume 23

    " None "

Volume 24

    Asterisks indicate that a resolution was passed.

Volume 25

    " None "

Volume 26

    " None "

Volume 27

    " None "

Volume 28

    " None "

Volume 29

    " None "

Volume 30

    " None "

Volume 31

    " None "

Volume 32

    " None "

Tables

U. S. Statutes at Large

Congress, session and dates

Volume 1

    1st Congress, 1st session; March 4, 1789 - September 29, 1789
               2nd session; January 4, 1790 - August 12, 1790
               3rd session; December 6, 1790 - March 3, 1791

    2nd Congress, 1st session; October 24, 1791 - May 8, 1792
               2nd session; November 5, 1792 - March 2, 1793

    3rd Congress, 1st session; December 2, 1793 - June 9, 1794
               2nd session; November 3, 1794 - March 3, 1795

    4th Congress, 1st session; December 7, 1795 - June 1, 1796
               2nd session; December 5, 1796 - March 3, 1797

    5th Congress, 1st session; May 15, 1797 - July 10, 1797
               2nd session; November 13, 1797 - July 16, 1798
               3rd session; December 3, 1798 - March 3, 1799

Volume 2

    6th Congress, 1st session; December 2, 1799 - May 14, 1800
               2nd session; November 17, 1800 - March 3, 1801

    7th Congress, 1st session; December 7, 1801 - May 3, 1802
               2nd session; December 6, 1802 - March 3, 1803

    8th Congress, 1st session; October 17, 1803 - March 27, 1804
               2nd session; November 5, 1804 - March 3, 1805

    9th Congress, 1st session; December 2, 1805 - April 21, 1806
               2nd session; December 1, 1806 - March 3, 1807

    10th Congress, 1st session; October 26, 1807 - April 25, 1808
               2nd session; November 7, 1808 - March 3, 1809

    11th Congress, 1st session; May 22, 1809 - June 28, 1809
               2nd session; November 27, 1809 - May 1, 1810
               3rd session; December 3, 1810 - March 3, 1811

    12th Congress, 1st session; November 4, 1811 - July 6, 1812
               2nd session; November 2, 1812 - March 3, 1813

Volume 3

13th Congress, 1st session; May 24, 1813 - August 2, 1813
            2nd session; December 6, 1813 - April 18, 1814
            3rd session; September 19, 1814 - March 3, 1815

14th Congress, 1st session; December 4, 1815 - April 30, 1816
            2nd session; December 2, 1816 - March 3, 1817

15th Congress, 1st session; December 1, 1817 - April 20, 1818
            2nd session; November 16, 1818 - March 3, 1819

16th Congress, 1st session; December 6, 1819 - May 15, 1820
            2nd session; November 13, 1820 - March 3, 1821

17th Congress, 1st session; December 3, 1821 - May 8, 1822
            2nd session; December 2, 1822 - March 3, 1823

Volume 4

18th Congress, 1st session; December 1, 1823 - May 27, 1824
            2nd session; December 6, 1824 - March 3, 1825

19th Congress, 1st session; December 5, 1825 - May 22, 1826
            2nd session; December 4, 1826 - March 3, 1827

20th Congress, 1st session; December 3, 1827 - May 26, 1828
            2nd session; December 1, 1828 - March 3, 1829

21st Congress, 1st session; December 7, 1829 - May 31, 1830
            2nd session; December 6, 1830 - March 3, 1831

22nd Congress, 1st session; December 5, 1831 - July 16, 1832
            2nd session; December 3, 1832 - March 2, 1833

23rd Congress, 1st session; December 2, 1833 - June 30, 1834
            2nd session; December 1, 1834 - March 3, 1835

Volume 5

24th Congress, 1st session; December 7, 1835 - July 4, 1836
            2nd session; December 5, 1836 - March 3, 1837

25th Congress, 1st session; September 4, 1837 - October 16,1837
            2nd session; December 4, 1837 - July 9, 1838
            3rd session; December 3, 1838 - March 3, 1839

26th Congress, 1st session; December 2, 1839 - July 21, 1840
            2nd session; December 7, 1840 - March 3, 1841

27th Congress, 1st session; May 31, 1841 - September 13, 1841
            2nd session; December 6, 1841 - August 31, 1842
            3rd session; December 5, 1842 - March 3, 1843

28th Congress, 1st session; December 4, 1843 - June 17, 1844
            2nd session; December 2, 1844 - March 3, 1845

Volume 6

1st to 28th Congress, 1780-1845; Private Acts

Volume 7

Treaties, 1778-1845; Indian Tribes

Volume 8

Treaties, 1778-1845; Between the United States and Foreign Nations

Volume 9

29th Congress, 1st session; December 1, 1845 - August 10, 1846
              2nd session; December 7, 1846 - March 3, 1847

30th Congress, 1st session; December 6, 1847 - August 14, 1848
              2nd session; December 4, 1848 - March 3, 1849

31st Congress, 1st session; December 3, 1849 - September 30,1850
              2nd session; December 2, 1850 - March 3, 1851

Volume 10

32nd Congress, 1st session; December 1, 1851 - August 31, 1852
              2nd session; December 6, 1852 - March 3, 1853

33rd Congress, 1st session; December 5, 1853 - August 7, 1854
              2nd session; December 4, 1854 - March 3, 1855

Volume 11

34th Congress, 1st session; December 3, 1855 - August 18, 1856
              2nd session; August 21, 1856 - August 30, 1856
              3rd session; December 1, 1856 - March 3, 1857

35th Congress, 1st session; December 7, 1857 - June 14, 1858
              2nd session; December 6, 1858 - March 3, 1859

Volume 12

36th Congress, 1st session; December 5, 1859 - June 25, 1860
              2nd session; December 3, 1860 - March 3, 1861

37th Congress, 1st session; July 4, 1861 - August 6, 1861
              2nd session; December 2, 1861 - July 17, 1862
              3rd session; December 1, 1862 - March 3, 1863

Volume 13

38th Congress, 1st session; December 7, 1863 - July 4, 1864
              2nd session; December 5, 1864 - March 3, 1865

Volume 14

39th Congress, 1st session; December 4, 1865 - July 28, 1866
              2nd session; December 3, 1866 - March 3, 1867

Volume 15

40th Congress, 1st session; March 4, 1867 - December 2, 1867
             2nd session; December 2, 1867 - November 10, 1868
             3rd session; December 7, 1868 - March 3, 1869

Volume 16

41st Congress, 1st session; March 4, 1869 - April 10, 1869
             2nd session; December 6, 1869 - July 15, 1870
             3rd session; December 5, 1870 - March 3, 1871

Volume 17

42nd Congress, 1st session; March 4, 1871 - April 20, 1871
             2nd session; December 4, 1871 - June 10, 1872
             3rd session; December 2, 1872 - March 3, 1873

Volume 18

Part 1, Revised Statutes, 1873-1874
Part 2, Revised Statutes, D. C., 1873-1874
Part 3,

43rd Congress, 1st session; December 1, 1873 - June 23, 1874
             2nd session; December 7, 1874 - March 3, 1875

Volume 19

44th Congress, 1st session; December 6, 1875 - August 15, 1876
             2nd session; December 4, 1876 - March 3, 1877

Volume 20

45th Congress, 1st session; October 15, 1877 - December 3, 1877
             2nd session; December 3, 1877 - June 20, 1878
             3rd session; December 2, 1878 - March 3, 1879

Volume 21

46th Congress, 1st session; March 18, 1879 - July 1, 1879
             2nd session; December 1, 1879 - June 16, 1880
             3rd session; December 6, 1880 - March 3, 1881

Volume 22

47th Congress, 1st session; December 5, 1881 - August 8, 1882
             2nd session; December 4, 1882 - March 3, 1883

Volume 23

48th Congress, 1st session; December 3, 1883 - July 7, 1884
             2nd session; December 1, 1884 - March 3, 1885

Volume 24

49th Congress, 1st session; December 7, 1885 - August 5, 1886
             2nd session; December 6, 1886 - March 3, 1887

Volume 25

    50th Congress, 1st session; December 5, 1887 - October 20, 1888
                  2nd session; December 3, 1888 - March 3, 1889

Volume 26

    51st Congress, 1st session; December 2, 1889 - October 1, 1890
                  2nd session; December 1, 1890 - March 3, 1891

Volume 27

    52nd Congress, 1st session; December 7, 1891 - August 5, 1892
                  2nd session; December 5, 1892 - March 3, 1893

Volume 28

    53rd Congress, 1st session; August 7, 1893 - November 3, 1893
                  2nd session; December 4, 1893 - August 28, 1894
                  3rd session; December 3, 1894 - March 3, 1895

Volume 29

    54th Congress, 1st session; December 2, 1895 - June 11, 1896
                  2nd session; December 7, 1896 - March 3, 1897

Volume 30

    55th Congress, 1st session; March 15, 1897 - July 24, 1897
                  2nd session; December 6, 1897 - July 8, 1898
                  3rd session; December 5, 1898 - March 3, 1899

Volume 31

    56th Congress, 1st session; December 4, 1899 - June 7, 1900
                  2nd session; December 3, 1900 - March 3, 1901

Volume 32

    57th Congress, 1st session; December 2, 1901 - July 1, 1902
                  2nd session; December 1, 1902 - March 3, 1903

BIBLIOGRAPHY

Ames, John G. Comprehensive Index to the Publications of the
    United States Government, 1881-1893.
    Washington: Government Printing Office, 1905.

Congressional Information Service. U.S. Serial Set Index,
    Parts 1-5, 1789-1903.
    Washington: Congressional Information Service, 1975.

Greely, Adolphus W. Public Documents of the First Fourteen
    Congresses, 1789-1817.
    Washington: Government Printing Office, 1900.

Law Librarians' Society of Washington, D.C. Union list of
    legislative histories, 4th edition.
    Littleton: Fred B. Rothman and Company, 1977.

Ordway, Albert. General Index of the Journals of Congress,
    from the Eleventh to Sixteenth Congress, 1809-1821.
    Washington: Government Printing Office, 1883.

Ordway, Albert. General Index to the Journals of Congress
    for the First Ten Congresses, 1789-1809.
    Washington: Government Printing Office, 1880.

Poore, Benjamin Perley. A Descriptive Catalog of Government
    Publications of the United States, 1774-1881.
    Washington: Government Printing Office, 1885.

Schmeckebier, Laurence F., and Roy B. Eastin. Government
    Publications and Their Use.
    Washington: Brookings Institution, 1969.

Shepard's Acts and Cases By Popular Names.
    Colorado Springs: Shepard's Citations, 1968.

U. S. Congress. Congressional globe; sketches of the
    debates and proceedings - V. 1-46, 1833-1873.
    Washington: Globe Office for the editors.

U. S. Congress. Congressional record. V. 1- 43rd Congress,
    1873-
    Washington: Government Printing Office, 1873.

U. S. Congress. The Debates and proceedings in Congress of the
    United States, V. 1-42, 1789-1824. (Annals of Congress)
    Washington: Gales and Seaton, 1834.

U. S. Congress. Official Congressional Directory
    Washington: Government Printing Office, 1975.

U. S. Congress. Register of Debates in Congress, comprising the leading debates and incidents, V. 1-14, 1824-1837. Washington: Gales and Seaton, 1825.

U. S. Congress. House. Congressional Journals of the U. S. House of Representatives, 1789-1817. Washington: Michael Glazier, Inc., 1977.

U. S. Congress. House. Index to reports of committees of the House of Representatives, 14th - 49th Congress inclusive. Washington: Government Printing Office, 1887.

U. S. Congress. House. Journals of the U. S. House of Representatives, First thirteen Congresses, 1789-1815. Washington: Gales and Seaton, 1826.

U. S. Congress. Senate. Congressional Journals of the U. S. Senate, 1789-1817. Wilmington: Michael Glazier, Inc., 1977.

U. S. Congress. Senate. Index to reports of committees of the Senate, 14th - 49th Congress inclusive. Washington: Government Printing Office, 1887.

U. S. Congress. Senate. Journals of the U. S. Senate, First Thirteen Congresses, 1789-1815. Washington: Gales and Seaton, 1820.

United States. Laws, statutes, etc. (Indexes). Index analysis of the U.S. Federal statutes, 1789-1907. Washington: Government Printing Office, 1908.

United States. Laws, statutes, etc. Revised statutes of the United States, 2nd edition. Washington: Government Printing Office, 1878.

United States. Laws, statutes, etc. Statutes at large, V. 1-32, 1789-1903. Washington: Government Printing Office, 1845.

United States. Laws, statutes, etc. United States Code. Washington: Government Printing Office, 1977.

United States. Laws, statutes, etc. United States Code Annotated. St. Paul: West Publishing Company, 1927.

U. S. Superintendent of Documents. Catalog of the Public Documents of the Congress and of all Departments of the Government of the United States. V. 1-6, 1893-1903. Washington: Government Printing Office, 1895.

U. S. Superintendent of Documents. Checklist of the United States Public Documents, 1789-1909. Washington: Government Printing Office, 1911.